D1104917

Language, Cognition,
and Human Nature

Also by Steven Pinker

Language Learnability and Language Development
Learnability and Cognition
The Language Instinct
How the Mind Works
Words and Rules
The Blank Slate
The Stuff of Thought
The Better Angels of Our Nature

Edited by Steven Pinker

Visual Cognition
Connections and Symbols (with Jacques Mehler)
Lexical and Conceptual Semantics (with Beth Levin)
The Best American Science and Nature Writing 2004

Language, Cognition, and Human Nature

SELECTED ARTICLES

STEVEN PINKER

OXFORD
UNIVERSITY PRESS

Oxford University Press is a department of the University of Oxford.
It furthers the University's objective of excellence in research, scholarship,
and education by publishing worldwide.

Oxford   New York
Auckland   Cape Town   Dar es Salaam   Hong Kong   Karachi
Kuala Lumpur   Madrid   Melbourne   Mexico City   Nairobi
New Delhi   Shanghai   Taipei   Toronto

With offices in
Argentina   Austria   Brazil   Chile   Czech Republic   France   Greece
Guatemala   Hungary   Italy   Japan   Poland   Portugal   Singapore
South Korea   Switzerland   Thailand   Turkey   Ukraine   Vietnam

Oxford is a registered trademark of Oxford University Press
in the UK and certain other countries.

Published in the United States of America by
Oxford University Press
198 Madison Avenue, New York, NY 10016

Library of Congress Cataloging-in-Publication Data
Pinker, Steven, 1954-
Language, cognition, and human nature : Selected articles / Steven Pinker.
pages cm
Includes bibliographical references and index.
ISBN 978-0-19-932874-1 (hardcover : alk. paper)   1. Language acquisition.   2. Cognition.
3. Psycholinguistics.   I. Title.
P118.P53 2013
401'.9—dc23
2013010222

1 3 5 7 9 8 6 4 2
Printed in the United States of America
on acid-free paper

For Stephen Kosslyn
mentor, colleague, friend

Contents

Introduction

Scholars who write for a general audience are often asked how they reconcile their academic work with their popular writing. Is it hard to lurch back and forth between clear prose and academese? Do your jealous colleagues gong your submissions to the journals and blackball you from the prestigious societies? With all the fame and fortune that you get from popular writing, do you still have the time and desire to do research?

When Oxford University Press offered to publish a collection of my academic papers, these frequently asked questions about the tensions between the limelight and the ivory tower came to mind. Like the majority of professors who rate themselves above average, I tend to think that my academic work is interesting and important, and was predictably flattered by the invitation. But I would not have agreed to mislead book buyers or saddle university libraries with another tome of recycled articles if I did not think that some of my academic papers had crossover appeal. No one will confuse this book with popular science, but at least for me the line between academic and popular writing has never been sharp.

In *Stylish Academic Writing*, the literary scholar Helen Sword shows why a book with that title does not deserve a place on lists of The World's Thinnest Books, along with *America's Most Popular Lawyers* and *The Engineer's Guide to Fashion*. She analyzed the literary style of five hundred articles in academic journals, which may seem like an exercise in masochism. But Sword found that a healthy minority of articles in every field were written with grace and panache. Fortunately for me, this includes the sciences of language and mind. One of my graduate advisers, Roger Brown, the founder of the field of language acquisition, was a gifted stylist, and as a student I savored his prose and pored over his penciled marginalia on my own papers. Though I can crank out turgid mush with the best of them, Roger's example inspired me to strive in my own academic prose for clarity, forcefulness, and the occasional touch of flair. After I had published my second university press book, an editor told me (I am paraphrasing) that my writing did not suck and encouraged me to reach a wider audience. The result was *The Language Instinct*, the first of six trade books and a turning point in my professional life.

I have found that not only can academic writing be stylish but popular writing can be intellectually rigorous. Writing a trade book is an opportunity to develop ideas with a scope and depth that is impossible within the confines of a journal article or academic monograph. The demand for clarity can expose bad ideas that are obscured by murky academese, and the demand for concrete detail in recounting experiments ("Ernie and Bert puppets" not "stimuli") can uncover flaws in design that would otherwise be overlooked. Standards of fact-checking, too, are higher. A typical journal article is vetted by two or three arbitrarily chosen referees, working anonymously and grudgingly; a popular book is read by tens of thousands of readers who are all too happy to say "Gotcha!" at any lapse of logic or accuracy. In my popular books I've always held myself to the standard of not claiming anything that I would not be prepared to defend to my scientific peers, and I've often developed ideas that lent themselves to experiments and technical hypotheses. These books get more citations in the scholarly literature than my academic articles do.

As for repercussions in my professional life, I don't let my mind go there, because it would give me an excuse to produce second-class work. It's not that my recent experiences with peer review have been easy. The process of getting an article accepted for publication in an academic journal is by far the most unpleasant experience in intellectual life, since it requires devoting time and brainpower to making one's article *worse* in an abject effort to satisfy the whims of an anonymous referee who may nix the compromised version anyway.

But this is not just about me. In 2009 the journal *Perspectives on Psychological Science* devoted a special section to what many social scientists believe is a broken peer review process. Writer after writer bemoaned the systematic biases in the process and the anachronistic delays (on average, six years' elapse between the time an experiment is conceived and the time it sees the light of day). Two of them, David Trafimow and Stephen Rice, imagined the letters that would be sent to history's great scientists if they had been subjected to today's peer review process ("Dear Eratosthenes, I am sorry to be the bearer of bad news, but the reviewers were unanimous in their negative opinion and, based on my independent reading, I was forced to agree."). Better still is the viral YouTube video which retitles the bunker scene from the movie *Downfall* with Hitler's reaction to receiving the verdict of the dreaded Third Reviewer. In response to these incentives, I recently opted to submit a theoretical article to the on-line discussion forum www.edge.org rather than to an academic journal. It was published in a day rather than a year, appeared as I had written it rather than with baffling sops to the Third Reviewer, and was subjected to far more rigorous scientific scrutiny: my scientific peers were invited to go after me hammer and tongs in full view of the public.

For all that, I continue to expose myself to the indignities of peer review. Academic research forces me to stay current with the methods and findings of the field and offers the irreplaceable pleasure of empirical discovery and scientific puzzle-solving. And in this volume, I serve up some of my past and recent contributions to the annals of research in cognitive science.

My selections are eclectic. They cover the major topics of my research career: models of language acquisition; topics in visual cognition, particularly mental imagery and shape recognition; the meaning and syntax of verbs; regular and irregular phenomena in language and their implications for the mechanisms of cognition; and the social psychology of direct and indirect speech. With two exceptions I excluded papers reporting primary experimental data, since they have less interest to general readers and because they tend to be more ephemeral, valuable only insofar as they are absorbed into an ongoing research enterprise. I've always liked to write big theoretical papers—sometimes to outline a theory, sometimes to analyze a big idea (evolution, cognitive architecture, nature and nurture), sometimes to take up an argument with other thinkers such as Stephen Jay Gould, Noam Chomsky, Jerry Fodor, Richard Dawkins, and H. Paul Grice. Some of the selections are highly cited; others are personal favorites that have lain in obscurity either because I published them in obscure places to discharge some academic debt, or, more commonly, because no one else seemed to think they were as interesting as I did.

In the pitiless process of assembling a collection which optimized scientific diversity, continuing relevance, and the overall page count, I ended up without any of the articles I coauthored with my most important scientific influence of all, my thesis adviser Stephen M. Kosslyn. This volume is dedicated to him, with gratitude and affection.

S.P.

Language, Cognition, and Human Nature

1

Formal Models of Language Learning

Scientists are often asked what led them to go into their fields, and the more creative among them will proffer some childhood narrative, such as Stephen Jay Gould's thanking his father for taking him to see the dinosaurs at the American Museum of Natural History when he was 5. Though I don't begrudge Gould that charming anecdote, I doubt that this kind of explanation is true for most scientists. How many children are even aware of the specialties that will become their life's calling: mycologist, crystallographer, tribologist, condensed matter physicist? Certainly I can think of no childhood inspiration for a career in psycholinguistics. Though I'm sometimes tempted to confabulate a narrative for how I came to study language (I grew up in bilingual Quebec, I was forced to go to Hebrew school, and so on), the truth lies in the prosaic combination of happenstance events that I suspect explains most career pathways.

When I began graduate school at Harvard in 1976, I thought of language as just one of many topics in my chosen field, cognitive psychology. But Harvard had recently denied tenure to most of its cognitive psychologists, and one of the only available courses in the general area of cognition was dedicated to language acquisition. I found the readings frustrating—there was plenty of research on the cute things that children say, but the theories of how they actually ended up learning the language were vague and squishy, quite unlike the computational models of vision and memory I was familiar with. No one really seemed to know what they were talking about when they slung around concepts like "innate knowledge," "general cognitive learning mechanisms," or "parental input." At the same time, a course on reasoning assigned a short paper in the mathematical theory of computation by the obscure mathematician E. M. Gold, which tried to formalize the problem of language learning. As an undergraduate I had taken a course in the mathematical theory of computation, so I understood the jargon, and the proofs themselves were simple. With nothing else to do I put the two topics together and wrote a course paper on mathematical and computational models of language learning and how they could make theories of language acquisition in children more concrete and precise. Two years and three revisions later, it became my first single-authored publication.

Though I still thought of language as a sideline, and did my dissertation research on visual imagery, the world kept telling me that my ideas on language were more interesting. My first job, my first book, and eventually my entire research program centered on ideas that I first explored in this paper. After having reviewed the extant models of language acquisition and found each of them wanting in a different way, I developed my own theory, presented in Language Learnability and Language Development *and in* Learnability and Cognition, *and tried to test it in experiments and corpus analyses.*

The paper shaped me not just professionally but intellectually, by sensitizing me to the importance of innate mechanisms in cognition. Innate mechanisms are important not because everything is innate and learning is unimportant, but because the only way to explain learning is to identify the innate mechanisms that make learning possible. It was an appreciation of this logical point that began a lifelong fascination with the nature of human nature—not just the parts that make language possible, but those that underlie cognition, emotion, aesthetics, and violence. This paper also revealed my impatience with the common assumption that because learning and culture are important, the mind should be treated as a blank slate—an assumption that I took on a quarter-century later in The Blank Slate.

I started rereading this 35-year-old article with trepidation, but I think it has held up well. Though many cognitive scientists have recently warned of the danger of misunderstanding Gold's theorems and applying them to children's language acquisition in simplistic ways, all these warnings were already in this article. Also to be found in those pages is an explanation of approximate, probabilistic, and Bayesian models of acquisition, which nowadays are often described as the new new thing. I also stand by the paper's analyses of general-purpose learning mechanisms, of innate language acquisition abilities, of distributional analysis, of artificial grammar experiments, and of semantic, pragmatic, and simplified parental input. And though this paper helped to launch the "learnability approach" to language acquisition that became influential in the 1980s and early 1990s, I sometimes despair that the caveat by Roger Brown with which I ended the article has come to pass: the field of language acquisition today has become as atheoretical and unmechanistic as it was in 1970s.

A whimsical touch in the paper is its use of the word "googol" in the original sense of the number 10^{100}, decades before Sergei Brin and Larry Page co-opted it (with a change in spelling) as a name for their search engine. When I wrote the first draft in 1977, the term was unfamiliar enough that my teacher John Macnamara commented in the margins:

> The googol is a nasty little multi-zeroed beast
> Which will not serve the language-learner's purpose in the least.
> Though its many-zeroed tail looks harmless, still you see
> It packs a sting that's every bit as painful as a bee.

I. Introduction

How children learn to speak is one of the most important problems in the cognitive sciences, a problem both inherently interesting and scientifically promising. It is *interesting* because it is a species of the puzzle of induction: how humans are capable of forming valid generalizations on the basis of a finite number of observations. In this case, the generalizations are those that allow one to speak and understand the language of one's community, and are based on a finite amount of speech heard in the first few years of life. And language acquisition can claim to be a particularly *promising* example of this puzzle, promising to the extent that empirical constraints on theory construction promote scientific progress in a given domain. This is because any plausible theory of language learning will have to meet an unusually rich set of empirical conditions. The theory will have to account for the fact that all normal children succeed at learning language, and will have to be consistent with our knowledge of what language is and of which stages the child passes through in learning it.

It is instructive to spell out these conditions one by one and examine the progress that has been made in meeting them. First, since all normal children learn the language of their community, a viable theory will have to posit mechanisms powerful enough to acquire a natural language. This criterion is doubly stringent: though the rules of language are beyond doubt highly intricate and abstract, children uniformly *succeed* at learning them nonetheless, unlike chess, calculus, and other complex cognitive skills. Let us say that a theory that can account for the fact that languages can be learned in the first place has met the *Learnability Condition*. Second, the theory should not account for the child's success by positing mechanisms narrowly adapted to the acquisition of a particular language. For example, a theory positing an innate grammar for English would fail to meet this criterion, which can be called the *Equipotentiality Condition*. Third, the mechanisms of a viable theory must allow the child to learn his language within the time span normally taken by children, which is in the order of three years for the basic components of language skill. Fourth, the mechanisms must not require as input types of information or amounts of information that are unavailable to the child. Let us call these the *Time* and *Input Conditions*, respectively. Fifth, the theory should make predictions about the intermediate stages of acquisition that agree with empirical findings in the study of child language. Sixth, the mechanisms described by the theory should not be wildly inconsistent with what is known about the cognitive faculties of the child, such as the perceptual discriminations he can make, his conceptual abilities, his memory, attention, and so forth. These can be called the *Developmental* and *Cognitive Conditions*, respectively.

It should come as no surprise that no current theory of language learning satisfies, or even addresses itself to, all six conditions. Research in psychology has by and large focused on the last three, the Input, Developmental, and Cognitive Conditions, with much of the research directed toward further specifying or articulating the conditions themselves. For example, there has been research on the nature of the speech available to children learning language (see Snow and Ferguson, 1977), on the nature of children's early word combinations (e.g., Braine, 1963), and on similarities between linguistic and cognitive abilities at various ages (e.g., Sinclair de-Zwart, 1969). Less often, there have been attempts to construct theoretical accounts for one or more of such findings, such as the usefulness of parental speech to children (e.g., Newport, Gleitman, and Gleitman, 1977), the reasons that words are put together the way they are in the first sentences (e.g., Brown, 1973; Schlesinger, 1971), and the ways that cognitive development interacts with linguistic development (e.g., Slobin, 1973). Research in linguistics that has addressed itself to language learning at all has articulated the Equipotentiality Condition, trying to distinguish the kinds of properties that are universal from those that are found only in particular languages (e.g., Chomsky, 1965, 1973).

In contrast, the attempts to account for the acquisition of language itself (the Learnability Condition) have been disappointingly vague. Language Acquisition has been attributed to everything from "innate schematisms" to "general multipurpose learning strategies"; it has been described as a mere by-product of cognitive development, of perceptual development, of motor development, or of social development; it has been said to draw on "input regularities," "semantic relations," "perceived intentions," "formal causality," "pragmatic knowledge," "action schemas," and so on. Whether the mechanisms implicated by a particular theory are adequate to the task of learning human languages is usually left unanswered.

There are, however, several bodies of research that address themselves to the Learnability criterion. These theories try to specify which learning mechanisms will succeed in which ways, for which types of languages, and with which types of input. A body of research called *Grammatical Induction,* which has grown out of mathematical linguistics and the theory of computation, treats languages as formal objects and tries to prove theorems about when it is possible, in principle, to learn a language on the basis of a set of sentences of the language. A second body of research, which has grown out of artificial intelligence and cognitive simulation, consists of attempts to program computers to acquire languages and/or to simulate human language acquisition. In a third research effort, which has grown out of transformational linguistics, a learning model capable of acquiring a certain class of transformational grammars has been described. However, these bodies of research are seldom cited in the psychological literature, and researchers in developmental psycholinguistics for the most part do not seem to be familiar with them. The present paper is an attempt to remedy this situation. I will try to give a critical review of these formal models of language acquisition, focusing on their relevance to human language learning.

There are two reasons why formal models of language learning are likely to contribute to our understanding of how children learn to speak, even if none of the models I will discuss satisfies all of our six criteria. First of all, a theory that is powerful enough to account for the *fact* of language acquisition may be a more promising first approximation of an ultimately viable theory than one that is able to describe the *course* of language acquisition, which has been the traditional focus of developmental psycholinguistics. As the reader shall see, the Learnability criterion is extraordinarily stringent, and it becomes quite obvious when a theory cannot pass it. On the other hand, theories concerning the mechanisms responsible for child language per se are notoriously underdetermined by the child's observable linguistic behavior. This is because the child's knowledge, motivation, memory, and perceptual, motor, and social skills are developing at the same time that he is learning the language of his community.

The second potential benefit of formal models is the explicitness that they force on the theorist, which in turn can clarify many conceptual and substantive issues that have preoccupied the field. Despite over a decade and a half of vigorous debates, we still do not know that sort of a priori knowledge, if any, is necessary to learn a natural language; nor whether different sorts of input to a language learner can make his task easy or difficult, possible or impossible; nor how semantic information affects the learning of the syntax of a language. In part this is because we know so little about the mechanisms of language learning, and so do not know how to translate vague terms such as "semantic information" into the information structures that play a causal role in the acquisition process. Developing explicit, mechanistic theories of language learning may be the only way that these issues can be stated clearly enough to evaluate. It seems to be the consensus in other areas of cognitive psychology that mechanistic theories have engendered enormous conceptual advances in the understanding of mental faculties, such as long-term memory (Anderson and Bower, 1973), visual imagery (Kosslyn and Schwartz, 1977), and problem solving (Newell and Simon, 1973).

The rest of the paper is organized into eight sections. In Section II, I will introduce the vocabulary and concepts of mathematical linguistics, which serve as the foundation for research on language learnability. Sections III and IV present E. Gold's seminal theorems on language learnability, and the subsequent research they inspired. Section V describes the so-called "heuristic" language learning models, several of which have been implemented as computer simulations of human language acquisition. Sections VI and VII discuss the rationale for the "semantic" or "cognitive" approach to language learning, focusing on John R. Anderson's computer simulation of a semantics-based learner. Section VIII describes a model developed by Henry Hamburger, Kenneth Wexler, and Peter Culicover that is capable of learning transformational grammars for languages. Finally, in Section IX, I discuss the implications of this research for developmental psycholinguistics.

II. Formal Models of Language

In this section I define the elementary concepts of mathematical linguistics found in discussions of language learnability. More thorough accounts can be found in Gross (1972) and in Hopcroft and Ullman (1969).

LANGUAGES AND GRAMMARS

To describe a language in mathematical terms, one begins with a finite set of *symbols,* or a *vocabulary.* In the case of English, the symbols would be English words or morphemes. Any finite sequence of these symbols is called a *string,* and any finite or infinite collection of strings is called a *language.* Those strings in the language are called *sentences;* the strings not in the language are called *non-sentences.*

Languages with a finite number of sentences can be exhaustively described simply by listing the sentences. However, it is a celebrated observation that natural and computer languages are infinite, even though they are used by beings with finite memory. Therefore the languages must have some finite characterization, such as a recipe or program for specifying which sentences are in a given language. A *grammar,* a set of rules that generates all the sentences in a language, but no non-sentences, is one such characterization. Any language that can be generated by a set of rules (that is, any language that is not completely arbitrary) is called a *recursively enumerable* language.

A grammar has four parts. First of all, there is the vocabulary, which will now be called the *terminal vocabulary* to distinguish it from the second component of the grammar, called the *auxiliary vocabulary.* The auxiliary vocabulary consists of another finite set of symbols, which may not appear in sentences themselves, but which may act as stand-ins for groups of symbols, such as the English "noun," "verb," and "prepositional phrase." The third component of the grammar is the finite set of *rewrite rules,* each of which replaces one sequence of symbols, whenever it occurs, by another sequence. For example, one rewrite rule in the grammar for English replaces the symbol "noun phrase" by the symbols "article noun"; another replaces the symbol "verb" by the symbol "grow." Finally, there is a special symbol, called the *start symbol,* usually denoted S, which initiates the sequence of rule operations that generate a sentence. If one of the rewrite rules can rewrite the "S" as another string of symbols it does so; then if any rule can replace part or all of that new string by yet another string, it follows suit. This procedure continues, one rule taking over from where another left off, until no auxiliary symbols remain, at which point a sentence has been generated. The language is simply the set of all strings that can be generated in this way.

CLASSES OF LANGUAGES

There is a natural way to subdivide grammars and the languages they generate into classes. First, the grammars of different sorts of languages make use of different types of rewrite rules. Second, these different types of languages require different sorts of computational machinery to produce or recognize their sentences, using various amounts of working memory and various ways of accessing it. Finally, the theorems one can prove about language and grammars tend to apply to entire classes of languages, delineated in these ways. In particular, theorems on language learnability refer to such classes, so I will discuss them briefly.

These classes fall into a hierarchy (sometimes called the *Chomsky hierarchy*), each class properly containing the languages in the classes below it. I have already mentioned the largest class, the recursively enumerable languages, those that have grammars that generate all their member sentences. However, not all of these languages have a *decision procedure*, that is, a means of determining whether or not a given string of symbols is a sentence in the language. Those that have decision procedures are called *decidable* or *recursive* languages. Unfortunately, there is no general way of knowing whether a recursively enumerable language will turn out to be decidable or not. However, there is a very large subset of the decidable languages, called the *primitive recursive* languages, whose decidability *is* known. It is possible to *enumerate* this class of languages, that is, there exists a finite procedure called a *grammar-grammar* capable of listing each grammar in the class, one at a time, without including any grammar not in the class. (It is not hard to see why this is impossible for the class of decidable languages: one can never be sure whether a given language is decidable or not.)

The primitive recursive languages can be further broken down by restricting the form of the rewrite rules that the grammars are permitted to use. *Context-sensitive* grammars contain rules that replace a single auxiliary symbol by a string of symbols whenever that symbol is flanked by certain neighboring symbols. *Context-free* grammars have rules that replace a single auxiliary symbol by a string of symbols regardless of where that symbol occurs. The rules of *finite state* grammars may replace a single auxiliary symbol only by another auxiliary symbol plus a terminal symbol; these auxiliary symbols are often called *states* in discussions of the corresponding sentence-producing machines. Finally, there are grammars that have no auxiliary symbols, and hence these grammars can generate only a finite number of strings altogether. Thus they are called *finite cardinality* grammars. This hierarchy is summarized in Table 1.1, which lists the classes of languages from most to least inclusive.

NATURAL LANGUAGES

Almost all theorems on language learnability, and much of the research on computer simulations of language learning, make reference to classes in the Chomsky hierarchy. However, unless we know where natural languages fall in the classification, it is obviously of little psychological interest. Clearly, natural languages are not of finite cardinality; one can always produce a new sentence by adding, say, "he insists that" to the beginning of an old sentence. It is also not very difficult to show that natural languages are not finite state: as Chomsky (1957) has demonstrated, finite state grammars cannot generate sentences with an arbitrary number of embeddings, which natural languages permit (e.g., "he works," "either he works or he plays," "if either he works or he plays, then he tires," "since if either he ...," etc.).

Table 1.1 **Classes of Languages**

Class	Learnable from an informant?	Learnable from a text?	Contains natural languages?
Recursively Enumerable	no	no	yes[*]
Decidable (Recursive)	no	no	?
Primitive Recursive	yes	no	?
Context-Sensitive	yes	no	?
Context-Free	yes	no	no
Finite State	yes	no	no
Finite Cardinality	yes	yes	no

[*]by assumption.

It is more difficult, though not impossible, to show that natural languages are not context-free (Gross, 1972; Postal, 1964). Unfortunately, it is not clear how much higher in the hierarchy one must go to accomodate natural languages. Chomsky and most other linguists (including his opponents of the "generative semantics" school) use *transformational* grammars of various sorts to describe natural languages. These grammars generate bracketed strings called *deep structures,* usually by means of a context-free grammar, and then, by means of rewrite rules called *transformations,* permute, delete, or copy elements of the deep structures to produce sentences. Since transformational grammars are constructed and evaluated by a variety of criteria, and not just by the ability to generate the sentences of a language, their place in the hierarchy is uncertain. Although the matter is by no means settled, Peters and Ritchie (1973) have persuasively argued that the species of transformational grammar necessary for generating natural languages can be placed in the context-sensitive class, as Chomsky conjectured earlier (1965, p. 61). Accordingly, in the sections following, I will treat the set of all existing and possible human languages as a subset of the context-sensitive class.

III. Grammatical Induction: Gold's Theorems

LANGUAGE LEARNING AS GRAMMATICAL INDUCTION

Since people presumably do not consult an internal list of the sentences of their language when they speak, knowing a particular language corresponds to knowing a particular set of rules of some sort capable of producing and recognizing the sentences of that language. Therefore learning a language consists of inducing that set of rules, using the language behavior of the community as evidence of what the rules must be. In the paragraphs following I will treat such a set of rules as a grammar. This should not imply the belief that humans mentally execute rewrite rules one by one before uttering a sentence. Since every grammar can be translated into a left-to-right sentence producer or recognizer, "inducing a grammar" can be taken as shorthand for acquiring the ability to produce and recognize just those sentences that the grammar generates. The advantage of talking about the grammar is that it allows us to focus on the process by which a particular language is learned (i.e., as opposed to some other language), requiring no commitment as to the detailed nature of the production or comprehension process in general (i.e., the features common to producers or recognizers for *all* languages).

The most straightforward solution to this induction problem would be to find some algorithm that produces a grammar for a language given a sample of its sentences, and then to attribute some version of this algorithm to the child. This would also be the most *general* conceivable solution. It would not be necessary to attribute to the child any a priori knowledge about the particular type of language that he is to learn (except perhaps that it falls into one of the classes in the Chomsky hierarchy, which could correspond to some putative memory or processing limitation). We would not even have to attribute to the child a special language acquisition faculty. Since a grammar is simply one way of talking about a computational procedure or set of rules, an algorithm that could produce a grammar for a language from a sample of sentences could also presumably produce a set of rules for a different sort of data (appropriately encoded), such as rules that correctly classify the exemplars and non-exemplars in a laboratory concept attainment task. In that case it could be argued that the child learned language via a general induction procedure, one that simply "captured regularity" in the form of computational rules from the environment.

Unfortunately, the algorithm that we need does not exist. An elementary theorem of mathematical linguistics states that there are an infinite number of different grammars that can generate any finite set of strings. Each grammar will make different predictions about the strings not in the set. Consider the sample consisting of the single sentence "the dog barks." It could have been taken from the language consisting of: 1) all three-word strings; 2) all article-noun-verb sequences; 3) all sentences with a noun phrase; 4) that sentence alone; 5) that sentence plus all those in the July 4, 1976 edition of the New York Times; as well as 6) all English sentences. When the sample consists of more than one sentence, the class of possible languages is reduced but is still infinitely large, as long as the number of sentences in the sample is finite. Therefore it is impossible for *any* learner to observe a finite sample of sentences of a language and always produce a correct grammar for the language.

LANGUAGE IDENTIFICATION IN THE LIMIT

Gold (1967) solved this problem with a paradigm he called *language identification in the limit*. The paradigm works as follows: time is divided into discrete trials with a definite starting point. The teacher or environment "chooses" a language (called the *target language*) from a predetermined class in the hierarchy. At each trial, the learner has access to a single string. In one version of the paradigm, the learner has access sooner or later to all the sentences in the language. This sample can be called a *text*, or *positive information presentation*. Alternately, the learner can have access to both grammatical sentences and ungrammatical strings, each appropriately labelled. Because this is equivalent to allowing the learner to receive feedback from a native informant as to whether or not a given string is an acceptable sentence, it can be called *informant* or *complete information presentation*. Each time the learner views a string, he must guess what the target grammar is. This process continues forever, with the learner allowed to change his mind at any time. If, after a finite amount of time, the learner always guesses the same grammar, and if that grammar correctly generates the target language, he is said to have *identified the language in the limit*. It is noteworthy that by this definition the learner can never know when or even whether he has succeeded. This is because he can never be sure that future strings will not force him to change his mind.

Gold, in effect, asked: How well can a completely general learner do in this situation? That is, are there any classes of languages in the hierarchy whose members can all be identified in the limit? He was able to prove that language learnability depends on the information available: if both sentences and non-sentences are available to a learner (informant presentation), the class of primitive recursive languages, and all its subclasses (which include the natural languages) are learnable. But if only sentences are available (text presentation), *no* class of languages other than the finite cardinality languages is learnable.

The proofs of these theorems are straightforward. The learner can use a maximally general strategy: he enumerates every grammar of the class, one at a time, rejecting one grammar and moving on to the next whenever the grammar is inconsistent with any of the sample strings (see Figure 1.1). With informant presentation, any incorrect grammar will eventually be rejected when it is unable to generate a sentence in the language, or when it generates a string that the informant indicates is not in the language. Since the correct grammar, whatever it is, has a definite position in the enumeration of grammars, it will be hypothesized after a finite amount of time and there will never again be any reason to change the hypothesis. The class of primitive recursive languages is the highest learnable class because it is the highest class whose languages are decidable, and whose grammars and decision procedures can be enumerated, both necessary properties for the procedure to work.

The situation is different under text presentation. Here, finite cardinality languages are trivially learnable—the learner can simply guess that the language is the set of sentences that have appeared in the sample so far, and when every sentence in the language has appeared at least once, the learner will be correct. But say the class contains

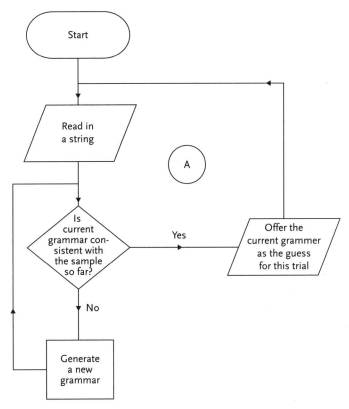

Figure 1.1 A flowchart for Gold's enumeration procedure. Note that there is no "stop" symbol; the learner samples strings and guesses grammars forever. If the learner at some point enters loop "A" and never leaves it, he has identified the language in the limit.

all finite languages and at least one infinite language (as do classes higher than finite cardinality). If the learner guesses that the language is just the set of sentences in the sample, then when the target language is infinite the learner will have to change his mind an infinite number of times. But if the learner guesses only infinite languages, then when the target language is finite he will guess an incorrect language and will never be forced to change his mind. If non-sentences were also available, any overgeneral grammar would have been rejected when a sentence that it was capable of generating appeared, marked as a non-sentence. As Gold put it, "the problem with text is that if you guess too large a language, the sample will never tell you're wrong."

IMPLICATION OF GOLD'S THEOREMS

Do children learn from a text or an informant? What evidence we have strongly suggests that children are not usually corrected when they speak ungrammatically, and when they are corrected they take little notice (Braine, 1971; Brown and Hanlon,

1970; McNeill, 1966). Nor does the child seem to have access to more indirect evidence about what is not a sentence. Brown and Hanlon (1970) were unable to discern any differences in how parents responded to the grammatical versus the ungrammatical sentences of their children. Thus the child seems to be in a text situation, in which Gold's learner must fail. However, all other models must fail in this situation as well—there can be no learning procedure more powerful than the one that enumerates all the grammars in a class.

An even more depressing result is the astronomical amount of time that the learning of most languages would take. The enumeration procedure, which gives the learner maximum generality, exacts its price: the learner must test astronomically large numbers of grammars before he is likely to hit upon the correct one. For example, in considering all the finite state grammars that use seven terminal symbols and seven auxiliary symbols (states), which the learner must do before going on to more complex grammars, he must test over a googol (10^{100}) candidates. The learner's predicament is reminiscent of Jorge Luis Borges's "librarians of Babel," who search a vast library containing books with all possible combinations of alphabetic characters for the book that clarifies the basic mysteries of humanity. Nevertheless, Gold has proved that *no* general procedure is uniformly faster than his learner's enumeration procedure. This is a consequence of the fact that an infinite number of grammars is consistent with any finite sample. Imagine a rival procedure of any sort that correctly guessed a certain language at an earlier trial than did the enumeration procedure. In that case the enumeration procedure must have guessed a different language at that point. But the sample of sentences up to that point could have been produced by many different grammars, including the one that the enumeration procedure mistakenly guessed. If the target language had happened to be that other language, then at that time the enumeration procedure would have been correct, and its rival incorrect. Therefore, for every language that a rival procedure identifies faster than the enumeration procedure, there is a language for which the reverse is true. A corollary is that every form of enumeration procedure (i.e., every order of enumeration) is, on the whole, equivalent in speed to every other one.

Gold's model can be seen as an attempt to construct some model, any model, that can meet the Learnability Condition. But Gold has shown that even if a model is unhindered by psychological considerations (i.e., the Developmental, Cognitive, and Time Conditions), learnability cannot be established (that is, unless one flagrantly violates the Input Condition by requiring that the learner receive negative information). What's more, no model can do better than Gold's, whether or not it is designed to model the child. However, since children presumably do have a procedure whereby they learn the language of their community, there must be some feature of Gold's learning paradigm itself that precludes learnability, such as the criterion for success or access to information. In Section IV, I will review research inspired by Gold's theorems that tries to establish under what conditions language learnability from a sample of sentences is possible.

IV. Grammatical Induction: Other Results

GRAMMATICAL INDUCTION FROM A TEXT

This section will describe four ways in which languages can be learned from samples of sentences. One can either restrict the order of presentation of the sample sentences, relax the success criterion, define a statistical distribution over the sample sentences, or constrain the learner's hypotheses.

Order of Sentence Presentation

In Section III it was assumed that the sample strings could be presented to the learner in any order whatsoever. Gold (1967) proved that if it can be known that the sample sentences are ordered in some way as a function of time, then all recursively enumerable languages are learnable from a positive sample. Specifically, it is assumed that the "teacher" selects the sentence to be presented at time t by consulting a *primitive recursive function* that accepts a value of t as input and produces a sentence as output. Primitive recursive functions in this case refer to primitive recursive grammars that associate each sentence in the language with a unique natural number. Like primitive recursive grammars, they can be enumerated and tested, and the learner merely has to identify in the limit which function the teacher is using, in the same way that the learner discussed in Section III (and illustrated in Figure 1.1) identified primitive recursive grammars. This is sufficient to generate the sentences in the target language (although not necessarily sufficient to recognize them). Although it is hard to believe that every sentence the child hears is uniquely determined by the time that has elapsed since the onset of learning, we shall see in Section VI how a similar learning procedure allows the child to profit from semantic information.

Another useful type of sequencing is called *effective approximate ordering* (Feldman, 1972). Suppose that there was a point in time by which every grammatical sentence of a given length or less had appeared in the sample. Suppose further that the learner can calculate, for any length of sentence, what that time is. Then, at that point, the learner can compute all the strings of that length or less that are *not* in the language, namely, the strings that have not yet appeared. This is equivalent to having access to non-sentences; thus learning can occur. Although it is generally true that children are exposed to longer and longer sentences as language learning proceeds (see Snow and Ferguson, 1977), it would be difficult to see how they could take advantage of this procedure, since there is never a point at which short sentences are excluded altogether. More generally, though, it is possible that the fairly systematic changes in the speech directed to the developing child (see Snow and Ferguson, 1977) contain information that is useful to the task of inducing a grammar, as Clark (1973) and Levelt (1973) have suggested. For example, if it were true that sentences early in the sample were always generated by fewer rules or needed fewer derivational steps than sentences later in the sample, perhaps a learner could reject any candidate grammar that used more rules or steps for the earlier sentences than for the later ones. However, the attempts to discern such an ordering in parental speech have been disappointing (see Newport *et al.*, 1977) and it remains to be seen whether the speech directed to the child is sufficiently well-ordered with respect to this or any other syntactic dimension for an order-exploiting strategy to be effective. I will discuss this issue in greater depth in Section IX.

Relaxing the Success Criterion

Perhaps the learner should not be required to identify the target language exactly. We can, for example, simply demand that the learner *approach* the target language, defining approachability as follows (Biermann and Feldman, 1972; Feldman, 1972): 1) Every sentence in the sample is eventually included in the language guessed by the learner; 2) any incorrect grammar will at some point be permanently rejected; and 3) the correct grammar will be guessed an infinite number of times (this last condition defining *strong approachability*). The difference between strong approachability and identifiability is that, in the former case, we do not require the learner to stick to the correct grammar once he has guessed it. Feldman has shown that the class of primitive recursive languages is approachable in the limit from a sample of sentences.

The success criterion can also be weakened so as to allow the learner to identify a language that is an *approximation* of the target language. Wharton (1974) proposes a way to define a *metric* on the set of languages that use a given terminal vocabulary, which would allow one to measure the degree of similarity between any two languages. What happens, then, if the learner is required to identify any language whatsoever that is of a given degree of similarity to the target language? Wharton shows that a learner can approximate any primitive recursive language to any degree of accuracy using only a text. Furthermore, there is always a degree of accuracy that can be imposed on the learner that will have the effect of making him choose the target language exactly. However, there is no way of knowing how high that level of accuracy must be (if there were, Gold's theorem would be false). Since it is unlikely that the child ever duplicates exactly the language of his community, Wharton and Feldman have shown that a Gold-type learner *can* meet the Learnability condition if it is suitably redefined.

There is a third way that we can relax the success criterion. Instead of asking for the *only* grammar that fits the sample, we can ask for the *simplest* grammar from among the infinity of candidates. Feldman (1972) defines the *complexity* of a grammar, given a sample, as a joint function (say, the sum) of the *intrinsic complexity* of the grammar (say, the number of rewrite rules) and the *derivational complexity* of the grammar with respect to the sample (say, the average number of steps needed to generate the sample sentences). He then describes a procedure which enumerates grammars in order of increasing intrinsic complexity, thereby finding the simplest grammar that is consistent with a positive sample. However it is important to point out that such a procedure will *not* identify or even strongly approach the target language when it considers larger and larger samples. It is easy to see why not. There is a grammar of finite complexity that will generate every possible string from a given vocabulary. If the target language is more complex than this *universal grammar*, it will never even be considered, because the universal grammar will always be consistent with the text and occurs earlier in the enumeration than the target grammar (Gold, 1967). Thus equipping the child with Occam's Razor will not help him learn languages.

Bayesian Grammar Induction

If a grammar specifies the probabilities with which its rules are to be used, it is called a *stochastic* grammar, and it will generate a sample of sentences with a predictable statistical distribution. This constitutes an additional source of information that a learner can exploit in attempting to identify a language.

Horning (1969) considers grammars whose rewrite rules are applied with fixed probabilities. It is possible to calculate the *probability of a sentence given a grammar* by multiplying together the probabilities of the rewrite rules used to generate the sentence. One can calculate the *probability of a sample of sentences* with respect to the grammar in the same way. In Horning's paradigm, the learner also knows the *a priori probability* that any grammar will have been selected as the target grammar. The learner enumerates grammars in approximate order of decreasing a priori probability, and calculates the probability of the sample with respect to each grammar. He then can use the equivalent of Bayes's Theorem to determine the *a posteriori probability* of a grammar given the sample. The learner always guesses the grammar with the highest a posteriori probability. Horning shows how an algorithm of this sort can converge on the most probable correct grammar for any text.

Constraining the Hypothesis Space

In its use of a priori knowledge concerning the likelihood that certain types of languages will be faced, Horning's procedure is like a stochastic version of Chomsky's (1965) abstract description of a language acquisition device. Chomsky, citing the infinity of grammars consistent with any finite sample, proposes that there is a *weighting function* that represents the child's selection of hypothesis grammars in the face of a finite sample. The weighting function assigns a "scattered" distribution of probabilities to grammars, so that the candidate grammars that incorporate the basic properties of natural languages are assigned high values, while those (equally correct) grammars that are not of this form are assigned extremely low or zero values. In weighting grammars in this way, the child is making assumptions about the probability that he will be faced with a particular type of language, namely, a natural language. If his weighting function is so constructed that only one highly-weighted grammar will be consistent with the sample once it has grown to a certain size, then learnability from a text is possible. To take an artificial example, if the child gave high values only to a set of languages with completely disjoint vocabularies (e.g., Hindi, Yiddish, Swahili, etc.), then even a single sentence would be sufficient evidence to learn a language. However, in Gold's paradigm, a learner that assigned weights of zero to some languages would fail to learn those languages should they be chosen as targets. But in the case of the child, this need not be a concern. We need only show how the child is able to learn human languages; it would not be surprising if the child was thereby rendered unable to learn various gerrymandered or exotic languages.

There are two points to be made about escaping Gold's conclusions by constraining the learner's hypothesis set. First, we lose the ability to talk about a general rule-inducing strategy constrained only by the computation-theoretic "lines of fracture" separating classes of languages. Instead, we are committed to at least a weak form of nativism, according to which "the child approaches the data with the presumption that they are drawn from a language of an antecedently well-defined type" (Chomsky, 1965, p. 27). Second, we are begging the question of whether the required weighting function exists, and what form it should take. It is not sufficient simply to constrain the learner's hypotheses, even severely. Consider Figure 1.2, a Venn diagram representing the set of languages assigned high a priori values (Circle A) and the set of languages that are consistent with the sample at a given point in the learning process (Circle B). To ensure learnability, the set of languages in the intersection between the two circles must shrink to a single member as more and more of the sample is considered. Circle B must not encompass Circle A completely, nor coincide with it, nor overlap with it to a large degree (a priori set too broad); nor can it be disjoint from it (a priori set too narrow). Specifying an a priori class of languages with these properties corresponds to the *explanatory adequacy* requirement in transformational linguistics. In Section VIII I shall examine an attempt to prove learnability in this way.

We have seen several ways to achieve learnability, within the constraint that only grammatical sentences be available to the learner. However, in severing one head of this hydra, we see that two more have grown in its place. The learning procedures discussed in this section still require astronomical amounts of time. They also proceed in an implausible manner, violating both the Developmental and the Cognitive

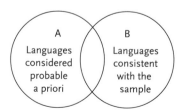

Figure 1. 2. Achieving learnability by constraining the learner's hypothesis set.

criteria. First, children do not adopt and jettison grammars in one piece; they seem to add, replace, and modify individual rules (see Brown, 1973). Second, it is unreasonable to suppose that children can remember every sentence they have heard, which they must do to test a grammar against "the sample." In the next paragraphs I will review some proposals addressed to the Time Condition, and in Section V, research addressed more directly to the Developmental and Cognitive Conditions.

REDUCING LEARNING TIME

Efficient Enumeration

The learners we have considered generate grammars rather blindly, by using a grammar-grammar that creates rules out of all possible combinations of symbols. This process will yield many grammars that can be shown to be undesirable even before they are tested against the sample. For example, grammars could be completely equivalent to other grammars except for the names of their auxiliary symbols; they could have some rules that grind to a halt without producing a sentence, and others that spin freely without affecting the sentence that the other rules produce; they could be redundant or ambiguous, or lack altogether a certain word known to appear in the language. Perhaps our estimate of the enormous time required by an enumeration procedure is artificially inflated by including various sorts of silly or bad grammars in the enumeration. Wharton (1977) has shown that if a learner had a "quality control inspector" that rejected these bad grammars before testing them against the sample, he could save a great deal of testing time. Furthermore, if the learner could reject not one but an entire set of grammars every time a single grammar failed a quality control test or was incompatible with the sample, he could save even more time, a second trick sometimes called *grammatical covering* (Biermann and Feldman, 1972; Horning, 1969; Wharton, 1977; Van der Mude and Walker, 1978). Horning and Wharton have implemented various enumeration techniques as computer programs in order to estimate their efficiency, and have found that these "quality control" and "covering" strategies are faster than blind enumeration by many orders of magnitude. Of course, there is no simple way to compare computation time in a digital computer with the time the brain would take to accomplish an analogous computation, but somehow, the performance of the efficient enumeration algorithms leaves little cause for optimism. For example, these techniques in one case allowed an IBM 360 computer to infer a finite state grammar with two auxiliary symbols and two terminal symbols after several minutes of computation. However natural languages have on the order of 10–100 auxiliary symbols, and in general the number of grammars using 2^{n^3} auxiliary symbols grown as . Clearly, stronger medicine is needed.

Ordering by a priori Probability

The use of an a priori probability metric over the space of hypothesis grammars, which allowed Horning's procedure to learn a language without an informant, also reduces the average time needed for identification. Since Horning's learner must enumerate grammars in approximate order of decreasing a priori probability, the grammars most likely to have been chosen as targets are also the ones first hypothesized. Thus countless unlikely grammars need never be considered. Similarly, if the learner could enumerate the "natural grammars" before the "unnatural" ones, he would learn more quickly than he would if the enumeration order was arbitrary. Unfortunately, still not quickly enough. Despite its approximate ordering by a priori probability, Horning's procedure requires vast amounts of computation in learning even the simplest grammars; as he puts it, "although the enumeration procedure...is formally optimal, its Achilles's heal is efficiency." Similarly, the set of natural languages is presumably enormous, and more or less equiprobable as far as the neonate is concerned; thus even enumerating only the natural languages would not be a shortcut to learning. In general, the problem of learning by enumeration within a reasonable time bound is likely to be intractable. In the following section I describe the alternative to enumeration procedures.

V. Heuristic Grammar Construction

ALGORITHMS AND HEURISTICS FOR LANGUAGE LEARNING

Like many other computational problems, language learning can be attempted by *algorithmic* or *heuristic* techniques (see Newell and Simon, 1973). The enumerative procedures we have been discussing are algorithmic in that they guarantee a solution in those cases where one exists.[1] Unfortunately they are also prohibitively time-consuming and wildly implausible as models of children. Heuristic language learning procedures, on the other hand, may hold greater promise in these regards. They differ from the enumerative procedures in two respects. First, the grammars are not acquired and discarded whole, but are built up rule by rule as learning proceeds. Second, the input sentences do not just contribute to the binary decision of whether or not a grammar is consistent with the sample, but some property possessed by sample sentences is used as a hint, guiding the process of rule construction. Thus heuristic language learning procedures are prima facie candidates for theories of human language acquisition. They acquire language piecemeal, as children do (Brown, 1973), and they have the potential for doing so in a reasonable amount of time, drawing their power from the exploitation of detailed properties of the sample sentences instead of the exhaustive enumeration of a class of grammars.

Many heuristic procedures for acquiring rules of finite state and context-free grammars have been proposed (for examples see Biermann and Feldman, 1972; Fu and Booth, 1975; and Knobe and Knobe, 1977). The following example should give the reader the flavor of these procedures. Solomonoff (1964) suggested a heuristic for inferring recursive context-free rules from a sample, in this case with the aid of an informant to provide negative information. *Recursive rules* (not to be confused with the "recursive grammars" discussed earlier) rewrite a symbol as a string containing the original symbol, i.e., rules of the form A → BAC. They are important because they can be successively applied an infinite number of times, giving the grammar the power to generate an infinite number of sentences. An English example might rewrite the symbol for an adjective "A" as the sequence "very A." Solomonoff's learner would delete flanking substrings from an acceptable sample string, and ascertain whether the remaining string was grammatical. If so, he would sandwich that string repetitively with the substrings that were initially deleted, testing each multi-layered string for grammaticality. If they were all grammatical, a recursive rule would be constructed. For example, given the string XYZ in the original sample, the learner would test Y, then if successful, XXYZZ, XXXYZZZ, and so on. If a number of these were acceptable, the rules A → XAZ and A → Y would be coined.

Caveats Concerning Heuristic Methods

Several points must be made about heuristic methods, lest it appear that in trading enumerative procedures for heuristic ones one gets something for nothing. First, as I have mentioned, no procedure can do better than Gold's, either in overall success or in speed, when the set of target languages consists of one of the classes in the Chomsky hierarchy. If the heuristic procedures succeed in learning some languages in a reasonable amount of time, they must take large amounts of time or fail altogether for many other ones. Thus we must again abandon the notion of a general rule learner who is constrained only by the sorts of processing or memory limits that implicitly define classes of computational procedures. Second, heuristic procedures commit the learner to assumptions not only about the target languages, but about the sentences that find their way into the sample. That is, the procedures could be fooled by using unusual or unrepresentative sets of sentences as the basis for rule construction. Consider Solomonoff's heuristic. If the target language permitted no more than three levels of embedding, the learner would have erred by constructing a rule that permitted an infinite number of embeddings. On the other hand, if the sample was a text lacking the multiply-embedded sentences that in Solomonoff's case were provided by the informant, the learner would have erred by constructing the overly-narrow rule which simply generates the original string XYZ. In the natural language case, of course, these problems are less worrisome. Not only will the child do well by "assuming" that the target language is a member of a relatively constrained set (viz., the natural languages), but he will do well in "assuming" that his sample will be a well-defined subset of the target language, not some capricious collection of sentences. Whatever its exact function may turn out to be, the dialect of speech addressed to children learning language has been found to have indisputably consistent properties across different cultures and learning environments (see Snow and Ferguson, 1977).

However, one difference between algorithmic and heuristic procedures advises caution. Whereas enumeration procedures guarantee success in learning an entire language, each heuristic at best gives hope for success in acquiring some piece of the grammar. But one can never be sure that a large collection of heuristics will be sufficient to acquire all or even a significant portion of the language. Nor can one know whether a heuristic that works well for simple constructions or small samples (e.g., the research on the construction of context-free and finite state rules cited earlier) will continue to be successful when applied to more complex, and hence more realistic tasks. In other words, in striving to meet the Developmental, Cognitive, or Time Conditions, we may be sacrificing our original goal, Learnability. The research to be discussed in the remainder of this section illustrates this tradeoff.

The Computer Simulation of Heuristic Language Acquisition

Since one cannot prove whether or not a set of heuristics will succeed in learning a language, several investigators have implemented heuristic strategies as computer programs in order to observe how effective the heuristics turn out to be when they are set to the task of acquiring rules from some sample. Constructing a learning model in the form of a computer program also gives the designer the freedom to tailor various aspects of the program to certain characteristics of human language learners, known or hypothesized. Thus the theorist can try to meet several of our conditions, and is in a better position to submit the model as a *theory* of human language acquisition.

KELLEY'S PROGRAM

Kalon Kelley (1967) wrote the first computer simulation of language acquisition. His priority was to meet the Developmental criterion, so his program was designed to mimic the very early stages of the child's linguistic development.

Kelley's program uses a heuristic that we may call *word-class position learning*. It assumes that the words of a language fall into classes, and that each class can be associated with an absolute or relative ordinal position in the sentence. At the time that Kelley wrote the program, an influential theory ("pivot grammar," Braine, 1963) asserted that early child language could be characterized in this way. As an example of how the heuristic works, consider the following sentences:

1. (a) He smokes grass.
    (b) He mows grass.
    (c) She smokes grass.
    (d) She smokes tobacco.

A learner using the word-class position heuristic would infer that "he" and "she" belong to one word class, because they both occur as the first word of the sentence (or perhaps because they both precede the word "smokes"); similarly, "smokes" and "mows" can be placed in another word class, and "grass" and "tobacco" can be placed into a third. The learner can also infer that a sentence can be composed of a word from the first class, followed by a word from the second class, followed by a word from the third class. A learner who uses this heuristic can now produce or recognize eight sentences after having heard only four.

Kelley's program is equipped with three sets of hypotheses, corresponding to the periods in which the child uses one-, two-, and three-word utterances, respectively. The program advances from one stage to the next at arbitrary moments designated by the programmer. Its first strategy is to count the number of occurrences of various "content" words in the sample sentences; these words are explicitly tagged as content words by the "adult." It retains the most frequent ones, and can produce them as one-word sentences. In its second stage, it looks for two word classes, called "things" and "actions." Kelley assumes that children can tell whether a word refers to a thing or an action by the non-linguistic context in which it was uttered. To model this assumption, his program guesses arbitrarily that a particular word is in one or the other class, and has access to its "correct" classification. If the guess is correct, it is strengthened as a hypothesis; if incorrect, it is weakened. At the same time, the program tabulates the frequency with which the word classes precede or follow each other, thereby hypothesizing rules that generate the frequent sequences of word classes (e.g., S → thing action; S → thing thing). Like the hypotheses that assign words to classes, these rules increase or decrease in strength according to how frequently they are consistent with the input sentences. In its third state, the program retains its two word classes, and adds a class consisting of two-item sequences (e.g., thing-action) from the previous stage. As before, it accumulates evidence regarding which of these classes can occur in which sentence positions relative to one another, thereby hypothesizing rules that generate frequent sequences of classes (e.g., S → thing-action thing). A separate feature of the program is its ability to learn the "functions" of the individual sentence constituents, such as which is the subject and which is the predicate. As before, the program learns these by making rather arbitrary guesses and checking them against the "correct" answer, to which it has access.

An Evaluation

Though Kelley's program was a brave first attempt, it is unsatisfactory on many counts. For one thing, children seem unaffected by the frequency of syntactic forms in adult speech (Brown, 1973), whereas frequency of input forms is the very life-blood of Kelley's learning procedure. Second, the role of the "correct" structural descriptions of sentences given to the program is puzzling. Kelley intends them to be analogous to the child's perception that a word uttered in the context of some action is an "action" word, that a part of a sentence denoting an object being attended to is the "subject" of the sentence, and so on. But in the context of the program, this is reduced to the trivial process of guessing the class or function of a word, and being told whether or not the guess is correct. I will review more systematic attempts to simulate perceptual and pragmatic clues in Sections VI-VIII. Finally, the heuristics that the program uses are inadequate to advance beyond the three-word stage since, as we shall see, natural languages cannot be characterized by sequences of word classes. In any case, one must question whether there is really any point in doing simulations that address themselves only to the Developmental Condition. The early stages of language development can easily be accounted for by all sorts of ad hoc models; it is the acquisition of the full adult grammar that is the mystery.

THE DISTRIBUTIONAL ANALYSIS HEURISTIC

The problem with the word-class position heuristic when it is applied to learning natural languages is that it analyzes sentences at too microscopic a level. It is practically impossible to state natural language regularities in terms of contiguous word classes in sentences. Consider the following sentences:

2. (a) That dog bothers me.
    (b) What she wears bothers me.
    (c) Cheese that is smelly bothers me.
    (d) Singing loudly bothers me.
    (e) The religion she belongs to bothers me.

In the different sentences, the word "bothers" is preceded by a noun, a verb, an adjective, an adverb, and a preposition. Clearly there is a generalization here that an astute learner should make: in all the sentences, "bothers" is preceded by a noun phrase. But noting that certain word classes precede "bothers" will not capture that generalization, and will only lead to errors (e.g., "Loudly bothers me").

A more general heuristic should look for more flexible contexts than either ordinal position in a sentence or position relative to an adjacent item, and should define classes more broadly, so that each class can consist of strings of words or subclasses instead of single words. Kelley's program moved in this direction in its third stage. Heuristics of this sort are often called *distributional analysis* procedures (see Harris, 1964), and exploit the fact that in context-free languages, the different instantiations of a grammatical class are interchangeable in the same linguistic context. Thus it is often a good bet that the different strings of words that all precede (or follow, or are embedded in) the same string of words all fall into the same class, and that if one member of such a class is found in another context, the other members of that class can be inserted there, too. Thus in sentences 2(a-e), a distributional analysis learner would recognize that all strings that precede "bothers me" fall into a class, and that a member of that class followed by the phrase "bothers me" constitutes a sentence. If the learner then encounters the sentence "That dog scares me," he can place "scares me" and "bothers me" into a class, and "scares" and "bothers" into a subclass. If he were to encounter "Sol hates that dog," he could place all the noun phrases in the first class after the phrase "Sol hates." By this process, the learner could build up categories at different levels of abstraction, and catalogue the different ways of combining them in sentences.

Problems with Distributional Analysis

There are several hurdles in the way of using distributional analysis to learn a natural language. First, it requires a great many sets of minimally-contrasting sentences as input. We know that American children often do hear closely-spaced sets of sentences with common constituents (e.g., Brown, Cazden, and Bellugi, 1969; Snow, 1972; see Snow and Ferguson, 1977), but we do not know whether this pattern is universal, nor whether it occurs with enough grammatical constituents to determine uniquely every rule that the child can master. Second, a distributional analysis of a sample of a natural language is fraught with the possibility for serious error, because many words belong to more than one word class, and because virtually any subsequence of words in a sentence could have been generated by many different rules. For example, sentences 3(a-d)

3. (a) Hottentots must survive.
    (b) Hottentots must fish.
    (c) Hottentots eat fish.
    (d) Hottentots eat rabbits.

would seduce a distributional analysis learner into combining heterogeneous words such as "must" and "eat" into a single class, leading to the production of "Hottentots must rabbits," "Hottentots eat survive," and other monstrosities.

Finally, there is a combinatorial explosion of possibilities for defining the context for a given item. Given n words in a sentence other than the item of interest, there are $2^n - 1$ different ways of defining the "context" for that item—it could be the word on the immediate right, the two words on the immediate left, the two flanking words, and so on. In combination with the multiple possibilities for focusing on an item to be generalized, and with the multiple ways of comparing items and contexts across large sets of sentences, these tasks could swamp the learner. However by restricting the types of contexts that a learner may consider, one can trade off the first and third problems against the second. An extremely conservative learner would combine two words in different sentences into the same class only if all the remaining words in the two sentences were identical. This would eliminate the explosion of hypotheses, and sharply reduce the chances of making overgeneralization errors, but would require a highly overlapping sample of sentences to prevent undergeneralization errors (for example, considering every sentence to have been generated by a separate rule). Siklóssy (1971, 1972) developed a model that relies on this strategy. On the other hand, a bolder learner could exploit more tenuous similarities between sentences, making fewer demands on the sample but risking more blunders, and possibly having to test for more similarities. It is difficult to see whether there is an "ideal" point along this continuum. In any case no one has reported a successful formalization or computer implementation of a "pure" distributional analysis learner. Instead, researchers have been forced to bolster a distributional analysis learner with various back-up techniques.

AN "AUTOMATED LINGUIST"

Klein and Kuppin (1970) have devised what they call "an automatic linguistic fieldworker intended to duplicate the functions of a human fieldworker in learning a grammar through interaction with a live human informant." Though never intended as a model of a child, "Autoling," as they call it, was the most ambitious implementation of a heuristic language learner, and served as a prototype for later efforts at modelling the child's language learning (e.g., Anderson, 1974; Klein, 1976).

Use of Distributional Analysis

The program is at heart a distributional analysis learner. As it reads in a sentence, it tries to parse it using the grammar it has developed up until that point. At first each rule simply generates a single sentence, but as new sentences begin to overlap with old ones, the distributional heuristics begin to combine words and word strings into classes, and define rules that generate sequences of classes and words. Out of the many ways of detecting similar contexts across sentences, Autoling relies most heavily on two: identical strings of words to the left of different items, and alternating matching and mismatching items.

Generalizing Rules

Autoling also has heuristics for generalizing rules once they have been coined. For example, if one rule generates a string containing a substring that is already generated by a second rule (e.g., X → ABCD and Y → BC), the first rule is restated so as to mention the left-hand symbol of the second rule instead of the substring (i.e., X → AYD; note that this is a version of Solomonoff's heuristic). Or, if a rule generates a string composed of identical substrings (e.g., X → ABCABC), it will be converted to a recursive pair of rules (i.e., X → ABC; X → XABC). Each such generalization increases the range of sentences accepted by the grammar.

Taming Generalizations

In constructing rules in these ways, Autoling is generalizing beyond the data willy-nilly, and if left unchecked, would soon accept or generate vast numbers of bad strings. Autoling has three mechanisms to circumvent this tendency. First, whenever it coins a rule, it uses it to generate a test string, and asks the informant whether or not that string is grammatical. If not, the rule is discarded and Autoling tries again, deploying its heuristics in a slightly different way. If this fails repeatedly, Autoling tries its second option: creating a transformational rule. It asks its informant now for a correct version of the malformed string, and then aligns the two strings, trying to analyze the correct string into constituents similar to those of the malformed string. It then generates a rule that transforms the malformed into the correct string, permuting or deleting the most inclusive common constituents. As before, it uses the new transformation to generate a test string, and asks the informant for a verdict on its grammaticality, discarding the rule and trying again if the verdict is negative. Finally, if nothing succeeds, the entire grammar self-destructs, and the heuristics begin again from scratch on the entire collection of acceptable sentences, which have been retained since the beginning of the learning session.

An Evaluation

Autoling was not meant to be a model of the child, and needless to say, it is far from one. Unlike children, it scans back and forth over sentences, makes extensive use of negative feedback and corrections from an informant (cf., Brown *et al.,* 1969), tests each new rule methodically, remembers every sentence it hears, and gives up and restarts from scratch when in serious trouble. But it is important as a vivid illustration of the pitfalls of building a language learning model around a collection of heuristics. It is bad enough that Autoling resembles one of Rube Goldberg's creations, with its battery of heuristics (only a few of which I have mentioned), its periodic checkings and recheckings for overlapping, redundant, or idle rules, its various cleanup routines, its counters tabulating its various unsuccessful attempts, and so on. But even with all these mechanisms, Autoling's success as a language learner is very much in doubt. Klein and Kuppin do present records of the program successfully inducing grammars for artificial languages such as a set of well-formed arithmetic expressions. But as an illustration of its ability to learn a natural language, they present a rather unparsimonious grammar, constructed on its second attempt, which generates a finite fragment of English together with a variety of gibberish such as "need she" and "the want take he." Klein and Kuppin are simply unable to specify in any way what Autoling can or cannot learn. Thus Autoling—and, I would argue, any other attempt to model grammar acquisition via a large set of ad hoc heuristics—does not seem a promising start for an adequate theory of language learning. Not only does it violate the Developmental, Cognitive, and Input Conditions, but it does not even come close to meeting the Learnability Condition—the chief motivation for designing learning simulations in the first place.

VI. Semantics and Language Learning

I have postponed discussing the role of semantics in language learning for as long as possible, so as to push the purely syntactic models as far as they can go. But the implausibility of both the enumerative and the heuristic learners seems to indicate that the time has come.

THE "COGNITIVE THEORY" OF LANGUAGE LEARNING

The semantic approach to language learning is based on two premises. First, when children learn a language, they do not just learn a set of admissible sentences; they also learn how to express meanings in sentences. Second, children do not hear sentences in isolation; they hear them in contexts in which they can often make out the intended meanings of sentences by non-linguistic means. That is, they can see what objects and actions are being referred to in the sentences they hear, and they can discern what their parents are trying to communicate as they speak. (Kelley incorporated a version of this assumption into his model.) An extremely influential theory in developmental psycholinguistics (often called the "Cognitive Theory") asserts that children learn syntax by inferring the meanings of sentences from their non-linguistic contexts, then finding rules to convert the meanings into sentences and vice-versa (Macnamara, 1972; Schlesinger, 1971). Several considerations favor the Cognitive Theory. The first (though rarely cited) consideration is that semantic information can substitute for information about non-sentences to make classes of languages formally learnable. The second is that there is some empirical evidence that both children and adults use semantic information when they learn syntactic rules. The third consideration is that this task is thought to be "easier" than inferring a grammar from a set of strings alone, because the mental representations corresponding to sentence meanings are thought to resemble the syntactic structures of sentences. I will discuss each justification for the semantic approach in turn.

LEARNABILITY WITH SEMANTIC INFORMATION

John Anderson (1974, 1975, 1976) has described a semantic version of Gold's language acquisition scenario, formalizing an earlier speculation by Clark (1973). First, he assumes that whatever "sentence meanings" are, they can be expressed in a formal symbolic notation, and thus can be put into one-to-one correspondence with the set of natural numbers by the mathematical technique known as "Gödelization." Second, he assumes that a natural language is a function that maps sentences onto their meanings, or equivalently, well-formed strings onto natural numbers, and vice-versa. (In contrast, we have been assuming that natural languages are functions that map strings onto the judgments "grammatical" and "non-grammatical," or equivalently, "1" and "0.") Third, he assumes that children have access to a series of pairs consisting of a sentence and its meaning, inferred from the non-linguistic context. The child's task is to identify in the limit a function which maps sentences onto their meanings.

Recall that Gold (1967) proved that the class of primitive recursive functions, which map strings onto numbers, is learnable provided that the learner has eventual access to all number-string pairs. For Gold, the numbers represented the trial number or time since the start of learning, but in Anderson's model, the numbers correspond to sentence meanings. The learner enumerates the primitive recursive functions, testing each one against the sample of sentence-meaning pairs, retaining a function if it is consistent with the sample (see Figure 1.1). In this way the learner will identify the function (and hence the language) in the limit, since all incorrect functions will be rejected when they pair a meaning with a different string than the one in the sample.

Although in this version the learner can be proved to succeed without requiring information as to what is not a sentence, all of Gold's other conclusions remain in force. It will take the learner an astronomical amount of time until he arrives at the correct function, but there is no quicker or more successful method, on the whole, than enumerating functions one by one. By suitably restricting the learner's hypothesis space, learning time can be reduced, and by using heuristic procedures that exploit properties of individual meaning-sentence pairs, it can be reduced even further. But once again the learner ceases to be a multipurpose rule learner—he makes tacit assumptions about the syntax of the target language, about the way that meanings are mapped onto strings, and about the representativeness of the meaning-sentence pairs in the sample at a given time. He will fail to learn any language that violates these assumptions. As Chomsky (1965) has noted, the hypothesis that the child uses semantics in learning syntax is in some senses stronger, not weaker, than the hypothesis that sentences alone are used.

EVIDENCE FOR THE COGNITIVE THEORY

Cognitive Development and Language Acquisition

Two sorts of evidence have been martialled in support of the view that humans base their learning of syntax upon their conceptualization or perception of the meanings of sentences. The first consists of various correlations between language development and cognitive development, which are thought to imply that the non-linguistic mental representations available to the child constrain the linguistic hypotheses that he will entertain. For example, the early two- and three-word utterances of children seem to reflect closely certain semantic relations such as agent-action, possessor-possessed, etc. (Bowerman, 1973; Brown, 1973; Schlesinger, 1971). As well, the "cognitive complexity" of the semantic functions underlying various grammatical rules has been shown to predict in a rough way the order of the child's mastery of those rules (Brown, 1973). Similarly, it has been found that some syntactically simple rules (such as the conditional in Russian) are not acquired until the underlying semantic functions (in this case, implication) have been mastered (Slobin, 1973).

Semantics and Artificial Language Learning

The second sort of evidence comes from a set of experiments in which adult subjects are required to learn artificial languages, that is, they must learn to discriminate grammatical from ungrammatical test strings as defined by a grammar concocted by the experimenter. In early experiments of this type (e.g., Miller, 1967), where subjects saw various strings of nonsense syllables, even the simplest grammars were extremely difficult for the subjects to learn. However, in a famous set of experiments, Moeser and Bregman (1972, 1973) presented some subjects with a sample of strings, and other subjects with a sample in which each string was paired with a picture of geometric forms such that the shapes, colors, and spatial relations of the forms corresponded to the words and syntactic relations in the sentences (that is, the pictures were intended to serve as the semantic referents of the strings). After more than 3000 strings had been presented, the subjects who saw only strings failed utterly to discriminate grammatical from ungrammatical test strings, while those who saw strings and pictures had no trouble making the discrimination. This finding has led many theorists to conclude that it is intrinsically easier for humans to learn syntactic rules if they use semantic information in addition to sentences.

However Anderson (1974, 1975) has pointed out that semantics-based learners, including the subjects in Moeser and Bregman's studies, learn by virtue of specific assumptions they make about the way the target language uses syntactic structures to express semantic relations. For example, he notes that natural languages require an adjective to predicate something about the referent of the noun in its own noun phrase, never a noun in another noun phrase in the sentence. That is, in no natural language could a phrase such as "the blue stripes and the red rectangle" refer to an American flag, even though the sentences of such a language might be identical to the sentences of (say) English, and the semantic relations expressible in that language might be identical to those expressible in (say) English. Anderson performed an experiment in which subjects saw strings of English words (referring to shapes, colors, and spatial relations) generated by an artificial grammar. A second group saw the same strings paired with pictures in such a way that each adjective in the sentence modified the noun in its phrase; a third group saw the same strings and pictures, but they were paired in such a way that each adjective modified a noun in a different phrase (like our example with the flag). Only the second group of subjects, with the "natural semantics," were later able to discriminate grammatical from ungrammatical test strings. Thus, Anderson argues, it is not the availability of semantic information per se that facilitates syntax learning in humans, but semantic information that corresponds to the syntactic structures in the target language in some assumed way.[2] These correspondences will be explained in the next section, in which semantics-based learning heuristics are discussed.

HEURISTICS THAT USE SEMANTICS

The most important fact about the natural language acquisition task is that the units composing linguistic rules are abstract, and cannot be derived from sample strings in any simple way. The problem with distributional analysis was that these units or "constituents" do not uniquely reveal themselves in the patterns of sentence overlappings in a sample. However, if the semantic representation of a sentence corresponds in a fairly direct way to the syntactic description of that sentence, semantic information can serve the same purpose as distributional regularities. The syntactic structure of a sentence in a context-free or context-sensitive language can be depicted as a tree, with each node representing a constituent, and the set of branches emanating from a node representing the application of a rule rewriting that constituent as a sequence of lower-order constituents. Similarly, the mental representational structures corresponding to percepts and sentence meanings are also often represented as trees or similar graph structures (e.g., Anderson and Bower, 1973; Norman and Rumelhart, 1975; Winston, 1975). The top nodes of such trees usually correspond to logical propositions, and the branches of these trees correspond to the breakdown of propositions into their subjects and predicates, and to the successive breakdown of the subject and predicate into concepts and relations, or into further propositions. If the tree representing a sentence meaning is partially isomorphic to the constituent structure of the sentence, presumably there is a way that a child can use the meaning structure, which by assumption he has, to discern the constituent structure of the sentence, which he does not have. Anderson (1974, 1975, 1977) has demonstrated precisely how such heuristics could work. In the following paragraphs I shall explain the operation of these heuristics; then, in Section VII, I shall show how Anderson has embodied these heuristics in a computer model of the language learner.

Using Semantics to Delineate Constituents: The Tree-Fitting Heuristic

This heuristic begins with the assumption that the child knows the meaning of all the "content" words in the sentence, that is, he knows to which concept node in the meaning structure each word corresponds. The learner matches the concepts in the meaning structure to the words in the sentence, and attempts to fit the tree structure for the meaning onto the sentence, spatially rearranging the nodes and branches as necessary but preserving all links between nodes. The learner now has a tree-structure for the sentence, and can deduce what the constituents are and how the rules of the grammar rewrite the major constituents as sequences of minor ones.

An example will make this heuristic clearer. Say the child saw a white cat eating a mouse. His perceptual system might construct the propositions "X is a CAT," "X is WHITE," "Y is a MOUSE," and "X EATS Y," which can be depicted as a single tree-structure like the one in Figure 1.3(a). Say the child simultaneously heard the string of words "the white cat eats a mouse." By matching the word "white" onto the concept "WHITE" (and so on for the other words), reversing the order of the respective links to "CAT" and to "MOUSE," and straightening out continuous series of links, the child can arrive at the tree-structure for the sentence which is depicted in Figure 1.3(c). He can then hypothesize rules specifying that a sentence can be broken down into two constituents, that one constituent can be broken down into a class containing the word "white" and another containing the word "cat," and that the second main constituent can be broken down into the word "eats" and a constituent containing a class containing the word "mouse." Furthermore, the child can construct rules translating syntactic constituents into semantic propositions and vice-versa. In this example, he could hypothesize that the first major constituent of a sentence refers to some individual that is the subject of an underlying proposition, the first word class in this constituent refers to some property predicated of that individual, and so on.

The problem with this heuristic is that there are usually many ways to fit a semantic structure onto a string of words, only one of which will correspond to the correct breakdown of the sentence into its syntactic constituents. For example, nothing would have prevented the child in our example from constructing the syntactic trees depicted in Figures 1.3(d) and (e) instead of the one in Figure 1.3(c). Anderson has proposed two mechanisms by which the heuristic could "know" the best way to fit the semantic tree onto the string. First, the learner must know which node of the semantic tree should be highest in the syntactic tree, in order to distinguish between the possibilities represented in Figures 1.3(c) and (d). This corresponds to knowing the main proposition of the sentence, that is, what is the major topic of the sentence and what is the major thing being asserted of it. Anderson suggests that this pragmatic information is communicated to the child during his normal interactions with adults; in other words, the social and communicative context in which a sentence is uttered makes it clear what the adult intends to assert about what (see Bruner, 1975, for supporting arguments and evidence). For the tree-fitting heuristic, this means that one of the propositions in the semantic structure is tagged as the "principal" one, and its node will be highest when the semantic tree is fitted onto the string of words. The nodes connected to this "root" node by one link are placed one level lower, followed by the nodes connected to the root by two links, and so on. Thus if the main proposition concerns what the cat did to the mouse, the heuristic will fit the tree depicted in Figure 1.3(c) onto the string. On the other hand, if it is the whiteness of the mouse-eating cat that is being asserted (e.g., "white is the cat that eats the mouse"), the heuristic will fit the tree depicted in Figure 1.3(d) onto the string.

The second constraint on the heuristic is that no branches be allowed to cross. Thus the heuristic would be prohibited from fitting the tree depicted in Figure 1.3(e) onto the string. No set of context-free rules can generate a tree like this, and in fact what the constraint does is prevent the heuristic from constructing trees from which no context-free rules can possibly be derived. Thus this constraint, which Anderson

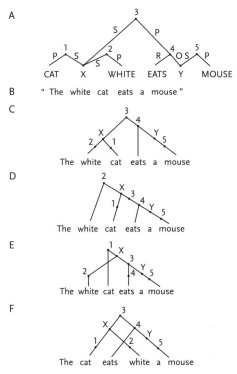

Figure 1.3. Semantic structure (a) to be fitted onto the string (b) in various ways by the Tree-fitting heuristic. In this formalism for semantic structures (HAM; Anderson and Bower, 1973), S = subject, P = predicate, R = relation, O = object, X and Y represent individuals, and capitalized terms are concepts, which correspond to words.

calls the *Graph Deformation Condition,* will prevent the learner from learning languages that use certain rules to transform meaning structures into sentences. For example, it cannot learn a language that could express the semantic structure in Figure 1.3(a) by the string of words "the cat eats white a mouse." Nor could it learn the "unnatural semantics" language that the subjects in Anderson's experiment failed to learn. In each case it would be unable to fit the semantic structure onto the string without crossing branches, as Figure 1.3(f) shows. In general, the heuristic is incapable of learning languages that permit elements from one constituent to interrupt the sequence of elements in another constituent. As Anderson argues, this is a particularly telling example of how a semantics-based heuristic in effect assumes that the language it faces maps meanings onto sentences only in certain ways. In this case, the Tree-fitting heuristic "assumes" that the language meets the Graph Deformation Condition. Anderson believes that natural languages obey this constraint for the most part, and that both children and adults (such as his experimental subjects) tacitly assume so as they use the Tree-fitting heuristic. I will discuss these claims in Section VII.

Using Semantics to Generalize Rules

Once the learner has broken down sentences into their constituents and hypoth-esized the corresponding rewrite rules, he must combine rules that have been derived from different sentences—otherwise he is left with one set of rules for each sentence, not much better than a learner who simply memorized the sentences whole. Rule-merging is a particularly rocky step for distributional analysis heuris-tics (as sentences 3(a-d) showed), since sentences from natural languages provide countless temptations to merge dissimilar constituents owing to the syntactic ambi-guity of most short substrings. Klein and Kuppin's program tentatively merged rules with overlapping constituents, used the newly-merged rules to generate a sentence, and submitted the sentence to the informant for approval before it would declare the merger permanent. But this is an unrealistic way to keep overgeneralizations in check. Not only do children not have access to such an informant, but even if they did, it is unlikely that the Autoling strategy would work as required. A merged rule can usually generate many sentences, sometimes an infinite number, so the knowl-edge that one string is acceptable does not mean that all the strings generated by the rule will be acceptable.

However information in the semantic representation might be used instead to decide whether rules can safely be merged. First, Anderson suggests that words in the same positions in different sentences whose concepts have identical roles in the semantic structure can be merged into one class. For example, say the learner, after processing the meaning–sentence pair in Figure 1.3(c), encountered the sen-tence "The green snail nibbles the leaf," together with its semantic structure, as shown in Figure 1.4(a) and (b). After fitting the semantic tree onto the string (see Figure 1.4(c)) and deriving the corresponding rules, the learner can use the simi-larities between the semantic representations in Figures 1.3(a) and 1.4(a) to merge the two sets of rules. For example, "EATS" in Figure 1.3(a) corresponds to the "rela-tion" branch of the predicate of the main proposition, and so does "NIBBLES" in Figure 1.4(a). The learner can then merge the corresponding words into one class, and by similar means can merge "white" and "green," "eat" and "snail," and so on.

Now the learner must recognize that the higher constituents in the two sen-tences can also be merged, such as the ones embracing "the white cat" and "the green snail." Anderson suggests a double criterion for when to merge higher-order constituents: they must decompose into identical sub-constituents, and they must serve the same semantic role. In this example, both are satisfied: the word classes in the two constituents have already been merged, and both constituents serve as the subject of their respective main propositions. Once all the parallel constituents in the two sentences have been merged, the learner will end up with a grammar that generates sixteen different sentences: "the green cat eats a leaf," "the white snail nibbles a mouse," and so on. Anderson calls this heuristic (and the putative prop-erty of natural languages that it exploits) *Semantics-Induced Equivalence of Syntax.* He asserts that the heuristic exploits the tendency of natural languages always to

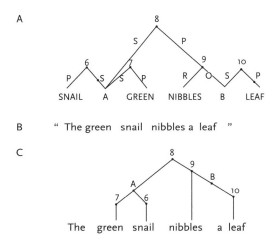

Figure 1.4. Semantic structure (A), string (B), and tree (C) which, in conjunction with Figure 1.3 illustrate the Semantics-Induced Equivalence Heuristic.

use the same syntactic construction to express a particular semantic relation within a given higher-order constituent. Whether or not this claim is true of English will be discussed in Section VII.

It is interesting to note that the Semantics-Induced Equivalence of Syntax heuristic is neither more nor less conservative, on the whole, than Distributional Analysis. Each will try to merge in situations where the other would not. Thus the Distributional Analysis heuristic would make no generalization embracing the sentences in Figures 1.3 and 1.4, since they share no content words. Instead it would have to wait until some sentence like "the green snail eats a mouse" appeared. On the other hand, the Semantics-Induced Equivalence heuristic, upon encountering the sentence "the white cat eats slowly," would not merge "slowly" with "the mouse" (as would Distributional Analysis), since "MOUSE" and "SLOWLY" would not have the same roles in their semantic structures. It should be clear from these examples that the Semantics-Induced Equivalence heuristic will, in general, make the wiser generalization.

VII. Anderson's Language Acquisition System

THE COMPUTER SIMULATION OF SEMANTICS-BASED HEURISTIC LANGUAGE ACQUISITION

Heuristics that exploit syntax-semantics correlations, like those that exploit properties of sentences alone, are often implemented as computer programs (Anderson, 1974, 1975, 1977; Fabens and Smith, 1975; Klein, 1976; Klein and Rozencvejg, 1974; McMaster, Sampson, and King, 1976; Reeker, 1976; Siklóssy, 1971, 1972).

In a sense, these programs are incarnations of the informal Cognitive Theories of the Schlesinger and Macnamara sort. As such, they serve as a testing ground for the adequacy of those theories, especially at meeting the Learnability Condition, and can also contribute to the goal of specifying more precisely and explicitly the mechanisms that these theories implicate. Unfortunately, many of the programs that have been developed succumb to the same syndrome that afflicted Klein and Kuppin's model: unreasonable assumptions about the learner and the information available to him, ad hoc and unparsimonious learning mechanisms, and dubious success at learning. For example, the program of Fabens and Smith (1975) modifies its rules in accordance with environmental approval and disapproval, which Brown and Hanlon (1970) have shown is probably irrelevant to the learning of syntax. Other programs (e.g., Klein, 1976; Reeker, 1976; Siklóssy, 1971, 1972) avoid this device but only learn to produce meager, ill-defined fragments of natural languages, often generating many non-sentences at the same time. The exception among these efforts is Anderson's Language Acquisition System (LAS; 1974, 1975, 1977). As we have seen, Anderson has carefully defined certain heuristics that his program employs and the properties of natural languages that make these heuristics useful. As well, the program can acquire well-defined infinite subsets of natural languages, its semantic representations have an independent theoretical motivation, and it avoids for the most part psychologically unrealistic strategies. For these reasons, I will discuss only Anderson's simulation from among the many that have been reported (which in any case rely on heuristics remarkably similar to the ones Anderson uses).

HOW LAS WORKS

General Architecture

LAS uses a formalism for semantic representations that Anderson has used elsewhere as a theory of information representation in long term memory (the Human Associative Memory system (HAM) of Anderson and Bower, 1973). Its grammar is in the form of an Augmented Transition Network (ATN), which is held by many to be a plausible model of human language processing (see Kaplan, 1975). The ATN that LAS uses corresponds rule-for-rule to a context-free grammar, but can be incorporated more easily into a left-to-right sentence recognizer or producer. LAS has a subroutine corresponding to sentence production, which uses the ATN to convert a semantic structure into a sentence. It also has a subroutine that corresponds to sentence comprehension, which uses the ATN to convert a sentence into its semantic structure. Finally, it has a learning program that uses pairs consisting of semantic structures and sentences to build the ATN piece-by-piece. The latter program is the one of interest here.

Like Kelley's and Klein and Kuppin's programs, LAS is driven by the comprehension process. It tries to interpret a sentence from left-to-right with its current grammar, and alters parts of the grammar if it fails. If a particular rule gets the learner part way in interpreting a sentence, it is the one that will be expanded. LAS also forgets the exact sentences that it hears, so that a sentence contributes to grammatical development only in the way that it alters the grammar as it is being understood. These features give LAS a psychologically realistic flavor compared to other models I have discussed.

Use of the Tree-Fitting Heuristic

When LAS receives its first sentence-meaning pair, there is no grammar to interpret it yet, so it must build the first pieces of the grammar relying entirely on the Tree-fitting heuristic. But in general, the HAM structure representing the learner's perception of the situation in which the sentence has been uttered is not really suitable for fitting onto the string right away. It contains too many sentence-irrelevant propositions, and has no way of indicating the proposition corresponding to the principle assertion of the sentence (see Section VI). Thus the program is forced to compute an intermediate representation, called the *Prototype Structure,* which omits propositions whose concepts have no counterparts among the words of the sentence, and highlights the principle proposition (in line with supposed pragmatic cues). It is this Prototype structure, not the meaning structure itself, that the Tree-fitting heuristic tries to fit onto the string of words. Once an acceptable tree has been derived by the heuristic, LAS constructs ATN *arcs,* each one corresponding to a left-to-right sequence of constituents composing a higher constituent, and the corresponding rules that map these syntactic constituents onto their semantic counterparts.

Use of the Semantics-Based Equivalence Heuristic

When subsequent pairs come in, LAS tries to interpret the strings using all its rules simultaneously. Using the Semantics-Induced Equivalence heuristic, it unites into a single class words whose concepts serve the same role in their respective HAM structures. Similarly, it merges any two arcs (i.e., higher-order constituents) that simultaneously assign the same semantic role to their respective sentence constituents. These mechanisms were discussed in Section VI. In addition, LAS will merge two arcs if one is a proper subsequence of another, as long as they both specify the same semantic role. For example, assume that LAS has induced an arc that will parse sequences like "the mouse" in Figure 1.3, and that it is forced by a subsequent sentence to construct an arc that will parse "the mouse that nibbles the house." Then the old arc will be swallowed into the new one automatically (with the last four words marked as "optional"). In this way, LAS can construct recursive rules, allowing it to generate infinite languages. In the present example, it would construct a low-level arc to parse "the house"; however, this substring can already be parsed with the higher-level arc built to parse "the mouse that nibbles the house" (since "mouse" and "house" would presumably be merged, and the last four words are marked as optional). Consequently it would merge the two arcs, ending up with the recursive arc corresponding to the rule *"noun phrase → the noun that nibbles noun phrase."* Now it can generate "the mouse that nibbles the cat that eats the mouse that nibbles the house" and so on.

Finally, LAS has a special heuristic with which it handles the so-called "grammatical morphemes" such as articles, auxiliaries, relative pronouns, and so on, which have no direct counterparts in the semantic representations. This heuristic will be discussed in a later paragraph.

Learning Powers of LAS

How well does LAS do? Anderson presents several examples in which LAS is faced with artificial languages or fragments of natural languages, all context-free, which can be used to describe arrangements of two-dimensional shapes of various colors and sizes. In all cases LAS succeeded in acquiring a grammar for the language, including infinitely large subsets of English and French, after taking in 10-15 meaning-sentence pairs. For example, it could handle sentences like "the large blue square which is below the triangle is above the red circle which is small," and other sentences using these grammatical constructions. Anderson conjectures that LAS could learn any context-free language with a semantic system that respected the Graph Deformation Condition and the Semantics-Induced Equivalence of Syntax Condition.

AN EVALUATION OF LAS

LAS is unquestionably an impressive effort. Anderson is alone in showing how a learner with semantics-based heuristics can succeed in learning chunks of natural languages in a plausible manner. Furthermore, there are possibilities for extending the powers of LAS. If LAS were built like Winograd's (1972) program to converse with another speaker instead of receiving sentences passively, it would have representational structures that conceivably could be useful in acquiring rules for interrogatives, conditionals, imperatives, and so on. And if it had a more childlike semantic representational system, which categorized the world into actors, actions, and recipients of actions, possessors and possessed, objects and locations, and so on, its linguistic abilities might even resemble those of young children (cf., Brown, 1973). By enriching the semantic system gradually, it might even be possible to generate a sequence of stages parallel to the child's linguistic development, which would be a unique accomplishment among formal models of language learning (outside of Kelley's limited attempts). Of course, all of this remains to be shown.

In any case, rather than spelling out the various ways that LAS can be extended, I shall focus in this section on the *limits* of LAS's abilities, on Anderson's claim that "the weakness of LAS ... is sufficiently minor that I am of the opinion that LAS-like learning mechanisms, with the addition of some correcting procedures, could serve as the basis for language learning" (1977, pp. 155–156). Since LAS is an incarnation of the currently popular Cognitive Theory of language learning, Anderson's claim is an important one. If true, it would support the contention that the child's perceptual and cognitive representations are sufficiently rich data structures to support language acquisition (e.g., Bowerman, 1973; Sinclair-de Zwart, 1969; Schlesinger, 1971), obviating the need for innate language-specific data structures (e.g., Chomsky, 1965; Fodor, 1966; McNeill, 1966). On this view, the innate constraints on the learner derive only from his cognitive representational structures and, as Anderson points out, his tacit assumptions about how these correspond to syntactic structures. For this reason I will examine LAS's abilities in some detail. In particular, I shall scrutinize Anderson's central claim, that most syntactic rules can be derived from distinctions made at the semantic level, while the rest can be derived with the help of a few miscellaneous heuristics.

Do Natural Languages Obey the Graph Deformation Condition?

This condition, on which the Tree-fitting heuristic depends, decrees in effect that natural languages must be context-free, a conclusion that Anderson explicitly supports (despite its near-universal rejection by linguists). There are a number of natural language constructions which cross branches, and Anderson must find reason to dismiss them as counter-examples to the omnipotence of the Tree-fitting heuristic. One example is the "respectively" construction. As Figures 1.5(a) and (b) show, the semantic structures for these sentences cannot be fitted onto the strings without branches crossing. A second example can be found in languages that indicate semantic roles by case markers instead of by word order (e.g., Russian, Latin, Wolbiri). In these languages it is possible for an element that belongs to one phrase to interrupt a sequence of elements in a second phrase, provided that the intruding element is suitably marked as belonging to its phrase. Anderson cites both these counter-examples, and argues that they are atypical constructions, possibly acquired by special problem-solving strategies outside the normal language induction mechanisms. While the rarity of constructions of the "respectively" sort make this conclusion tenable for these constructions, it is less easy to forgive the paucity of mechanisms in LAS for acquiring case-inflection rules, prevalent in languages other than English, which naturally give rise to constructions with crossing branches.

A second class of counter-examples consists of discontinuous elements, which give rise to crossing syntactic dependencies in a sentence. For example, in the sentence "Irving threw the meat out that had green spots," the phrase "the meat" is part of a constituent that includes "that had green spots," whereas the word "threw" is part of a constituent that includes the word "out." Figure 1.5(c) and (d) show how these branches must cross (similar crossing dependencies can occur with auxiliary and tense morphemes under certain analyses, see Gross, 1972). Anderson exempts the Tree-fitting heuristic from having to deal with such constructions on the grounds that they involve "non-meaning bearing morphemes" which are

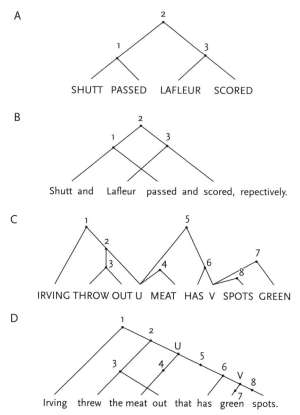

Figure 1.5. Violations of the Graph Deformation Condition.

outside its province. But this is not quite true—the morpheme "out" in the sentence in Figure 1.5(d) conveys a different meaning than would the morphemes "up" or "around" or "down" if one were substituted in its place. But it is not clear how the morpheme "out" would have been mapped onto the semantic structure in the first place—if "THROW-OUT" were represented as a unitary node, and the morpheme "out" introduced into the sentence by some other means, the tree-fitting heuristic would not have to deal with the morpheme. As a putative universal for natural languages, the Graph Deformation Condition can be criticized in that the HAM structures representing the meanings of various sentence types are not specified a priori, but seem to be made up as they are needed. For this reason it is hard to disconfirm the Condition with the present examples, though.

Do Natural Languages Permit Semantics-Induced Generalizations?

The Tree-fitting heuristic has a function other than giving a tree-structure to the sentence. The heuristic attaches semantic labels to the branches of the tree, and the Semantics-Induced Equivalence of Syntax heuristic uses these labels as criteria for merging rules derived from different sentences. These heuristics serve LAS well, but only because the subset of English grammar and the subset of HAM structures that Anderson has chosen correspond almost feature for feature. For example, the grammatical rule that specifies that sentences consist of a noun phrase and a verb phrase corresponds to the breakdown of HAM propositions into a subject and a predicate; the grammatical rule that breaks the predicate phrase into a spatial preposition and a noun phrase corresponds to the breakdown of a HAM predicate into a relation and an object, and so on. However, whenever syntax and semantics diverge, I will show, LAS errs, either over- or undergeneralizing.

Semantics-Induced Undergeneralizations
LAS's powers to generate more sentences than it has seen reside in its abilities to merge the different exemplars of a constituent type into a single class. Thus one would want LAS to recognize, say, that (to a first approximation) all noun phrases in English are generated by the same set of rules, regardless of the type of sentence or the position in a sentence in which the noun phrase is found. However LAS fails to do so even with the restricted subset of English it is given. For example, it fails to recognize the equivalence of subject noun phrases in sentences using the word "above" with those using the word "below." This is because the concepts "above" and "below" are represented identically in the propositions at the semantic level, with the subject of such a proposition interpreted by other procedures as the higher of the two objects in space. Thus the counterpart to "the square" in "the square is above the circle" is the subject in the underlying proposition, whereas in "the square is below the triangle" it is the object. For this reason the two occurrences of the phrase are mistakenly treated as different syntactic units.

   Although Anderson suggests a solution to this particular problem, related problems will pop up when different subsets of languages are attempted. This is because natural languages frequently use the same constituents to express different underlying logical functions (which is one of the chief motivations for developing transformational grammars, with their distinction between deep and surface structures). Thus the Semantics-Induced Equivalence heuristic would never realize that the different tokens of the phrase "the cop" in 4(a-e)

4. (a) The cop frightens the thief.
    (b) The cop is frightened by the thief.
    (c) The cop tends to like thieves.
    (d) The cop who arrests thieves...
    (e) The cop who thieves frighten...

are examples of the same type of sentence constituent, since in the different sentences and phrases it functions variously as subject or object of the underlying proposition, or as part of the principal proposition or one of the secondary propositions.

LAS would develop ad hoc rules for the different types of sentences, and would be unable to conclude that a subject noun phrase in an active sentence can also appear as the subject of a passive sentence, a "tend"-type sentence, and so on.

One interesting way to remedy this problem would be to posit distinct mental predicates corresponding to the different syntactic constructions that a verb can enter into. Thus there would be mental predicates for "FRIGHTEN," "IS-FRIGHTENED-BY," "TENDS-TO-FRIGHTEN," "IS-EASY-TO-FRIGHTEN," and so on (which is similar to a proposal Anderson has made elsewhere in discussing memory for sentences, see Anderson and Bower, 1973). Since the subjects of the sentences with all these constructions are also the subjects of their underlying propositions at the semantic level, LAS would have grounds to merge them. Unfortunately, this raises the problem of how the learner could tell when to encode a situation using one type of mental predicate rather than another. For example, how would the learner know to use the "FRIGHTEN" predicate just when hearing "It is easy to frighten the cat," but the "IS-EASY-TO-FRIGHTEN" predicate when hearing "That cat is easy to frighten"? This "encoding problem" and its possible solutions will be discussed further in Section IX.

Semantics-Induced Overgeneralizations

In relying on semantic criteria, LAS also generalizes in cases where it should not. For example, the proposition asserting that an entity is square-shaped can appear in a sentence either as "the square" or "the square thing," but the proposition asserting that an entity is colored red can appear only as "the red thing." Nonetheless, since the two propositions have the same format, LAS overgeneralizes and accepts "the red." Anderson solves this problem by providing LAS with an innate schema for noun phrases, including the stipulation that a noun phrase must contain at least one noun. If indeed the general form of the noun phrase is innate, it cannot have the format Anderson proposes, however, since many noun phrases lack nouns—consider the subject noun phrases in the sentences "Jogging exhausts me," "It is a total bore," and "That he chortles is irritating."

A similar overgeneralization problem follows from the fact that verbs with similar semantic representations have different case structures, that is, require different numbers and arrangements of noun phrases in the sentences in which they appear. Thus "give" might appear in a semantic structure with a subject and two objects, corresponding to the giver, gift, and recipient. Using this structure, LAS could build rules that parsed "Rockefeller gave Brown a million dollars," with two consecutive noun phrases after the verb; it would also construct rules to parse "Rockefeller gave a million dollars to Brown," with a noun phrase and a prepositional phrase. However when LAS later encounters sentences like "The IMF transferred a billion dollars to Ghana," or "Rockefeller donated a Wyeth to the museum," it would merge "give," "transfer," and "donate" into a single class, since they would have similar roles in their semantic representations, and would mistakenly produce "Rockefeller donated the museum a Wyeth," "The IMF transferred Ghana a billion dollars," and so on. Anderson does suggest a heuristic that might help LAS in learning the case structures of verbs: placing all the concepts that are causally related to the verb at the same level of embedding in the Prototype structure. This would not help for the present examples, however, since the different verbs have the same causal relation to the noun phrases, but have different case structures nonetheless. Many similar examples can be found in English: "throw" versus "propel," "show" versus "display," "teach" versus "instruct," and so on.

Learning Grammatical Morphemes

The class of grammatical morphemes (e.g., articles, inflections, conjunctions, relative pronouns, etc.) poses special problems for LAS, since they have no counterparts in its semantic structures. Anderson argues that learning the rules for ordering these terms in the absence of semantic information is *not* problematic, at least in a formal sense. Since grammatical morphemes occur in sub-sequences of finite length, they constitute a finite cardinality language, which, according to Gold's theorems, can be learned with neither an informant nor a semantic referent. This argument is misleading, however, because whether or not a string of grammatical morphemes is acceptable will depend on its context. Since the relevant context can be indefinitely long, there would be an infinite number of cases for the finite cardinality learner to memorize. Thus what the learner faces is *not* a finite cardinality language after all. For example, the occurrence of the string "to which" in sentence 5(a) is grammatical only because the verb "give," which can take a prepositional phrase beginning with "to," appears later in the sentence (compare the same sentence with "spent" in place of "gave"). But as sentences 5(b-d) show, that verb can be an arbitrary distance away, resulting in an infinite number of contexts to learn.

5. (a) The museum to which he gave a million dollars is in Chicago.
   (b) The museum to which it is obvious he gave a million dollars is in Chicago.
   (c) The museum to which I think it is obvious he gave a million dollars is in Chicago.
   (d) The museum to which I think without any justification whatsoever it is obvious he gave a million dollars is in Chicago.

Thus learning rules for these classes of items is formally far from a trivial matter, and it is worth examining the heuristic solutions to the problem that Anderson proposes.

To begin with, it should be noted that LAS faces a language with few grammatical morphemes: only the articles "the" and "a," the copula "is," and the relative pronoun "which." The spatial prepositions such as "above" are treated as content words, since they correspond directly to nodes in the semantic representation, and to simplify matters even further, the expression "to the left of" has been collapsed into the single word "left-of." With this simple language, LAS can survive with a single heuristic: when it encounters one or more grammatical morphemes, it brackets them with the content word immediately to the right, creating a new constituent.

Problems with the Grammatical Morpheme Heuristic
Although this heuristic works well enough to prevent LAS from making any gross errors, it prevents it from making important generalizations as well. For example, LAS cannot recognize the equivalence in its grammar of predicate phrases in the main clause of a sentence and predicate phrases in relative clauses, because the latter have the word "which" grafted onto them. This also seems to be the reason that LAS fails to merge its class for prenominal adjectives (*"red* square") with its identical class for predicate adjectives ("the square *is red*"). In any case, the heuristic clearly would not work for larger subsets of natural languages. As Anderson notes, in sentences like

6. The woman that he ran after is nimble.

LAS would create the nonsense constituent "after is nimble," leading to many possibilities for error (e.g., "The woman he loved after is nimble").

"Correcting Procedures" for Handling Grammatical Morphemes
Anderson does suggest remedies for some of these problems. For example, the first problem could be solved by allowing LAS to merge arcs with identical subconstituents, whether or not one arc is wholly contained in the other. However this procedure would still not make the required generalization in the general case—it would not help detect the similarities between main clauses and other sorts of relative clauses, such as those in which the objects have been deleted. For example, in 7(b), there is no constituent corresponding to the "the monster devoured" in 7(a), as the brackets indicate. Nonetheless one would want a learner to be able to generalize that whatever can be expressed in a main clause like 7(b)

7. (a) The cookie that the monster devoured is huge.
   (b) (The monster) (devoured (the cookie))

can also be expressed in a relative clause like the one in 7(a).

Anderson also suggests that redundant word classes, such as the predicate and prenominal adjective classes in our example, should be merged if they have enough members in common. But this would only lead to trouble. In natural languages, many if not most nouns can also serve as verbs and adjectives, but it would be disastrous to merge those classes outright, since many adjectives and verbs *cannot* serve as nouns.

Finally, Anderson suggests that the incorrect parse of sentences like 6 could be avoided if the learner would exploit the pause often found after the preposition in spoken speech as a cue to the correct location of the constituent boundary. However, natural speech is full of pauses that do *not* signal phrase boundaries (see Rochester, 1973), so such a heuristic would not, in general, do much good.

CONCLUSION

In sum, careful scrutiny of the learning mechanisms of LAS does not bear out Anderson's claim that such mechanisms are sufficient to learn natural languages. We have seen a number of cases in which the semantics-based heuristics are inadequate in principle to learn important features of English. This would not be a serious criticism if there were principled ways of extending LAS to handle these features. But virtually all of Anderson's proposals for extending LAS would at best work for the particular glitches they were designed to fix, and would be ineffective if applied to larger subsets of natural languages.

None of this diminishes the importance of Anderson's contribution. In the traditional psycholinguistic literature, the "Cognitive" theory of language learning is usually discussed in such vague terms that it is impossible to evaluate. In embodying this theory in a computer program, Anderson has shown what assumptions the theory rests on, which aspects of language learning the theory can account for, and which aspects are beyond its reach. In Section IX, I will discuss further the implications of LAS and other models for theories of human language learning.

VIII. A Theory of Learning Transformational Grammars

The features of natural language that give LAS the most trouble are precisely those features that cannot easily be handled by context-free grammars, and that motivated the development of transformational grammars (Chomsky, 1957, 1965). Examples are discontinuous constituents, "respectively"-type constructions, case- and complement structures of various verbs, the divergence of semantic roles and syntactic constituent structures, the placement of "grammatical morphemes," and generalizations that hold across related syntactic constructions. An adequate theory of language learning will have to account for the acquisition of languages with these sorts of properties. Henry Hamburger, Kenneth Wexler, and Peter Culicover have taken a large step in this direction by constructing a mathematical model which incorporates some reasonable assumptions about the language learner, and which they prove is capable of learning transformational grammars of a certain type (Hamburger and Wexler, 1975; Wexler, Culicover, and Hamburger, 1975; Culicover and Wexler, 1977).

Central to Hamburger, Wexler, and Culicover's theory is the assumption that the learner is innately constrained to entertain hypotheses of a certain sort, and is therefore capable of acquiring only certain types of languages. As I have mentioned, this assumption could conceivably enable an enumerative language learner to learn a language with access only to a sample of sentences. The assumption is also implicit in a weak form in the heuristic approach to language learning, and is explicitly embraced by Anderson when he claims that the learner "assumes" that the target language conforms to the Graph Deformation Condition and to the Semantics-Induced Equivalence of Syntax Condition. But Hamburger *et al.* take the strongest view, originally proposed by Chomsky (1962, 1965), that innate, language-specific constraints cause the child to consider only a very narrowly-defined class of transformational grammars. Hamburger, Wexler, and Culicover's feat was to define these constraints in a precise way, show why they contribute to learnability, and make the case that natural languages fall into the class they define.

Hamburger *et al.* begin with a version of Chomsky's transformational grammar, in which a set of context-free *base rules* generates a *deep structure* tree which *transformations* operate upon to produce a sentence. The base rules can generate arbitrarily large deep structures only by rewriting sentences within sentences, that is, by repetitively applying one of the rules that rewrites the "S" symbol. Each occurrence of an "S" delineates a *level* in the deep structure. Transformational rules are applied first at the lowest level (i.e., the most deeply embedded subsentence), then to the second lowest level, and so on.

LEARNABILITY OF TRANSFORMATIONAL GRAMMARS FROM A TEXT

Wexler and Hamburger (1973) first attempted to prove that a constrained class of transformational grammars was identifiable in the limit from a sample of sentences (see the section on "Constraining the Hypothesis Space" in Section IV). They made the assumption, known to be overly strong, that all languages have identical base rules and differ only in their transformational rules. Thus they made the base rules innate, and required the learner to identify in the limit a set of transformations that generated the target language. This they proved to be impossible. Therefore, in their next attempts (Hamburger and Wexler, 1975; Wexler, Culicover, and Hamburger, 1975) they assumed, with Anderson and the "Cognitive" theorists, that the child has simultaneous access to a string and its meaning, and must learn rules that translate one into the other.

SEMANTIC REPRESENTATIONS AND THE INVARIANCE PRINCIPLE

In Hamburger *et al.*'s model, a sentence meaning is represented by a tree structure that has the same hierarchical breakdown of constituents as the deep structure of the sentence, but with no particular left-to-right ordering of the constituents (such a structure is similar to Anderson's "Prototype structure"). Since deep structure constituents are ordered differently in different languages, the first task for the learner is to learn the base rules which define the orderings his language uses. Wexler and Culicover note that this can be accomplished in a number of simple ways (in fact, Anderson's Tree-fitting heuristic is one such way). Like Anderson, they point out that this assumes that in all natural languages the deep structures *will* preserve the hierarchical connectivity of nodes in semantic structures, differing only in their linear order (i.e., branches may not cross, nor may links be severed and re-attached elsewhere). They justify this *Invariance Condition* (similar, of course, to Anderson's Graph Deformation Condition) by showing that out of all the combinatorial possibilities for ordering constituents of a certain type in deep structures, only those that respect the Invariance Condition are found in natural languages (over 200 of which they examine, Culicover and Wexler, 1974).

THE LEARNING PROCEDURE

From then on the learner must hypothesize a set of transformations, or a *transformational component*, that in combination with the base rules generates the target language. The procedure is simple. The learner undergoes an infinite series of trials in which he is presented with a meaning-sentence pair and is required to guess a grammar. For each pair, the learner applies his current transformational rules to the deep structure (which he computes from the meaning structure), and compares the result against the input string. If they match, the learner leaves his grammar untouched and proceeds to the next pair. If they do not match, the learner randomly decides between two courses of action. He can discard, at random, any of the transformations he used to derive the incorrect string; or, he can hypothesize a set consisting of all the transformations capable of transforming the deep structure to the input string in conjunction with the rest of the grammar, and select one of these transformations at random for inclusion in the grammar. Hamburger *et al.* prove that with suitable constraints on the transformations used by the target language (and hypothesized by the learner), the learner will converge on a correct grammar for the language (i.e., the probability that the learner will have guessed a correct grammar becomes arbitrarily close to 1 as time passes). The proof is long and complex and will not be outlined here. Instead I will summarize how the constraints that Hamburger *et al.* propose function to guarantee learnability. This, of course, is the crux of the Chomskian claim that learnability considerations favor a strongly nativist theory of language acquisition.

PROVING LEARNABILITY

As I have mentioned in Section IV, restricting the learner's hypothesis space only yields learnability if the intersection between the grammars in the hypothesis space and the grammars consistent with the sample becomes smaller and smaller as learning proceeds (see Figure 1.2). Hamburger *et al.* must show that when the learner has guessed an incorrect transformational component, he need not wait an arbitrarily long time before discovering his error, that is, encountering a semantic structure that the Component does not properly transform into the corresponding sentence. This in turn implies that the learner must not have to wait until an arbitrarily *complex* meaning-sentence pair appears in the sample before knowing that his transformational component is incorrect, since by the laws of probability he would have to wait an arbitrarily long time for an arbitrarily complex pair. In other words, if the learner has an incorrect transformational component, that component must make an error on a sentence-meaning pair that is no more complex than a certain bound (where complexity is measured by the number of S-nodes or levels in the deep structure).

This condition is not satisfied for unconstrained transformational grammars. In transformational grammars, each transformation is triggered by a particular configuration of symbols in a deep structure, or *structural description*. If a structural description can be arbitrarily complex for a transformation in the grammar, then the learner would have to wait until a meaning-sentence pair of that (arbitrary) complexity appeared in the sample before having occasion to hypothesize such a transformation. It would then be impossible to prove that the probability of the learner having hypothesized a complete, correct grammar approaches unity with increasing exposure to the sample. So Hamburger *et al.* proposed the following constraint on transformations: no transformation may have a structural description that refers to symbols in more than two adjacent levels in the deep structure. Consider the deep structure-sentence pair in Figure 1.6 (the example has been simplified drastically from Chomsky, 1973). Assuming that the learner's transformational component does not yet correctly map one onto the other, the learner could hypothesize something like the following transformation (assuming that other transformations place the grammatical morphemes properly):

NP VP NP VP NP VP what → what NP VP NP VP NP VP.

However this transformation would be forbidden by Hamburger *et al.*'s constraint, because the symbols on the left hand side span across three levels in the deep structure. Instead, the learner could hypothesize something like the following:

NP VP what → what NP VP

which, applied successively from the deepest level upward, would produce the same string. (It is interesting to note that in this example the learner would not even have had to wait until encountering a pair this complex to hypothesize the transformation—an interrogative sentence with one level would have sufficed.) Hamburger *et al.* argue that virtually all transformations in English and other languages conform to this condition, which they call the *Binary Principle.* Although they proposed the principle because, without it, they could not have proved learnability, they point out that Chomsky (1973) independently proposed an identical constraint, the *Subjacency Condition,* which he justified on descriptive grounds. That is, there seems to be independently motivated evidence that the Binary Principle is true of natural languages.

THE FREEZING PRINCIPLE

The Binary Principle is not sufficient, however, to guarantee that an incorrect transformational component will make a telltale error on a meaning-sentence pair less complex than a certain bound. The base rules of a grammar can generate only a finite number of structures within a single level, by definition. Together with the Binary Principle, this would seem to ensure that input data of bounded complexity would suffice to exhaust all the structural descriptions that could trigger transformations. Unfortunately, whenever a transformation is applied at one level, it can alter the configuration of symbols within another level, creating new potential structural descriptions for transformations. Thus a series of transformations starting arbitrarily far down in a deep structure can alter the configuration of symbols within another level (as, in fact, the example in Figure 1.6 showed), creating new potential structural descriptions for transformations. A learner whose transformational component was in error only when applied to this altered configuration would never discover the error until coming across this arbitrarily complex structure. To remedy this situation, Culicover, Wexler, and Hamburger (1975) proposed a new constraint, the *Freezing Principle,* which forbids a transformation to apply to a configuration of symbols that could only have been created by the previous application of another transformation. The artificial example in Figure 1.7 shows how the constraint works. Say

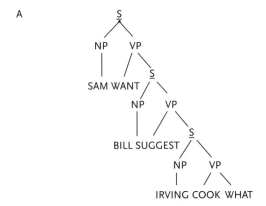

B   "What does Sam want Bill to suggest Irving cook?"

Figure 1.6. Deep structure (A) and string (B) illustrating the Binary Principle.

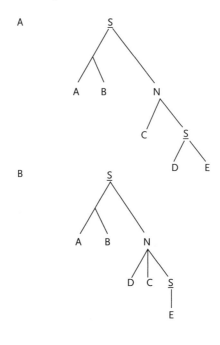

C   " B A D C E "

Figure 1.7. Deep structure (A) and string (C) illustrating the Freezing Principle.

the learner must transform the deep structure 7(a) into the string 7(c), and already has a transformation that reverses the two morphemes C and B, as shown in 7(b). Now he must coin a transformation that reverses the morphemes A and B. The following transformation, for example, would accomplish this reversal:

ABDC → BADC.

However, the Freezing Principle forbids this hypothesis, since it refers to the symbol sequence DC, which was not generated by a base rule but was created by another transformation. Instead, the learner can hypothesize the following transformation:[3]

AB → BA.

With the Binary and Freezing Principles, Hamburger, Wexler, and Culicover not only prove that the learner will converge on a correct grammar, but that he can do so without even having to consider any structure with more than two levels of embedded sentences (i.e., three S-nodes).

Of course, Hamburger, Wexler, and Culicover must show that their constraint does not prevent their learner from acquiring any natural language. In Wexler, Culicover, and Hamburger (1975) and Culicover and Wexler (1977), examples of many sorts of English constructions are adduced to support the contention that natural languages obey the Freezing Principle. Moreover, Wexler *et al.* argue that in some cases the Freezing Principle does a better job than other constraints proposed in the linguistics literature at explaining why certain types of sentences are judged ungrammatical, and that in other cases, it mandates a choice between competing, hitherto equally plausible theories.

AN EVALUATION

In evaluating the Hamburger *et al.* model, it is important to note that I have changed the emphasis somewhat from their presentation. Their chief goal was to develop an "explanatorily adequate" linguistic theory (see Chomsky, 1965), which not only accounts for various linguistic phenomena, but *explains* why they must be one way and not another. Thus Hamburger, Wexler, and Culicover claim that the reason why natural languages conform to the Invariance, Binary, and Freezing Principles is that if they did not, they would not be learnable. Their model of a language learner was their means of justifying the claim.

Secondarily, they present their learning model as a first step toward an adequate theory of language learning (which is what I have been emphasizing). As such, they can claim no more than that their model is (at least) "minimally plausible." It requires no information about non-sentences, does not have to remember the entire sample, requires sentences no more complex than those with two levels of subsentences, employs semantic information in learning, processes sentences one at a time, and changes its grammar rule by rule. In other words, it does not flagrantly contradict some of the obvious facts of human language development. However, since the model is only a specification of the boundary conditions of a theory of language learning (i.e., they are claiming that the child's hypotheses must be *no less constrained* than those of the model), many features would have to be fleshed out before it could be considered any more than "minimally plausible." First, there is no indication at present that the learner would converge in a time-span comparable to a human childhood. It seems inefficient and implausible to have the child enumerating sets of transformations and mentally rolling dice to decide which to keep or discard. What is needed is a theory showing how the child's hypotheses are guided in a more direct way by the meaning-sentence pair under consideration, and how these hypotheses are computed during the left-to-right processing of a sentence. Third, unordered deep structures are questionable candidates for a theory of the child's representational system (although this will be discussed further in Section IX). Finally, we are left with few suggestions as to how the transformational component, once acquired, is used in producing and comprehending sentences.

In any case the Hamburger, Wexler, and Culicover model is a unique and extremely impressive achievement. Theirs is the only model that is capable of learning natural languages in all their complexity and that at the same time is not blatantly counter to what we know about the child and his learning environment. They also have clarified and justified, more clearly than anyone else has, two central tenets of transformational linguistics: that considerations of language learnability can dictate a choice between rival linguistic theories, and that learnability considerations imply strong innate constraints of a certain type on the child's language learning faculties. As they put it, "The bridge that Chomsky has re-erected between psychology and linguistics bears two-way traffic" (Hamburger and Wexler, 1975).

IX. Implications for Developmental Psycholinguistics

TOWARD A THEORY OF LANGUAGE LEARNING

Among the models of language learning that I have considered, two seem worthy upon examination to serve as prototypes for a *theory* of human language acquisition. Anderson's LAS program roughly meets the Cognitive, Input, and Time Conditions, while faring less well with the Learnability and Equipotentiality Conditions. Hamburger, Wexler, and Culicover's transformational model meets the Learnability and Equipotentiality Conditions (clearly), and the Input Condition (perhaps), while faring less well with the Cognitive and Time Conditions. I hope it is not too banal to suggest that we need a theory that combines the best features of both models. It must incorporate a psychologically realistic comprehension process, like Anderson's system, since language acquisition is most plausibly thought of as being driven by the comprehension process. But at the same time, the model's semantic structures must be rich enough, and the hypothesization procedure constrained enough, that any natural language can be shown to be learnable (like the Hamburger *et al.* model), so that the model does not become buried under a pile of ad hoc, semi-successful heuristics when it is extended to more and more linguistic domains. Of course, developing such a theory has been hampered by the lack of a suitable theory of language itself, one that both gives a principled explanation for linguistic phenomena in various domains and languages, and that can be incorporated in a reasonable way into a comprehension model (see Bresnan, 1978, for a step in this direction). Of course, here is not the place to attempt to present a new theory synthesizing the best features of previous efforts. Instead, I will attempt to point out the implications that the formal study of language learning has for current issues in developmental psycholinguistics.

DEVELOPMENTAL PSYCHOLINGUISTICS AND LANGUAGE ACQUISITION DEVICES

Current attitudes toward language acquisition models among developmental psycholinguists have been strongly influenced by the fate of a research framework adopted during the 1960's that went under the name of the Language Acquisition Device, or LAD. There were in fact two different meanings to the expression Language Acquisition Device, and I think it is important to distinguish them. In one formulation (Chomsky, 1962), the child was idealized as an abstract device that constructed rules for an unknown language on the basis of a sample of sentences from that language; characterizing the workings of that "device" was proposed as a goal for linguistics and psychology. As an analogy, we could think of a physiologist interested in electrolyte regulation who idealized the brain as "a bag of salt water," proceeding then to study the structure of the membrane, concentration of ions, and so on. Of course, in this sense, I have been talking about language acquisition devices throughout the present paper. However there is a second, stronger sense in which LAD is taken to describe a specific theory of language acquisition (e.g., Clark, 1973; Levelt, 1973). In this sense (Fodor, 1966; McNeill, 1966), the child is said to possess an innate mental faculty containing highly specific knowledge about transformational grammars, which extracts deep structures from the speech around him and adopts transformational rules, one at a time, culminating in a transformational grammar for the language. Pursuing the analogy with physiology, LAD would correspond in this sense to our physiologist proposing that the brain accomplished electrolyte regulation by means of a special purpose structure, "a bag of salt water," with various properties. In support of this theory, it was claimed that the child based his learning on a sample of speech composed largely of fragments and complex, semi-grammatical expressions (Chomsky, 1965), that the early utterances of the child displayed mastery of highly abstract syntactic relations (McNeill, 1966), and that the linguistic progress of the child seemed to reflect the accretion of transformations (e.g., Brown and Hanlon, 1970). However the entire approach quickly fell into disfavor when it was found that the speech directed to children was well-formed and structurally simple (Snow, 1972), that the child might exploit semantic information in addition to sentences themselves (e.g., Macnamara, 1972), that the early speech of children might be better broken down into "cognitive" or semantic relations than into abstract syntactic ones (e.g., Bowerman, 1973; Brown, 1973), and that in many cases children learned transformationally complex constructions before they learned their simpler counterparts (e.g., Maratsos, 1978). As a result, LAD has been abandoned by developmental psycholinguists as a *theory,* and in its place I think there has developed a rough consensus that semantic and pragmatic information, together with the simplified speech of parents, allows children to learn language by using general cognitive skills rather than a special language-specific faculty. However, LAD has also been rejected in its more general sense as a *problem* to be addressed, and it also seems to me that most debates in developmental psycholinguistics are, unfortunately, no longer carried out with an eye toward ultimately specifying the mechanisms of syntax acquisition. When specific proposals concerning such mechanisms are considered, I shall argue, the substance of many of these debates can change significantly.

NATIVISM VERSUS EMPIRICISM: TWO EXTREME PROPOSALS

Formal results from the study of language learnability give us grounds for dismissing quite decisively two general proposals concerning what sort of mechanisms are necessary and sufficient for language learning, one empiricist, one nativist.

The extreme empiricist proposal is that there are no language-specific a priori constraints on the types of rules that humans can acquire. In this vein, it is argued that once a sufficient number of sentences has been observed, languages can be learned by "general multipurpose learning strategies" (Putnam, 1971), by "discovery procedures" (Braine, 1971), or by "learning algorithms" like a "discretizer-plus-generalizer" that "extracts regularity from the environment" (Derwing, 1973). As I have mentioned, Gold's enumeration procedure is the most powerful imaginable realization of a general learning algorithm. Nevertheless, even this procedure is inadequate in principle to acquire rules on the basis of a sample of sentences. And if the criterion for "acquisition" is weakened (by requiring only approachability, approximations to the target language, etc.), then learning is possible, but not within a human lifespan.

At the other extreme is the proposal that innate knowledge of the properties of natural languages, especially those of deep structures, allows the child to learn a language from a sample of sentences (e.g., Fodor, 1966; McNeill, 1966). In one of Hamburger and Wexler's early models (Wexler and Hamburger, 1973), they imposed constraints on the learner's hypotheses that were known to be unrealistically stringent (e.g., that all languages share identical deep structure rules). Nevertheless they proved that this class of languages is unlearnable on the basis of a sample of sentences, and therefore, that the same must be true of classes that are specified more weakly (and hence more realistically). Of course, it is still possible that a different sort of innate constraint might guarantee learnability, but this will remain a matter of speculation until someone puts forth such a proposal.

PROBLEMS FOR THE COGNITIVE THEORY OF LANGUAGE ACQUISITION

The inability of these procedures to induce grammars from samples of sentences suggests strongly that semantic and pragmatic information is used in language learning. The moderate success of the models of Anderson and of Hamburger *et al.* also lends credence to this conclusion. However, despite the great popularity of the Cognitive Theory among developmental psycholinguists, there has been little discussion of what I believe to be the foundation of the theory: the precise nature of the child's internal representations. The Cognitive Theory requires that children have available to them a system of representational structures similar enough in format to syntactic structures to promote language learning, and at the same time, flexible and general enough to be computable by children's cognitive and perceptual faculties on the basis of nonlinguistic information. Until we have a theory of the child's mental representations that meets these conditions, the Cognitive Theory will remain an unsupported hypothesis. Unfortunately, designing a representational system with the desired properties will be far from a simple task. The two main problems, which I call the "encoding problem" and the "format problem," pit the Cognitive Condition against the Learnability and Equipotentiality Conditions.

The Encoding Problem

This problem is a consequence of the fact that languages can describe a situation in a number of ways, and that humans can perceive a situation in a number of ways. One might plausibly attribute many different representational structures to a child perceiving a given situation, but only one of these structures will be the appropriate one to try to convert into the sentence being heard simultaneously. Barring telepathy, how does the child manage to encode a situation into just the structure that underlies the sentence that the adult is uttering?

Consider an earlier example. Anderson assumes that when a child sees, say, a white cat eating a mouse, his mind constructs a structure something like the one in Figure 1.3(a). This is fortunate for the child (and for the model-builder), since in the example the sentence arriving concurrently happens to be "The white cat eats a mouse," whose meaning corresponds to that structure. But what if the sentence were "The mouse is being eaten by the cat," "That's the second mouse that the cat has eaten," "Some cats don't eat mice," "What's that white cat doing with the mouse?" and so on? To put it differently, assuming that the original sentence was the one uttered, what if the child were to have constructed a cognitive structure containing propositions asserting that the mouse was 'all gone', or that the cat and mouse were playing, or that the mouse looked easy for the cat to eat, and so on? In any of these cases, the child would face the task of trying to map a meaning structure onto a string with which it has only a tenuous connection. Thus the semantic representation would offer few clues, or misleading ones, about how to hypothesize new rules.[4]

I have already mentioned that Anderson would face this problem if he were to multiply the number of available mental predicates that correspond to a given verb, in order to foster certain generalizations. Hamburger *et al.* face a similar problem. In their model, the structures underlying synonymous sentences, such as actives and passives, are presumably identical except for a marker triggering a transformation in cases like the passive (since each transformation is obligatorily triggered by some deep structure configuration). Again, it is not clear how the child knows when to insert into his semantic structure the markers that signal the transformations that the adult happens to have applied.

Possible Solutions to the Encoding Problem

I see three partial solutions to the encoding problem that together would serve to reduce the uncertainty associated with typical language learning situations, ensuring that the child will encode situations into unique representations appropriate to the sentences the adult is uttering. The first relies on the hypothesis that the representational system of the child is less powerful and flexible than that of the adult, and is capable of representing a given situation in only a small number of ways. Thus in the preceding example, the child is unlikely to encode the scene as propositions asserting that the mouse was not eating the cat, that all cats eat mice, etc. As the child develops, presumably his representational powers increase gradually, and so does the range of syntactic constructions addressed to him by his parents. If, as is often suggested (e.g., Cross, 1977), parents "fine-tune" their speech to the cognitive abilities of their children, that is, they use syntactic constructions whose semantics correspond to the representations most likely to be used by the child at a given moment, then the correspondence between the adult's sentence meaning and the child's encoding of the situation would be closer than we have supposed.

The second solution would posit that the child's social perception is acute enough to detect all the pragmatic or communicative differences that are concurrently signaled by syntactic means in different sentences (see Bruner, 1975). That is, the child knows from the conversational context what the adult is presupposing, what he or she is calling attention to, what is being asserted of what, and so on. For example, the child must not only *see* that the cat is eating the mouse, but must know that the adult is asserting of the cat that it is eating a mouse, instead of asserting of the mouse that it is disappearing into the cat, or many other possibilities. (As mentioned earlier, Anderson used this rationale in developing LAS, when he marked one of the propositions in each semantic structure as the intended "main proposition" of the sentence.) If this line of reasoning is correct, strong conditions are imposed both on the language and on the learner. The syntax of languages must not allow synonymy, in a strict sense: any two "base" structures (i.e., Anderson's Prototype structure or Hamburger *et al.*'s deep structure) that do not differ semantically (i.e., instantiate the same propositions) must differ pragmatically in some way. Conversely, the pragmatic and perceptual faculties of the child must be capable of discriminating the types of situations that occasion the use of different syntactic devices.

The third solution would equip the child with a strategy that exploited some simple property of the sentence to narrow down the possible interpretations of what the adult is asserting. Anderson implicated a strategy of this sort when LAS examined the set of words in a sentence and retained only the propositions in its meaning structure whose concepts corresponded to those words. In the present example, the child might always construct a proposition whose subject corresponds to the first noun in the sentence, and then choose (or, if necessary, create) some mental predicate that both corresponds to the verb and is consistent with his perception of the scene. Thus, when hearing an active sentence, the child would construct a proposition with the cat as the subject and "EATS" as part of the predicate; when hearing the passive version, the proposition would have the mouse as the subject and "IS-EATEN-BY" as part of the predicate.[5] One can even speculate that such a strategy is responsible for Bever's (1970) classic finding that children of a certain age interpret the referent of the first noun of both active and passive sentences as the agent of the action designated by the verb. The children may have set up the concept corresponding to the first noun as the subject of a proposition, but, lacking mental predicates like "IS-EATEN-BY" at that stage in their development, they may have mistakenly chosen predicates like "EATS" by default.

I hope to have shown how consideration of the requirements and implications of formal theories of language learning (in this case, those of Anderson and of Hamburger *et al.*) lead one to assign more precise roles to several phenomena studied intensively by developmental psycholinguists. Specifically, I suggest that the primary role in syntax learning of cognitive development, "fine-tuning" of adult speech to children learning language, knowledge of the pragmatics of a situation, and perceptual strategies is to ensure that the child encodes a situation into the same representational structure that underlies the sentence that the adult is uttering concurrently (cf. Bruner, 1975; Bever, 1970; Sinclair de-Zwart, 1969; and Snow, 1972; for different interpretations of the respective phenomena).

The Format Problem

Once we are satisfied that the child has encoded the situation into a unique representation, corresponding to the meaning of the adult's sentence, we must ensure that that representation is of the appropriate *format* to support the structural analyses and generalizations required by the learning process.

To take an extreme example of the problem, imagine that the study of perceptual and cognitive development forced us to conclude that the internal representations of the child were simply lists of perceptual features. Using a semantics-based generalization heuristic, the learner would have no trouble merging words like "cat" and "mouse," since both are objects, furry, animate, four-legged, etc. But the learner would be unable to admit into this class nouns like "flutter" or "clang," which have no perceptual features in common with "cat," nor "fallacy" or "realization," which have no perceptual features at all. The difficulties would intensify with more abstract syntactic structures, since there are no conjunctions of perceptual features that correspond to noun phrases, relative clauses, and so on. The problem with this representational format is that even if it were adequate for perception, it is not adaptable to syntax learning. It does not provide the units that indicate how to break a sentence into its correct units, and to generalize to similar units across different sentences.

In other words, what is needed is a theory of representations whose elements correspond more closely to the elements of a grammar. In Anderson's theory, for example, a representation is composed of a "subject" and a "predicate," which in turn is composed of a "relation" and an "object." These correspond nicely to the syntactic rules that break down a sentence into a noun phrase and a verb phrase, then the verb phrase into a verb and another noun phrase. Furthermore, propositions encoded for different situations in which syntactically similar sentences would be uttered would all have the same format, regardless of whether they represent furry things, square things, events, actions, abstract mathematical concepts, or other propositions. Hamburger *et al.* posit a cognitive representation with a format even more suitable to language learning: unordered deep structures. This is one of the reasons why their model is more successful at acquiring syntactic rules than LAS is. In sum, these theorists posit that the syntax of the language of thought is similar to the syntax of natural languages.

However, this solution might create problems of its own. It is possible for theorists to use "cognitive" representations with a format so suitable to syntactic rule learning that the representations may no longer be plausible in a theory of perception or cognition. To take a hypothetical example, in standard transformational grammars a coordinated sentence such as "Jim put mustard and relish on his hot dog" is derived from a two-part deep structure, with trees corresponding to the propositions "Jim put mustard on his hot dog" and "Jim put relish on his hot dog." However a theory of cognitive or perceptual representations based on independent evidence (e.g., reaction times, recall probabilities, etc.), when applied to this situation, might not call for two separate propositions, but for a single proposition in which one of the arguments was divided into two parts, corresponding to the two conjoined nouns (which is the way it is done in Anderson and Bower, 1973, for example). Cases like this, if widespread and convincing, would undermine Hamburger *et al.*'s premise that unordered deep structures are plausible as cognitive representations.

In this vein, it is noteworthy that even though Anderson's semantic structures were lifted from his theory of long term memory, they too are more similar to linguistic deep structures than those of any other theory of memory representation, incorporating features like a binary subject-predicate division, distinct labels for each proposition, and a hierarchical arrangement of nodes (cf., Norman and Rumelhart, 1975; Winston, 1975). In fact, many of these features are not particularly well-supported by empirical evidence (see Anderson, 1976), and others may be deficient on other grounds (see Woods, 1975). Concerning other computer models in which "the designer feeds in what he thinks are the semantic representations of utterances," McMaster *et al.* (1976, p. 377) remark that "the risk is that [the designer] will define semantics in such a way that it is hardly different from syntax. He is actually providing high-level syntactic information. This gives the grammar-inferrer an easy task, but makes the process less realistic...."[6]

Implications of the Format Problem

Faced with possibly conflicting demands on a theory of the form of mental representation from the study of language learning and the study of other cognitive processes, we have two options. One is to assert that, all other considerations notwithstanding, the format of mental representations *must* be similar to syntactic structures, in order to make language learning possible. Fodor (1975), for example, has put forth this argument.[7] The second is to posit at least two representational formats, one that is optimally suited for perception and cognition, and one that is optimally suited for language learning, together with a conversion procedure that transforms a representation from the former to the latter format during language learning. Anderson and Hamburger *et al.* already incorporate a version of this hypothesis. In LAS, the semantic structures are not entirely suitable for rule learning, so there is a procedure that converts them into the "prototype structures." And in the Hamburger *et al.* model, the deep structures are not entirely suitable as cognitive representations (being too specific to particular languages), so there is a procedure whereby they are derived from "semantic structures." Ultimately the Cognitive Theory of language learning must posit one or more representational formats appropriate to cognition in general and to language learning in particular, and, if necessary, the procedures that transform one sort of representation into the other.

NATIVISM AND EMPIRICISM REVISITED

It is often supposed that if children indeed base their rule learning on cognitive representational structures, the traditional case for nativism has been weakened (e.g., Schlesinger, 1971; Sinclair de-Zwart, 1969). According to this reasoning, cognitive structures already exist for other purposes, such as perception, reasoning, memory, and so forth, so there is no need to claim that humans possess an innate set of mental structures specific to language. However, this conclusion is at best premature. It is far from obvious that the type of representational structures motivated by a theory of perception or memory is suitably adaptable to the task of syntactic rule learning. For if the foregoing discussion is correct, the requirements of language learning dictate that cognitive structures are either language-like themselves, or an innate procedure transforms them into structures that are language-like. When one considers as well the proposed innate constraints on how these structures enter into the rule hypothesization process (i.e., Anderson's Graph Deformation and Semantics-Induced Equivalence Principles, and Hamburger *et al.*'s Binary and Freezing Principles), one must conclude that the Cognitive Theory of language learning, in its most successful implementations, vindicates Chomsky's innateness hypothesis if it bears on it at all.[8]

LANGUAGE LEARNING AND OTHER FORMS OF LEARNING

It might be conjectured that if one were to build models of other instances of human induction (e.g., visual concept learning, observational learning of behavior patterns, or scientific induction), one would be forced to propose innate constraints identical to those proposed by the designers of language learning models.

If so, it could be argued that the constraints on language learning are necessitated by the requirements of *induction* in general, and not natural language induction in particular. While it is still too early to evaluate this claim, the computer models of other types of induction that have appeared thus far do not seem to support it. In each case, the representational structures in which data and hypotheses are couched are innately tailored to the requirements of the *particular domain of rules being induced.* Consider Winston's (1975) famous program, which was designed to induce classes of block-structures, such as arches and tables, upon observing exemplars and non-exemplars of the classes. The units of the program's propositional structures can designate either individual blocks, blocks of triangular or rectangular shape, or any block whatsoever; the connecting terms can refer to a few spatial relations (e.g., adjacency, support, contact) and a few logical relations (e.g., part-whole, subset-superset). The program literally cannot conceive of distance, angle, color, number, other shapes, disjunction, or implication. This removes the danger of the program entertaining hypotheses other than the ones the programmer is trying to teach it. Similarly, Soloway and Riseman's (1977) program for inducing the rules of baseball upon observing sample plays is fitted with innate knowledge of the kind of rules and activities found in competitive sports in general. Langley's (1977) program for inducing physical laws upon observing the behavior of moving bodies is confined to considering assertions about the values of parameters for the positions, velocities, and accelerations of bodies, and is deliberately fed only those attributes of bodies that are significant in the particular mock universe in which it is "placed" for a given run. These restrictions are not just adventitious shortcuts, of course. Induction has been called "scandalous" because any finite set of observations supports an intractably large number of generalizations. Constraining the type of generalizations that the inducer is allowed to consider in a particular task is one way to defuse the scandal.

PARENTAL SPEECH TO CHILDREN

Frequently it is argued that the special properties of parents' speech to children learning language reduces the need for innate constraints on the learning process (e.g., Snow, 1972). Since these claims have not been accompanied by discussions of specific learning mechanisms that benefit from the special speech, they seem to be based on the assumption that something in the formal properties of the language learning task makes short, simple, grammatical, redundant sentences optimal for rule learning. However a glance at the models considered in the present paper belies this assumption: the different models in fact impose very different requirements on their input.

Consider the effects of interspersing a few ungrammatical strings among the sample sentences. Gold's enumeration learner would fail miserably if a malformed string appeared in the sample—it would jettison its correct hypothesis, never to recover it, and would proceed to change its mind an infinite number of times. On the other hand, Horning's Bayesian learner can easily tolerate a noisy sample, because here the sample does not mandate the wholesale acceptance or rejection of grammars, but a selection from among them of the one with the highest posterior probability. The Hamburger *et al.* model would also converge despite the occasional incorrect input datum, since at any point in the learning process at which it has an incorrect grammar (e.g., if it were led astray by a bad string), there is a nonzero probability that it will hypothesize a correct grammar within a certain number of trials (assuming, of course, that it does not encounter another bad string before converging).

Similarly, it is doubtful that the length or complexity of sentences has a uniform effect on different models. Feldman described a procedure requiring that the sample sentences be ordered approximately by increasing length, whereas Gold's procedure is completely indifferent to length. In the Hamburger *et al.* model, contrary to the intuition of some, learning is facilitated by *complex* sentences—not only will the learner fail to converge if he does not receive sentences with at least two levels of embedded sentences, but he will converge faster with increasingly complex sentences, since in a complex sentence there are more opportunities for incorrect transformations or the absence of correct transformations to manifest themselves by generating the wrong string. Nevertheless, short and simple sentences may indeed facilitate learning in humans, but for a different reason. Since children have limited attention and memory spans, they are more likely to retain a short string of words for sufficient time to process it than they would a long string of words. Similarly, they are more likely to encode successfully a simple conceptualization of an event than a complex one. Thus short, simple sentences may set the stage for rule hypothesization while playing no role (or a detrimental role) in the hypothesization process itself.

Other models are sensitive to other features of the input. Since Klein and Kuppin's Autoling relies on distributional analysis, it thrives on sets of minimally-contrasting sentences. Since Anderson's LAS merges constituents with the same semantic counterparts, it progresses with sets of sentences with similar or overlapping propositional structures.

In sum, the utility of various aspects of the input available to a language learner depends entirely on the learning procedure he uses. A claim that some feature of parental speech facilitates rule learning is completely groundless unless its proponent specifies some learning mechanism.

Conclusions

In an address called "Word from the Language Acquisition Front," Roger Brown (1977) has cautioned:

Developmental psycholinguistics has enjoyed an enormous growth in research popularity... which, strange to say, may come to nothing. There have been greater research enthusiasms than this in psychology: Clark Hull's principles of behavior, the study of the Authoritarian personality, and, of course, Dissonance Theory. And in all these cases, very little advance in knowledge took place.... A danger in great research activity which we have not yet surmounted, but which we may surmount, is that a large quantity of frequently conflicting theory and data can become cognitively ugly and so repellent as to be swiftly deserted, its issues unresolved.

It is my belief that one way to surmount this danger is to frame issues in the context of precise models of the language learning process, following the lead of other branches of the cognitive sciences. I hope to have shown in this section why it may be necessary to find out how language learning *could* work in order for the developmental data to tell us how it *does* work.

Notes

1. Strictly speaking, they are not "algorithms" in the usual sense of effective procedures, since they do not compute a solution and then halt, but compute an infinite series of guesses.
2. Of course, in this particular case the assumption about semantics and syntax need not have been innate, since the subjects' tacit knowledge of English could have constrained their hypotheses.
3. As the example suggest, the Binary and Freezing Principles tend to reduce the context-sensitivity of rules in grammars by preventing large parts of tree structures from entering into the structural descriptions of transformations. This is not a coincidence, since in general context-free rules are more easily learnable than context-sensitive rules. See also Kaplan (1978) who argues that the reduction of context-sensitivity afforded by the Subjacency (i.e., Binary) Principle contributes to efficient sentence parsing.
4. Dan Slobin (1978; personal communication) has pointed out that the child faces a similar problem in learning the morphology of his language. Natural languages dictate that certain semantic features of the sentence referent (e.g. number, person, gender, definiteness, animacy, nearness to the speaker, completedness, and so on) must be signalled in prefixes, suffices, alternate vowel forms, and other means. However, these features are by no means all that a child *could* encode about an event: the color, absolute position, and texture of an object, the time of day, the temperature, and so on, though certainly perceptible to the child, are ignored by the morphology of languages, and hence should not be encoded as part of the semantic structure that the child must learn to map onto the string. To make matters worse, the morphological rules of different languages select different subsets of these features to signal obligatorily, and disagree further over which features should be mapped one-to-one onto morphological markers, and which sets of features should be conflated in a many-to-one fashion in particular markers. Thus there has to be some mechanism in the child's rule-hypothesization faculty whereby his possible conceptualizations of an event are narrowed down to only those semantic features that languages signal, and ultimately, down to only those semantic features that his target language signals.
5. This example follows the Anderson model with the "multiple predicate" modification I suggested. In the Hamburger *et al.* model, the child could insert a "transformation marker" into

his deep structure whenever the subject of the deep structure proposition was not the first noun in the sentence.

6. This discussion has assumed that the language-specific structures posited as cognitive representations are specific to languages in general, not to particular languages. If the representations are tailored to *one* language (e.g., when predicates in LAS's propositions take the same number of arguments as the verb they correspond to, even though the same verbs in different languages take different numbers of arguments), a second and equally serious problem results.

7. Incidentally, it is ironic that Anderson, in a different context, fails to mention this argument when he examines the case for propositional theories of mental representation in general (Anderson, 1978).

8. One could contest this conclusion by pointing out that it has only been shown that the various nativist assumptions are *sufficient* for learnability, not that they are *necessary*. But as Hamburger and Wexler put it (1975), "anyone who thinks the assumption[s are] not necessary is welcome to try to devise proofs corresponding to ours without depending on [those] assumptions."

References

Anderson, J. (1974) Language acquisition by computer and child. (Human Performance Center Technical Report No. 55.) Ann Arbor, University of Michigan.

Anderson, J. (1975) Computer simulation of a Language Acquisition System: A first report. In R. Solso (ed.), *Information processing and cognition: The Loyola Symposium*. Washington, Erlbaum.

Anderson, J. (1976) *Language, Memory, and Thought*. Hillsdale, N.J.: Erlbaum.

Anderson, J. (1977) Induction of augmented transition networks. *Cog. Sci., 1*, 125–157.

Anderson, J. (1978) Arguments concerning representations for mental imagery. *Psychol. Rev., 85*, 249–277.

Anderson, J. and G. Bower (1973) *Human Associative Memory*. Washington, Winston.

Bever, T. (1970) The cognitive basis for linguistic structures. In J. Hayes (ed.), *Cognition and the Development of Language*. New York, Wiley.

Biermann, A. and J. Feldman (1972) A survey of results in grammatical inference. In S. Watanabe (ed.), *Frontiers in Pattern Recognition*. New York, Academic Press.

Bowerman, M. (1973) *Learning to talk: A Cross-sectional Study of Early Syntactic Development, with Special Reference to Finnish*. Cambridge, U.K., Cambridge University Press.

Braine, M. (1963) The ontogeny of English phrase structure: The first phrase. *Lang., 39*, 1–14.

Braine, M. (1971) On two models of the internalization of grammars. In D. Slobin (ed.), *The Ontogenesis of Grammar*. New York, Academic Press.

Bresnan, J. (1978) A realistic transformational grammar. In G. Miller, J. Bresnan and M. Halle (eds.), *Linguistic Theory and Psychological Reality*. Cambridge, Mass., MIT Press.

Brown, R. (1973) *A First Language: The Early Stages*. Cambridge, Mass., Harvard University Press.

Brown, R. (1977) Word from the language acquisition front. Invited address at the meeting of the Eastern Psychological Association, Boston.

Brown, R, C. Cazden and U. Bellugi (1969) The child's grammar from I to III. In J. Hill (ed.), *Minnesota Symposium on Child Psychology, Vol. II*. Minneapolis, University of Minnesota Press.

Brown, R. and C. Hanlon (1970) Derivational complexity and order of acquisition in child speech. In J. Hayes (ed.), *Cognition and the Development of Language*. New York, Wiley.

Bruner, J. (1975) The ontogenesis of speech acts. *J. child Lang., 2*, 1–19.

Chomsky, N. (1957) *Syntactic Structures*. The Hague, Mouton.

Chomsky, N. (1962) Explanatory models in linguistics. In E. Nagel and P. Suppes (eds.), *Logic, Methodology, and Philosophy of Science*. Stanford, Stanford University Press.

Chomsky, N. (1965) *Aspects of the Theory of Syntax*. Cambridge, Mass., MIT Press.

Chomsky, N. (1973) Conditions on transformations. In S. Anderson and P. Kiparsky (eds.), *A Festschrift for Morris Halle*. New York, Holt, Rinehart and Winston.

Clark, E. (1973) What should LAD look like? Some comments on Levelt. In *The Role of Grammar in Interdisciplinary Linguistic Research*. Colloquium at the University of Bielefeld, Bielefeld, W. Germany.

Cross, T. (1977) Mothers' speech adjustments: The contribution of selected child listener variables. In C. Snow and C. Ferguson (eds.), *Talking to Children: Input and Acquisition*. New York, Cambridge University Press.

Culicover, P. and K. Wexler (1974) The Invariance Principle and universals of grammar. (Social Science Working Paper No. 55.) Irvine, Cal., University of California.

Culicover, P. and K. Wexler (1977) Some syntactic implications of a theory of language learnability. In P. Culicover, T. Wasow, and A. Akmajian (eds.), *Formal Syntax*. New York, Academic Press.

Derwing, B. (1973) *Transformational Grammar as a Theory of Language Acquisition*. Cambridge, UK, Cambridge University Press.

Fabens, W. and D. Smith (1975) A model of language acquisition using a conceptual base. (Technical Report CBM-TR-55, Department of Computer Science.) New Brunswick, N.J., Rutgers—The State University.

Feldman, J. (1972) Some decidability results on grammatical inference and complexity. *Information and Control, 20*, 244–262.

Fodor, J. (1966) How to learn to talk: Some simple ways. In F. Smith and G. Miller (eds.), *The Genesis of Language*. Cambridge, Mass., MIT Press.

Fodor, J. (1975) *The Language of Thought*. New York, Thomas Crowell.

Fu, K. and T. Booth (1975) Grammatical inference: Introduction and survey. *IEEE Transactions on Systems, Man, and Cybernetics, SMC-5(1)*, 95–111; *SMC-5(4)*, 409–423.

Gold, E. (1967) Language identification in the limit. *Information and Control, 16*, 447–474.

Gross, M. (1972) *Mathematical models in linguistics*. Englewood Cliffs, N.J., Prentice-Hall.

Hamburger, H. and K. Wexler (1975) A mathematical theory of learning transformational grammar. *J. Math. Psychol., 12*, 137–177.

Harris, Z. (1964) Distributional structure. In J. Fodor and J. Katz (eds.), *The Structure of Language*. Englewood Cliffs, N.J., Prentice Hall.

Hopcroft, J. and J. Ullman (1969) *Formal languages and their relation to automata*. Reading, Mass., Addison Wesley.

Horning, J. (1969) A study of grammatical inference. (Technical Report No. CS 139, Computer Science Dept.) Stanford, Stanford University.

Kaplan, R. (1975) On process models for sentence analysis. In D. Norman and D. Rumelhart (eds.), *Explorations in cognition*. San Francisco, W. H. Freeman.

Kaplan, R. (1978) Computational resources and linguistic theory. Paper presented at the Second Theoretical Issues in Natural Language Processing Conference, Urbana, Ill.

Kelley, K. (1967) Early syntactic acquisition. (Report No. P-3719.) Santa Monica, Cal., The Rand Corporation.

Klein, S. (1976) Automatic inference of semantic deep structure rules in generative semantic grammars. In A. Zampoli (ed.), *Computational and Mathematical Linguistics: Proceedings of 1973 International Conference on Computational Linguistics, Pisa*. Florence, Italy, Olschki.

Klein, S. and M. Kuppin (1970) An interactive program for learning transformational grammars. *Computer Studies in the Humanities and Verbal Behavior, III*, 144–162.

Klein, S. and V. Rozencvejg (1974) A computer model for the ontogeny of pidgin and creole languages. (Technical Report No. 238, Computer Science Dept.) Madison: University of Wisconsin.

Knobe, B. and K. Knobe (1977) A method for inferring context-free grammars. *Information and Control, 31*, 129–146.

Kosslyn, S. and S. Schwartz (1977) A simulation of visual imagery. *Cog. Sci., 1*, 265–296.

Langley, P. (1977) BACON: A production system that discovers empirical laws. (CIP Working Paper No. 360.) Pittsburg, Carnegie Mellon University.

Levelt, W (1973) Grammatical inference and theories of language acquisition. In *The role of Grammar in Interdisciplinary Linguistic Research*. Colloquium at the University of Bielefeld, Bielefeld, W. Germany.

Macnamara, J. (1972) Cognitive basis for language learning in infants. *Psychol. Rev.*, 79, 1–13.

Maratsos, M. (1978) New models in linguistics and language acquisition. In G. Miller, J. Bresnan and M. Halle (eds.), *Linguistic Theory and Psychological Reality*. Cambridge, Mass., MIT Press.

McMaster, I., J. Sampson and J. King (1976) Computer acquisition of natural language: A review and prospectus. *Intern. J. Man-Machine Studies*, 8, 367–396.

McNeill, D. (1966) Developmental psycholinguistics. In F. Smith and G. Miller (eds.), *The genesis of language*. Cambridge, Mass., MIT Press.

Miller, G. (1967) Project Grammarama. In *The Psychology of Communication*. Hammonsworth, NY: Basic Books.

Moeser, S. and A. Bregman (1972) The role of reference in the acquisition of a miniature artificial language. *J. verb. Learn. verb. Behav.*, 12, 91–98.

Moeser, S. and A. Bregman (1973) Imagery and language acquisition. *J. verb. Learn. verb. Behav.*, 12, 91–98.

Newell, A. and H. Simon (1973) *Human problem solving*. Englewood Cliffs, N.J., Prentice Hall.

Newport, E., H. Gleitman and L. Gleitman (1977) Mother, I'd rather do it myself: Some effects and non-effects of maternal speech style. In C. Snow and C. Ferguson (eds.), *Talking to Children: Input and Acquisition*. New York, Cambridge University Press.

Norman, D. and D. Rumelhart (1975) *Explorations in Cognition*. San Francisco, W. H. Freeman.

Peters, S. and R. Ritchie (1973) On the generative power of transformational grammars. *Infor. Sci.*, 6, 49–83.

Postal, P. (1964) Limitations of phrase structure grammars. In J. Fodor and J. Katz (eds.), *The Structure of Language*. Englewood Cliffs, N.J., Prentice Hall.

Putnam, H. (1971) The "Innateness Hypothesis" and explanatory models in linguistics. In J. Searle (ed.), *The Philosophy of Language*. London, Oxford University Press.

Reeker, L. (1976) The computational study of language acquisition. In M. Yovits and M. Rubinoff (eds.), *Advances in Computers, Vol. 15*. New York, Academic Press.

Rochester, S. (1973) The significance of pauses in spontaneous speech. *J. Psycholing. Res.*, 2, 51–81.

Schlesinger, 1. (1971) Production of utterances and language acquisition. In D. Slobin (ed.), *The Ontogenesis of Grammar*. New York, Academic Press.

Siklóssy, L. (1971) A language learning heuristic program. *Cog. Psychol.*, 2, 279–295.

Siklóssy, L. (1972) Natural language learning by computer. In H. Simon and L. Siklóssy (eds.), *Representation and Meaning: Experiments with Information-processing Systems*. Englewood Cliffs, N.J., Prentice Hall.

Sinclair de-Zwart, H. (1969) Developmental psycholinguistics. In D. Elkind and J. Flavell (eds.), *Studies in Cognitive Development: Essays in Honor of Jean Piaget*. New York, Oxford University Press.

Slobin, D. (1973) Cognitive prerequisites for the development of grammar. In C. Ferguson and D. Slobin (eds.), *Studies in Child Language Development*. New York, Holt, Rinehart and Winston.

Slobin, D. (1978) Universal and particular in the acquisition of language. In *Language Acquisition: State of the Art*. Conference at the University of Pennsylvania, Philadelphia, May 1978.

Snow, C. (1972) Mothers' speech to children learning language. *Child Devel.*, 43, 549–565.

Snow, C. and C. Ferguson (1977) *Talking to children: Language Input and Acquisition*. New York: Cambridge University Press.

Solomonoff, R. (1964) A formal theory of inductive inference. *Infor. Control*, 7, 1–22; 224–254.

Soloway, E. and E. Riseman (1977) Levels of pattern description in learning. (COINS Technical Report 77-5), Computer and Information Science Dept., Amherst, Mass., University of Massachusetts.

Van der Mude, A. and A. Walker (1978) On the inference of stochastic regular grammars. *Infor. Control*, 38, 310–329.

Wexler, K., P. Culicover and H. Hamburger (1975) Learning-theoretic foundations of linguistic universals. *Theoret. Ling.*, 2, 215–253.

Wexler, K. and H. Hamburger (1973) On the insufficiency of surface data for the learning of transformational languages. In K. Hintikka, J. Moravcsik and P. Suppes (eds.), *Approaches to Natural Languages*. Dordrecht, Netherlands: Reidel.

Wharton, R. (1974) Approximate language identification. *Infor. Control*, 26, 236–255.

Wharton, R. (1977) Grammar enumeration and inference. *Infor. Control*, 33, 253–272.

Winograd, T. (1972) A program for understanding natural languages. *Cog. Psychol.*, 3, 1–191.

Winston, P. (1975) Learning structural descriptions from examples. In P. Winston (ed.), *The Psychology of Computer Vision*. New York, McGraw-Hill.

Woods, W. (1975) What's in a link: Foundations of semantic networks. In D. Bobrow and A. Collins (eds.), *Representation and Understanding: Studies in Cognitive Science*. New York, Academic Press.

2

A Computational Theory of the Mental Imagery Medium

My research program on mental imagery began with a worry about a paradox. The signature experiment on mental imagery in the 1970s had been Roger Shepard's demonstration that people can mentally rotate three-dimensional shapes in depth as easily as they could rotate them around the line of sight. My research adviser, Stephen Kosslyn, had designed a computer model of imagery in which images were represented as patterns of filled cells in a two-dimensional matrix of pixels. In an aside in one of his papers, he suggested that the model could be extended to account for images of 3-D shapes by adding a dimension of cells to the matrix, yielding a 3-D array of what today we would call voxels.

Upon reading this comment a problem immediately sprang to mind. A 3-D representation of 3-D space should have no perspective effects arising from projecting the scene onto a 2-D surface such as the retina. After all, it's not as if there is a beam of light that illuminates the filled voxels in the computer's memory (or the neurons in the brain), which is somehow reflected off of those numbers and then focused onto the retina of a little man inside the head. Yet human mental imagery really does seem to have perspective effects, depicting a scene as it would appear from a specific vantage point. In the mind's eye, imagined railroad tracks seem to converge, receding objects seem to shrink, and occluded surfaces are invisible.

After having shown in my thesis that mental images do have both 3-D and perspective-specific properties, I was faced with the puzzle of what kind of mental representation could capture them both. This obscure theoretical paper, which incorporated ideas from two of the major vision theorists of the mid-twentieth century, J. J. Gibson and David Marr, is my best attempt to solve the problem. The concept of a "2 1/2-D representation," which I borrowed from Marr, has been kept alive in my colleague Ken Nakayama's theory of a "visible surface representation," and the idea of an object-centered reference frame is still around in Irv Biederman's influential "geon" theory of shape recognition. (That theory is subjected to an empirical test in the paper reproduced as chapter 6 in this collection.) Two other foundational ideas in cognitive science are aired in this article. One is

the "imagery debate," with Shepard and Kosslyn on one side and the cognitive psychologist Zenon Pylyshyn, joined by many philosophers and artificial intelligence researchers,
on the other. The second is and the computational theory of mind, which is the key idea
of cognitive science and a major bridge in our understanding of the relationship of mind
and matter.

Introduction

As a recent book title has put it (Gardner, 1985), the mind has a new science. Over
the past 25 years, the field called "Cognitive Science" has revolutionized our understanding of mental processes. At the heart of this discipline is a "central dogma"
which plays a role analogous to the doctrine of atomism in physics, the germ theory
of disease in medicine, and plate tectonics in geology. This central dogma is the
"Computational Theory of Mind": that mental processes are formal manipulations
of symbols, or programs, consisting of sequences of elementary processes made
available by the information-processing capabilities of neural tissue. The computational theory of mind has led to rapid progress because it has given a precise
mechanistic sense to formerly vague terms such as "memory," "meaning," "goal,"
"perception," and the like, which are indispensable to explaining intelligence. It has
also fostered the experimental investigation of mental processes in the laboratory,
because computational theories allow one to predict the relative ease or difficulty
people will have in performing various tasks by assessing the number and type of
computational steps and the amount of memory required by the mechanisms of the
theory as it simulates the task in question. (Fodor (1968, 1975), Newell and Simon
(1973), and the papers in Haugeland (1981), outline the logic of cognitive science
in detail.)

Mental imagery is one of the topics that have benefited the most from this new
approach to the mind. Through much of this century philosophers and psychologists have argued that the common sense notion of a mental image is scientifically
useless at best and incoherent or misleading at worst (see Kosslyn, 1980; Block,
1981). But the formulation of computational models of imagery has clarified the
issues to such an extent that debates over imagery have now shifted to empirical
discussions about which theory is correct, rather than logical discussions about
which concepts are coherent. In this paper, I discuss how one apparent paradox
in imagery—that "mental pictures" imply a two-dimensional medium, whereas
people's images can contain 3D objects—can be resolved by thinking in computational terms. In particular, I propose a theory of the brain mechanism in which
images occur and how 3D spatial information is put into it and read out of it.
I also show how the theory is compatible with the computational demands of
other spatial abilities such as pattern recognition, perceptual stability, attention,
and intersensory coordination.

2. Background: The Array Theory of Imagery

At least since Plato's time, visual memories have been likened to physical pictures. Though a literal reading of this "picture metaphor" leads to absurd consequences (see Pylyshyn, 1973), Stephen Kosslyn (Kosslyn, 1980; Kosslyn, Pinker, Smith, and Shwartz, 1979; Pinker and Kosslyn, 1983) has shown that there is a sensible interpretation of the metaphor that is compatible with the principles of modern computational psychology. Briefly, this "array theory" is based on the following tenets. The structure underlying our experience of visual perception and imagery can best be characterized by a two-dimensional array of cells, each mapping onto a local region of the visual field. Objects and scenes are depicted in the array by patterns of filled cells isomorphic in shape to the object or scene. The array cells are filled with information arriving from the eyes during perception and from labelled, hierarchically structured long-term memory (LTM) files, corresponding to objects and their parts, during imagination. Information from memory placed in the array fades quickly unless refreshed periodically. The elements filling the cells can be thought of as primitive elements representing the lightness, color, texture, and presence and orientation of edges in small local regions of the visual field. Pattern-matching procedures can operate on the array patterns to construct symbolic descriptions of the objects and scenes depicted therein, and transformation procedures can alter the patterns by moving elements from cell to cell, simulating translations, rotations, size scalings, and so forth. Figure 2.1 shows the overall organization of the imagery system according to the array theory. (For a more detailed account, see Kosslyn, Pinker, Smith, & Shwartz, 1979).

EVIDENCE FOR THE ARRAY THEORY

The Array Theory is supported by four categories of experimental data.

2.1. First, if there really exists a fixed medium supporting spatial patterns in imagery and perception, one should be able to obtain stable measures of the intrinsic spatial properties of the array, such as its shape, size, grain, isotropy, homogeneity,

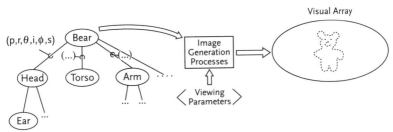

Figure 2. 1. The array theory of imagery. The LTM representation of a shape is on the left; the information in parentheses specifies the position of a part relative to the whole.

dimensionality, and brain locus. Since the theory posits a single array used in imagery and perception, estimates of the array properties derived when subjects imagine patterns should be similar to analogous estimates made when subjects perceive those patterns, and it should be possible to obtain evidence that some of the visual areas of the brain are used in visual imagery. As predicted, Kosslyn (1978) and Weber and Malmstrom (1979) were able to estimate the maximum size of images; Finke & Kosslyn (1980) and Finke and Kurtzman (1981) estimated the fall-off of resolution with eccentricity in the visual field for images and percepts; and Kosslyn, Brunn, Cave, and Wallach (1984) measured the resolution of imagined and perceived patterns of different orientations and spatial frequencies, observing an "oblique effect" for imagery as well as for perception. Recent studies in human neuropsychology have supported the idea that there are neural structures that represent and manipulate information in imagery, which are often shared by perceptual processes. Farah (1984) reviewed literature showing that an inability to generate visual images, with preserved abilities to process visual information, can result from damage to certain areas of the left hemisphere. She also cited cases of an inability to imagine particular classes of objects (e.g. animals) accompanied by an inability to recognize those classes when they are presented visually. Bisiach and Luzatti (1978) documented neglect patients that not only failed to report the contents of the left half of their visual field but failed to report objects that were in the left sides of scenes imagined from specific vantage points. Peronnet, Farah, and Gonon (this volume) showed altered event-related potentials from early stages of visual processing resulting from exact matches between images and visual stimuli.

2.2. The second body of evidence is useful in attempting to distinguish the array theory from theories that hold that abstract propositions are the only form of internal representation. When a visual pattern is represented as a set of propositions, its size, shape, location, and orientation are factored apart into separate propositions, one per attribute. For example, a slightly tilted square might be represented as follows: SHAPE(x,square); SIZE(x,27); LOCATION(x,50,75); ORIENTATION(x,75) (e.g., Anderson, 1978; Miller & Johnson-Laird, 1976). In contrast, an array representation of a pattern conflates these four attributes into one and the same collection of dots or elements in the array. Thus if the representation underlying imagery is an array, when one of these attributes of an image must be compared with a remembered attribute value, the others can be expected to interfere. This prediction has been borne out many times. For example, Shepard & Metzler (1971) found that subjects could not decide whether two depicted 3D objects had the same shape until they mentally rotated one object into the orientation of the other, taking proportionally more time to perform the rotation when the objects were separated by greater angles (see also Cooper & Shepard, 1973). This shows that orientation can interfere with shape judgments. Kosslyn (1975) found that subjects took longer to verify the presence of parts of imagined animals when either the part was intrinsically small or the animal was imagined at a small size.

This shows that size can interact with shape judgments. Shwartz (1979) has shown that when subjects prepare for a visual stimulus whose shape must be discriminated from a remembered pattern, they rotate an image of the remembered pattern into the anticipated orientation of the stimulus, doing so at a faster rate when the image is smaller. I have replicated this effect in two unpublished experiments, one using 3D shapes, another using a Cooper-Shepard paradigm with 2D shapes. The dependence of mental rotation rate on size shows that size, orientation, and shape mutually interact in visual imagery, as one would expect if normalizing orientation was an operation performed iteratively on a bounded region of array cells, with smaller regions of cells requiring fewer operations per iteration. Finke & Pinker (1982, 1983) and Pinker, Choate, and Finke (1984; see also Spoehr & Williams, 1978) showed that when subjects are asked to determine whether a visible arrow points to the position of an imagined dot, the time they require is a linear function of how far the arrow is from the dot position (as if subjects were mentally extrapolating the arrow until it hit or missed the image of the dot). All of these findings can be explained under the theory that images are two-dimensional distributions of local elements that can be matched against templates constructed from memory, but only after being transformed so as to normalize the irrelevant attributes (e.g., differences in size, orientation, or location) that would otherwise vitiate the template match. In contrast, a propositions-only model would lead one to expect that each spatial attribute could be interrogated directly, without displaying effects of the values of other attributes, since each attribute is defined in a separate, modular proposition.

2.3. The third body of evidence concerns the facilitation of perception by imagery in a way that is sensitive to the precise spatial distribution of the imagined and physical patterns in the visual field. Brooks (1967) and Segal & Fusella (1970) showed that mental images and perceptual processing mutually interfere if both are in the same sensory modality. Cooper & Shepard (1973), Metzler (1973), Shwartz (1979), and many others (see Kosslyn et al., 1979) have shown that classification latencies for visual stimuli are greatly reduced, and the need to normalize irrelevant attributes is eliminated, if subjects form an image of the stimulus in advance for use as a template against the stimulus when it appears. But if image and stimulus differ in orientation, size, or location, or if the information given the subject in advance does not allow an image of a determinate shape, size, orientation, and location to be formed (e.g., information about orientation but not shape, as in Cooper & Shepard, 1973, or information about shape but not location, as in Posner, Snyder, & Davidson, 1980), the benefits are reduced or nonexistent. The most dramatic illustration of the template-like properties of images come from Farah (1985), who found that forming an image facilitated the sensitivity of detecting near-threshold visual stimuli but only if they were of the same shape and location as the image. A different kind of facilitation was demonstrated by Freyd and Finke (1984), who showed that imagining a context frame around a set of line segments facilitated discriminating the lengths of those segments in the same way that a visually presented frame would have led to such facilitation. All this implies that preparation for a stimulus is maximally effective only if one can prime or fill in the set of cells that will be occupied by the stimulus when it appears. Again, this argues against a representation factoring visual attributes apart, since in that case, any attribute, spatially localizable or not, should be primable. Together with the rest of the evidence cited here, it also argues for a single array structure representing specifically visual information in imagery and perception.

2.4. Finally, there is evidence related to the function of imagery. People report using images to "see" patterns that they had not encoded explicitly when they originally inspected a scene, such as the shape of a beagle's ears (Kosslyn, 1980), how many windows are in one's living room (Shepard and Cooper, 1982), or the emergent properties that objects would display when juxtaposed or positioned in various ways (Pinker & Finke, 1980; Shepard, 1978). Many of these properties could only be detected if images represented the basic geometric properties of local parts of a shape in a single frame of reference, as opposed to descriptions of the parts in terms of their function or identity with respect to the object as a whole. For example, Finke, Pinker, and Farah (1987) read descriptions of arrangements of objects to people, such as "Imagine a capital letter 'D'. Rotate the figure 90 degrees to the left. Now place a capital letter 'J' at the bottom." Most subjects could "see" that the result was a depiction of an umbrella, a symbolic description that was not in the original instructions. This ability required undoing the mental description of the curved segment of the 'D' as being to the right of its spine with its concave region pointing left, the description of the top of the 'J' as being part of the same object as the hooked segment and distinct from the spine of the 'D', and so on. It required "seeing" a pattern that cut across the original description of each part as belonging to a whole, and representing each part neutrally in terms of its overall position and orientation in the visual field (technically, in a global, viewer-centered coordinate system, rather than in a set of distributed object-centered coordinate systems; see Hinton, 1979a; Pinker, 1984). An array, in which parts are represented in terms of a single frame of reference, makes the detection of parts that cut across the description or parse of an object easy to do; a conceptual description of parts relative to the objects that they are parts of does not. See Hollins (1985), Pinker and Finke (1980), Slee (1980), and Shepard and Feng (reported in Shepard & Cooper, 1982) for other demonstrations of the ability to detect novel geometric patterns in images, and Kosslyn (1980), Kosslyn et al. (1979), Pinker and Kosslyn (1983), Pinker (1984), Shepard (1978), Finke (1980), and Finke and Shepard (1986), for extensive general reviews of the experimental literature on the properties of images.

3. Problems for the Array Theory

The evidence outlined above suggests that the array theory is a plausible account of the short-term mental representation of visuospatial information. The theory, however, remains controversial. For example, Pylyshyn (1981) argues that the theory as a whole has too many free parameters to be explanatory, and that the supporting experiments can be given alternative explanations in terms of subjects' tacit knowledge about the physical world and their perceptual systems. Hinton (1979a, b) and Chambers and Reisberg (1985) point out that certain image inspection processes seem to operate on the interpretation of an object as a whole, or upon the role that a part plays in a reference frame aligned with the object, rather than being able to access arbitrary local regions of a pattern.

Though these counterarguments are important, I will focus here upon a different and equally serious class of criticisms: that the array theory is ill-suited to represent information about three-dimensional objects and scenes. In particular, there are two problems with the two-dimensional array. The first is that mental rotation in depth, which yields just as precise a linear relation between reaction time and angular disparity as rotation in the frontal plane (Shepard & Metzler, 1971), is difficult to model within a 2D array, for three reasons: a) 2D depictions of 3D objects are ambiguous—an ellipse in a 2D array could represent an ellipse viewed head-on or a circle tilted about its vertical axis. Rotating it in depth would yield very different results on the different interpretations (e.g., a narrowing in one case and a widening in the other), so the rotation operator could not proceed correctly if all it accessed was the array. b) One can formulate accounts of the incremental nature of mental rotation for picture-plane rotations (e.g., perhaps because of a constraint that cell contents can only be shifted to neighboring cells in a given iteration, or because small increments of rotation minimize shape distortion introduced by noise in the rotation operation), but not for depth rotations, since for each increment of rotation, different points in the rotated pattern shift by very different amounts across the array. c) As an object rotates in depth, new surfaces come into view. This information was not in the array to begin with, and so the rotation cannot be accomplished solely by operations on array cells.

The second problem with the 2D array (e.g., Neisser, 1979) is that of perceptual stability: If the experience of imagery is analogous to perceptual experience, as introspection as well as much of the empirical imagery literature suggests, both experiences should be of a world of meaningful solid objects, available to all sensory modalities, and stable despite changes in eye position, head position, or body movement in any direction. But these properties are difficult, if not impossible, to simulate on an internal two-dimensional "screen" or array.

Clearly, the array theory (and the age-old picture metaphor that preceded it) will stand or fall depending on its ability to account for the representation of the three-dimensional world in perception and imagery. I will first present, and reject, a series of simple extensions of the array theory that might give it an ability to deal with the representation of 3D information. Then I will propose a new theory, which I believe solves the problems inherent in the earlier approaches.

4. Simple Extensions of the Array Theory to Handle the Third Dimension

4.1. 3D ARRAY

The most natural way to extend the array theory to handle the three-dimensional case is to build the third dimension right into the array, giving it the equivalent of rows, columns, and layers instead of just rows and columns. In contrast to the 2D array, this allows one to model rotation in depth as a set of uniform displacements of elements from cell to cell, and allows one to explain the incremental nature of the rotation by a putative constraint on how far (i.e., across how many intervening cells) an element can be displaced in a single computational step (see also Attneave & Block, 1973; Shepard & Judd, 1976). Similarly, it can account for people's ability to scan mentally along a straight trajectory in any direction in an imagined 3D scene, a performance that requires proportionally more time for greater 3D Euclidean distances between the source and destination of scanning (Pinker & Kosslyn, 1978; Pinker, 1980b; see also Attneave and Pierce, 1978).

Despite the intuitive appeal of the "sandbox in the head" theory (Attneave, 1972), it faces several major problems (Pinker and Kosslyn, 1978; Pinker, 1980a, b). The introspective experience of imagery is of a perspective glimpse of a scene from a particular vantage point (Pinker, 1980a, b; Hinton, 1979a). Furthermore, experimental evidence supports this introspection: imagined objects are reported by subjects to "loom large" as one imagines moving toward them (Kosslyn, 1978); and objects that are imagined as concealed, out of view, distant, or foreshortened are recalled less frequently in an incidental memory test than objects imagined to be visible (Abelson, 1976; Fiske, Taylor, Etcoff, & Laufer, 1979; Keenan & Moore, 1979; Pinker, Nimgade, and Wiesenfeld, 1982). Perspective information is easily accessed in scenes imagined "from a vantage point": for example, when subjects are asked to scan mentally across an image of a 3D scene by imagining a rifle sight sweeping from one object to another, their scan times are proportional to the separation between the objects in the 2D projection of the scene orthogonal to the "line of sight" (Pinker, 1980b; Pinker & Finke, 1980), showing the accuracy of the representation of projective interpoint distances in images. Other experiments, involving psychophysical and pattern-matching tasks, reported in Pinker and Finke (1980), confirm the availability of accurate perspective information. Barring the absurd interpretation that the "mind's eye" has a lens and a retina onto which "images of images" are projected, data on perspective effects in imagery are hard to reconcile with the 3D array theory, for perspective effects arise when a 3D scene is accessed via its projection onto a 2D surface, not when the scene or a 3D representation thereof is accessed directly.

4.2. 2D ARRAY + MEMORY FILES

This hypothesis, suggested by results in Pinker (1980b) and Pinker and Finke (1980), keeps the array two-dimensional, but puts information about the three-dimensional shapes of objects and scenes in the long-term memory files from which array patterns are generated. The process that "paints in" the array would accept as input not just a memory file containing information about the intrinsic 3D shape of the object (say, in the form of a list of object-centered 3D coordinates defining the object's surface), but also a vector specifying the intended "viewing" angle and distance. The process would then use a perspective transformation to compute the coordinates of the cells that would have to be filled in to depict the object accurately with respect to that "vantage point." Mental transformations would consist of successively repainting the array pattern, feeding in a slightly different value for the vantage point each time.

Unfortunately, this account has its own problems. First, it posits that the image painting process can immediately generate a depiction of a pattern at any orientation. Empirical evidence suggests otherwise. Pinker, Stromswold, and Beck (1984) found that subjects were unable to generate images of remembered 3D objects at arbitrary orientations given an orientation cue; rather, they first imagined the object in the orientation at which they had studied it, or in its canonical orientation, and then mentally rotated it into the target orientation. In any case, if humans *could* generate images at prespecified orientations, we would not be able to explain the incremental nature of mental rotation: if subjects can generate an image at a desired orientation immediately, why do they take proportionally longer to match stimulus pairs separated by greater disparities? In addition, if objects are mentally transformed by altering the viewer's vantage point relative to the scene, these transformations would resemble movements of the observer relative to the entire scene, as opposed to movements of parts of the scene relative to the rest. This is contrary both to subjects' introspections, and to data showing that subjects can imagine parts of an image moving with respect to a perceived (hence stationary) display (Pinker, 1980b; Pinker & Finke, 1980).

4.3. 2 1/2D ARRAY

In Pinker (1980a), I proposed that the 2D array be enriched along the lines of Marr and Nishihara's (1978) "2 1/2D sketch," a structure sometimes used in computer vision systems at an intermediate stage of the shape recognition process. This would involve filling each cell in the array not just with elements representing the lightness, color, texture, or edge-orientation of the corresponding local region of the depicted surface, but with quantities specifying its depth and surface orientation with respect to the viewer as well. In the simple 2D array theory of Kosslyn (1980), the rotation operator computed the trajectories of elements by sweeping across the array, and using the address of each filled cell (specifying its 2D position) to compute the address of the cell to which its contents must be moved in that iteration. In the 2 1/2D array theory, the rotation operator would access not just the cell address, but also the contents of the cell (specifying its depth from the vantage point). This additional piece of information is all that is needed mathematically for the rotation operator to compute the address and depth value of the destination cell for that element. Thus this account satisfies the three conditions that in combination strained the earlier approximations: it represents perspective effects (since the array cells are isomorphic to the two-dimensional layout of the visual field as experienced from a particular vantage point); it contains information about the third dimension (making 3D transformations such as rotation or translation in depth possible); and it allows such transformations to be performed by operating on the information displayed in the array, rather than by constructing the array pattern from scratch repeatedly.

Still, the theory is not wholly satisfactory. First, there is no simple mechanism for bringing new material into the array at the trailing edge of an object rotating in depth. But another problem is more fundamental. Since the addresses and depth values in the array are specified relative to the viewer (that is, in a viewer-centered coordinate system), the perspective appearance of objects are represented explicitly: a given visual angle corresponds to a precise number of adjacent array cells. On the other hand, objects' intrinsic sizes and shapes, and their locations in the world, are represented implicitly and must be computed indirectly from the cell addresses and contents using a set of coordinate transforms (that is, a given real world size corresponds to a large number of adjacent cells with "near" depth values or a small number of adjacent cells with "far" depth values). This predicts that tasks accessing perspective information about objects in immediate visual memory should be easier and less consuming of mental effort than those accessing objective information about intrinsic size and shape. Though both perspective ("visual field") and objective ("visual world") percepts are possible (see Gibson, 1950, 1952; Boring, 1952; Pinker, 1980a), contrary to the prediction of the 2 1/2D array theory, the latter are clearly more primary in several ways. Children see objects as three-dimensional long before they can use perspective information, say, in drawings (Spelke, in press; Phillip, Hobbs & Pratt, 1978); our primary phenomenal experience is of a world of solid objects laid out in a fixed 3D framework despite the wildly fluctuating retinal images, the properties of which we are usually unaware of (Gibson, 1950; Neisser, 1976, 1979); and judgments about shape and size seem to be chronometrically sensitive to three-dimensional properties of objects such as intrinsic shape and intrinsic size, and relatively insensitive to factors such as depth and occlusion that affect perspective properties (Metzler & Shepard, 1974; Uhlarik, Pringle, Jordan, & Misceo, 1980; Pringle & Uhlarik, 1979). Though the primacy of objective over perspective judgments can be handled by making certain assumptions about the temporal properties of the processes that operate on the information in the 2 1/2D array (i.e., that accessing a cell address is as time-consuming as accessing its contents, or that deriving object-centered from viewer-centered coordinates is a computationally primitive step invariably invoked while transforming images), the resulting theory becomes unparsimonious and counterintuitive.

5. A New Theory: Dual-Address Array

The chief problem for each of the theories outlined above is an inability to deal parsimoniously with the dual nature of visual experience: The visual field, such as when railroad tracks stretching to the horizon are seen to converge, and the visual world, such as when those same tracks are seen as parallel (Gibson, 1950, 1952; Boring, 1952; Pinker, 1980a). Each of these mental sets plays a role in perception and in imagery. The theory to be outlined in this section tries to capture this duality within the confines of a single array structure.

In a 2 1/2D array as described here, the depth of a local region of a surface is specified by filling an array cell with a number representing that depth. Say we took the array and replaced each cell by a string of cells, so that each cell in the string would represent a specific depth from the viewer when filled with a primitive element or mark. The mapping between physical depth and the cells in the string could be nonlinear, like the focusing scale on a camera lens barrel, so that objects at apparently infinite distances (e.g., heavenly bodies) would be represented by elements in the last cell of each string. Furthermore, one could stipulate that only one cell in a string can be filled at one time, so that only visible, not occluded surfaces, would be represented (though the fact that we can perceive transparency might call for a weaker assumption than this). If we consider cells representing the same depth in adjacent strings to be adjacent to one another, then this array is half-way between a 2 1/2D array and a 3D array (though I will resist the temptation to christen it a "2 3/4D array"). The array cells map topographically onto distinct regions of visible three-dimensional space, as in the 3D or sandbox theory. But unlike that theory, the mapping from array cell to physical region is nonlinear and nonhomogeneous; only visible surfaces are represented; and the cell addresses are in viewer-centered coordinates (i.e., horizontal visual angle, vertical visual angle, and depth, all relative to the "Cyclopean" fovea), therefore displaying the perspective, not intrinsic, sizes and shapes of objects. In fact, Downing and Pinker (1985) showed that the accessing of visual space by focal attention seems to be determined by this type of coordinate system: when people attend to a location, they detect a stimulus presented at that location more quickly; for stimuli presented at various distances from the attended locus, this enhancement falls off as a function of distance in terms of visual angle and distance in depth.

So far the theory is barely different from the 2 1/2D model. But say we now gave each cell in the array a *second* address, reflecting its coordinates in a 3D,

(Depth from the vantage point)		−90°	−60°	−30°	0°	30°	60°	90°
	∞	−∞, 0	−∞, ∞	−∞, ∞	0, ∞	∞, ∞	∞, ∞	∞, 0
	1000	−1000, 0	−900, 500	−500, 900	0, 1000	500, 900	900, 500	1000, 0
	100	−100, 0	−90, 50	−50, 90	0, 100	50, 90	90, 50	100, 0
	10	−10, 0	−9, 5	−5, 9	0, 10	5, 9	9, 5	10, 0
	1	−1, 0	−.9, .5	−.5, .9	0, 1	.5, .9	.9, .5	1, 0
	.1	−.1, 0	−.09, .05	−.05, .09	0, .1	.05, .09	.09, .05	.1, 0

Visual angle from the fixation point

Figure 2.2. Schematic diagram of the dual-address array. The Y- or height dimension is collapsed, yielding a "top-view," so to speak, of the array. The grain is vastly enlarged, and the known physiological characteristics of the visual field, like anisotropy and nonhomogeneity with eccentricity, are ignored. Viewer-centered addresses are listed in the margins; world-centered addresses are listed in each cell (no theoretical difference is implied by this notational difference). The origin of the world-centered system has been placed on the origin of the viewer-centered system.

world-centered, homogeneous, isotropic coordinate system mapping linearly into physical space. Such an array is represented schematically in Figure 2.2. It should be apparent from the figure that the mapping from world-centered to viewer-centered addresses is nonlinear and nonhomogeneous, so that a given number of adjacent array cells are assigned a small range of horizontal world-centered addresses in the "front" of the array and a large range in the "rear." Let us posit, as a final assumption, that the world-centered addresses can be specified in "base + index" format, like modern computer memories, which is equivalent to being able to move the origin of the coordinate system to lie on any cell of the array. (Thus what I am calling a "world-centered" coordinate system can be centered on or aligned with salient environmental surfaces such as walls and floors, or upon an object being attended to.) Since "mental arrays" of any sort owe many of their functional properties to their addressing or coordinate system (Pylyshyn, 1984), providing each cell with two addresses, one perspective-specific, and one world-centered, provides the advantages of separate 2D and 3D arrays without having to posit an additional structure plus processes linking it to all the others.

Marr and Nishihara (1978) and Hinton (1979b) point out that a variety of visual and inferential processes require a transformation from retinal or viewer-centered coordinates to object- or world-centered coordinates or vice-versa. The substantive hypothesis submitted here is that these translations are accomplished in effect as simple lookup operations on array cells, each cell pairing a viewer-centered coordinate triple with an object-centered coordinate triple for a distinct local region of the visual field. In the following sections I show how the theory provides succinct and plausible prima facie accounts of each of these processes, at the same time raising testable empirical hypotheses about various aspects of the mechanisms involved.

6. How the Dual-Address Theory Handles Spatial Information Processing

6.1. THE VISUAL FIELD AND THE VISUAL WORLD

In the dual-address theory, the processing of visual patterns via the world-centered addresses of the cells they fill yields visual world percepts (and hence is used in judgments about objects' real world shapes, sizes, and locations); processing the viewer-centered addresses yields visual field percepts. The current theory allows both mental sets to operate in imagery as well as perception, consistent with dem-onstrations that imagery transformations can obey either set (see Pinker, 1980a, for a review). For example, while driving on the highway, when I mentally place five cars between my car and the one up ahead to maintain the proper following distance, I can be confident that the judged distance really is five times one car length in the world though I can "see" each car as smaller than the one behind it.

6.2. MENTAL TRANSFORMATIONS

In performing transformations like rotation in depth, the world-centered coordinate system is first centered upon the object to be rotated. The rotation operator sweeps through cells in a bounded region of the array encompassing the object, and looks up the world-centered or object-centered address. Assuming that the object-centered coordinate system can be either cylindrical or spherical (see Marr, 1982; Pinker, 1984), the operator subtracts a constant from the angular coordinate of the address, fetches the contents of the cell with that new world/object-centered address, and deposits them into the cell being worked upon. A constraint that the fetched-from and deposited-into cells must be in close proximity within the array is one way to guarantee the incremental nature of the rotation. Sometimes the desired "source" cell is blocked because another cell in its string, representing an occluding surface at a nearer distance, is filled (i.e., at the trailing edge of a rotating object). In that case, the object-centered coordinates of the blocked cell are passed to the long-term memory file for the object's shape, which is assumed to be specified with respect to an object-centered coordinate system (e.g., as in Marr & Nishihara, 1978; Kosslyn & Shwartz, 1977). The desired sur-face element can now be retrieved from the LTM file by subtracting the angle through which the object has been rotated so far from the angular coordinate of the blocked cell. In contrast, the 2 1/2D array theory outlined earlier is far more complex, involv-ing viewer-to-object-centered translations at every step, and the theory fails to provide concise accounts of the incremental nature of the rotation or of the approximately equal rates for depth and picture-plane rotations. And unlike the 3D array theory, the current theory correctly implies that new 2D perspective patterns will emerge as an object rotates in depth (Pinker & Finke, 1980), since these patterns will be accessible via the viewer-centered coordinates of the rotated pattern.

6.3. MENTAL IMAGE GENERATION

In the Kosslyn & Shwartz (1977) version of the array theory, images are generated from LTM files hierarchically organized in terms of (a) the skeletal shape of the object, and (b) the details or parts attached to it, with additional information specifying the spatial relations of parts to the skeleton. Say the skeletal image is generated by first aligning the world-centered coordinate system with the desired position of the object, then by using these coordinate addresses to fill in the cells as specified by the skeletal file (this is a simple identity mapping on the aforementioned assumption that surface information in the LTM files is specified in object-centered coordinates). It is now straightforward to find the portion of the array that will be the destination of the points depicting the object's parts, since all the array cells have addresses relative to the object's skeleton, and the LTM specification of the proper location of the part is specified relative to the skeleton as well. This eliminates Kosslyn & Shwartz's somewhat cumbersome process of searching over the partially constructed image until attachment points for to-be-generated parts are recognized via their depicted shapes.

6.4. BOTTOM-UP PATTERN RECOGNITION

The position of a receptor in the retina determines the two angular viewer-centered coordinates of a local region of stimulation, and the retinal disparity of corresponding local regions of the stimulus pattern determines its depth (together with information about eye position). Thus the mapping from visual input to the array cells (addressed by their viewer-centered coordinates) is fairly direct. However, an efficient bottom-up pattern recognition system requires a description of the input shape that is insensitive to the orientation, location, projected size, and projected shape of the object, so that the description can be matched against a single or a small number of canonical descriptions of the object's intrinsic shape (Marr & Nishihara, 1978; Pinker, 1984). In the current theory, once the depth of every point has been established, the positions of parts of the objects in world-centered coordinates preserving size and shape constancy are available. If the origin (and possibly axes) of the world-centered coordinate system is then shifted to coincide with the natural axis of the object, each local surface region is specified in object-centered coordinates, so a global object-centered description of the object and its parts for input into the recognition process can be computed with a relatively small number of steps.

6.5. TOP-DOWN PATTERN RECOGNITION

Marr and Nishihara (1978) have suggested that when bottom-up procedures are inadequate to delineate the orientation in depth of a part of an object, one might use something like the following procedure: a) select, by bottom-up means, a long-term memory description of the object which specifies the relation between the principal axis (or skeleton) and each part; b) use that description to generate a set of possible two-dimensional projections of the part that are consistent both with the perceived orientation of the main axis of the object and with the spatial relations between the part and the main axis; and c) choose the part orientation from that set that yields the best match between predicted projection and actual input projection. This "image space processor" (and other top-down recognition processes, e.g., Waltz, 1979; Horn & Bachman, 1979; Pinker, 1980a) could be implemented as a template-matching process in the current theory by a) using the LTM shape description to generate a skeletal image; b) using the world/object-centered coordinates to rotate one of the parts in depth; and c) using the viewer-centered coordinates of the resulting pattern to determine when the rotated part best matches the silhouette of the input pattern.

6.6. EYE MOVEMENTS AND ATTENTION SHIFTS

Eye movements between objects in 3D space have been found to consist of two separate phases (Graham, 1965): a yoked movement of the eyes bringing the bisector of the angle they form into alignment with the target, and a convergence movement bringing the vertex of that angle onto the target. Together with information about the current eye positions, a command for the former motion can be derived directly from the first two viewer-centered coordinates of the target (i.e., the location of the depth string); a command for the convergence motion can be derived simply from the third (i.e., the location of the target cell within the depth string). Similarly, internal attention shifts seem to enhance a region of visual space defined by a range of visual angle and depth (Downing and Pinker, 1985); this would correspond to priming a cluster of adjacent cells in the array defined by the viewer-centered coordinate system.

6.7. PERCEPTUAL STABILITY

As mentioned, the world/object-centered coordinates of visual patterns are used to assess the physical layout of scenes. Say people mentally represent their positions in space by linking some portion of the world/object-centered coordinate system to a semantic memory structure for a known world location and direction (e.g., facing north in a familiar room). Now, when they move their eyes, head, or body, they can take a copy of the motor commands and use them to displace the origin of the world-centered coordinate system a corresponding amount and direction within the array. This preserves the perception that the visible world objectively stayed put (since objects are linked to the same world-centered coordinates as before), but also is consistent with the fact that the surfaces in the world that are currently visible, and their relation to the eyes, have changed as a result of the movement (since the array cells are in fact filled with a different pattern than before).

6.8. PERCEPTUAL ADAPTATION

It is well-known that with practice, humans can adapt to wearing prisms that distort the visual input in a variety of ways (Dodwell, 1970). In the current model, this could consist of altering the cell-by-cell linkages between world-centered addresses (which are accessed in intersensory and sensorimotor coordination) and the viewer-centered addresses (which are linked to specific field locations), based on discrepancies between the coordinates of objects or limbs in haptic or auditory representational structures and the object/world-centered coordinates in the visual array. Interestingly, Finke (1979) has shown that mismatches between intended and *imagined* hand locations can cause sensorimotor adaptation, and Kubovy (1979) has conjectured that the class of mathematical functions available for visuomotor adaptation is just the class available for mental image transformations. Both support the current argument that a common array structure underlies both mental images and the visual percepts that tie in to other sensory and motor systems.

7. Conclusion

In any field of science, metaphors are double-edged swords. They can serve a heuristic function, inspiring and organizing experimental research. On the other hand, they can lead one to confuse one's everyday familiarity with the metaphorical object with true explanations of the object under investigation. The metaphor of "a mind's eye looking at a mental picture" has had both roles in the study of imagery. No one denies that the metaphor has inspired important discoveries, such as the study of mental rotation. But some of the most vehement disagreements in philosophy and experimental psychology during this century have centered on the purported misuse of the metaphor, such as the absurd notions of homunculi in the skull and pictures painted onto the surface of the brain.

Happily, the application of computational cognitive science to the study of imagery has taken imagery theory and research out of the realm of metaphor. The array theory and its implementation as a computer simulation have exorcised the sense of paradox that surrounded the notion of images being picture-like entities that are inspected by perception-like processes. I hope to have shown how the paradox of squeezing a stable three-dimensional world into a two-dimensional mental picture can also be eliminated by a careful consideration of the ways in which computational processes can access and manipulate information about the geometric properties of objects and space. Such consideration led to a theory that, I hope, preserves the intuitive appeal and the empirical support of the picture metaphor while being capable of handling the inherent computational problems of representing and reasoning about 3D space. Whether the theory can be convincingly shown to be *true* is another story, but if we can focus our attention on whether theories are true, rather than on whether they are possible or logically coherent, then the study of imagery has truly made progress.

References

Abelson, R. P. Script processing in attitude formation and decision making. In J. S. Carrol & J. W. Payne (Eds.), *Cognition and Social Behavior*. Hillsdale, New Jersey: Erlbaum, 1976.

Anderson, J. R. Arguments concerning representations for mental imagery. *Psychological Review*, 1978, *85*, 249–277.

Attneave, F. Representation of physical space. In A. W. Melton & E. J. Martin (Eds.), *Coding Processes in Human Memory*. Washington, D.C.: V. H. Winston, 1972.

Attneave, F. & Block, N. Apparent motion in tridimensional space. *Perception & Psychophysics*, 1973, *13*, 301–307.

Attneave, F. & Pierce, C. R. Accuracy of extrapolating a pointer into perceived and imagined space. *American Journal of Psychology*, 1978, *91*, 371–387.

Bisiach, E. & Luzatti, C. Unilateral neglect of representational space. *Cortex*, 1978, *14*, 129–133.

Block, N. (Ed.) *Imagery*. Cambridge, MA: MIT Press, 1981.

Boring, E. G. The Gibsonian visual field. *Psychological Review*, 1952, *59*, 246–247.

Brooks, L. R. The suppression of visualization by reading. *Quarterly Journal of Experimental Psychology*, 1967, *19*, 289–299.

Chambers, D. & Reisberg, D. Can mental images be ambiguous? *Journal of Experimental Psychology: Human Perception and Performance*, 1985, *11*, 317–328.

Cooper, L. A. & Shepard, R. N. Chronometric studies of the rotation of mental images. In W. Chase (Ed.), *Visual Information Processing*. New York: Academic Press, 1973.

Dodwell, P. *Perceptual Adaptation*. New York: Holt, Rinehart, & Winston, 1970.

Downing, C. & Pinker, S. The spatial structure of visual attention. In M. Posner & O. Marin (Eds.), *Attention and Performance XI: Mechanisms of Attention and Visual Search*. Hillsdale, NJ: Erlbaum, 1985.

Farah, M. J. The neurological basis of mental imagery: A componential analysis. *Cognition*, 1984, *18*, 245–272.

Farah, M. J. Psychophysical evidence for a shared representational medium for visual images and percepts. *Journal of Experimental Psychology: General*, 1985, *114*, 91–103.

Finke, R. A. The functional equivalence of mental images and errors of movement. *Cognitive Psychology*, 1979, *11*, 235–264.

Finke, R. A. Levels of equivalence in imagery and perception. *Psychological Review*, 1980, *87*, 113–132.

Finke, R. A. & Kosslyn, S. M. Mental imagery acuity in the peripheral visual field. *Journal of Experimental Psychology: Human Perception and Performance*, 1980, *6*, 126–139.

Finke, R. A. & Kurtzman, H. S. Mapping the visual field in mental imagery. *Journal of Experimental Psychology: General*, 1981, *110*, 501–517.

Finke, R. A. & Pinker, S. Spontaneous image scanning in mental extrapolation. *Journal of Experimental Psychology: Learning, Memory, and Cognition*, 1982, *8*, 142–147.

Finke, R. A. & Pinker, S. Directional scanning of remembered visual patterns. *Journal of Experimental Psychology: Learning, Memory, and Cognition*, 1983, *9*(3), 398–410.

Finke, R. A., Pinker, S., and Farah, M. J. Reinterpreting visual patterns in mental imagery. Submitted for publication, 1987.

Finke, R. A. & Shepard, R. N. Visual functions of mental imagery. In K. R. Boff, L. Kaufman, & J. Thomas (Eds.), *Handbook of Perception and Human Performance*, Vol. 2. New York: Wiley-Interscience, 1986.

Fiske, S. T., Taylor, S. E., Etcoff, N. L., and Laufer, J. K. Imaging empathy, and causal attribution. *Journal of Experimental Social Psychology*, 1979, *15*, 356–377.

Fodor, J. A. *Psychological Explanation*. New York: Random House, 1968.

Fodor, J. A., *The Language of Thought*. New York: Thomas Y. Crowell Company, 1975.

Freyd, J. J. & Finke, R. A. Facilitation of length discrimination using real and imagined context frames. *American Journal of Psychology*, 1984, *97*, 323–341.

Gardner, H. *The Mind's New Science*. New York: Basic Books, 1985.

Gibson, J. J. *The Perception of the Visual World*. Boston: Houghton Mifflin, 1950.

Gibson, J. J. The visual field and the visual world: A reply to Professor Boring. *Psychological Review*, 1952, *59*, 149–151.

Graham, C. Visual space perception. In C. Graham (Ed.), *Vision and Visual Perception*. New York: Wiley, 1965.

Haugeland, J. (Ed.) *Mind Design: Philosophy, Psychology, Artificial Intelligence*. Montgomery, VT: Bradford Books, 1981.

Hinton, G. E. Imagery without arrays. *The Behavioral and Brain Sciences*, 1979a, *2*, 555–556.

Hinton, G. E. Some demonstrations of the effects of structural descriptions in mental imagery. *Cognitive Science*, 1979b, *3*, 231–250.

Hollins, M. Styles of mental imagery in blind adults. *Neuropsychologia*, 1985, *23*, 561–566.

Horn, B. K. P. & Bachman, B. L. Registering real images using synthetic images. In P. H. Winston & R. H. Brown (Eds.), *Artificial Intelligence: An MIT Perspective*. Cambridge, MA: MIT Press, 1979.

Keenan, J. M. & Moore, R. E. Memory for images of concealed objects: A reexamination of Neisser and Kerr. *Journal of Experimental Psychology: Human Learning and Memory*, 1979, *5*, 374–385.

Kosslyn, S. M. Information representation in visual images. *Cognitive Psychology*, 1975, *7*, 341–370.

Kosslyn, S. M. Measuring the visual angle of the mind's eye. *Cognitive Psychology*, 1978, *10*, 356–389.

Kosslyn, S. M. *Image and Mind*. Cambridge, MA: Harvard University Press, 1980.

Kosslyn, S. M., Brunn, J., Cave, K. R., & Wallach, R. W. Individual differences in mental imagery ability: A computational analysis. *Cognition*, 1984, *18*, 195–243.

Kosslyn, S. M., Pinker, S., Smith, G. E., & Shwartz, S. P. On the demystification of mental imagery. *The Behavioral and Brain Sciences*, 1979, *2*, 535–581.

Kosslyn, S. M. & Shwartz, S. P. A simulation of visual imagery. *Cognitive Science*, 1977, *1*, 265–295.

Kubovy, M. Two hypotheses concerning the interrelation of perceptual spaces. In L. D. Harmon (Ed.), *Interrelations of the Communicative Senses.Washington*, DC: National Science Foundation, 1979. Marr, D. *Vision*. San Francisco: Freeman, 1982.

Marr, D. & Nishihara, H. K. Representation and recognition of the spatial organization of three-dimensional shapes. *Proceedings of the Royal Society*, 1978, *200*, 269–294.

Metzler, J. Cognitive analogues of the rotation of three-dimensional objects. Unpublished doctoral dissertation, Stanford University, 1973.

Metzler, J. & Shepard, R. N. Transformational studies of the internal representation of three-dimensional space. In R. Solso (Ed.), *Theories in Cognitive Psychology: The Loyola Symposium*. Potomac, MD: Lawrence Erlbaum, 1974.

Miller, G. A. & Johnson-Laird, P. *Language and Perception*. Cambridge, MA: Harvard University Press, 1976.

Neisser, U. *Cognition and Reality*. San Francisco: W. H. Freeman, 1976.

Neisser, U. Images, models, and human nature. *The Behavioral and Brain Sciences*, 1979, *2*, 561.

Newell, A. & Simon, H. *Human Problem Solving*. Englewood Cliffs, NJ: Prentice Hall, 1973.

Phillip, W. A., Hobbs, S. B., Pratt, F. R. Intellectual realism in children's drawings of cubes. *Cognition*, 1978, *6*, 15–33.

Pinker, S. Mental imagery and the visual world. Center for Cognitive Science Occasional Paper #4, MIT, 1980. (a)

Pinker, S. Mental imagery and the third dimension. *Journal of Experimental Psychology: General*, 1980, *109*, 354–371. (b)

Pinker, S. Visual cognition: An introduction. *Cognition*, 1984, *16*, 1–63.

Pinker, S., Choate, P., & Finke, R. A. Mental extrapolation in patterns reconstructed from memory. *Memory and Cognition*, 1984, *12*(3), 207–218.

Pinker, S. & Finke, R. A. Emergent two-dimensional patterns in images rotated in depth. *Journal of Experimental Psychology: Human Perception and Performance*, 1980, *6*, 244–264.

Pinker, S. & Kosslyn, S. M. The representation and manipulation of three-dimensional space in mental images. *Journal of Mental Imagery*, 1978, *2*, 69–84.

Pinker, S. & Kosslyn, S. M. Theories of mental imagery. In A. Sheikh (Ed.), *Imagery: Current Theory, Research and Application*. New York: Wiley, 1983, 43–71.

Pinker, S., Nimgade, A., & Wiesenfeld, H. C. Memory for pictures imagined at different sizes, distances, and orientations. Paper presented at the 62nd Annual Meeting of the Western Psychological Association, Sacramento, CA, April 8-11, 1982.

Pinker, S., Stromswold, K., & Beck, L. Visualizing objects at prespecified orientations. Paper presented at the annual meeting of the Psychonomic Society, San Antonio, November, 1984.

Posner, M. I., Snyder, C. R., & Davidson, B. J. Attention and the detection of signals. *Journal of Experimental Psychology: General*, 1980, *109*, 160–174.

Pringle, R. & Uhlarik, J. Chronometric analysis of comparative size judgments with two-dimensional pictorial arrays. Paper presented at the annual meeting of the Psychonomic Society, Phoenix, Arizona, 1979.

Pylyshyn, Z. What the mind's eye tells the mind's brain: A critique of mental imagery. *Psychological Bulletin*, 1973, *80*, 1–24.

Pylyshyn, Z. The imagery debate: Analogue media versus tacit knowledge. *Psychological Review*, 1981, *88*, 16–45.

Pylyshyn, Z. *Computation and Cognition: Toward a Foundation for Cognitive Science*. Cambridge, MA: Bradford Books/MIT Press, 1984.

Segal, S. J. & Fusella, V. Influence of imaged pictures and sounds on detection of visual and auditory signals. *Journal of Experimental Psychology*, 1970, *83*, 458–464.

Shepard, R. N. The mental image. *American Psychologist*, 1978, *33*, 125–137.

Shepard, R. N. & Cooper, L. A. *Mental Images and Their Transformations*. Cambridge, MA: Bradford Books/MIT Press, 1982.

Shepard, R. N. & Judd, S. A. Perceptual illusion of rotation of three-dimensional objects. *Science*, 1976, *191*, 952–954.

Shepard, R. N. & Metzler, J. Mental rotation of three-dimensional objects. *Science*, 1971, *171*, 701–703.

Shwartz, S. P. Studies of mental image rotation: Implications of a computer simulation model of mental imagery. Unpublished doctoral dissertation, The Johns Hopkins University, 1979.

Slee, J. A. Individual differences in visual imagery ability and the retrieval of visual appearances. *Journal of Mental Imagery*, 1980, *4*, 93–113.

Spelke, E. S. Where perceiving ends and thinking begins: The apprehension of objects in infancy. In A. Yonas (Ed.), *Minnesota Symposia on Child Psychology*, in press.

Spoehr, K. T. & Williams, B. E. Retrieving distance and location information from mental maps. Paper presented at the nineteenth annual meeting of the Psychonomic Society, San Antonio, Texas, November 9-11, 1978.

Uhlarik, J., Pringle, R., Jordan, D., & Misceo, G. Size scaling in two-dimensional pictorial arrays. *Perception & Psychophysics*, 1980, *27*, 60–70.

Waltz, D. L. On the function of mental imagery. *The Behavioral and Brain Sciences*, 1979, *2*, 569–570.

Weber, R. J. & Malmstrom, F. V. Measuring the size of mental images. *Journal of Experimental Psychology: Human Perception & Performance*, 1979, *5*, 1–12.

3

Rules and Connections in Human Language

with A L A N P R I N C E

At least since the empiricist and rationalist philosophers of the Age of Reason, human intelligence has been explained in two different ways: as learned associations between sensory impressions and as the application of logical rules to symbolic representations. In the twentieth century the associationist theory lay behind the stimulus-response models of the behaviorists, the neural-network models of D. O. Hebb (an emeritus professor at McGill University when I was an undergraduate there), and the "perceptron" computer simulations by Frank Rosenblatt and Oliver Selfridge. The symbol-processing approach, meanwhile, had been revived during the cognitive revolution of the 1950s and 1960s. It was adopted by the artificial intelligence pioneers Marvin Minsky, Herbert Simon, and Allen Newell, by importers of information theory into psychology such as George Miller and Donald Broadbent, and by the linguist Noam Chomsky.

In the first decades of cognitive science, symbol-processing models pretty much carried the day. But in the 1980s, computer simulations of neural-network models were revived under the rubric of "connectionism" and "parallel distributed processing." These models, which used simplified models of neurons and synapses as a metaphor for their computational elements, seemed to bridge the levels of neurons and cognition, and in the eyes of many cognitive scientists seemed to render the symbolic approach obsolete. Even in the second decade of the twenty-first century, statistical learning models, many of them implemented as artificial neural networks, are often touted as the next wave in machine intelligence, and some can be found in consumer applications such as Google Translate and telephone speech recognition.

Yet as anyone who has been trapped in voice-mail jail or who has struggled with the word salad in a Google-translated Web page can attest, there are limitations to systems that are driven by sheer associations, unaided by the power of symbolic reasoning. These limitations are the topic of the paper reprinted here. David Rumelhart and James McClelland had developed a model of the acquisition of the past-tense construction in English, which was one of the first, and one of the most impressive, of the new wave of neural-network models appearing in the 1980s. In 1988 the linguist Alan Prince and

I published a lengthy critical analysis of it in the journal Cognition, *entitled "On Language and Connectionism: Analysis of a Parallel Distributed Processing Model of Language Acquisition." Together with an article by Jerry Fodor and Zenon Pylyshyn which appeared in the same issue, and a new preface to the book* Perceptrons *by Minsky and Seymour Papert, it became the most prominent analysis of the limitations of neural-network models of language and cognition, and remains my second-most cited paper.*

"On Language and Connectionism" was a very, very long article (121 pages). Shortly after it was published, the editor of the journal Trends in Neuroscience *asked if we could condense it for an audience of neuroscientists. Rather than devoting a third of this volume to the original article, I've included this one, which captures its most important points.*

Everyone hopes that the discoveries of neuroscience will help explain human intelligence, but no one expects such an explanation to be done in a single step. Neuroscience and cognitive science, it is hoped, will converge on an intermediate level of 'cognitive architecture' which would specify the elementary information processes that arise as a consequence of the properties of neural tissue and that serve as the building blocks of the cognitive algorithms that execute intelligent behavior. This middle level has proven to be elusive. Neuroscientists study firing rates, excitation, inhibition, plasticity; cognitive scientists study rules, representations, symbol systems. Although it's relatively easy to imagine ways to run cognitive symbol systems on digital computers, how they could be implemented in neural hardware has remained obscure. Any theory of this middle level faces a formidable set of criteria: it must satisfy the constraints of neurophysiology and neuroanatomy, yet supply the right kind of computational power to serve as the basis for cognition.

Recently there has been considerable enthusiasm for a theory that claims to do just that. Connectionist or Parallel Distributed Processing (PDP) models try to model cognitive systems using networks of large numbers of densely interconnected units. The units transmit signals to one another along weighted connections; they 'compute' their output signals by weighting each of their input signals by the strength of the connection it comes in on, summing the weighted inputs, and feeding the result into a nonlinear output function, usually a threshold. Learning consists of adjusting the strengths of connections and the threshold-values, usually in a direction that reduces the discrepancy between an actual output and a 'desired' output provided by a set of 'teaching' inputs.[1,2] These are not meant to be genuine neural models; although some of their properties are reminiscent of the nervous system, others, such as the teaching and learning mechanisms, have no neural analogue, and much of what we know of the topology of neural connectivity plays no role.[3] However, their proponents refer to them as 'brain-style' or 'brain-metaphor' models, and they have attracted enormous interest among neuroscientists.[4] Much of this interest comes from demonstrations that show how the models can exhibit rule-like behavior without containing rules. The implication is that PDP networks eventually might be consistent with both neurophysiology and with a revised but adequate theory of cognition, providing the long-sought bridge.

The most dramatic and frequently-cited demonstration of the rule-like behavior of PDP systems comes from a model of the acquisition of the past tense in English.[5] It addresses a phenomenon that has served as a textbook example of the role of rules in cognitive behavior.[6] Young children use regular ('walked') and irregular ('broke') verbs early on, but then begin to generalize the regular 'ed' ending, saying 'breaked' and considerably later, 'broked' as well. By kindergarten they can convert a nonsense word 'jick' provided by an experimenter into 'jicked', and easily differentiate the three phonological variants of the regular suffix: 't' for words ending in an unvoiced consonant ('walked'), 'd' for words ending in a voiced phoneme ('jogged'), and 'ed' for words ending in a 't' or 'd' ('patted'). According to the traditional explanation of the developmental sequence, children first memorize past forms directly from their parents' speech, then coin a rule that generates them productively.

Remarkably, Rumelhart and McClelland's network model exhibits the same general type of behavior (and also several other developmental phenomena), but has no rules at all (see Box 3.1). It has no representations of words, regular versus irregular cases, roots, stems, or suffixes. Rather, it is a simple two-layer network, with a set of input units that are turned on in patterns that correspond to the verb stem, a set of output units that are turned on in patterns that correspond to the verb's past tense form, and connections between every input unit and every output unit. All that happens in learning is that the network compares its own version of the past tense form with the correct version provided by a 'teacher', and adjusts

---

Box 3.1 **How the Rumelhart–McClelland model works**

Rumelhart and McClelland's model, in its trained state, should take any stem as input and emit the corresponding past tense form. They assume that the acquisition process establishes a direct mapping from the phonetic representation of the stem to the phonetic representation of the past tense form. (In English, the stem is the same as the infinitive and the uninflected present tense). A graphical representation of the model is shown in this box; of its three components, the center one, the 'pattern associator', is the most important theoretically.

The model's pattern associator is a simple network with two layers of nodes (or 'units'), one layer for representing the input, the other for the output. Nodes in the R–M model may only be 'on' or 'off'; each node therefore represents a single binary feature, 'off' or 'on' marking the absence or presence of a certain property that a word may have. Every distinct stem must be encoded as a unique subset of input nodes; every distinct past tense form as a unique subset of output nodes.

Here a problem arises. The natural assumption would be that words are concatenations of phonemes, strings on an alphabet. But the pattern association network must analyse inputs as an unordered set of properties (codable as a set of turned-on units). Dedicating each unit to a phoneme would obliterate information about serial order, leading to the confusion of 'pit' and 'tip', 'cat' and 'tack', and so on. To overcome this problem, Rumelhart and McClelland turn to a scheme proposed by Wickelgren,[20] according to which a string is represented as the set of the trigrams (3-character sequences) that it contains. (In order to mark word edges, it is necessary to assume that word-boundary (#) is a character in the underlying alphabet.) Rumelhart and McClelland call such trigrams 'Wickelphones'. For example, the word 'strip' contains the following assortment of Wickelphones: {ip#, rip, str, tri, #st}; and 'strip' is uniquely reconstructible from this trigram set. Although certain trigram sets are consistent with more than one string, in particular those containing three Wickelphones ABC, BCA, and CAB, all words in their sample were uniquely encoded.

However, the Wickelphone itself is not suitable for the task at hand, for two compelling reasons. First, the number of possible Wickelphones for their representation of English would have multiplied out to over 43 000 nodes for the input stem, 43 000 nodes for the output past form, and two billion connections between them, too many to handle in present-day computers. Second, an interesting model must be able to generalize beyond the word set given to it, and provide past tense forms for new stems based on their similarities to the ones trained. Since phonological regularities (like those involved in past tense formation) do not treat phonemes as atomic, unanalysable wholes but pertain instead to their constituent phonetic properties like place and manner of articulation, voicing, the height and tenseness of vowels, stridency (noisiness), and so on, it is necessary that such fine-grained information be represented in the network. The Wickelphone is too coarse to support the necessary generalization. For example, any English speaker who had to provide a past tense form for the hypothetical verb 'to Bach' (as in the composer) would pronounce it bach-t, not bach-d or bach-ed, even though ch is not a consonant they have heard used in an English verb. This reaction is based on the similarity of ch to p, k, s, and so on, all of which share the feature 'unvoiced'; and the tacit knowledge that verbs ending in unvoiced consonants have their past tense suffix pronounced as t. Since atomic symbols for phonemes do not represent this similarity, decomposition of phonemes into features is a standard tool of phonology. Rumelhart and McClelland therefore assume a phonetic decomposition of segments into features which are in broad outline like those used by phonologists. Rather than dedicating nodes to Wickelphones, they use what they call 'Wickelfeatures', where a Wickelfeature is a trigram of features, one from each of the 3 elements of the Wickelphone. For example, the features, 'VowelUnvoicedlnterrupted' and 'HighStopStop' are two of the Wickelfeatures in the ensemble that would correspond to the Wickelphone 'ipt'. By simplifying the Wickelfeature set in a number of other ways that will not be discussed here, Rumelhart and McClelland pared down the number of Wickelfeature nodes to 460. (See Refs 5 and 8 for a complete description of the model.)

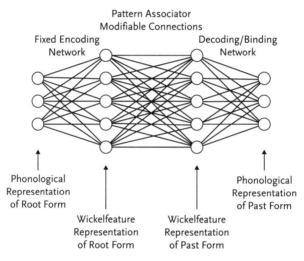

Each word is represented by a collection of turned-on nodes that correspond to its Wickelfeatures. This gives a 'distributed' representation: an individual word does not register on its own node, but is analysed as an ensemble of properties, Wickelfeatures. As the figure shows, an "encoder" of an unspecified nature is invoked to convert an ordered phonetic string into a set of activated Wickelfeature units.

In the pattern associator, every input node is connected to every output node, so that each input Wickelfeature can influence any Wickelfeature in the output set. Because of this, the device can record an immense variety of correlations between patterns of activation. How is an output generated? Suppose that a set of input nodes is turned on. Any given output node receives signals from the nodes in the active input set. The strength of each such signal is determined by a weight attached to the link along which the signal travels. The output node adds up the strengths of all incoming signals and compares this sum to a threshold value; if the sum exceeds the threshold, the node can turn on.

The decision is made probabilistically: the farther the weighted sum is above (below) the threshold, the more likely the node is to turn on (off).

The untrained pattern associator starts out with no preset relations between input and output nodes: the link weights are all zero. Training involves presenting the network with an input stem and comparing the output pattern actually obtained with the desired pattern, which is provided to the network by a 'teacher' as a distinct kind of 'teaching' input (not shown in the figure). The corresponding psychological assumption is that the child, through some unspecified process, has already figured out which past tense form is to be associated with which stem form.

The comparison between the output pattern obtained from the network's internal computation and the desired pattern provided by the 'teacher' is made on a node-by-node basis. Any output node that is in the wrong state becomes the target of adjustment. If the network ends up leaving a node off that ought to be on according to the teacher, changes are made to render that node more likely to fire in the presence of the particular input at hand. Specifically, the weights on the links connecting active input units to the recalcitrant output unit are increased slightly; this will increase the tendency for the currently active input units—those that represent the input form—to activate the target node. In addition, the target node's own threshold is lowered slightly, so that it will tend to turn on more easily across the board. If, on the other hand, the network incorrectly turns an output node *on*, the reverse procedure is employed: the weights of the connections from currently active input units are decremented (potentially driving the connection weight to a negative, inhibitory value) and the target node's threshold is raised; a hyperactive output node is thus made more likely to turn off given the same pattern of input node activation. Repeated cycling through input–output pairs, with concomitant adjustments, shapes the behavior of the pattern associator. This is the 'perceptron convergence procedure'[21] and it is known to produce, in the limit, a set of weights that successfully maps the input activation vectors onto the desired output activation vectors, as long as such a set of weights exists.

In fact, the R–M net, following about 200 training cycles of 420 stem-past pairs (a total of about 80,000 trials), is able to produce correct past forms for the stems when the stems are presented alone, that is, in the absence of 'teaching' inputs. A single set of connection weights in the network is able to map *look* to *looked*, *live* to *lived*, *melt* to *melted*, *hit* to *hit*, *make* to *made*, *sing* to *sang*, even *go* to *went*. The bits of stored information accomplishing these mappings are superimposed in the connection weights and node thresholds; no single parameter corresponds uniquely to a rule or to any single irregular stem-past pair.

The structure of the encoding and decoding networks is not the focus of Rumelhart and McClelland's efforts, but they must have several special properties for the model to work properly. The input encoder was deliberately designed to activate some incorrect Wickelfeatures in addition to the precise set of Wickelfeatures in the stem: specifically, a randomly selected subset of those Wickelfeatures that encode the features of the central phoneme properly but encode incorrect feature values for one of the two context phonemes. Because this 'blurring' is highly selective, the process that gives rise to it cannot be interpreted as random noise. Rather, the blurred representation is intended to foster a further kind of generalization of the right sort; blurring the input representations makes the connection weights in the R–M model less likely to be able to exploit the idiosyncrasies of the words in the training set and hence reduces the model's tendency towards conservatism.

The output decoder faces a formidable task. When an input stem is fed into the model, the result is a set of activated output Wickelfeature units characterizing properties of the predicted past tense form. Nothing in the model ensures that the set of activated output units will fit together to describe a legitimate word or even a unique, consistent, and well-formed string of phonemes. Since the output Wickelfeatures virtually never define such a string exactly, there is no clear sense in which one knows which word (if any) the output Wickelfeatures are defining. A special mechanism called the 'Whole-String Binding Network' was programmed to provide an estimate of the model's tendencies to output possible words. Basically, this network had one unit stand for every possible string of phonemes less than 20 phonemes long (obviously, the actual set had to be pruned considerably from this astronomically large number of possibilities; this was done with the help of another mechanism that will not be discussed here). Once the set of Wickelfeature units in the past tense vector is activated, the word-like nodes in the whole-string binding network 'compete' for them. Each whole-string 'word' unit has a transient strength value that increases with the number of activated Wickelfeatures that its associated 'word' uniquely contains. ('Credit' for activated Wickelfeatures contained in several words is split among the units standing for those words.) Conversely, activated Wickelfeatures that are not contained in a word cause the strength of that word's unit to diminish. Strings whose units exceed a threshold level of strength after this competition process stabilizes are interpreted as the final output of the model.

In sum, the R–M model works as follows. The phonological string is exchanged for a set of Wickelfeatures by an unspecified process that activates all the correct and some of the incorrect Wickelfeature units. The pattern associator excites the Wickelfeature units in the output; during the training phase its parameters (weights and thresholds) are adjusted to reduce the discrepancy between the excited Wickelfeature units and the desired ones provided by the teacher. The activated Wickelfeature units may then be decoded into an output word by a whole-string binding network.

the strengths of the connections and the thresholds so as to reduce the difference. Rumelhart and McClelland suggest, and many are quick to agree, that this shows the viability of associationist theories of language acquisition, despite their virtual abandonment by linguists 25 years ago.[7] A system can show rule-like behavior without actually containing rules; perhaps the more sophisticated PDP version of associationism can serve as the basis of a revised theory of the psychology of language at the same time as its underlying mechanisms are tuned to be more faithful to neurophysiology.

Of course, the fact that a computer model behaves intelligently without rules does not show that humans lack rules, any more than a wind-up mouse shows that real mice lack motor programs. Recently, a set of papers has argued that the most prominent PDP models of language are incorrect on empirical grounds.[8–10] The evidence comes from a number of sources: the nature of children's language, as observed both in experiments and naturalistic studies; regularities in the kinds of words and sentences people judge to be natural-sounding or ill-formed in their colloquial speech; and the results of the simulation runs of the models themselves. If true, the implications are important, for they bear on the claims that associative networks can explain human rule-governed intelligence. We review here the most prominent evidence, which falls into three groups: the design of the model, its asymptotic performance (which ought to approximate an adult's command of everyday English), and its child-like intermediate behavior.

Evidence for the Linguistic Constructs Lacking from the Rumelhart–McClelland Model

The Rumelhart-McClelland model owes its radical look to the fact that it has nothing corresponding to the formal linguistic notions 'segment', 'string', 'stem', 'affix', 'word', 'root', 'regular rule', or 'irregular exception'. However, in standard psycholinguistic theories these entities are not mere notational conveniences but constructs designed to explain facts about the organization of language. By omitting the constructs without adequate substitutes, the R–M model is inconsistent with these facts.

STRINGS AND SEGMENTS

According to standard theories, a word's phonological representation contains a string of segments (phonemes), each segment decomposed into features that correspond to aspects of the articulation or sound of the segment (e.g. voiced/unvoiced, nasal/oral, front/back). Rumelhart and McClelland, in contrast, use a completely 'distributed' representation,[2] in which a word is a (simultaneous) pattern of activation over a single vector of units. This leads to an immediate problem for them: representing linear order. If each unit simply represented a phoneme or feature, the model would not be able to distinguish words in which the same sounds appear in different orders, for example 'apt', 'pat', and 'tap'. Thus Rumelhart and McClelland are led to use context-sensitive units, each of which encodes the presence of a substring of three adjacent phonological features in a word. For example, 'unvoiced-unvoiced-voiced' and 'fricative-stop-low–vowel' are two of the context-sensitive features activated for the word 'stay'. The input and output vectors each consist of 460 of these units; by activating subsets of them, it is possible to define unique patterns for the common English verbs.

There is good evidence that people don't use context-sensitive units of this kind, however. First, trisegmental units cannot uniquely encode all linguistic strings: though such units may work for English, they won't work generally. For example, the Australian language Oykangand contains distinct words 'algal' and 'algalgal'. These decompose into the very same set of context-sensitive features, and hence the model is incapable of distinguishing them. Second, the features make the wrong predictions about psychological similarity. Pairs of strings that differ in terms of the order of two phonemes, such as 'slit' and 'silt', are judged to sound similar, and indeed confusions among them are the probable cause of certain changes in the history of English such as 'brid' to 'bird' or 'thrid' to 'third'. However, if the atomic units of description correspond to (what we usually think of as) triples, then <abc> and <acb>, as atoms, are entirely distinct (one mustn't be misled by the fact that we, the theorists, use three-letter mnemonic abbreviations for them). Without introducing arbitrary tricks into the model, it is impossible to account for perceived similarities between words defined by them.[8,9] Third, the model makes the wrong prediction about the kinds of rules that should be easy to learn, hence prevalent in languages, and those rules that should be absent from languages. It is as easy for the model to learn bizarre, cross-linguistically non-existent rules for forming the past tense (such as reversing the order of the phonemes of the stem, which involves the simple association of each input unit <abc> with the output unit <cba>; or changing every phoneme to the next one in English alphabetical order; or adding a 'g' to end of a word if it begins with 'st' but a 'p' if it begins in 'sk') as it is to learn common rules (e.g. do nothing to the stem; add a 'd' to the stem)[8].

The basic problem is that in their simple associationist architecture, the same units must represent both the decomposition of a string into phonetic components and the order in which the components are concatenated. These are conflicting demands and ultimately the units can satisfy neither successfully. The Rumelhart–McClelland representational system is a case study in the difficulty of meeting the known constraints on cognitive structure. The actual units of phonological structure—from phonetic features, to segments, to syllables and stress-groups—are reasonably well understood. Abandoning them in favor of a unit—the feature triplet—that demonstrably has no role in linguistic processes is sure to lead to empirical problems.

MORPHOLOGY AND PHONOLOGY

The R–M model computes a one-step mapping from the phonological features of the stem to the phonological features of the past tense form. This allows it to dispense with many of the rules and abstract representations one finds in familiar theories of language. But there is overwhelming evidence that the mapping is actually computed in several layers. Consider the pattern of differences in the suffixes in 'walked', 'jogged', and 'patted', which are contingent on the last phoneme of the stem. These differences are not unique to the past tense form: they also occur in the passive participle ('he was kicked', 'he was slugged', 'he was patted') and in adjectives ('sabre-toothed', 'long-nosed', 'one-handed'). They also occur with different suffixes altogether, such as the plural ('hawks', 'dogs', 'hoses') and the possessive ('Pat's', 'Fred's', 'George's'). They even occur in simple words lacking inflection: there are words like 'ax' and 'act', with two unvoiced consonants in a row, and words like 'adze', with two voiced consonants in a row, but no words pronounced like 'acd' or 'agt', with an unvoiced consonant followed by a voiced consonant or vice-versa. The obvious explanation is that the t-d-ed pattern has nothing to do with the past tense at all; it belongs to a different system—phonology—that adjusts words and strings so as to conform to the sound pattern of English, regardless of how the words or strings were formed. (Basically, the phonological rules here force consonant clusters at the ends of words to be either consistently voiced or consistently unvoiced, and they insert a vowel between adjacent consonants if they are too similar). The regular past tense pattern, belonging to the 'morphological' system, is simply that /d/ gets added to the end of a verb; the threefold variation is handled by a different phonological component. By collapsing the distinction into a single component, the model cannot account for the fact that the pattern of threefold variation follows from general constraints on the language as a whole.

STEM AND AFFIX

Linguistic processes tend to 'copy' stems with only minor modifications: 'walk/walked' is a pervasive pattern; 'go/went' is extremely rare. In some languages, the stem is copied twice, a phenomenon called 'reduplication': the past of 'go' would be 'gogo'. Similarly, the identity of an affix tends to be preserved across its variants: the endings for 'jog' and 'pat' are 'd' and 'ed', respectively, not 'd' and 'ob' or 'iz' and 'gu'. A subtle but important property of network models is that there is no such thing as pure copying, just modifiable connections between one set of units and another set. Only the consistency of the pairings among units can affect the operation of the model, not what the units stand for (the labels next to the units are visible to the theorist, but not to the model). Hence the prevalence of copying operations in linguistic mappings is inexplicable; the network model could just as easily learn rules that change all a's to e's, all b's to c's, and so on.

LEXICAL ITEMS

In standard psychological theories, a word has an 'entry' in a mental lexicon that is distinct from its actual sound. This is necessary because of homophones such as 'ring' and 'wring' or 'lie' (prevaricate) and 'lie' (recline). Crucially, homophones can have different past tense forms, for example, 'rang' and 'wrung', or 'lied' and 'lay'. The R–M model, because it simply maps from phonological units to phonological units, is incapable of handling such words.

A natural reaction to this phenomenon might be to suppose that the past tense form is associated with meaning as well as with sound; perhaps the different semantic feature representations of the meanings of 'ring' and 'wring' can be directly associated with their different past tense forms. Somewhat surprisingly, it turns out that meaning is almost completely irrelevant to the past tense form; such forms are sensitive to distinctions at a level of representation at which verb roots are distinct but meaningless symbols. For example, verbs like 'come, go, do, have, set, get, put, stand…' each have dozens of meanings, especially in combination with 'particles' like 'in, out, up' and 'off', but they have the same irregular past tense forms in each of these semantic incarnations. This even occurs when these stems appear in combination with meaningless prefixes—'stood/understood', 'get/forget', 'come/overcome'. (Though the prefixes are meaningless, they must be real prefixes, appearing in other words: 'overcome' and 'become', which contain intuitively recognizable prefixes, are transformed to 'overcame' and 'became', but 'succumb', which sounds similar but lacks a genuine prefix, is not transformed into 'succame'). Conversely, synonyms need not have the same kind of past tense forms: compare 'hit/hit' versus 'strike/struck' versus 'slap/slapped', which have similar meanings, but different kinds of past tenses. Thus the similarity space relevant to the irregular past tenses has no semantic dimensions in it; all that matters is gross distinctness—'wring is not the same word as ring'—not actual meaning.

Even the distinction between a 'verb' and a 'verb root' is psychologically significant. Somewhat to the puzzlement of non-scientific prescriptive grammarians, people find it natural to say 'broadcasted', not 'broadcast', 'joy-rided', not 'joy-rode', 'grandstanded', not 'grandstood', 'high-sticked' (in ice hockey) not 'high-stuck'. The reason is that 'irregularity' is a property attached to verb roots, not verbs. For each of these verbs, speakers have a sense, usually unconscious, that they were derived from nouns ('a joy-ride', 'a high-stick', etc.). Since it makes no sense for a noun to be marked in a person's mental dictionary as having an irregular 'past tense form', any verb that is felt to be derived from nouns or adjectives automatically becomes regular, hence 'joy-rided'.

What all these examples suggest is that the mental processes underlying language are sensitive to a system of representation—traditionally called 'morphology'—at which there are lawful regularities among entities that are neither sounds nor meanings, specifically, lexical items, stems, affixes, roots, and parts-of-speech.

REGULAR VERSUS IRREGULAR PASTS

A revolutionary aspect of the Rumelhart–McClelland model is that the regular and irregular past tense alternations are collapsed into a single network. This is an example of one of the frequently claimed advantages of connectionist systems in general: that rule-governed cases, partially rule-governed cases, and isolated exceptions are all treated uniformly.[11] But of course this is only an advantage if people show no clear-cut distinction between rule-governed and exceptional behavior. In the case of the past tense system, however, qualitative differences can be documented. Consider these four:

(1) Irregular verbs cluster into 'family resemblance groups' that are phonologically similar: ('blow/blew' 'grow/grew', 'throw/threw') ('take/took', 'shake/shook') ('sting/stung', 'fling/flung', 'stick/stuck'). Regular verbs have nothing in common phonologically; any string can be a regular verb.

(2) Irregular pasts can be fuzzy in their naturalness or acceptability, depending on how similar they are to the central tendency of a cluster: 'wept', 'knelt', 'rent', and 'shod' sound stilted to many speakers, especially speakers of American English. In the extreme case, irregular past tense forms can sound totally bizarre: 'Last night I forwent the pleasure of grading papers' or 'I don't know how she bore it' have a very strange sound to most ears. In contrast, regular verbs, unless they are similar to an irregular cluster, have no gradient of acceptability based on their phonology: even phonologically unusual stems such as 'genuflect' yield past tense forms that sound as natural in the past tense as they are in the present tense; 'She eked out a living' is no worse-sounding than 'she ekes out a living'; 'They prescinded' no worse than 'They prescind' (even if one has no idea what 'prescind' means).

(3) There are no sufficient conditions for a verb to be in any irregular class: although 'blow' becomes 'blew' in the past, 'flow' becomes 'flowed'; although 'ring'

becomes 'rang', 'string' becomes 'strung' and 'bring' becomes 'brought'. In contrast, a sufficient condition for a verb to be regular is that it not be irregular; if it is regular, its past tense form is 100 percent predictable.

(4) Most of the irregular alternations can only apply to verbs with a certain structure: the pattern in 'send/sent', namely to change a 'd' to a 't', requires that there be a 'd' in the stem to begin with. The regular rule, which adds a 'd' to the stem, regardless of what the stem is, can cover all possible cases by its very nature.

These differences, though subtle, all point to the same conclusion. There is a psychologically significant difference between regular and irregular verbs: the former seem to be governed by an all-or-none process—a rule—that applies across the board except where specifically pre-empted by the presence of an irregular past tense form; the latter consist of several memorized lists of similar-sounding words forming fuzzy family resemblance classes.

The Model's Degree of Success

Despite the optimistic claims of success for the model, its actual performance is limited in significant ways. After 80,000 training trials (about 200 presentations each of 420 pairs of verb stems and their correct past tense forms), the model was given 72 new verbs in a test of its ability to generalize. It made errors on 33 percent of these verbs. In some cases, it emitted no response at all; in others, it offered a single incorrect form; in still others, it offered both a correct and an incorrect form, unable to decide between them (these cases must count as errors: a crucial aspect of the psychology of language is that irregular forms pre-empt regular ones in people's speech—not only do people say 'went' and 'came', but they avoid saying 'goed' and 'comed').

The model's errors can be traced to several factors. First, it associates past tense features with specific stem features; it has no concept of an abstract entity 'stem' independent of the features it is composed of. Hence, if there are gaps in the phonological space defined by the stems that the model was trained on, it could fail to generalize to newly presented items occupying those gaps and emit no response at all, even to common words such as 'jump' or 'warm'. Second, the model soaks up any degree of regularity in the training set, leading it to overestimate the generality of some of the vowel changes found among English irregular verbs, and resulting in spurious overregularizations such as 'shipped' as the past of 'shape' or 'brawned' as the past of 'brown'. Third, the model has no way of keeping track of separate competing responses, such as 'type' and 'typed'; hundreds of mutually incompatible features associated with a stem are all activated at once in the output feature vector, with no record of which ones cohere as target responses. Though Rumelhart and McClelland constructed a temporary, separate response-competition module to extract a cohesive response, the module could not do so effectively, producing blended hybrids such as 'typeded' for 'typed', 'membled' for 'mail', and 'squakt' for 'squat'.

Children's Language

The most dramatic aspect of the past tense model is its apparent ability to duplicate the stages that children pass through: first using 'ate', then both 'ate' and 'eated' (and occasionally 'ated'), finally 'ate' exclusively. This is especially surprising because nothing changes in the model itself; it just responds passively to the teacher's input.

For this reason, it turns out that the model's changes are caused by changes in its input. Rumelhart and McClelland note that high-frequency verbs tend to be irregular and vice versa. Children, they reasoned, are likely to learn a few high-frequency verbs first, then a large number of verbs, of which an increasing proportion would probably be regular. Hence in simulating children with their model, they defined two stages. In the first stage they fed in ten high-frequency verbs (two regular and eight irregular), paired with their correct past tense forms, ten times each. In the second stage they fed it 420 high-frequency and medium-frequency verb pairs, 190 times each, of which 336 (80 percent) were regular. Frequencies were determined by published statistics of a large corpus of written English. The model responded accordingly: in the first stage, the regular pattern was only exemplified by two verbs, only one more than each of the eight irregular patterns, and the model in effect recorded ten separate patterns of associations between stem and past. Thus it performed perfectly on irregular verbs. In the second stage, there was a huge amount of evidence for the regular pattern, which swamped the associations specific to the irregular verbs, resulting in overgeneralization errors such as 'breaked'. Finally, as the 420 word corpus was presented over and over, the model was able to strengthen connections between features unique to irregular stems and features unique to its past forms, and to inhibit connections to the features of the regular ending, so as to approach correct performance.

The prediction, then, is that children's overgeneralization should also be triggered by changes in the ratio of irregular to regular forms in their vocabularies. The prediction is completely false. Figure 3.1 shows data from four children at six different stages of development; overgeneralization typically occurs in the stage marked III. The proportion of regular verbs in the children's vocabularies remains essentially unchanged throughout this period, and there is never a point at which regular verbs predominate.[8] The same is true of token frequencies, and of frequencies in parental speech.[8,12] The cause of the onset of overgeneralization is not a change in vocabulary statistics, but some endogenous change in the child's language mechanisms.

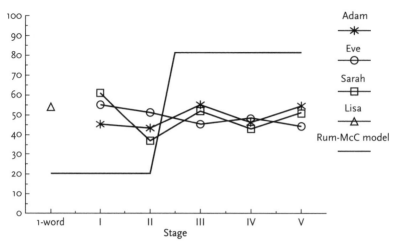

Figure 3.1. Percentage of regular verbs in the vocabulary of four children over six stages of development, and in the Rumelhart–McClelland model. The model predicts that 'overgeneralization errors'—i.e., giving an irregular verb a regular past tense form, like 'bring/bringed'—would result from a high incidence of regular verbs in the vocabulary, which strengthens the connections for this regular pattern. While the model showed overgeneralization errors after the introduction of a high percentage of regular verbs, there is no evidence that children use a high percentage of regular verbs at the stage at which they first make overgeneralization errors. (Taken with permission, from Ref. 8.)

This is also shown by the fact that across a sample of children, use of the regular pattern correlates with general measures of grammatical sophistication, though not with chronological age. The use of irregular past forms, in contrast, correlates with chronological age.[13] This is exactly what one would expect if, contrary to the predictions of the model, rote (for the irregulars) and rule (for the regulars) were distinct mechanisms, the former depending on sheer quantity of exposure to the language, the latter on mastery of the grammatical system in general.

A second interesting way in which the model appears to mimic children is in the late appearance of doubly marked errors such as 'ated'. The model becomes prone to such errors because of response blending: when the responses for 'ate' and 'eated' each attain a sufficient level of strength at the same time, the model has no way of keeping track of which segments belong to which target and blends them. The alternative hypothesis is that children misconstrue 'ate' as itself being a stem and mistakenly attach the regular ending to it—basically, they think there are two distinct English verbs, 'eat' and 'ate'.[14,15] The data favor this hypothesis. Unambiguous blends of irregular vowel changes and the regular ending (e.g. 'sepped' for 'sip') are extremely rare in children's speech.[8] However, errors involving a past form misconstrued as a stem are common: children often say 'ating', 'he ates', and 'to ate'.[15] Moreover, when children are simply asked to convert 'eat' to a past tense form in experiments, they virtually never say 'ated', showing that when children do say 'ated',

it is because of something they do to an input consisting of 'ate', not an input consisting of 'eat'. Apparently children do not derive inflected forms by haphazardly assembling them out of bits and pieces associated with the stem; they largely respect the
integrity of words and the systematic modifications that can be applied to them.[16]
In sum, the mechanisms invoked by the Rumelhart–McClelland model to account
for children's behavior—lack of distinct mechanisms for memorization and rules,
sensitivity to input frequency, and response blending—are inconsistent with the
data from developmental psycholinguistics.

Implications for Neuroscience

The Rumelhart–McClelland model is an extremely important contribution to
our understanding of human language mechanisms. For the same reason that its
impressive performance at first seemed to vindicate associative networks lacking
implemented rules, the empirical flaws revealed by closer scrutiny provide valuable
lessons about the kinds of mechanisms that language—and probably many other
aspects of cognition—requires.

(1) *Elements versus their positions.* Lashley's problem of serial order in behavior
applies in full force to language, and it is not solved by invoking feature units
that conflate a feature and its immediate context. Such units cannot encode
certain words at all, and they cannot explain patterns of psychological similarity defined by a given feature appearing in different serial positions.

(2) *Variables.* A variable is a symbol that can stand for a group of individuals
regardless of their individual properties; in arithmetic '$x + 1 > x$' is true regardless of whether x is even, odd, prime, and so on. Languages use variables in
many of their operations; the regular past tense rule in English, which adds
'd' to the variable "stem," is a perfect example. Associating response features
with the concrete features of a class of inputs is not the same thing as linking
them to a symbol or variable that represents the class itself, because the associations are sensitive to the properties of the particular sample of inputs in a
way that a genuine variable is not.

(3) *Individuals.* Two objects may share all their relevant features yet may be distinct in the world, hence their representations must be kept distinct in the
brain. The case of 'lie/lay' versus 'lie/lied' shows that it must be possible to
represent two identical patterns of features as corresponding to distinct entities. It is not enough to have large numbers of units with different perceptual
receptive fields; some structures must be dedicated to representing an entity
as simply being a distinct entity *per se*.

(4) *Binding.* Vision researchers have recently been made aware of one of the
inherent problems of representing objects simply as patterns of activation

over feature maps: it is impossible to keep the bindings of two simultaneously presented objects distinct, and a pressured perceiver is liable to illusory conjunctions whereby a red circle plus a green square is perceived as a green circle plus a red square.[17] A serial attentional mechanism is invoked in such cases to glue features into objects. Similarly, it is not sufficient that words be produced solely by activating patterns of features associated with an input, because when there are competing targets, there is no way of keeping the competing alternatives from blending. Simple connectionist models of language have this problem, but children's inflectional systems, apparently, do not.

(5) *Modularity.* It has recently become apparent that the visual system is not a single black box but is composed of many partially autonomous subsystems.[18] This conclusion was suggested by the methodology of 'dissection by psychophysics' even before it was corroborated by neuroanatomical and neurophysiological techniques. Though the neuroanatomy of language is not well understood, the equivalent psychophysical investigations strongly support a functional decomposition of language skill into subcomponents, and any model of language abilities will have to reflect this rather than mapping from input to output in a single link. Furthermore, the internal 'links' are organized in specific ways. In the present case, phonology and morphology reveal themselves as distinct subsystems, and that is only the most obvious cut.

(6) *Independence from correlational statistics of the input.* Connectionist networks, like all associationist models, learn by recording patterns of correlation among perceptual features. Language acquisition almost certainly does not work that way; in many cases, children ignore pervasive environmental correlations and make endogenously driven generalizations that are in some cases surprising with respect to the correlational statistics of the input but are consistent with subtle grammatical principles.[19] This can be seen in the case of the past tense, where the onset of overgeneralization is clearly independent of input statistics, and the extent of generalization in the adult state (e.g. avoiding it if an irregular form exists; but overriding the irregular form if the verb is derived from a noun root) is not a reflection of any simple correlational property of the input. More generally, to the extent that language is composed of separate subsystems, the role of environmentally driven changes must be quite circumscribed: if a subsystem's inputs and outputs are not connected to the environment, but to other internal subsystems, then they are invisible to the environment and there is no direct way for the connectionist's 'teaching inputs' to tune them to the correct state via incremental changes from a *tabula rasa*.

Overall, there is a more general lesson. Theories attempting to bridge neuroscience and cognition must be consistent with the data of both. The data of human language in particular are extremely rich, and theories of considerable sophistication and explanatory power have been developed in response to them. Though it may be convenient to impose a revisionist associationist theory on the phenomena of language, such a move is not scientifically defensible. Building the bridge will be more difficult, and more interesting, than it might first appear.

Selected References

1. Feldman, J. A. and Ballard, D. H. (1982) *Cognit. Sci. 6*, 205–254
2. Hinton, G. E., McClelland, J. L. and Rumelhart, D. E. (1986) in *Parallel Distributed Processing: Explorations in the Microstructure of Cognition* (Vol. 1: *Foundations*) (Rumelhart, D. E., McClelland, J. L. and the PDP Research Group, eds), pp. 77–109, MIT Press
3. Crick, F. and Asanuma, C. (1986) in *Parallel Distributed Processing: Explorations in the Microstructure of Cognition* (Vol. 2: *Psychological and Biological Models*) (McClelland, J. L., Rumelhart, D. E. and the PDP Research Group, eds), pp. 333–371, MIT Press
4. Sejnowski, T. (1987) *Trends Neurosci. 10*, 304–305
5. Rumelhart, D. E. and McClelland, J. L. (1986) in *Parallel Distributed Processing: Explorations in the Microstructure of Cognition* (Vol. 2: *Psychological and Biological Models*) (McClelland, J. L., Rumelhart, D. E. and the PDP Research Group, eds), pp. 216–271, MIT Press
6. Berko, J. (1958) *Word 14*, 150–177
7. Chomsky, N. (1959) *Language 3*, 26–58
8. Pinker, S. and Prince, A. (1988) *Cognition 28*, 73–193
9. Lachter, J. and Bever, T. G. (1988) *Cognition 28*, 195–247
10. Fodor, J. A. and Pylyshyn, Z. (1988) *Cognition 28*, 3–71
11. McClelland, J. L. and Rumelhart, D. E. (1985) *J. Exp. Psychol. Gen. 114*, 159–188
12. Slobin, D. I. (1971) in *The Ontogenesis of Grammar: A Theoretical Symposium* (Slobin, D. I., ed.), pp. 215–223, Academic Press
13. Kuczaj, S. A. (1977) *J. Verbal Learning Verbal Behav. 16*, 589–600
14. Kuczaj, S. A. (1978) *Child Dev. 49*, 319–326
15. Kuczaj, S. A. (1981) *J. Child Lang. 8*, 485–487
16. Slobin, D. I. (1985) in *The Crosslinguistic Study of Language Acquisition* (Vol. II *Theoretical Issues*) (Slobin, D. I. ed.), pp. 1157–1249, Erlbaum Associates
17. Treisman, A. and Schmidt, H. (1982) *Cog. Psych. 14*, 107–141
18. Van Essen, D. C. and Maunsell, J. (1983) *Trends Neurosci. 6*, 370–375
19. Pinker, S. (1984) *Language Learnability and Language Development*, Harvard University Press
20. Wickelgren, W. A. (1969) *Psychol. Rev. 76*, 1–15
21. Rosenblatt, F. (1962) *Principles of Neurodynamics*, Spartan

4

When Does Human Object Recognition Use a Viewer-Centered Reference Frame?

with MICHAEL TARR

This is one of my favorite articles from my empirical oeuvre. As a postdoctoral fellow at MIT in 1980-81, I was fortunate to have interacted with the brilliant computational neuroscientist David Marr, shortly before his death from leukemia when he was still in his thirties. Marr had proposed that people are good at recognizing objects, despite wild variations in the objects' retinal projections when seen from different angles, because the brain stores the arrangement of the object's parts with respect to a coordinate system centered on the object itself rather than on the viewer's eyes, head, or body. The theory struck me as so beautiful that it had to be true, and in the theory presented in chapter 2 in this collection, I assumed that it was true. But in a series of experiments on shape recognition that I carried out with Michael Tarr when he was a graduate student working with me at MIT (he is now a distinguished cognitive neuroscientist at Carnegie-Mellon University), the theory did not seem to be true: people took longer to recognize a shape when they saw it at orientations different from the one in which they had originally learned it, suggesting that they had stored the shape in something like its original appearance, rather than having stored its inherent geometric structure.

In the experiments reported in this paper, Tarr and I replicated the orientation-dependence of human shape recognition, but with an important twist. When a shape is what we called "bilaterally redundant"—it can be distinguished from other shapes without keeping track of the relative arrangement of its parts along a dimension other than its primary axis—people can recognize the shape equally quickly at any orientation. So Marr was half-right: the brain stores information about a shape relative to one intrinsic axis of that shape, just not, as he had thought, relative to all of its axes. Another way of putting it is that the brain can mentally skewer an object with one axis of a coordinate system and can register how far along that axis its parts are, and how close or far away from that axis the parts are, but it cannot simultaneously keep track of whether those parts are above, below, to the left, or to the right of that axis.

I like this article because it succinctly captures the pleasures of experimental research: testing and refining a hypothesis through a succession of systematic manipulations across a series of experiments. It also partly vindicates my prejudice that elegant theories are often correct, albeit in a more circumscribed form than the one in which it had originally been conceived.

Object constancy, the ability to recognize an object despite changes in its retinal image produced by displacements and rotations, is an important problem in both human vision and computer vision systems (Marr, 1982; Rock, 1983). A prominent proposal by Marr and Nishihara (1978) is that the visual system first aligns a coordinate system on an input object based on its axes of symmetry, elongation, or movement, describes the arrangement of the object's parts within that system (resulting in the same description regardless of the object's orientation relative to the viewer), and matches the description against memory representations stored in the same format. An alternative is that the input is transformed into a canonical orientation and then is matched against a representation in memory of the appearance of the object in that orientation (Rock, 1974; Tarr & Pinker, 1989). We present data from experiments designed to determine if and when people use such mechanisms. The experiments rely on the discovery by Shepard and his collaborators (Shepard & Cooper, 1982; Shepard & Metzler, 1971) that humans possess an analogue visual transformation process, "mental rotation." The principal empirical signature of mental rotation is that people take more time to classify a shape that is oriented farther from the upright, and take more time to match two objects that differ by greater orientation differences. Other evidence confirms that this chronometric pattern reflects an incremental rotation process. For example, during the interval between stimulus presentation and the response, the subject can quickly classify a probe stimulus displayed at an intermediate orientation; the optimal intermediate orientation changes continuously during the stimulus-response interval. There is also evidence from single-cell recordings in the monkey motor cortex for an analogous transformation process in the motor planning system (Georgopoulos, Lurito, Petrides, Schwartz, & Massey, 1989).

The fact that mental rotation exists, however, does not mean that it is used to recognize objects. Most mental rotation tasks require the subject to discriminate shapes from their mirror-images. It is possible that people generally use object-centered coordinate systems to recognize shapes, but that such coordinate systems can be of either handedness, so that objects and their mirror-images have equivalent representations. If coordinate systems are not explicitly labeled as right-handed or left-handed, mental rotation would be needed when handedness must be discriminated (and only then). Input shapes would be rotated into alignment with the up–down axis of the perceiver, so that the right and left sides of the shape would align with the right and left sides of the person, which are explicitly labeled as "right" and "left," making the handedness discrimination possible (Corballis, 1988; Hinton & Parsons, 1981).

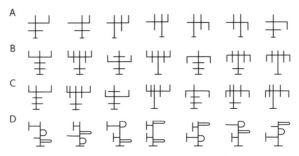

Figure 4.1. Shapes presented to subjects for identification. (A) Asymmetrical shapes.
(B) Symmetrical shapes. (C) Skewed-symmetrical shapes. (D) Bilaterally redundant shapes.

In fact when subjects are simply required to name objects, orientation effects on response time greatly diminish (Corballis, Zbrodoff, Shetzer, & Butler, 1978). However, such results are inconclusive. If shapes can be discriminated on the basis of orientation-independent local features, such as a curved segment present in only one object, subjects could name objects via this shortcut. Furthermore, the alphanumeric characters typically used are highly overlearned and might be stored in multiple representations, each specific to an orientation, so input shapes at any of these orientations could be matched directly in constant time (Jolicoeur, 1985; Tarr & Pinker, 1989).

We present data from experiments that avoid these problems. Subjects learned names for three novel shapes (a subset of those shown in Fig. 4.1A), each studied only at the upright orientation. The seven shapes were composed of similar configurations of line segments in different spatial arrangements, so no local feature could serve as a unique cue. No shape was the mirror-image of any other, and each shape had a clearly marked base and vertical axis, minimizing the time needed to locate the shape's intrinsic axis and bottom. Subjects saw the shapes on a CRT at different orientations and identified them by pressing one of three buttons labeled with the shape names. On 25 percent of the trials one of the other four shapes in Figure 4.1A was presented, and subjects pressed a foot pedal.[1]

Results, shown in Figure 4.2A (test orientations at 0°, 45°, −90°, and 135°), suggest that people employed mental rotation to recognize the shapes: Recognition time was linearly related to orientation from the upright, and the .95 confidence interval for the obtained slope of 2.42 ms/deg (an estimate of the rotation rate) includes the slope values obtained in the Cooper and Shepard experiments,[2] but does not include zero.[3],[4]

Viewer-Centered Object Recognition

The fact that people show orientation effects even when the task does not require handedness to be assigned is evidence that mental rotation, not the computation of an object-centered viewpoint-independent description, is the mechanism

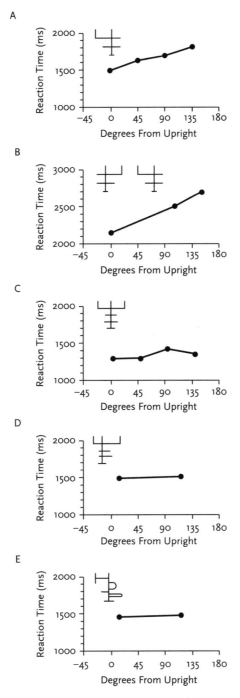

Figure 4.2. Response times to identify shapes as a function of orientation. (A) Asymmetrical shapes. (B) Asymmetrical shapes and their mirror images. (C) Symmetrical shapes. (D) Skewed-symmetrical shapes. (E) Bilaterally redundant shapes.

used.[5] An alternative is that subjects attempted to determine the handedness of the stimuli despite its irrelevance to the task, anticipating that there might be mirror-image distractors. This alternative can be eliminated by an experiment (originally reported as Condition 0/105/−150 of Experiment 3 in Tarr & Pinker, 1989) in which subjects saw both handedness versions of the shapes, and were required to ignore the difference, identifying each object and its mirror image by the same response.[6] Here handedness information is by definition irrelevant to the task. Nonetheless, orientation effects were found once again for standard versions of the shapes (Fig. 4.2B; test orientations at 0°, 105°, and −150°; slope for standard versions: 3.65 ms/deg).[7]

Under some circumstances, however, orientation-invariant recognition does occur. The same experimental procedure run with symmetrical shapes (Fig. 4.1B), which cannot be assigned a handedness, shows that people can recognize such shapes equally quickly at all orientations[8] (Fig. 4.2C; test orientations at 0°, 45°, −90°, and 135°; slope: 0.63 ms/deg). This is not an effect of geometric symmetry itself. Additional experiments show that the crucial property is that one side be redundant with the other, so only a single side need be examined to discriminate among shapes within the set. When the shapes are skewed so that they are not symmetrical (Fig. 4.1C), there is still no effect of orientation (Fig. 4.2D; test orientations at 15° and 120° or −15° and −120°; slope: 0.29 ms/deg). Even when there is no similarity between the shapes' right and left sides, but the arrangement of parts on each side is unique to that shape so only a single side need be examined to identify it, as in Figure 4.1D, there are no effects of orientation (Fig. 4.2E; test orientations at 15° and 120° or −15° and −120°; slope: 0.18 ms/deg).[9,10]

Why is mental rotation needed to recognize asymmetrical shapes, even when handedness is irrelevant to recognition, but not needed to recognize shapes whose two sides are redundant? For the symmetrical, skewed-symmetrical, and bilaterally redundant shapes, it is sufficient to keep track of the one-dimensional ordering of parts on either side of the shape from bottom to top. For example, "two small cross-bars underneath a longer crossbar with upright bends" is sufficient to discriminate the first shape from the second shape in Figure 4.3A. This suggests that perceivers can assign a one-dimensional vector to a shape's axis defining a top-to-bottom ordering of parts equally quickly regardless of the shape's orientation. In contrast, shapes requiring rotation have parts whose locations must be specified along two dimensions simultaneously. For example, to identify the first shape in Figure 4.3B, the perceiver must encode the fact that the top crossbar is shorter on one side of the shape and longer on the other, and that the right-angle upward bend is on the side with the short crossbar segment. Absolute handedness information is not required: it does not matter whether the first side is remembered as the right side and the second as the left or vice-versa. But discriminating between sides is required: it matters that the side with the long crossbar segment is remembered as being a *different* side than the side with the bend. This is necessary in order that the shape not be confused

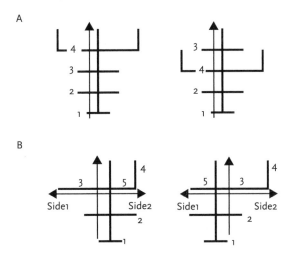

Figure 4.3. One-dimensional and two-dimensional descriptions of shapes. (A) A pair of shapes where one-dimensional descriptions are sufficient for distinguishing between them. (B) A pair of shapes where one-dimensional descriptions are insufficient to make the discrimination, necessitating the use of two-dimensional descriptions.

with the second shape in Figure 4.3B, which also has a crossbar that is longer on one side than the other, but in which it is the side with the longer crossbar segment that has the bend. Thus the mere requirement that two sides be kept distinct is enough to require that subjects mentally rotate.

This result suggests that the part of the visual system subserving object recognition lacks an object-centered 2D (and presumably 3D) coordinate system. The reference frame aligned with the viewer's egocentric upright, with its body-defined up–down and right–left directions, is the only one in which two dimensions are simultaneously specified. There is an object-centered mode of description, but it is insufficient to represent the arrangement of parts along two dimensions simultaneously; all that can be specified is the order of parts along a single foreaft dimension (or at most, the distance of each part from the midline along an independent medial-lateral "half-dimension," but with no specification of separate sides).

These data do not imply that all misoriented objects are recognized through mental rotation. For highly familiar objects, multiple orientation-specific representations can be directly matched against the input (Jolicoeur, 1985; Tarr & Pinker, 1989), and for many objects, sets of distinctive features or parts may suffice for identification. Even different objects composed of the same parts may be distinguished without mental rotation if the objects differ in how their parts are arranged along a single dimension. But determining the 2D and 3D relational structure of an object appears to require that the object be represented in a familiar orientation with respect to the viewer's upright. It is unclear how many cases of object recognition in natural settings require the computation of multidimensional spatial relations.

Jolicoeur (1985) found that pictures of everyday objects are recognized more slowly as they are misoriented farther from the upright. Perhaps this is because many common shapes, although symmetrical about one axis, are not symmetrical about their other axes. For example, to recognize quadrupeds depicted in side view line drawings, one must encode properties of the head, tail, and limbs, which in the general case are fully distinguished only by their positions both along the foreaft axis and above or below it. This suggests that mental rotation may not be an uncommon strategy for recognizing misoriented complex objects.

Acknowledgments

We thank Jigna Desai and Greg Wolff for assistance and Irving Biederman and Pierre Jolicoeur for their helpful comments. Supported by NSF Grant BNS 8518774.

Notes

1. Nine subjects learned the shapes by tracing them and then drawing them from memory. Different subsets of shapes were taught to different subjects. The 3 target shapes were shown 8 times in the orientations 0°, 45°, −90°, and 135°, and the 4 distractors were shown 2 times at these orientations, for a total of 128 trials, preceded by 12 practice trials.
2. Mean slopes ranged from 1.61 ms/deg to 3.06 ms/deg in the summary of experiments compiled by S. Shepard and D. Metzler (1988).
3. Error rates for the four orientations were 5%, 3%, 6%, and 6%.
4. Orientation effects in this experiment cannot be attributed to the prominent vertical axis of the shapes being aligned with subjects' retinal or head axis during the initial teaching of the shapes. Tarr and Pinker (1989) found effects of orientation on naming times even when shapes were taught at an orientation of 15°, which did not coincide with the subjects' retinal or head-defined upright (Experiments 3 and 4; Condition 15/120).
5. There is no paradox in the suggestion that people know the direction in which to rotate an object before they have recognized it. For example, if three noncollinear landmarks can be extracted from the input shape independently of orientation, and analogous landmarks are indicated in memory representations, the optimal axis and direction of rotation can be computed, though the degree of shape match for the rest of the object cannot be assessed until the transformation is executed. See Ullman (1989) and Tarr and Pinker (1989) for discussion.
6. The procedure was identical to that of Experiment 1 except that 13 subjects were run, both handedness versions of each shape were shown (consequently half of the trials presented mirror images of the shapes), and a different and smaller set of orientations were used. For the data on the recognition of mirror image versions, which are not relevant here, see Experiment 3 of Tarr and Pinker (1989).
7. Orientation effects in this experiment cannot be attributed to subjects' not having had sufficient practice to realize that each shape and its mirror-image were to be treated equivalently. After the trials reported, an additional 1408 trials were administered, followed by 768 trials in which the shapes were shown at 24 new orientations separated by 15° increments. We found comparable effects on recognition time of the difference between the stimulus orientation and the nearest well-learned orientation (slope for standard versions = 4.14 ms/deg). This shows that rotation was still necessary for shapes in new orientations even after extensive

practice at treating the shape and its mirror image as equivalent. See Tarr and Pinker (1989) for details.

8. The slope of the line shown in Figure 4.2C (0.63 ms/deg) is significantly different from the slope of the line shown in Figure 4.2A (2.42 ms/deg; $F(1, 19) = 5.18$, $p < .05$) and from the slope of the line shown in Figure 4.2B (3.65 ms/deg; $F(1, 23) = 12.2$, $p < .01$).

9. Apart from the specified changes in the stimuli, the use of new orientations, and slight variations in the number of trials, the method was unchanged from previous experiments.

10. The orientation-independence effect holds not only for the set of orientations shown in Figure 4.2C-E, but for a larger set of orientations, presented to the subjects for the first time after they had undergone many more trials (>1000). Slopes for new orientations were: 0.53 ms/deg (symmetrical shapes); 0.57 ms/deg (skewed-symmetrical); 1.07 ms/deg (bilaterally redundant).

References

Corballis, M. C. (1988). Recognition of disoriented shapes. *Psychological Review, 95*(1), 115–123.

Corballis, M. C., Zbrodoff, N. J., Shetzer, L. I., & Butler, P. B. (1978). Decisions about identity and orientation of rotated letters and digits. *Memory & Cognition, 6*, 98–107.

Georgopoulos, A. P., Lurito, J. T., Petrides, M., Schwartz, A. B., & Massey, J. T. (1989). Mental rotation of the neuronal population vector. *Science, 243*, 234–236.

Hinton, G. E., & Parsons, L. M. (1981). Frames of reference and mental imagery. In J. Long & A. Baddeley (Eds.), *Attention and performance IX*. Hillsdale, NJ: Erlbaum.

Jolicoeur, P. (1985). The time to name disoriented natural objects. *Memory & Cognition, 13*(4), 289–303.

Marr, D. (1982). *Vision: A computational investigation into the human representation and processing of visual information*. San Francisco: Freeman.

Marr, D., & Nishihara, H. K. (1978). Representation and recognition of the spatial organization of three-dimensional shapes. *Proceedings of the Royal Society of London Ser. B, 200*, 269–294.

Rock, I. (1974). The perception of disoriented figures. *Scientific American, 230*(Jan), 78–85.

Rock, I. (1983). *The logic of perception*. Cambridge, MA: MIT Press.

Shepard, R. N., & Cooper, L. A. (1982). *Mental images and their transformations*. Cambridge, MA: MIT Press.

Shepard, R. N., & Metzler, J. (1971). Mental rotation of three-dimensional objects. *Science, 171*, 701–703.

Shepard, S., & Metzler, D. (1988). Mental rotation: Effects of dimensionality of objects and type of task. *Journal of Experimental Psychology: Human Perception and Performance, 14*(1), 3–11.

Tarr, M. J., & Pinker, S. (1989). Mental rotation and orientation-dependence in shape recognition. *Cognitive Psychology, 21*(2), 233–282.

Ullman, S. (1989). Aligning pictorial descriptions: An approach to object recognition. *Cognition, 32*, 193–254.

5

Natural Language and Natural Selection

with PAUL BLOOM

This article, coauthored with Paul Bloom (then a graduate student, now a distinguished author and cognitive scientist at Yale), is my most frequently cited paper. One reason it attracted attention is that it broke the century-long taboo on discussing the evolution of language. Our heresy was all the more noteworthy given that we were at MIT, an institution which had been associated with Noam Chomsky and his staunchly anti-Darwinist view on language. One of the thirty-odd commentaries published with this article was entitled "Liberation!" and our article deserves some of the credit (or blame, depending on how you look at it) for the revival of the study of language evolution in the 1990s and early twenty-first century. For me it began an interest in the evolution of cognition and emotion, also nearly taboo at the time, which has colored my work ever since.

The article was newsworthy for a second reason: it picked a fight with three of the alpha males of the era. One was Chomsky, with whom I resumed the debate more than a decade later (see chapter 10). A second was the beloved evolutionary biologist Stephen Jay Gould, who at the time was treated as an infallible seer on evolution because of his engaging Natural History *column and his bestselling books. The third was Gould's comrade Richard Lewontin, the brilliant population geneticist and prolific leftist writer, who, like Superman, the Lone Ranger, and Jim in the eponymous Jim Croce song, you didn't mess around with. (Lewontin took up our challenge in a wittily dismissive commentary in the journal.)*

Like my article with Prince, this one originated in a public debate at MIT's Center for Cognitive Science, which for two decades hosted a standing-room-only seminar which inverted the usual colloquium format by first allowing two commentators to give their best shots at a paper and then having the author reply. The target article that evening was an application of Gould's ideas on evolution to language and cognition by the cognitive scientist Massimo Piatelli-Palmarini, and he and Gould squared off against Bloom and me. In the audience that evening was the philosopher Dan Dennett, who credits the evening as the impetus to write his 1995 book Darwin's Dangerous Idea. *Dennett was struck by the discrepancy between his own reaction to the debate, which he thought we had won, and the reaction of most of the audience, who thought that Gould and Piatelli-Palmarini had won it. He wrote the book to clarify what he thought were widespread misunderstandings of the theory of evolution and its implications for human affairs.*

> Language could not have begun in the form it was said to have taken in the first recorded utterance of Thomas Babbington Macaulay (the infant Lord Macaulay): once when he was taken out, his hostess accidently spilled hot tea on him. The little lad first bawled his head off, but when he had calmed he said in answer to his hostess' concern, "Thank you Madam, the agony is sensibly abated."
>
> —P. B. and J. S. Medawar

1. Introduction

All human societies have language. As far as we know they always did; language was not invented by some groups and spread to others like agriculture or the alphabet. All languages are complex computational systems employing the same basic kinds of rules and representations, with no notable correlation with technological progress: the grammars of industrial societies are no more complex than the grammars of hunter-gatherers; Modern English is not an advance over Old English. Within societies, individual humans are proficient language users regardless of intelligence, social status, or level of education. Children are fluent speakers of complex grammatical sentences by the age of three, without benefit of formal instruction. They are capable of inventing languages that are more systematic than those they hear, showing resemblances to languages that they have never heard, and they obey subtle grammatical principles for which there is no evidence in their environments. Disease or injury can make people linguistic savants while severely retarded, or linguistically impaired with normal intelligence. Some language disorders are genetically transmitted. Aspects of language skill can be linked to characteristic regions of the human brain. The human vocal tract is tailored to the demands of speech, compromising other functions such as breathing and swallowing. Human auditory perception shows complementary specializations toward the demands of decoding speech sounds into linguistic segments.

This list of facts (see Pinker, 1989a) suggests that the ability to use a natural language belongs more to the study of human biology than human culture; it is a topic like echolocation in bats or stereopsis in monkeys, not like writing or the wheel. All modern students of language agree that at least some aspects of language are due to species-specific, task-specific biological abilities, though of course there are radical disagreements about specifics. A prominent position, outlined by Chomsky (1965, 1980, 1981, 1986, 1988a), Fodor (1983), Lenneberg (1964, 1967), and Liberman (Liberman, Cooper, Shankweiler, & Studdert-Kennedy, 1967; Liberman and Mattingly, 1989), is that the mind is composed of autonomous computational modules—mental faculties or "organs"—and that the acquisition and representation of language is the product of several such specialized modules.

It would be natural, then, to expect everyone to agree that human language is the product of Darwinian natural selection. The only successful account of the origin of complex biological structure is the theory of natural selection, the view that the differential reproductive success associated with heritable variation is the primary organizing force in the evolution of organisms (Darwin, 1859; see Bendall, 1983 for a contemporary perspective). But surprisingly, this conclusion is contentious. Noam Chomsky, the world's best-known linguist, and Stephen Jay Gould, the world's best-known evolutionary theorist, have repeatedly suggested that language may not be the product of natural selection, but a side effect of other evolutionary forces such as an increase in overall brain size and constraints of as-yet unknown laws of structure and growth (e.g., Chomsky, 1972, 1982a, 1982b, 1988a, 1988b; Gould, 1987a; Gould and Piattelli-Palmarini, 1987). Recently Massimo Piattelli-Palmarini (1989), a close correspondent with Gould and Chomsky, has done the field a service by formulating a particularly strong version of their positions and articulating it in print. Premack (1985, 1986) and Mehler (1985) have expressed similar views.

In this paper we will examine this position in detail, and will come to a very different conclusion. We will argue that there is every reason to believe that language has been shaped by natural selection as it is understood within the orthodox "synthetic" or "neo-Darwinian" theory of evolution (Mayr, 1982). In one sense our goal is incredibly boring. All we argue is that language is no different from other complex abilities such as echolocation or stereopsis, and that the only way to explain the origin of such abilities is through the theory of natural selection. One might expect our conclusion to be accepted without much comment by all but the most environmentalist of language scientists (as indeed it is by such researchers as Bickerton, 1981, Liberman and Mattingly, 1989, Lieberman, 1984, and, in limited respects, by Chomsky himself in some strands of his writings.[1] On the other hand, when two such important scholars as Chomsky and Gould repeatedly urge us to consider a startling contrary position, their arguments can hardly be ignored. Indeed these arguments have had a strong effect on many cognitive scientists, and the nonselectionist view has become the consensus in many circles.

Furthermore, a lot is at stake if our boring conclusion is wrong. We suspect that many biologists would be surprised at the frequent suggestion that the complexity of language cannot be explained through natural selection. For instance, Chomsky has made the following statements:

> [an innate language faculty] poses a problem for the biologist, since, if true, it is an example of true 'emergence'—the appearance of a qualitatively different phenomenon at a specific stage of complexity of organization. (1972: 70)

It is perfectly safe to attribute this development [of innate mental structure] to "natural selection," so long as we realize that there is no substance to this assertion, that it amounts to nothing more than a belief that there is some naturalistic explanation for these phenomena. (1972: 97)

Evolutionary theory is informative about many things, but it has little to say, as of now, of questions of this nature [e.g., the evolution of language]. The answers may well lie not so much in the theory of natural selection as in molecular biology, in the study of what kinds of physical systems can develop under the conditions of life on earth and why, ultimately because of physical principles. (1988a: 167)

It does seem very hard to believe that the specific character of organisms can be accounted for purely in terms of random mutation and selectional controls. I would imagine that the biology of a 100 years from now is going to deal with the evolution of organisms the way it now deals with the evolution of amino acids, assuming that there is just a fairly small space of physically possible systems that can realize complicated structures....Evolutionary theory appears to have very little to say about speciation, or about any kind of innovation. It can explain how you get a different distribution of qualities that are already present, but it does not say much about how new qualities can emerge. (1982a: 23)

If findings coming out of the study of language forced biologists to such conclusions, it would be big news.

There is another reason to scrutinize the nonselectionist theory of language. If a current theory of language is truly incompatible with the neo-Darwinian theory of evolution, one could hardly blame someone for concluding that it is not the theory of evolution that must be questioned, but the theory of language. Indeed, this argument has been the basis of critiques of Chomsky's theories by Bates, Thal, and Marchman (1989), Greenfield (1987), and Lieberman (1984, 1989), who are nonetheless strange bedfellows with Chomsky in doubting whether an innate generative grammar could have evolved by natural selection. Since we are impressed both by the synthetic theory of evolution and by the theory of generative grammar, we hope that we will not have to choose between the two.

In this paper, we first examine arguments from evolutionary biology about when it is appropriate to invoke natural selection as an explanation for the evolution of some trait. We then apply these tests to the case of human language, and conclude that language passes. We examine the motivations for the competing nonselectionist position, and suggest that they have little to recommend them. In the final section, we refute the arguments that have claimed that an innate specialization for grammar is incompatible with the tenets of a Darwinian account and thus that the two are incompatible.

2. The Role of Natural Selection in Evolutionary Theory

Gould has frequently suggested that evolutionary theory is in the throes of a scientific revolution (e.g., Eldredge & Gould, 1972; Gould, 1980). Two cornerstones of the Darwinian synthesis, adaptationism and gradualism, are, he argues, under challenge. Obviously if strict Darwinism is false in general it should not be used to explain the origin of language.

2.1. NONSELECTIONIST MECHANISMS OF EVOLUTIONARY CHANGE

In a classic paper, Gould and Lewontin (1979) warn against "naive adaptationism," the inappropriate use of adaptive theorizing to explain traits that have emerged for other reasons (see also Kitcher, 1985; Lewontin, 1978). The argument is illustrated by an analogy with the mosaics on the dome and spandrels of the San Marco basilica in Venice:

> Spandrels—the tapering triangular spaces formed by the intersection of two rounded arches at right angles...are necessary architectural by-products of mounting a dome on rounded arches. Each spandrel contains a design admirably fitted into its tapering space. An evangelist sits in the upper part flanked by the heavenly cities. Below, a man representing one of the four biblical rivers...pours water from a pitcher in the narrowing space below his feet.
>
> The design is so elaborate, harmonious, and purposeful that we are tempted to view it as the starting point of any analysis, as the cause in some sense of the surrounding architecture. But this would invert the proper path of analysis. The system begins with an architectural constraint: the necessary four spandrels and their tapering triangular form. They provide a space in which the mosaicists worked; they set the quadripartite symmetry of the dome above.
>
> Such architectural constraints abound, and we find them easy to understand because we do not impose our biological biases upon them....Anyone who tried to argue that the structure [spandrels] exists because of [the designs laid upon them] would be inviting the same ridicule that Voltaire heaped on Dr. Pangloss: "Things cannot be other than they are....Everything is made for the best purpose. Our noses were made to carry spectacles, so we have spectacles. Legs were clearly intended for breeches, and we wear them."...Yet evolutionary biologists, in their tendency to focus exclusively on immediate adaptation to local

conditions, do tend to ignore architectural constraints and perform just such an inversion of explanation. (pp. 147-149)

Unconvincing adaptationist explanations, which Gould and Lewontin compare to Kipling's "Just-so stories," are easy to find. In the Science and Technology section of the *Boston Globe* in March 1987, an article noted that the number of teats in different mammals ought to correspond not to the average litter size but to the largest litter size that can occur for that species within some bound of probability. Since humans ordinarily bear single children but not infrequently have twins, we have an explanation for why humans have two breasts, not one. The author did not discuss the possibility that the bilateral symmetry that is so basic to the mammalian body plan makes the appearance of one-breasted humans rather unlikely. Gould and Lewontin describe a number of nonadaptationist mechanisms that they feel are frequently not tested within evolutionary accounts: genetic drift, laws of growth and form (such as general allometric relations between brain and body size), direct induction of form by environmental forces such as water currents or gravity, the effects of accidents of history (which may trap organisms in local maxima in the adaptive landscape), and "exaptation" (Gould and Vrba, 1982), whereby new uses are made of parts that were originally adapted to some other function or of spandrels that had no function at all but were present for reasons of architecture, development, or history. They point out that Darwin himself had this pluralistic view of evolution, and that there was an "unfairly maligned" nonadaptationist approach to evolution, prominent in continental Europe, that stressed constraints on "Baupläne" (architectural plans) flowing from phyletic history and embryological development. This body of research, they suggest, is an antidote to the tendency to treat an organism as a bundle of traits or parts, each independently shaped by natural selection.

2.2. LIMITATIONS ON NONSELECTIONIST EXPLANATIONS

The Gould and Lewontin argument could be interpreted as stressing that since the neo-Darwinian theory of evolution includes nonadaptationist processes it is bad scientific practice not to test them as alternatives to natural selection in any particular instance. However, they are often read as having outlined a radical new alternative to Darwin, in which natural selection is relegated to a minor role. Though Gould and Lewontin clearly eschew this view in their paper, Gould has made such suggestions subsequently (e.g., Gould, 1980), and Piattelli-Palmarini (1989: 1) has interpreted it as such when he talks of Darwinian natural selection being replaced by "a better evolutionary theory (one based on 'exaptation')." The reasons why we should reject this view were spelled out clearly by Williams (1966), and have been amplified recently by Dawkins (1983, 1986).

The key point that blunts the Gould and Lewontin critique of adaptationism is that *natural selection is the only scientific explanation of adaptive complexity*. "Adaptive complexity" describes any system composed of many interacting parts where the details of the parts' structure and arrangement suggest design to fulfill some function. The vertebrate eye is the classic example. The eye has a transparent refracting outer cover, a variable-focus lens, a light-sensitive layer of neural tissue lying at the focal plane of the lens, a diaphragm whose diameter changes with illumination level, muscles that move it in precise conjunction and convergence with those of the other eye, and elaborate neural circuits that respond to patterns defining edges, colors, motion, and stereoscopic disparity. It is impossible to make sense of the structure of the eye without noting that it appears as if it was designed for the purpose of seeing—if for no other reason that the man-made tool for image formation, the camera, displays an uncanny resemblance to the eye. Before Darwin, theologians, notably William Paley, pointed to its exquisite design as evidence for the existence of a divine designer. Darwin showed how such "organs of extreme perfection and complication" could arise from the purely physical process of natural selection.

The essential point is that no physical process other than natural selection can explain the evolution of an organ like the eye. The reason for this is that structures that can do what the eye does are extremely low-probability arrangements of matter. By an unimaginably large margin, most objects defined by the space of biologically possible arrangements of matter cannot bring an image into focus, modulate the amount of incoming light, respond to the presence of edges and depth boundaries, and so on. The odds that genetic drift, say, would result in the fixation within a population of just those genes that would give rise to such an object are infinitesimally small, and such an event would be virtually a miracle. This is also true of the other nonselectionist mechanisms outlined by Gould and Lewontin. It is absurdly improbable that some general law of growth and form could give rise to a functioning vertebrate eye as a by-product of some other trend such as an increase in size of some other part. Likewise, one need not consider the possibility that some organ that arose as an adaptation to some other task, or a spandrel defined by other body parts, just happened to have a transparent lens surrounded by a movable diaphragm in front of a light-sensitive layer of tissue lying at its focal plane. Natural selection—the retention across generations of whatever small, random modifications yield improvements in vision that increase chances of survival and reproduction—is the only physical process capable of creating a functioning eye, because it is the only physical process in which the criterion of being good at seeing can play a causal role. As such it is the only process that can lead organisms along the path in the astronomically vast space of possible bodies leading from a body with no eye to a body with a functioning eye.

This argument is obviously incomplete, as it relies on the somewhat intuitive notion of "function" and "design." A skeptic might accuse the proponent of circularity, asking why a lump of clay should not be considered well-designed to fulfill the function of taking up exactly the region of space that it in fact takes up. But the circle can be broken in at least three ways. First, biologists need posit far fewer functions than there are biological systems; new functions are not invented for each organ of each organism. Furthermore, each legitimate function can be related via a direct plausible causal chain to other functions and—critically—to the overall function of survival and reproduction. Finally, convergent evolution and resemblance to human artifacts fulfilling the same putative function give independent criteria for design. But regardless of the precise formulation of the modern argument from design (see, e.g., Cummins, 1984), it is not controversial in practice. Gould himself readily admits that natural selection is the cause of structures such as the vertebrate eye, and he invokes the criterion of engineering design, for example, to rescue Darwinism itself from the charge of circularity (Gould, 1977a). Presumably this is why Gould and Lewontin concede that they agree with Darwin that natural selection is "the most important of evolutionary mechanisms."

What, then, is the proper relation between selectionist and nonselectionist explanations in evolution? The least interesting case involves spandrels that are not involved in any function or behavior, such as the redness of blood, the V-shaped space between a pair of fingers, the hollow at the back of a knee, the fact there are a prime number of digits on each limb, and so on. The mere presence of these *epiphenomenal spandrels*, which play no direct role in the explanation of any species-typical behavior or function, says nothing about whether the structures that they are associated with were shaped by selection. There are as many of them as there are ways of describing an organism that do not correspond to its functional parts.

Much more important are cases where spandrels are modified and put to use. However, in such cases of *modified spandrels*, selection plays a crucial role. Putting a dome on top of four arches gives you a spandrel, but it does not give you a mosaic depicting an evangelist and a man pouring water out of a pitcher. That would *really* be a miracle. To get the actual mosaic you need a designer. The designer corresponds to natural selection. Spandrels, exaptations, laws of growth, and so on can explain the basic plans, parts, and materials that natural selection works with—as Jacob (1977) put it, nature is a tinkerer, not an engineer with a clean drawing board. The best examples of structures produced entirely by nonadaptationist mechanisms are generally one-part or repetitive shapes or processes that correspond to simple physical or geometric laws, such as chins, hexagonal honeycombs, large heads on large bodies, and spiral markings. But, as Darwin stressed, when such parts and patterns are modified and combined into complex biological machines fulfilling some delicate function, these subsequent modifications and arrangements must be explained by natural selection.

The real case of evolution without selection consists of the use of *unmodified spandrels*. Gould (1987a) describes a kind of wading bird that uses its wings primarily to block reflections on the surface of water while looking for fish. The possibility that some useful structure is an unmodified spandrel is the most interesting implication of the Gould-Lewontin argument, since Darwinian natural selection would really play no role. Note, though, that unmodified spandrels have severe limitations.

A wing used as a visor is a case where a structure designed for a complex engineering task that most arrangements of matter do not fulfill, such as controlled flight, is exapted to a simple engineering task that many arrangements of matter do fulfill, such as screening out reflections (we are reminded of the paperweight and aquarium depicted in *101 Uses for a Dead Computer*). When the reverse happens, such as when a solar heat exchanger is retooled as a fully functioning wing in the evolution of insects (Kingsolver and Koehl, 1985), natural selection must be the cause.

We are going over these criteria for invoking natural selection in such detail because they are so often misunderstood. We hope we have made it clear why modern evolutionary biology does *not* license Piattelli-Palmarini's conclusion that "since language and cognition probably represent the most salient and the most novel biological traits of our species, ... it is now important to show that they may well have arisen from totally extra-adaptive mechanisms." And Piattelli-Palmarini is not alone. In many discussions with cognitive scientists we have found that adaptation and natural selection have become dirty words. Anyone invoking them is accused of being a naive adaptationist, or even of "misunderstanding evolution." Worst of all, he or she is open to easy ridicule as a Dr. Pangloss telling Just-so stories. (Premack's 1986 reply to Bickerton, 1986, is typical.) Given the uncontroversially central role of natural selection in evolution, this state of affairs is unfortunate. We suspect that many people have acquired much of their knowledge of evolutionary theory from Gould's deservedly popular essays. These essays present a view of evolution that is vastly more sophisticated than the 19th-Century versions of Darwin commonly taught in high schools and even colleges. But Gould can easily be misread as fomenting a revolution rather than urging greater balance within current biological research, and his essays do not emphasize the standard arguments for when it is appropriate, indeed necessary, to invoke natural selection.

Also lurking beneath people's suspicions of natural selection is a set of methodological worries. Isn't adaptationism fundamentally untestable, hence unscientific, because adaptive stories are so easy to come by that when one fails, another can always be substituted? Gould and Lewontin may be correct in saying that biologists and psychologists have leapt too quickly to unmotivated and implausible adaptationist explanations, but this has nothing to do with the logic of adaptationist explanations per se. Glib, unmotivated proposals can come from all kinds of theories. To take an example close to home, the study of the evolution of language attained its poor reputation precisely because of the large number of silly *non*adaptationist hypotheses that were proposed. For instance, it has been argued that language arose from mimicry of animal calls, imitations of physical sounds, or grunts of exertion (the infamous "bow-wow," "ding-dong," and "heave-ho" theories).

Specific adaptationist proposals are testable in principle and in practice (see Dennett, 1983; Kitcher, 1983; Maynard Smith, 1984, Mayr, 1982; Sober, 1984; Williams, 1966). Supplementing the criterion of complex design, one can determine whether putatively adaptive structures are correlated with the ecological conditions that make them useful, and under certain circumstance one can actually measure the reproductive success of individuals possessing them to various degrees (see, e.g., Clutton-Brock, 1983). Of course, the entire theory of natural selection may be literally unfalsifiable in the uninteresting sense that elaborations can always rescue its empirical failings, but this is true of all large-scale scientific theories. Any such theory is supported to the extent that the individual elaborations are mutually consistent, motivated by independent data, and few in number compared to the phenomena to be explained.[2]

Indeed one could argue that it is nonadaptationist accounts that are often in grave danger of vacuity. Specific adaptationist proposals may be unmotivated, but they are within the realm of biological and physical understanding, and often the problem is simply that we lack the evidence to determine which account within a set of alternative adaptive explanations is the correct one. Nonadaptationist accounts that merely suggest the possibility that there is some hitherto-unknown law of physics or constraint on form—a "law of eye-formation," to take a caricatured example—are, in contrast, empty and nonfalsifiable.

2.3. TWO ISSUES THAT ARE INDEPENDENT OF SELECTIONISM

There are two other issues that Gould includes in his depiction of a scientific revolution in evolutionary theory. It is important to see that they are largely independent of the role of selection in evolutionary change.

2.3.1. Gradualism

According to the theory of "punctuated equilibrium" (Eldredge and Gould, 1972; Gould and Eldredge, 1977), most evolutionary change does not occur continuously within a lineage but is confined to bursts of change that are relatively brief on the geological time scale, generally corresponding to speciation events, followed by long periods of stasis. Gould has suggested that the theory has some very general and crude parallels with approaches to evolution that were made disreputable by the neo-Darwinian synthesis, approaches that go by the names of "saltationism," "macromutations," or "hopeful monsters" (e.g., Gould, 1981). However, he is emphatic that punctuated equilibrium is "a theory about ordinary speciation (taking tens of thousands of years) and its abrupt appearance at low scales of geological resolution, not about ecological catastrophe and sudden genetic change" (Gould, 1987b: 234). Many other biologists see evolutionary change in an even more orthodox light. They attribute the sudden appearance of fully formed new kinds of organisms in the fossil record to the fact that speciation typically takes place in small, geographically isolated populations. Thus transitional forms, even if evolving over very long time-spans, are unlikely to appear in the fossil record until they reinvade the ancestral territory; it is only the invasion that is sudden (see, e.g., Ayala, 1983; Dawkins,

1986; Mayr, 1982; Stebbins and Ayala, 1981). In any case it is clear that evolutionary change is gradual from generation to generation, in full agreement with Darwin. Thus Piattelli-Palmarini (1989: 8) expresses a common misunderstanding when he interprets the theory of punctuated equilibrium as showing that "many incomplete series in the fossil record are incomplete, not because the intermediate forms have been lost for us, but because they simply never existed."

Once again the explanation of adaptive complexity is the key reason why one should reject nongradual change as playing an important role within evolution. An important Darwinian insight, reinforced by Fisher (1930), is that the only way for complex design to evolve is through a sequence of mutations with small effects. Although it may not literally be impossible for an organ like the eye to emerge across one generation from no eye at all, the odds of this happening are unimaginably low. A random large leap in the space of possible organic forms is astronomically unlikely to land an organism in a region with a fully formed functioning eye. Only a hill-climbing process, with each small step forced in the direction of forms with better vision, can guide the lineage to such a minuscule region of the space of possible forms within the lifetime of the universe.

None of this is to deny that embryological processes can result in quite radical single-generation morphological changes. "Homeotic" mutations causing slight changes in the timing or positioning of epigenetic processes can result in radically new kinds of offspring, such as fruit flies with legs growing where their antenna should be, and it is possible that some speciation events may have begun with such large changes in structure. However there is a clear sense in which such changes are still gradual, since they only involve a gross modification or duplication of existing structure, not the appearance of a new kind of structure (see Dawkins, 1983).

2.3.2. Exaptation

Exaptation is another process that is sometimes discussed as if it was incompatible both with adaptationism and with gradualism. People often wonder whether each of the "numerous, successive, slight modifications" from an ancestor lacking an organ to a modern creature enjoying the fully-functioning organ leads to an improvement in function, as it should if the necessary evolutionary sequence is to be complete. Piattelli-Palmarini cites Kingsolver and Koehl's (1985) study of qualitative shifts during the evolution of wings in insects, which are ineffective for flight below a certain size, but effective as solar heat exchange panels precisely within that range. (The homology among parts of bat wings, seal flippers, horse forelimbs, and human arms is a far older example.) Nevertheless such exaptations are still gradual and are still driven by selection; there must be an intermediate evolutionary stage at which the part can subserve both functions (Mayr, 1982), after which the process of natural selection shapes it specifically for its current function. Indeed the very concept of exaptation is essentially similar to what Darwin called "preadaptation," and played an important role in his explanation of "the incipient stages of useful structures."

Furthermore, it is crucial to understand that exaptation is merely one empirical possibility, not a universal law of evolution. Gould is often quoted as saying "We avoid the excellent question, What good is 5 percent of an eye? by arguing that the possessor of such an incipient structure did not use it for sight" (1977b:107). (Of course no ancestor to humans literally had 5 percent of a human eye; the expression refers to an eye that has 5 percent of the complexity of a modern eye.) In response, Dawkins (1986: 81) writes: "An ancient animal with 5 per cent of an eye might indeed have used it for something other than sight, but it seems to me at least as likely that it used it for 5 per cent vision.... Vision that is 5 percent as good as yours or mine is very much worth having in comparison with no vision at all. So is 1 per cent vision better than total blindness. And 6 per cent is better than 5, 7 per cent better than 6, and so on up the gradual, continuous series." Indeed Darwin (1859) sketched out a hypothetical sequence of intermediate forms in the evolution of the vertebrate eye, all with counterparts in living organisms, each used for vision.

In sum, the positions of Gould, Lewontin, and Eldredge should not be seen as radical revisions of the theory of evolution, but as a shift in emphasis within the orthodox neo-Darwinian framework. As such they do not invalidate gradual natural selection as the driving force behind the evolution of language on a priori grounds. Furthermore, there are clear criteria for when selectionist and nonselectionist accounts should be invoked to explain some biological structure: complex design to carry out some reproductively significant function, versus the existence of a specific physical, developmental, or random process capable of explaining the structure's existence. With these criteria in hand, we can turn to the specific problem at hand, the evolution of language.

3. Design in Language

Do the cognitive mechanisms underlying language show signs of design for some function in the same way that the anatomical structures of the eye show signs of design for the purpose of vision? This breaks down into three smaller questions: What is the function (if any) of language? What are the engineering demands on a system that must carry out such a function? And are the mechanisms of language tailored to meet those demands? We will suggest that language shows signs of design for the communication of propositional structures over a serial channel.

3.1. AN ARGUMENT FOR DESIGN IN LANGUAGE

Humans acquire a great deal of information during their lifetimes. Since this acquisition process occurs at a rate far exceeding that of biological evolution, it is invaluable in dealing with causal contingencies of the environment that change within a lifetime, and provides a decisive advantage in competition with other species that can only defend themselves against new threats in evolutionary time (Brandon and Hornstein, 1986; Tooby and deVore, 1987). There is an obvious advantage in being able to acquire such information about the world second-hand: by tapping into the vast reservoir of knowledge accumulated by other individuals, one can avoid having to duplicate the possibly time-consuming and dangerous trial and error process that won that knowledge. Furthermore, within a group of interdependent, cooperating individuals, the states of other individuals are among the most significant things in the world worth knowing about. Thus communication of knowledge and internal states is useful to creatures who have a lot to say and who are on speaking terms. (In section 5.3, we discuss evidence that our ancestors were such creatures.)

Human knowledge and reasoning, it has been argued, is couched in a "language of thought" that is distinct from external languages such as English or Japanese (Fodor, 1975). The propositions in this representational medium are relational structures whose symbols pertain to people, objects, and events, the categories they belong to, their distribution in space and time, and their causal relations to one another (Jackendoff, 1983; Keil, 1979). The causal relations governing the behavior of other people are understood as involving their beliefs and desires, which can be considered as relations between an individual and the proposition that represents the content of that belief or desire (Fodor, 1985, 1987).

This makes the following kinds of contents as worthy of communication among humans. We would want to be able to refer to individuals and classes, to distinguish among basic ontological categories (things, events, places, times, manners, and so on), to talk about events and states, distinguishing the participants in the event or state according to role (agents, patients, goals), and to talk about the intentional states of ourselves and others. Also, we would want the ability to express distinctions of truth value, modality (necessity, possibility, probability, factivity), to comment on the time of an event or state including both its distribution over time (continuous, iterative, punctate) and its overall time of occurrence. One might also demand the ability to encode an unlimited number of predicates, arguments, and propositions. Further, it would be useful to be able to use the same propositional content within different speech acts; for instance, as a question, a statement, or a command. Superimposed on all of this we might ask for an ability to focus or to put into the background different parts of a proposition, so as to tie the speech act into its context of previously conveyed information and patterns of knowledge of the listener.

The vocal-auditory channel has some desirable features as a medium of communication: it has a high bandwidth, its intensity can be modulated to conceal the speaker or to cover large distances, and it does not require light, proximity, a face-to-face orientation, or tying up the hands. However it is essentially a serial interface, lacking the full two-dimensionality needed to convey graph or tree structures and typographical devices such as fonts, subscripts, and brackets. The basic tools of a coding scheme employing it are an inventory of distinguishable symbols and their concatenation.

Thus grammars for spoken languages must map propositional structures onto a serial channel, minimizing ambiguity in context, under the further constraints that the encoding and decoding be done rapidly, by creatures with limited short-term memories, according to a code that is shared by an entire community of potential communicants.

The fact that language is a complex system of many parts, each tailored to mapping a characteristic kind of semantic or pragmatic function onto a characteristic kind of symbol sequence, is so obvious in linguistic practice that it is usually not seen as worth mentioning. Let us list some uncontroversial facts about substantive universals, the building blocks of grammars that all theories of universal grammar posit, either as an explicit inventory or as a consequence of somewhat more abstract mechanisms.

- Grammars are built around symbols for major lexical categories (noun, verb, adjective, preposition) that can enter into rules specifying telltale surface distributions (e.g., verbs but not nouns generally take unmarked direct objects), inflections, and lists of lexical items. Together with minor categories that characteristically co-occur with the major ones (e.g., articles with nouns), the different categories are thus provided with the means of being distinguished in the speech string. These distinctions are exploited to distinguish basic ontological categories such as things, events or states, and qualities. (See, e.g., Jackendoff, 1983, 1990.)
- Major phrasal categories (noun phrase, verb phrase, etc.) start off with a major lexical item, the "head," and allow it to be combined with specific kinds of affixes and phrases. The resulting conglomerate is then used to refer to entities in our mental models of the world. Thus a noun like *dog* does not itself describe anything but it can combine with articles and other parts of speech to make noun phrases, such as *those dogs, my dog,* and *the dog that bit me,* and it is these noun phrases that are used to describe things. Similarly, a verb like *hit* is made into a verb phrase by marking it for tense and aspect and adding an object, thus enabling it to describe an event. In general, words encode abstract general categories and only by contributing to the structure of major phrasal categories can they describe particular things, events, states, locations, and properties. This mechanism enables the language-user to refer to an unlimited range of specific entities while possessing only a finite number of lexical items. (See, e.g., Bloom, 1989; Jackendoff, 1977.).
- Phrase structure rules (e.g., "X-bar theory" or "immediate dominance rules") force concatenation in the string to correspond to semantic connectedness in the underlying proposition, and thus provides linear clues of underlying structure, distinguishing, for example, *Large trees grow dark berries* from *Dark trees grow large berries.* (See, e.g., Gazdar, Pullum, Klein, and Sag, 1985; Jackendoff, 1977.)

- Rules of linear order (e.g., "directional parameters" for ordering heads, complements, and specifiers, or "linear precedence rules") allow the order of words within these concatenations to distinguish among the argument positions that an entity assumes with respect to a predicate, distinguishing *Man bites dog* from *Dog bites man*. (See, e.g., Gazdar et al., 1985; Travis, 1984.)
- Case affixes on nouns and adjectives can take over these functions, marking nouns according to argument role, and linking noun with predicate even when the order is scrambled. This redundancy can free up the device of linear order, allowing it to be exploited to convey relations of prominence and focus, which can thus mesh with the necessarily temporal flow of attention and knowledge acquisition in the listener.
- Verb affixes signal the temporal distribution of the event that the verb refers to (aspect) and the time of the event (tense); when separate aspect and tense affixes co-occur, they are in a universally preferred order (aspect closer to the verb; Bybee, 1985). Given that man-made timekeeping devices play no role in species-typical human thought, some other kind of temporal coordinates must be used, and languages employ an ingenious system that can convey the time of an event relative to the time of the speech act itself and relative to a third, arbitrary reference time (thus we can distinguish between *John has arrived, John had arrived* (when Mary was speaking), *John will have arrived* (before Mary speaks), and so on; Reichenbach, 1947). Verb affixes also typically agree with the subject and other arguments, and thus provide another redundant mechanism that can convey predicate-argument relations by itself (e.g., in many Native American languages such as Cherokee and Navajo) or that can eliminate ambiguity left open by other mechanisms (distinguishing, e.g., *I know the boy and the girl who like chocolate* from *I know the boy and the girl who likes chocolate*).
- Auxiliaries, which occur either as verb affixes (where they are distinguished from tense and aspect affixes by proximity to the verb) or in one of three sentence-peripheral positions (first, second, last), convey relations that have logical scope over the entire proposition (mirroring their peripheral position) such as truth value, modality, and illocutionary force. (See Steele, Akmajian, Demers, Jelinek, Kitagawa, Oehrle, & Wasow, 1981.)
- Languages also typically contain a small inventory of phonetically reducible morphemes—pronouns and other anaphoric elements—that by virtue of encoding a small set of semantic features such as gender and humanness, and being restricted in their distribution, can convey patterns of coreference among different participants in complex relations without the necessity of repeating lengthy definite descriptions (e.g., as in *A boy showed a dog to a girl and then he/she/it touched him/her/it/himself/herself*). (See Chomsky, 1981; Wexler and Manzini, 1984.)
- Mechanisms of complementation and control govern the expression of propositions that are arguments of other propositions, employing specific comple-

mentizer morphemes signaling the periphery of the embedded proposition and indicating its relation to the embedding one, and licensing the omission of repeated phrases referring to participants playing certain combinations of roles. This allows the expression of a rich set of propositional attitudes within a belief-desire folk psychology, such as *John tried to come, John thinks that Bill will come, John hopes for Bill to come, John convinced Bill to come,* and so on. (See Bresnan, 1982.)

- In *wh*-movement (as in *wh*-questions and relative clauses) there is a tightly constrained cooccurrence pattern between an empty element (a "trace" or "gap") and a sentence-peripheral quantifier (e.g., *wh*-words). The quantifier-word can be specific as to illocutionary force (question versus modification), ontological type (time, place, purpose), feature (animate/inanimate), and role (subject/object), and the gap can occur only in highly constrained phrase structure configurations. The semantics of such constructions allow the speaker to fix the reference of, or request information about, an entity by specifying its role within any proposition. One can refer not just to any dog but to *the dog that Mary sold __ to some students last year*; one can ask not only for the names of just any old interesting person but specifically *Who was that woman I saw you with __?* (See, e.g., Chomsky, 1981; Gazdar, Pullum, Klein, and Sag, 1985; Kaplan and Bresnan, 1982.)

And this is only a partial list, focusing on sheer expressive power. One could add to it the many syntactic constraints and devices whose structure enables them to minimize memory load and the likelihood of pursuing local garden paths in speech comprehension (e.g., Berwick and Weinberg, 1984; Berwick and Wexler, 1987; Bever, 1970; Chomsky and Lasnik, 1977; Frazier, Clifton, and Randall, 1983; Hawkins and Cutler, 1988; Kuno, 1973, 1974), or to ease the task of analysis for the child learning the language (e.g., Morgan, 1986; Pinker, 1984; Wexler and Culicover, 1980). On top of that there are the rules of segmental phonology that smooth out arbitrary concatenations of morphemes into a consistent sound pattern, juggling demands of ease of articulation and perceptual distinctness; the prosodic rules which disambiguate syntax and communicate pragmatic and illocutionary information; the articulatory programs that achieve rapid transmission rates through parallel encoding of adjacent consonants and vowels; and on and on. Language seems to be a fine example of "that perfection of structure and coadaptation which justly excites our admiration" (Darwin, 1859: 26).

As we write these words, we can hear the protests: "Pangloss! Just-so stories!" Haven't we just thought up accounts about functions post hoc after examining the structure? How do we know that the neural mechanisms were not there for other reasons, and that once they were there they were just put to various convenient uses by the first language users, who then conveyed their invention to subsequent generations?

3.2. IS THE ARGUMENT FOR LANGUAGE DESIGN A JUST-SO STORY?

First of all, there is nothing particularly ingenious, contorted, or exotic about our claims for substantive universals and their semantic functions. Any one of them could have been lifted out of the pages of linguistics textbooks. It is hardly the theory of evolution that motivates the suggestion that phrase structure rules are useful in conveying relations of modification and predicate-argument structure.

Second, it is not necessarily illegitimate to infer both special design and adaptationist origins on the basis of function itself. It all depends on the complexity of the function from an engineering point of view. If someone told you that John uses X as a sunshade or a paperweight, you would certainly be hard-pressed to guess what X is or where X came from, because all sorts of things make good sunshades or paperweights. But if someone told you that John uses X to display television broadcasts, it would be a very good bet that X is a television set or is similar in structure to one, and that it was designed for that purpose. The reason is that it would be vanishingly unlikely for something that was not designed as a television set to display television programs; the engineering demands are simply too complex.

This kind of reasoning is commonly applied in biology when high-tech abilities such as bat sonar are discovered. We suggest that human language is a similar case. We are not talking about noses holding up spectacles. Human language is a device capable of communicating exquisitely complex and subtle messages, from convoluted soap opera plots to theories of the origin of the universe. Even if all we knew was that humans possessed such a device, we would expect that it would have to have rather special and unusual properties suited to the task of mapping complex propositional structures onto a serial channel, and an examination of grammar confirms this expectation.

Third, arguments that language is designed for communication of propositional structures are far from logical truths. It is easy to formulate, and reject, specific alternatives. For example, occasionally it is suggested that language evolved as a medium of internal knowledge representation for use in the computations underlying reasoning. But while there may be a language-like representational medium—"the language of thought," or "mentalese" (Fodor, 1975)—it clearly cannot be English, Japanese, and so on. Natural languages are hopeless for this function: they are needlessly serial, rife with ambiguity (usually harmless in conversational contexts, but unsuited for long term knowledge representation), complicated by alternations that are relevant only to discourse (e.g., topicalization), and cluttered with devices (such as phonology and much of morphology) that make no contribution to reasoning. Similarly, the facts of grammar make it difficult to argue that language shows design for "the expression of thought" in any sense that is substantially distinct from "communication." If "expression" refers to the mere externalization of thoughts, in some kind of monologue or soliloquy, it is an unexplained fact that language contains mechanisms that presuppose the existence of a listener, such as rules of phonology and phonetics (which map sentences onto sound patterns, enhance confusable phonetic distinctions, disambiguate phrase structure with intonation, and so on.) and pragmatic devices that encode conversational topic, illocutionary force, discourse antecedents, and so on. Furthermore people do not express their thoughts in an arbitrary private language (which would be sufficient for pure "expression"), but have complex learning mechanisms that acquire a language highly similar in almost every detail to those of other speakers in the community.

Another example of the empirical nature of specific arguments for language design appears when we examine the specific expressive abilities that are designed into language. They turn out to constitute a well-defined set, and do not simply correspond to every kind of information that humans are interested in communicating. So although we may have some a priori intuitions regarding useful expressive capacities of grammar, the matter is ultimately empirical (see, e.g., Jackendoff, 1983, 1990; Pinker, 1989b; Talmy, 1983, 1988), and such research yields results that are specific enough to show that not just any intuition is satisfied. Grammar is a notoriously poor medium for conveying subtle patterns of emotion, for example, for which facial expressions and tones of voice are more informative (Ekman and Friesen, 1975; Etcoff, 1986). Although grammars provide devices for conveying rough topological information such as connectivity, contact, and containment, and coarse metric contrasts such as near/far or flat/globular, they are of very little help in conveying precise Euclidean relations: a picture is worth a thousand words. Furthermore, human grammar clearly lacks devices specifically dedicated to expressing any of the kinds of messages that characterize the vocal communication systems of cetaceans, birds, or nonhuman primates, such as announcements of individual identity, predator warnings, and claims of territory.

Finally, Williams (1966) suggests that convergent evolution, resemblance to man-made artifacts, and direct assessments of engineering efficiency are good sources of evidence for adaptation. Of course in the case of human language these tests are difficult in practice: significant convergent evolution has not occurred; no one has ever invented a system that duplicates its function (except for systems that are obviously parasitic on natural languages such as Esperanto or signed English); and most forms of experimental intervention would be unethical. Nonetheless, some tests are possible in principle, and this is enough to refute reflexive accusations of circularity.

For example, even the artificial languages that are focussed on very narrow domains of content and that are not meant to be used in a natural on-line manner by people, such as computer languages and symbolic logic, show certain clear parallels with aspects of human grammar. They have needed means of distinguishing types of symbols, predicate-argument relations, embedding, scope, quantification, and truth relations, and solve these problems with formal syntactic systems that specify arbitrary patterns of hierarchical concatenation, relative linear order, fixed positions within strings, and closed classes of privileged symbols. Of course there are vast dissimilarities, but the mere fact that terms like "language," "syntax," "predicate," "argument," and "statement" have clear meanings when applied to artificial systems, with no confusion or qualification, suggests that there are nonaccidental parallels that are reminiscent of the talk of diaphragms and lenses when applied to cameras and eyes. As for experimental investigation, in principle one could define sets of artificial grammars with and without one of the mechanisms in question, or with variations of it. The grammars would be provided or taught to pairs of communicators—formal automata, computer simulations, or college sophomores acting in conscious problem-solving mode—who would be required to convey specific messages under different conditions of speed, noise, or memory limitations. The proportion of information successfully communicated would be assessed and examined as a function of the presence and version of the grammatical mechanism, and of the different conditions putatively relevant to the function in question.

3.3. LANGUAGE DESIGN AND LANGUAGE DIVERSITY

A more serious challenge to the claim that grammars show evidence of good design may come from the diversity of human languages (Maratsos, 1989). Grammatical devices and expressive functions do not pair up in one-to-one fashion. For example, some languages use word order to convey who did what to whom; others use case or agreement for this purpose and reserve the use of word order to distinguish topic from comment, or do not systematically exploit word order at all. How can one say that the mental devices governing word order evolved under selection pressure for expressing grammatical relations if many languages do not use them for that purpose? Linguistic diversity would seem to imply that grammatical devices are very general-purpose tools. And a general-purpose tool would surely have a very generalized structure, and thus could be a spandrel rather than an adapted machine. We begin by answering the immediate objection that the existence of diversity, for whatever reason, invalidates arguments for universal language design; at the end of the section we offer some speculations as to why there should be more than one language to begin with.

First of all, the evolution of structures that serve not one but a small number of definite functions, perhaps to different extents in different environments, is common in biology (Mayr, 1982). Indeed, though grammatical devices are put to different uses in different languages, the possible pairings are quite circumscribed. No language uses noun affixes to express tense, or elements with the syntactic privileges of auxiliaries to express the shape of the direct object. Such universal constraints on structure and function are abundantly documented in surveys of the languages of the world (e.g., Bybee, 1985; Comrie, 1981; Greenberg, 1966; Greenberg, Ferguson, and Moravcsik, 1978; Hawkins, 1988; Keenan, 1976; and Shopen, 1985). Moreover, language universals are visible in language history, where changes tend to fall into a restricted set of patterns, many involving the introduction of grammatical devices obeying characteristic constraints (Kiparsky, 1976; Wang, 1976).[3]

But accounting for the evolution of a language faculty permitting restricted variation is only important on the most pessimistic of views. Even a smidgin of grammatical analysis reveals that surface diversity is often a manifestation of minor differences in the underlying mental grammars. Consider some of the supposedly radical typological differences between English and other languages. English is a rigid word-order language; in the Australian language Warlpiri the words from different logical units can be thoroughly scrambled, and case markers are used to convey grammatical relations and noun modification. Many Native American languages, such as Cherokee, use few noun phrases within clauses at all, and express grammatical relations by sticking strings of agreement affixes onto the verb, each identifying an argument by a set of features such as humanness or shape. Whereas "accusative" languages like English collapse subjects of transitive and intransitive sentences, "ergative" languages collapse objects of transitives with subjects of intransitives. Whereas English sentences are built around obligatory subjects, languages like Chinese are oriented around a position reserved for the discourse topic.

However, these variations almost certainly correspond to differences in the extent to which the same specific set of mental devices is put to use and not to differences in the kinds of devices that are put to use. English has free constituent order in strings of prepositional phrases (*The package was sent from Chicago to Boston by Mary; The package was sent by Mary to Boston from Chicago,* and so on). English has case, both in pronouns and in the genitive marker spelled *'s*. It expresses information about arguments in verb affixes in the agreement marker *-s*. Ergativity can be seen in verb alternations like *John broke the glass* and *The glass broke*. There is even a kind of topic position: *As for fish, I like salmon*. Conversely, Warlpiri is not without phrasal syntax. Auxiliaries go in second position (not unlike English, German, and many other languages). The constituents of a noun phrase must be contiguous if they are not case-marked; the constituents of a finite clause must be contiguous if the sentence contains more than one. Pinker (1984) outlines a theory of language acquisition in which the same innate learning mechanisms are put to use to different extents in children acquiring "radically" different languages.

When one looks at more abstract linguistic analyses, the underlying unity of natural languages is even more apparent. Chomsky has quipped that anything you find in one language can also be found in every other language, perhaps at a more abstract level of representation, and this claim can be justified without resorting to Procrustean measures. In many versions of his Government-Binding theory (1981), all noun phrases must be case marked; even those that receive no overt case-marking are assigned "abstract" case by an adjacent verb, preposition, or tense element. The basic order of major phrases is determined by the value of a language-varying parameter specifying the direction in which case assignment may be executed. So in a language like Latin, the noun phrases are marked with morphological case (and can appear in any position), while in a language like English, they are not so marked, and must be adjacent to a case-assigner such as a verb. Thus overt case marking in one language and word order in another are unified as manifestations of a single grammatical module. And the module has a well-specified function: in the terminology of the theory, it makes noun phrases "visible" for the assignment of thematic roles such as agent, goal, or location. Moreover, word order itself is not a unified phenomenon. Often when languages "use word order for pragmatic purposes," they are exploiting an underlying grammatical subsystem, such as stylistic rules, that has very different properties from that governing the relative order of noun phrases and their case-assigners.

Why is there more than one language at all? Here we can only offer the most tentative of speculations. For sound-meaning pairings within the lexicon, there are two considerations. First, one might suppose that speakers need a learning mechanism for labels for cultural innovations, such as *screwdriver*. Such a learning device is then sufficient for all vocabulary items. Second, it may be difficult to evolve a huge innate code. Each of tens of thousands of sound-meaning correspondences would have to be synchronized across speakers, but few words could have the nonarbitrary antecedents that would have been needed to get the standardization process started (i.e., analogous to the way bared fangs in preparation for biting evolved into the facial expression for anger.) Furthermore the size of such a code would tax the time available to evolve and maintain it in the genome in the face of random perturbations from sexual recombination and other stochastic genetic processes (Williams, 1966; Tooby and Cosmides, 1989). Once a mechanism for learning sound-meaning pairs is in place, the information for acquiring any particular pair, such as *dog* for dogs, is readily available from the speech of the community. Thus the genome can store the vocabulary in the environment, as Tooby and Cosmides (1989) have put it.

For other aspects of grammar, one might get more insight by inverting the perspective. Instead of positing that there are multiple languages, leading to the evolution of a mechanism to learn the differences among them, one might posit that there is a learning mechanism, leading to the development of multiple languages. That is, some aspects of grammar might be easily learnable from environmental inputs by cognitive processes that may have been in existence prior to the evolution of grammar, for example, the relative order of a pair of sequenced elements within a bounded unit. For these aspects there was no need to evolve a fixed value, and they are free to vary across communities of speakers. In Section 5.2.3 we discuss a simulation of evolution by Hinton and Nowlan (1987) that behaves in a way that is consistent with this conjecture.

3.4. LANGUAGE DESIGN AND ARBITRARINESS

Piattelli-Palmarini (1989) presents a different kind of argument: grammar is not completely predictable as an adaptation to communication, therefore it lacks design and did not evolve by selection. He writes, "Survival criteria, the need to communicate and plan concerted action, cannot account for our specific linguistic nature. Adaptation cannot even begin to explain any of these phenomena." Frequently cited examples of arbitrary phenomena in language include constraints on movement (such as subjacency), irregular morphology, and lexical differences in predicate-argument structure. For instance, it is acceptable to say *Who did John see Mary with?* but not *Who did John see Mary and?*; *John broke the glass* but not *John breaked the glass*; *John filled the glass with milk,* but not *John poured the glass with milk.* The arguments that language could not be an adaptation take two forms: (i) language could be better than it is, and (ii) language could be different than it is. We show that neither form of the argument is valid, and that the facts that it invokes are perfectly consistent with language being an adaptation and offer not the slightest support to any specific alternative.

3.4.1. Inherent Tradeoffs

In their crudest form, arguments about the putative functionlessness of grammar run as follows: "I bet you can't tell me a function for Constraint X; therefore language is a spandrel." But even if it could be shown that one part of language had no function, that would not mean that all parts of language had no function. Recall from Section 2.2 that many organs contain modified spandrels but that this does not mean that natural selection did not assemble or shape the organ. Worse, Constraint X may not be a genuine part of the language faculty but just a description of one aspect of it, an epiphenomenal spandrel. No adaptive organ can be adaptive in every aspect, because there are as many aspects of an organ as there are ways of describing it. The recent history of linguistics provides numerous examples where a newly-discovered constraint is first proposed as an explicit statement listed as part of a grammar, but is then shown to be a deductive consequence of a far more wide-ranging principle (see, e.g., Chomsky, 1981; Freidin, 1978.) For example, the ungrammaticality of sentences like *John to have won is surprising,* once attributed to a filter specifically ruling out [NP-to-VP] sequences, is now seen as a consequence of the Case Filter. Although one might legitimately wonder what good "*[NP-to-VP]" is doing in a grammar, one could hardly dispense with something like the Case Filter.

Since the mere appearance of some nonoptimal feature is inconclusive, we must examine specific explanations for why the feature exists. In the case of the nonselectionist position espoused by Piattelli-Palmarini, there is none: not a hint of how any specific aspect of grammar might be explained, even in principle, as a specific consequence of some developmental process or genetic mechanism or constraint on possible brain structure. The position gains *all* its support from the supposed lack of an adaptive explanation. In fact, we will show that there is such an explanation, well-motivated both within evolutionary theory and within linguistics, so the support disappears.

The idea that natural selection aspires toward perfection has long been discredited within evolutionary theory (Williams, 1966). As Maynard Smith (1984: 290) has put it, "If there were no constraints on what is possible, the best phenotype would live forever, would be impregnable to predators, would lay eggs at an infinite rate, and so on." Tradeoffs among conflicting adaptive goals are a ubiquitous limitation on optimality in the design of organisms. It may be adaptive for a male bird to advertise his health to females with gaudy plumage or a long tail, but not to the extent that predators are attracted or flight is impossible.

Tradeoffs of utility within language are also unavoidable (Bolinger, 1980; Slobin, 1977). For example, there is a conflict of interest between speaker and hearer. Speakers want to minimize articulatory effort and hence tend towards brevity and phonological reduction. Hearers want to minimize the effort of understanding and hence desire explicitness and clarity. This conflict of interest is inherent to the communication process and operates at many levels. Editors badger authors into expanding elliptical passages; parsimonious headline writers unwittingly produce *Squad Helps Dog Bite Victim* and *Stud Tires Out*. Similarly there is a conflict of interest between speaker and learner. A large vocabulary allows for concise and precise expression. But it is only useful if every potential listener has had the opportunity to learn each item. Again, this tradeoff is inherent to communication; one man's jargon term is another's *mot juste*.

Clearly, any shared system of communication is going to have to adopt a code that is a compromise among these demands, and so will appear to be arbitrary from the point of view of any one criterion. There is always a large range of solutions to the combined demands of communication which reach slightly different equilibrium points in this multidimensional space. Slobin (1977) points out that the Serbo-Croatian inflectional system is "a classic Indo-European synthetic muddle," suffixing each noun with a single affix from a paradigm full of irregularity, homophony, and zero-morphemes. As a result the system is perfected late and with considerable difficulty. In contrast the Turkish inflectional system is semantically transparent, with strings of clearly demarcated regular suffixes, and is mastered by the age of two. When it comes to production by an adult who has overlearned the system, however, Serbo-Croatian does have an advantage in minimizing the sheer number of syllables that must be articulated. Furthermore, Slobin points out that such tradeoffs can be documented in studies of historical change and borrowing. For example, changes that serve to enhance brevity will proceed until comprehension becomes impaired, at which point new affixes or distinctions are introduced to restore the balance (see also Samuels, 1972). A given feature of language may be arbitrary in the sense that there are alternative solutions that are better from the standpoint of some single criterion. But this does not mean that it is good for nothing at all!

Subjacency—the prohibition against dependencies between a gap and its antecedent which span certain combinations of phrasal nodes—is a classic example of an arbitrary constraint (see Freidin & Quicoli, 1989). In English you can say *What does he believe they claimed that I said?* but not the semantically parallel *What does he believe the claim that I said?.* One might ask why languages behave this way. Why not allow extraction anywhere, or nowhere? The constraint may exist because parsing sentences with gaps is a notoriously difficult problem and a system that has to be prepared for the possibility of inaudible elements anywhere in the sentence is in danger of bogging down by positing them everywhere. Subjacency has been held to assist parsing because it cuts down on the set of structures that the parser has to keep track of when finding gaps (Berwick and Weinberg, 1984). This bonus to listeners is often a hindrance to speakers, who struggle with resumptive pronouns in clumsy sentences such as *That's the guy that you heard the rumor about his wife leaving him.* There is nothing "necessary" about the precise English version of the constraint or about the small sample of alternatives allowed within natural language. But by settling on a particular subset of the range of possible compromises between the demands of expressiveness and parsability, the evolutionary process may have converged on a satisfactory set of solutions to one problem within language processing.

3.4.2. *Parity in Communications Protocols*
The fact that one can conceive of a biological system being different than it is says nothing about whether it is an adaptation (see Mayr, 1983). No one would argue that selection was not the key organizing force in the evolution of the vertebrate eye just because the compound eyes of arthropods are different. Similarly, pointing out that a hypothetical Martian language could do passivization differently is inconclusive. We must ask how well-supported specific explanations are.

In the case of features of human language structure that could have been different, again Piattelli-Palmarini presents no explanations at all and relies entirely on the putative inability of natural selection to provide any sort of motivated account. But in fact there is such an account: the nature of language makes arbitrariness of grammar itself part of the adaptive solution of effective communication. Any communicative system requires a coding protocol which can be arbitrary as long as it is shared. Liberman and Mattingly (1989) call this the requirement of *parity*, and we can illustrate it with the (coincidentally-named) "parity" settings in electronic communication protocols. There is nothing particularly logical about setting your printer's serial interface to the "even" as opposed to the "odd," parity setting. Nor is there any motivation to set your computer to odd as opposed to even parity. But there is every reason to set the computer and printer to the *same* parity, whatever it is, because if you don't, they cannot communicate. Indeed, standardization itself is far more important than any other adaptive feature possessed by one party. Many personal computer manufacturers in the 1980s boasted of the superior engineering and design of their product compared to the IBM PC. But when these machines were not IBM-compatible, the results are well-known.

In the evolution of the language faculty many "arbitrary" constraints may have been selected simply because they defined parts of a standardized communicative code in the brains of some critical mass of speakers. Piattelli-Palmarini may be correct in claiming that there is nothing adaptive about forming *yes-no* questions by inverting the subject and auxiliary as opposed to reversing the order of words in the sentence. But given that language must do one or the other, it is highly adaptive for each member of a community of speakers to be forced to learn to do it the same way as all the other members. To be sure, some combination of historical accidents, epiphenomena of other cognitive processes, and neurodevelopmental constraints must have played a large role in the breaking of symmetry that was needed to get the fixation process running away in one direction or another. But it still must have been selection that resulted in the convention then becoming innately entrenched.

The requirement of parity operates at all levels of a communications protocol. Within individual languages the utility of arbitrary but shared features is most obvious in the choice of individual words: there is no reason for you to call a dog *dog* rather than *cat* except for the fact that everyone else is doing it, but that is reason enough. Saussure (1959) called this inherent feature of language "l'arbitraire du signe," and Hurford (1989a), using evolutionary game theory, demonstrates the evolutionary stability of such a "Saussurean" strategy, whereby each learner uses the same arbitrary signs in production that it uses in comprehension (i.e., that other speakers use in production). More generally, these considerations suggest that a preference for arbitrariness is built into the language acquisition device at two levels. It only hypothesizes rules that fall within the (possibly arbitrary) set defined by universal grammar, and within that set, it tries to choose rules that match those used by the community, whatever they are.

The benefits of a learning mechanism designed to assess and adopt the prevailing parity settings become especially clear when we consider alternatives, such as trying to get each speaker to converge on the same standard by endogenously applying some rationale to predict form from meaning. There are many possible rationales for any form-meaning pairing, and that is exactly the problem—different rationales can impress different speakers, or the same speakers on different occasions, to different degrees. But such differences in cognitive style, personal history, or momentary interests must be set aside if people are to communicate. As mentioned, no grammatical device can simultaneously optimize the demands of talkers and hearers, but it will not do to talk in Serbo-Croatian and demand that one's listeners reply in Turkish. Furthermore, whenever cognition is flexible enough to construe a situation in more than one way, no simple correspondence between syntax and semantics can be used predictively by a community of speakers to "deduce" the most "logical" grammatical structure. For example, there is a simple and universal principle dictating that the surface direct object of a causative verb refers to an entity that is affected by the action. But the principle by itself is unusable. When a girl puts boxes in baskets she is literally affecting both: the boxes are changing location, and the baskets are changing state from empty to full. One would not want one perceiver interested in the boxes to say that *she is filling boxes* while another interested in the baskets to describe the same event as *filling baskets*; no one would know what went where. However by letting different verbs idiosyncratically select different kinds of entities as "affected" (e.g., *place the box/*basket* versus *fill the basket/*box*), and forcing learners to respect the verbs' wishes, grammar can allow speakers to specify different kinds of entities as affected by putting them in the direct object position of different verbs, with minimal ambiguity. Presumably this is why different verbs have different arbitrary syntactic privileges (Pinker, 1989b), a phenomenon that Piattelli-Palmarini (1989) describes at length. Even iconicity and onomatopoeia are in the eye and ear of the beholder. The ASL sign for "tree" resembles the motion of a tree waving in the wind, but in Chinese Sign Language it is the motion of sketching the trunk (Newport & Meier, 1985). In the United States, pigs go "oink"; in Japan, they go "boo-boo."

3.4.3. Arbitrariness and the Relation between Language Evolution and Language Acquisition

The need for arbitrariness has profound consequences for understanding the role of communicative function in language acquisition and language evolution. Many psychologists and artificial intelligence researchers have suggested that the structure of grammar is simply the solution that every child arrives at in solving the problem of how to communicate with others. Skinner's reinforcement theory is the strongest version of this hypothesis (Skinner, 1957), but versions that avoid his behaviorism and rely instead on general cognitive problem-solving abilities have always been popular within psychology. Both Skinner and cognitive theorists such as Bates et al. (1989) explicitly draw parallels between the role of function in learning and evolution. Chomsky and many other linguists and psycholinguists have argued against functionalism in ontogeny, showing that many aspects of grammar cannot be reduced to being the optimal solution to a communicative problem; rather, human grammar has a universal idiosyncratic logic of its own. More generally, Chomsky has emphasized that people's use of language does not tightly serve utilitarian goals of communication but is an autonomous competence to express thought (see, e.g., Chomsky, 1975). If communicative function does not shape language in the individual, one might conclude, it probably did not shape language in the species.

We suggest that the analogy that underpins this debate is misleading. It is not just that learning and evolution need not follow identical laws, selectionist or otherwise. (For example, as Chomsky himself has stressed, the issue never even comes up in clearer cases like vision, where nobody suggests that all infants' visual development is related to their desire to see or that visual systems develop with random variations that are selected by virtue of their ability to attain the child's goals.) In the case of language the arguments of section 3.4 suggest that language evolution and language acquisition not only *can* differ but that they *must* differ. Evolution has had a wide variety of equivalent communicative standards to choose from; there is no reason for it to have favored the class of languages that includes Apache and Yiddish, but not Old High Martian or Early Vulcan. But this flexibility has been used up by the time a child is born; the species and the language community have already made their choices. The child cannot learn just any useful communicative system; nor can he or she learn just any natural language. He or she is stuck with having to learn the particular kind of language the species eventually converged upon and the particular variety the community has chosen. Whatever rationales may have influenced these choices are buried in history and cannot be recapitulated in development.

Moreover, any code as complex and precise as a grammar for a natural language will not wear its protocol on its sleeve. No mortal computer user can induce an entire communications protocol or programming language from examples; that's why we have manuals. This is because any particular instance of the use of such a protocol is a unique event accompanied by a huge set of idiosyncratic circumstances, some relevant to how the code must be used, most irrelevant, and there is no way of deciding which is which. For the child, any sentence or set of sentences is compatible with a wide variety of very different grammars, only one of them correct (Chomsky, 1965, 1975, 1980, 1981; Pinker, 1979, 1984; Wexler and Culicover, 1980). For example, without prior constraints, it would be natural to generalize from input sentences like *Who did you see her with?* to **Who did you see her and?*, from *teethmarks* to **clawsmarks*, from *You better be good* to **Better you be good?*. The child has no manual to consult, and presumably that is why he or she needs innate constraints.

So we see a reason why functionalist theories of the evolution of language can be true while functionalist theories of the acquisition of language can be false. From the very start of language acquisition, children obey grammatical constraints that afford them no immediate communicative advantage. To take just one example, 1- and 2-year-olds acquiring English obey a formal constraint on phrase structure configurations concerning the distinction between lexical categories and phrasal categories and as a result avoid placing determiners and adjectives before pronouns and proper names. They will use phrases like *big dog* to express the belief that a particular dog is big, but they will never use phrases like *big Fred* or *big he* to express the belief that a particular person is big (Bloom, 1990). Children respect this constraint despite the limits it puts on their expressive range.

Furthermore, despite unsupported suggestions to the contrary among developmental psychologists, many strides in language development afford the child no locally-discernible increment in communicative ability (Maratsos, 1983, 1989). When children say *breaked* and *comed,* they are using a system that is far simpler and more logical than the adult combination of a regular rule and 150 irregular memorized exceptions. Such errors do not reliably elicit parental corrections or other conversational feedback (Brown and Hanlon, 1970; Morgan and Travis, 1989). There is no deficit in comprehensibility; the meaning of *comed* is perfectly clear. In fact the child's system has greater expressive power that the adult's. When children say *hitted* and *cutted,* they are distinguishing between past and nonpast forms in a manner that is unavailable to adults, who must use *hit* and *cut* across the board. Why do children eventually abandon this simple, logical, expressive system? They must be programmed so that the mere requirement of conformity to the adult code, as subtle and arbitrary as it is, wins over other desiderata.

The requirement that a communicative code have an innate arbitrary foundation ("universal grammar," in the case of humans) may have analogues elsewhere in biology. Mayr (1982: 612) notes that

> Behavior that serves as communication, for instance courtship behavior, must be stereotyped in order not to be misunderstood. The genetic program controlling such behavior must be "closed," that is, it must be reasonably resistant to any changes during the individual life cycle. Other behaviors, for instance those that control the choice of food or habitat, must have a certain amount of flexibility in order to permit the incorporation of new experiences; such behaviors must be controlled by an "open" program.

In sum, the requirement for standardization of communication protocols dictates that it is better for nature to build a language acquisition device that picks up the code of the ambient language than one that invents a code that is useful from a child's eye view. Acquiring such a code from examples is no mean feat, and so many grammatical principles and constraints must be hardwired into the device. Thus even if the functions of grammatical devices play an important role in evolution, they may play no role in acquisition.

4. Arguments for Language Being a Spandrel

Given that the criteria for being an adaptation appear to be satisfied in the case of language, we can examine the strength of the competing explanations that language is a spandrel suggested by Gould, Chomsky, and Piattelli-Palmarini.

4.1. THE MIND AS A MULTIPURPOSE LEARNING DEVICE

The main motivation for Gould's specific suggestion that language is a spandrel is his frequently-stated position that the mind is a single general-purpose computer. For example, as part of a critique of a theory of the origin of language, Gould (1979: 386) writes:

> I don't doubt for a moment that the brain's enlargement in human evolution had an adaptive basis mediated by selection. But I would be more than mildly surprised if many of the specific things it now can do are the product of direct selection "for" that particular behavior. Once you build

a complex machine, it can perform so many unanticipated tasks. Build a computer "for" processing monthly checks at the plant, and it can also perform factor analyses on human skeletal measures, play Rogerian analyst, and whip anyone's ass (or at least tie them perpetually) in tic-tac-toe.

The analogy is somewhat misleading. It is just not true that you can take a computer that processes monthly checks and use it to play Rogerian analyst; someone has to reprogram it first. Language learning is not programming: parents provide their children with sentences of English, not rules of English. We suggest that natural selection was the programmer.

The analogy could be modified by imagining some machine equipped with a single program that can learn from examples to calculate monthly checks, perform factor analyses, and play Rogerian analyst, all without explicit programming. Such a device does not now exist in artificial intelligence and it is unlikely to exist in biological intelligence. There is no psychologically realistic multipurpose learning program that can acquire language as a special case, because the kinds of generalizations that must be made to acquire a grammar are at cross-purposes with those that are useful in acquiring other systems of knowledge from examples (Chomsky, 1982; Pinker, 1979, 1984; Wexler and Culicover, 1980). The gross facts about the dissociability of language and other learned cultural systems, listed in the first paragraph of this paper, also belie the suggestion that language is a spandrel of any general cognitive learning ability.

4.2. CONSTRAINTS ON POSSIBLE FORMS

The theory that the mind is an all-purpose learning device is of course anathema to Chomsky (and to Piattelli-Palmarini), making it a puzzle that they should find themselves in general agreement with Gould. Recently, Gould (1989) has described some common ground. Chomsky, he suggests, is in the Continental tradition of trying to explain evolution by structural laws constraining possible organic forms. For example, Chomsky writes:

> In studying the evolution of mind, we cannot guess to what extent there are physically possible alternatives to, say, transformational generative grammar, for an organism meeting certain other physical conditions characteristic of humans. Conceivably, there are none—or very few—in which case talk about evolution of the language capacity is beside the point. (1972: 97-98)
>
> These skills [e.g., learning a grammar] may well have arisen as a concomitant of structural properties of the brain that developed for other reasons. Suppose that there was selection for bigger brains, more cortical surface, hemispheric specialization for analytic processing, or many

other structural properties that can be imagined. The brain that evolved might well have all sorts of special properties that are not individually selected; there would be no miracle in this, but only the normal workings of evolution. We have no idea, at present, how physical laws apply when 10^{10} neurons are placed in an object the size of a basketball, under the special conditions that arose during human evolution. (1982: 321)

In this regard [the evolution of infinite digital systems], speculations about natural selection are no more plausible than many others; perhaps these are simply emergent physical properties of a brain that reaches a certain level of complexity under the specific conditions of human evolution. (1988b: 22 in ms.)

Although Chomsky does not literally argue for any specific evolutionary hypothesis, he repeatedly urges us to consider "physical laws" as possible alternatives to natural selection. But it is not easy to see exactly what we should be considering. It is certainly true that natural selection cannot explain all aspects of the evolution of language. But is there any reason to believe that there are as-yet undiscovered theorems of physics that can account for the intricate design of natural language? Of course human brains obey the laws of physics, and always did, but that does not mean that their specific structure can be explained by such laws.

More plausibly, we might look to constraints on the possible neural basis for language and its epigenetic growth. But neural tissue is wired up by developmental processes that act in similar ways all over the cortex and to a lesser degree across the animal kingdom (Dodd and Jessell, 1988; Harrelson and Goodman, 1988). In different organisms it has evolved the ability to perform the computations necessary for pollen-source communication, celestial navigation, Doppler-shift echolocation, stereopsis, controlled flight, dam-building, sound mimicry, and face recognition. The space of physically possible neural systems thus can't be all *that* small, as far as specific computational abilities are concerned. And it is most unlikely that laws acting at the level of substrate adhesion molecules and synaptic competition, when their effects are projected upward through many levels of scale and hierarchical organization, would automatically result in systems that accomplish interesting engineering tasks in a world of medium-sized objects.

Changes in brain quantity could lead to changes in brain quality. But mere largeness of brain is neither a necessary nor a sufficient condition for language, as Lenneberg's (1967) studies of nanencephaly and craniometric studies of individual variation have shown. Nor is there reason to think that if you simply pile more and more neurons into a circuit, or more and more circuits into a brain, that computationally interesting abilities would just emerge. It seems more likely that you would end up with a very big random pattern generator. Neural network modeling efforts have suggested that complex computational abilities require either extrinsically imposed design or numerous richly structured inputs during learning or both

(Pinker & Prince, 1988; Lachter & Bever, 1988), any of which would be inconsistent with Chomsky's suggestions.

Finally, there may be direct evidence against the speculation that language is a necessary physical consequence of how human brains can grow. Gopnik (1990a, b) describes a syndrome of developmental dysphasia whose sufferers lack control of morphological features such as number, gender, tense, and case. Otherwise they are intellectually normal. One 10-year-old boy earned the top grade in his mathematics class and is a respectable computer programmer. This shows that a human brain lacking components of grammar, perhaps even a brain with the capacity of discrete infinity, is physically and neurodevelopmentally possible.

In sum, there is no support for the hypothesis that language emerges from physical laws acting in unknown ways in a large brain. While there are no doubt aspects of the system that can only be explained by historical, developmental, or random processes, the most likely explanation for the complex structure of the language faculty is that it is a design imposed on neural circuitry as a response to evolutionary pressures.

5. The Process of Language Evolution

For universal grammar to have evolved by Darwinian natural selection, it is not enough that it be useful in some general sense. There must have been genetic variation among individuals in their grammatical competence. There must have been a series of steps leading from no language at all to language as we now find it, each step small enough to have been produced by a random mutation or recombination, and each intermediate grammar useful to its possessor. Every detail of grammatical competence that we wish to ascribe to selection must have conferred a reproductive advantage on its speakers, and this advantage must be large enough to have become fixed in the ancestral population. And there must be enough evolutionary time and genomic space separating our species from nonlinguistic primate ancestors.

There are no conclusive data on any of these issues. However this has not prevented various people from claiming that each of the necessary postulates is false! We argue that what we do know from the biology of language and evolution makes each of the postulates quite plausible.

5.1. GENETIC VARIATION

Lieberman (1984, 1989) claims that the Chomskyan universal grammar could not have evolved. He writes:

> The premises that underlie current "nativist" linguistic theory...are out of touch with modern biology. Ernst Mayr (1982), in his definitive

work, *The Growth of Biological Thought*, discusses these basic principles that must structure any biologically meaningful nativist theory.... [one of the principles is:] Essentialistic thinking (e.g., characterizing human linguistic ability in terms of a uniform hypothetical universal grammar) is inappropriate for describing the biological endowment of living organisms. (1989: 203-205)

A true nativist theory must accommodate genetic variation. A detailed genetically transmitted universal grammar that is identical for every human on the planet is outside the range of biological plausibility. (1989: 223)

This is part of Lieberman's argument that syntax is acquired by general-purpose learning abilities, not by a dedicated module or set of modules. But the passages quoted above contain a variety of misunderstandings and distortions. Chomskian linguistics is the antithesis of the kind of essentialism that Mayr decries. It treats such disembodied interindividual entities as "The English Language" as unreal epiphenomena. The only scientifically genuine entities are individual grammars situated in the heads of individual speakers (see Chomsky, 1986, for extended discussion). True, grammars for particular languages, and universal grammar, are often provisionally idealized as a single kind of system. But this is commonplace in systems-level physiology and anatomy; for example the structure of the human eye is always described as if all individuals shared it and individual variation and pathology are discussed as deviations from a norm. This is because natural selection, while feeding on variation, uses it up (Ridley, 1986; Sober, 1984). In adaptively complex structures in particular, the variation we see does not consist of qualitative differences in basic design, and this surely applies to complex mental structures as well (Tooby and Cosmides, 1989).

Also, contrary to what Lieberman implies, there does exist variation in grammatical ability. Within the range that we would call "normal" we all know some individuals who habitually use tangled syntax and others who speak with elegance, some who are linguistically creative and others who lean on clichés, some who are fastidious conformists and others who bend and stretch the language in various ways. At least some of this variation is probably related to the strength or accessibility of different grammatical subsystems, and at least some, we suspect, is genetic, the kind of thing that would be shared by identical twins reared apart. More specifically, Bever, Carrithers, Cowart, and Townsend (1989) have extensive experimental data showing that right-handers with a family history of left-handedness show less reliance on syntactic analysis and more reliance on lexical association than do people without such a genetic background.

Moreover, beyond the "normal" range there are documented geneticallytransmitted syndromes of grammatical deficits. Lenneberg (1967) notes that specific language disability is a dominant partially sex-linked trait with almost complete penetrance (see also Ludlow and Cooper, 1983, for a literature review). More strikingly, Gopnik (1990b) has found a familial selective deficit in the use of morphological features (gender, number, tense, etc.) that acts as if it is controlled by a dominant gene.

This does not mean that we should easily find cases of inherited subjacency deficiency or anaphor blindness. Pleiotropy—single gene changes that cause apparently unrelated phenotypic effects—is ubiquitous, so there is no reason to think that every aspect of grammar that has a genetic basis must be controlled by a single gene. Having a right hand has a genetic basis, but genetic deficits do not lead to babies being born with exactly one hand missing. Moreover, even if there was a pure lack of some grammatical device among some people, it may not be easily discovered without intensive analysis of the person's perceptions of carefully constructed linguistic examples. Different grammatical subsystems can generate superficially similar constructions, and a hypothetical victim of a deficit may compensate in ways that would be difficult to detect. Indeed cases of divergent underlying analyses of a single construction are frequent causes of historical change.

5.2. INTERMEDIATE STEPS

Some people have doubted that an evolutionary sequence of increasingly complex and specialized universal grammars is possible. The intermediate links, it has been suggested, would not have been viable communication systems. These arguments fall into three classes.

5.2.1. Nonshared Innovations

Geschwind (1980), among others, has wondered how a hypothetical "beneficial" grammatical mutation could really have benefited its possessor, given that none of the person's less evolved compatriots could have understood him or her. One possible answer is that any such mutation is likely to be shared by individuals who are geneticallyrelated. Since much communication is among kin, a linguistic mutant will be understood by some of his or her relatives and the resulting enhancements in information sharing will benefit each one of them relative to others who are not related.

But we think there is a more general answer. Comprehension abilities do not have to be in perfect synchrony with production abilities. Comprehension can use cognitive heuristics based on probable events to decode word sequences even in the absence of grammatical knowledge. Ungrammatical strings like *skid crash hospital* are quite understandable, and we find we can do a reasonably good job understanding Italian newspaper stories based on a few cognates and general expectancies. At the same time grammatical sophistication in such sources does not go unappreciated. We are unable to duplicate Shakespeare's complex early Modern English but we can appreciate the subtleties of his expressions. When some individuals are making important distinctions that can be decoded with cognitive effort, it could set up a pressure for the evolution of neural mechanisms that would make this decoding process become increasingly automatic, unconscious, and undistracted by irrelevant aspects of world knowledge. These are some of the hallmarks of an innate grammatical "module" (Fodor, 1983). The process whereby environmentally induced responses set up selection pressures for such responses to become innate, triggering conventional Darwinian evolution that superficially mimics a Lamarckian sequence, is sometimes known as the Baldwin Effect.

Not all linguistic innovations need begin with a genetic change in the linguistic abilities of speakers. Former Secretary of State Alexander Haig achieved notoriety with expressions such as *Let me caveat that* or *That statement has to be properly nuanced.* As listeners we cringe at the ungrammaticality but we have no trouble understanding him and would be hard-pressed to come up with a concise grammatical alternative. The double standard exemplified by Haigspeak is fairly common in speech (Pinker, 1989b). Most likely this was always true, and innovations driven by cognitive processes exploiting analogy, metaphor, iconicity, conscious folk etymology, and so on, if useful enough, could set up pressures for both speakers and hearers to grammaticize those innovations. Note as well that if a single mental database is used in production and comprehension (Bresnan and Kaplan, 1982), evolutionary changes in response to pressure on one performance would automatically transfer to the other.

5.2.2. Categorical Rules

Many linguistic rules are categorical, all-or-none operations on symbols (see, e.g., Pinker and Prince, 1988, 1989). How could such structures evolve in a gradual sequence? Bates et al. (1989), presumably echoing Gould's "5% of an eye," (1989) write:

> What protoform can we possibly envision that could have given birth to constraints on the extraction of noun phrases from an embedded clause? What could it conceivably mean for an organism to possess half a symbol, or three quarters of a rule? (p. 3) ... monadic symbols, absolute rules and modular systems must be acquired as a whole, on a yes-or-no basis—a process that cries out for a Creationist explanation. (p. 30)

However, two issues are being collapsed here. While one might justifiably argue that an entire system of grammar must evolve in a gradual continuous sequence, that does not mean that every aspect of every rule must evolve in a gradual continuous sequence. As mentioned, mutant fruit flies can have a full leg growing where an antenna should be, and the evolution of new taxa with different numbers of appendages from their ancestors is often attributed to such homeotic mutations. No single mutation or recombination could have led to an entire universal grammar, but it could have led a parent with an *n*-rule grammar to have an offspring with an *n* + 1 rule grammar, or a parent with an *m*-symbol rule to have an offspring with an *m* + 1 symbol rule. It could also lead to a parent with no grammatical rules at all and just rote associations to have an offspring with a single rule. Grammatical rules are symbol-manipulations whose skeletal form is shared by many other mental systems. Indeed, discrete symbol manipulations, free from graded application based on similarity to memorized cases, is highly useful in many domains of cognition, especially those involving socially shared information (Freyd, 1983; Pinker and Prince, 1989; Smolensky, 1988). If a genetic change caused generic copies of a nonlinguistic symbol-replacement operation to pop up within the neural system underlying communication, such protorules could be put to use as parts of encoding and decoding schemes, whereupon they could be subject to selective forces tailoring them to specific demands of language. Rozin (1976) and Shepard (1986) have argued that the evolution of intelligence was made possible by just such sequences.

5.2.3. *Perturbations of Formal Grammars*

Grammars are thought to be complex computational systems with many interacting rules and conditions. Chomsky (1981) has emphasized how grammars have a rich deductive structure in which a minor change to a single principle can have dramatic effects on the language as a whole as its effects cascade through grammatical derivations. This raises the question of how the entire system could be viable under the far more major perturbations that could be expected during evolutionary history. Does grammar degrade gracefully as we extrapolate backwards in time? Would a universal grammar with an altered or missing version of some component be good for anything, or would it result in nothing but blocked derivations, filtered constructions, and partial structures? Lieberman (1989: 200) claims that "The only model of human evolution that would be consistent with the current standard linguistic theory is a sudden saltation that furnished human beings with the neural bases for language." Similarly, Bates et al. (1989: 2-3) claim that "If the basic structural principles of language cannot be learned (bottom up) or derived (top down), there are only two possible explanations for their existence: either Universal Grammar was endowed to us directly by the Creator, or else our species has undergone a mutation of unprecedented magnitude, a cognitive equivalent of the Big Bang."

But such arguments are based on a confusion. While a grammar for an existing language cannot tolerate minor perturbations and still be a grammar for a language that a modern linguist would recognize, that does not mean that it cannot be a grammar at all. To put it crudely, there is no requirement that the languages of *Homo erectus* fall into the class of possible *Homo sapiens* languages. Furthermore language abilities consist not just of formal grammar but also of such nonlinguistic cognitive processes as analogy, rote memory, and Haigspeak. Chomsky (1981) refers to such processes as constituting the "periphery" of grammar, but a better metaphor may put them in the "interstices," where they would function as a kind of jerry-rigging that could allow formally incomplete grammars to be used in generating and comprehending sentences.

The assertion that a natural language grammar either functions as a whole or not at all is surprisingly common. But it has no more merit than similar claims about eyes, wings, and webs that frequently pop up in the anti-Darwinian literature (see Dawkins, 1986, for examples), and which occasionally trigger hasty leaps to claims about exaptation. Pidgins, contact languages, Basic English, and the language of children, immigrants, tourists, aphasics, telegrams, and headlines provide ample proof that there is a vast continuum of viable communicative systems displaying a continuous gradation of efficiency and expressive power (see Bickerton, 1986). This is exactly what the theory of natural selection requires.

Our suggestions about interactions between learning and innate structure in evolution are supported by an interesting simulation of the Baldwin effect by Hinton and Nowlan (1987). They consider the worst imaginable scenario for evolution by small steps: a neural network with 20 connections (which can be either excitatory or inhibitory) that conveys no fitness advantage unless all 20 are correctly set. So not only is it no good to have 5 percent of the network; it's no good to have 95 percent. In a population of organisms whose connections are determined by random mutations a fitter mutant arises at a rate of only about once every million (2^{20}) genetically distinct organisms, and its advantages are immediately lost if the organism reproduces sexually. But now consider an organism where the connections are either genetically fixed to one or the other value or are settable by learning, determined by random mutation with an average of 10 connections fixed. The organism tries out random settings for the modifiable connections until it hits upon the combination that is advantageous; this is recognizable to the organism and causes it to retain those settings. Having attained that state the organism enjoys a higher rate of reproduction; the sooner it attains it, the greater the benefit. In such a population there *is* an advantage to having less than 100 percent of the correct network. Among the organisms with, say, 10 innate connections, the one in every thousand (2^{10}) that has the right ones will have some probability of attaining the entire network; in a thousand learning trials, this probability is fairly high. For the offspring of that organism, there are increasing advantages to having more and more of the correct connections innately determined, because with more correct connections to begin with, it takes less time to learn the rest, and the chances of going through life without having learned them get smaller.

Hinton and Nowlan confirmed these intuitions in a computer simulation, demonstrating nicely that learning can guide evolution, as the argument in this section requires, by turning a spike in fitness space into a gradient. Moreover they made an interesting discovery. Though there is always a selection pressure to make learnable connections innate, this pressure diminishes sharply as most of the connections come to be innately set, because it becomes increasingly unlikely that learning will fail for the rest. This is consistent with the speculation that the multiplicity of human languages is in part a consequence of learning mechanisms existing prior to (or at least independent of) the mechanisms specifically dedicated to language. Such learning devices may have been the sections of the ladder that evolution had no need to kick away.

5.3. REPRODUCTIVE ADVANTAGES OF BETTER GRAMMARS

David Premack (1985: 281-282) writes:

> I challenge the reader to reconstruct the scenario that would confer selective fitness on recursiveness. Language evolved, it is conjectured, at a time when humans or protohumans were hunting mastodons.... Would it be a great advantage for one of our ancestors squatting alongside the embers, to be able to remark: "Beware of the short beast whose front hoof Bob cracked when, having forgotten his own spear back at camp, he got in a glancing blow with the dull spear he borrowed from Jack"?
>
> Human language is an embarrassment for evolutionary theory because it is vastly more powerful than one can account for in terms of selective fitness. A semantic language with simple mapping rules, of a kind one might suppose that the chimpanzee would have, appears to confer all the advantages one normally associates with discussions of mastodon hunting or the like. For discussions of that kind, syntactic classes, structure-dependent rules, recursion and the rest, are overly powerful devices, absurdly so.

Premack's rhetorical challenge captures a conviction that many people find compelling, perhaps even self-evident, and it is worth considering why. It is a good example of what Dawkins (1986) calls the Argument from Personal Incredulity. The argument draws on people's poor intuitive grasp of probabilistic processes, especially those that operate over the immensities of time available for evolution. The passage also gains intuitive force because of the widespread stereotype of prehistoric humans as grunting cave men whose main reproductive challenge was running away from tigers or hunting mastodons. The corollary would seem to be that only humans in modern industrial societies—and maybe only academics, it is sometimes implied—need to use sophisticated mental machinery. But compelling as these common-sense intuitions are, they must be resisted.

5.3.1. Effects of Small Selective Advantages

First one must be reminded of the fact that tiny selective advantages are sufficient for evolutionary change. According to Haldane's (1927) classic calculations, for example, a variant that produces on average 1 percent more offspring than its alternative allele would increase in frequency from 0.1 percent to 99.9 percent of the population in just over 4,000 generations. Even in long-lived humans this fits comfortably into the evolutionary timetable. (Needless to say fixations of different genes can go on in parallel.) Furthermore the phenotypic effects of a beneficial genetic change need not be observable in any single generation. Stebbins (1982) constructs a mathematical scenario in which a mouselike animal is subject to selection pressure for increased size. The pressure is so small that it cannot be measured by human observers, and the actual increase in size from one generation to the next is also so small that it cannot be measured against the noise of individual variation. Nonetheless this mouse would evolve to the size of an elephant in 12,000 generations, a slice of time that is geologically "instantaneous." Finally, very small advantages can also play a role in macroevolutionary successions among competing populations of similar organisms. Zubrow (1987) calculates that a 1 percent difference in mortality rates among geographically overlapping Neanderthal and modern populations could have led to the extinction of the former within 30 generations, or a single millennium.

5.3.2. *Grammatical Complexity and Technology*

It has often been pointed out that our species is characterized by two features—technology and social relations among nonkin—that have attained levels of complexity unprecedented in the animal kingdom. Toolmaking is the most widely advertised ability, but the knowledge underlying it is only a part of human technological competence. Modern hunter-gatherers, whose lifestyle is our best source of evidence for that of our ancestors, have a folk biology encompassing knowledge of the life cycles, ecology, and behavior of wild plants and animals "that is detailed and thorough enough to astonish and inform professional botanists and zoologists" (Konner, 1982: 5). This ability allows the modern !Kung San, for example, to enjoy a nutritionally complete diet with small amounts of effort in what appears to us to be a barren desert. Isaacs (1983) interprets fossil remains of home bases as evidence for a lifestyle depending heavily on acquired knowledge of the environment as far back as two million years ago in *Homo habilis*. An oft-noted special feature of humans is that such knowledge can accumulate across generations. Premack (1985) reviews evidence that pedagogy is a universal and species-specific human trait, and the usefulness of language in pedagogy is not something that can be reasonably doubted. As Brandon and Hornstein (1986) emphasize, presumably there is a large selective advantage conferred by being able to learn in a way that is essentially stimulus-free (Williams, 1966, made a similar point). Children can learn from a parent that a food is poisonous or a particular animal is dangerous; they do not have to observe or experience this by themselves.

With regard to adult-to-adult pedagogy, Konner (1982: 171) notes that the !Kung discuss "everything from the location of food sources to the behavior of predators to the movements of migratory game. Not only stories, but great stores of knowledge are exchanged around the fire among the !Kung and the dramatizations—perhaps best of all—bear knowledge critical to survival. A way of life that is difficult enough would, without such knowledge, become simply impossible."

Devices designed for communicating precise information about time, space, predicate-argument relations, restrictive modification, and modality are not wasted in such efforts. Recursion in particular is extraordinarily useful. Premack repeats a common misconception when he uses tortuous phrases as an exemplification of recursive syntax; without recursion you can't say *the man's hat* or *I think he left*. All you need for recursion is an ability to embed a phrase containing a noun phrase within another noun phrase or a clause within another clause, which falls out of pairs of rules as simple as NP → det N PP and PP → P NP. Given such a capacity one can now specify reference to an object to an arbitrarily fine level of precision. These abilities can make a big difference. For example, it makes a big difference whether a far-off region is reached by taking the trail that is in front of the large tree or the trail that the large tree is in front of. It makes a difference whether that region has animals that you can eat or animals that can eat you. It makes a difference whether it has fruit that is ripe or fruit that was ripe or fruit that will be ripe. It makes a difference whether you can get there if you walk for three days or whether you can get there and walk for three days.

5.3.3. Grammatical Complexity and Social Interactions

What is less generally appreciated is how important linguistically supported social interactions are to a hunter-gatherer way of life. Humans everywhere depend on cooperative efforts for survival. Isaac (1983) reviews evidence that a lifestyle depending on social interactions among nonkin was present in *Homo habilis* more than two million years ago. Language in particular would seem to be deeply woven into such interactions, in a manner that is not qualitatively different from that of our own "advanced" culture. Konner (1982) writes:

> War is unknown. Conflicts within the group are resolved by talking, sometimes half or all the night, for nights, weeks on end. After two years with the San, I came to think of the Pleistocene epoch of human history (the three million years during which we evolved) as one interminable marathon encounter group. When we slept in a grass hut in one of their villages, there were many nights when its flimsy walls leaked charged exchanges from the circle around the fire, frank expressions of feeling and contention beginning when the dusk fires were lit and running on until the dawn. (p. 7)
>
> If what lawyers and judges do is work, then when the !Kung sit up all night at a meeting discussing a hotly contested divorce, that is also work. If what psychotherapists and ministers do is work, then when a !Kung man or woman spends hours in an enervating trance trying to cure people, that is also work. (p. 371)

Reliance on such exchanges puts a premium on the ability to convey socially-relevant abstract information such as time, possession, beliefs, desires, tendencies, obligations, truth, probability, hypotheticals, and counterfactuals. Once again, recursion is far from being an "overly powerful device." The capacity to embed propositions within other propositions, as in [$_S$ *He thinks that* S] or [$_S$ *She said that* [$_S$ *he thinks that* S]], is essential to the expression of beliefs about the intentional states of others.

Furthermore, in a group of communicators competing for attention and sympathies there is a premium on the ability to engage, interest, and persuade listeners. This in turn encourages the development of discourse and rhetorical skills and the pragmatically relevant grammatical devices that support them. Symons' (1979) observation that tribal chiefs are often both gifted orators and highly polygynous is a splendid prod to any imagination that cannot conceive of how linguistic skills could make a Darwinian difference.

5.3.4. *Social Use of Language and Evolutionary Acceleration*
The social value of complex language probably played a profound role in human evolution that is best appreciated by examining the dynamics of cooperative interactions among individuals. As mentioned, humans, probably early on, fell into a lifestyle that depended on extended cooperation for food, safety, nurturance, and reproductive opportunities. This lifestyle presents extraordinary opportunities for evolutionary gains and losses. On the one hand it benefits all participants by surmounting prisoners' dilemmas. On the other hand it is vulnerable to invasion by cheaters who reap the benefits without paying the costs (Axelrod and Hamilton, 1981; Cosmides, 1989; Hamilton, 1964; Maynard Smith, 1974; Trivers, 1971). The minimum cognitive apparatus needed to sustain this lifestyle is memory for individuals and the ability to enforce social contracts of the form "If you take a benefit then you must pay a cost" (Cosmides, 1989). This alone puts a demand on the linguistic expression of rather subtle semantic distinctions. It makes a difference whether you understand me as saying that if you give me some of your fruit I will share meat that I will get, or that you should give me some fruit because I shared meat that I got, or that if you don't give me some fruit I will take back the meat that I got.

But this is only a beginning. Cooperation opens the door to advances in the ability of cheaters to fool people into believing that they have paid a cost or that they have not taken a benefit. This in turn puts pressure on the ability to detect subtle signs of such cheating, which puts pressure on the ability to cheat in less detectable ways, and so on. It has been noted that this sets the stage for a cognitive "arms race" (e.g., Cosmides and Tooby, 1989; Dawkins, 1976; Tooby and DeVore, 1987; Trivers, 1971). Elsewhere in evolution such competitive feedback loops, such as in the struggle between cheetahs and gazelles, have led to the rapid evolution of spectacular structures and abilities (Dawkins, 1982). The unusually rapid enlargement of the human brain, especially the frontal lobes, has been attributed to such an arms race (Alexander, 1987; Rose, 1980). After all, it doesn't take all that much brain power to master the ins and outs of a rock or to get the better of a berry. But interacting with an organism of approximately equal mental abilities whose motives are at times outright malevolent makes formidable and ever-escalating demands on cognition. This competition is not reserved for obvious adversaries. Partial conflicts of reproductive interest between male and female, sibling and sibling, and parent and offspring are inherent to the human condition (Symons, 1979; Tooby and DeVore, 1987; Trivers, 1974).

It should not take much imagination to appreciate the role of language in a cognitive arms race. In all cultures human interactions are mediated by attempts at persuasion and argument. How a choice is framed plays a huge role in determining which alternative people choose (Tversky and Kahneman, 1981). The ability to frame an offer so that it appears to present maximal benefit and minimum cost to the buyer, and the ability to see through such attempts and to formulate persuasive counterproposals, would have been a skill of inestimable value in primitive negotiations, as it is today. So is the ability to learn of other people's desires and obligations through gossip, an apparently universal human vice (Cosmides and Tooby, 1989; Symons, 1979).

In sum, primitive humans lived in a world in which language was woven into the intrigues of politics, economics, technology, family, sex, and friendship which played key roles in individual reproductive success. They could no more live with a Me-Tarzan-you-Jane level of grammar than we could.

5.4. PHYLETIC CONTINUITY

Bates et al. (1989), Greenfield (1988), Lieberman (1976, 1984) argue that if language evolved in humans by natural selection, it must have antecedents in closely-related species such as chimpanzees, which share 99 percent of their genetic material with us and which may have diverged from a common ancestor as recently as 5-7 million years ago (King and Wilson, 1975; Miyamoto, Slightom, and Goodman, 1987). Similarly, since no biological ability can evolve out of nothing, they claim, we should find evidence of nonlinguistic abilities in humans that are continuous with grammar. Lieberman claims that motor programs are preadaptations for syntactic rules, while Bates (1976) and Greenfield (Greenfield and Smith, 1976) suggest that communicative gestures flow into linguistic naming. As Bates et al. (1989: 8) put it, "...we have to abandon any strong version of the discontinuity claim that has characterized generative grammar for thirty years. We have to find some way to ground symbols and syntax in the mental material that we share with other species."

The specific empirical claims have been disputed. Seidenberg and Petitto (Seidenberg, 1986; Seidenberg and Petitto, 1979, 1987) have reviewed the evidence of the signing abilities of apes and concluded that they show no significant resemblance to human language or to the process of acquiring it. In a study of the acquisition of sign language in deaf children, Petitto (1987) argues that nonlinguistic gestures and true linguistic names, even when both share the manual-visual channel, are completely dissociable. These conclusions could be fodder for the claim that natural language represents a discontinuity from other primate abilities and so could not have evolved by natural selection.

We find the Seidenberg and Petitto demonstrations convincing, but our argument is not based on whether they are true. Rather we completely disagree with the premise (not theirs) that the debate over ape signing should be treated as a referendum on whether human language evolved by natural selection. Of course human language, like other complex adaptations, could not have evolved overnight. But then there is no law of biology that says that scientists are blessed with the good fortune of being able to find evolutionary antecedents to any modern structure in some other living species. The first recognizably distinct mental system that constituted an antecedent to modern human language may have appeared in a species that diverged from the chimp-human common ancestor, such as *Australopithecus afarensis* or any of the subsequent hominid groups that led to our species. Moreover chimpanzees themselves are not generalized common ancestors but presumably have done some evolving of their own since the split. We must be prepared for the possible bad news that there just aren't any living creatures with homologues of human language, and let the chimp signing debate come down as it will.

As far as we know this would still leave plenty of time for language to have evolved: 3.5–5 million years, if early Australopithecines were the first talkers, or, as an absolute minimum, several hundred thousand years (Stringer and Andrews, 1988), in the unlikely event that early *Homo sapiens* was the first. (For what it's worth, Broca's area is said to be visible in cranial endocasts of two million year-old fossil hominids; Falk, 1983; Tobias, 1981.) There is also no justification in trying to squeeze conclusions out of the genetic data. On the order of forty million base pairs differ between chimpanzees and humans, and we see no reason to doubt that universal grammar would fit into these 10 megabytes with lots of room left over, especially if provisions for the elementary operations of a symbol-manipulation architecture are specified in the remaining 99 percent of the genome (see Seidenberg, 1986, for discussion).

In fact there is even more scope for design differences than the gross amount of nonshared genetic material suggests. The 1 percent difference between chimps and humans represents the fraction of base pairs that are different. But genes are long stretches of base pairs and if even one pair is different, the entire functioning product of that gene could be different. Just as replacing one bit in every byte leads to text that is 100 percent different, not 12.5 percent different, it is possible for the differing base pairs to be apportioned so that 100 percent of the genes of humans and chimps are different in function. Though this extreme possibility is, of course, unlikely, it warns us not to draw any conclusions about phenotypic similarity from degree of genomic overlap.[44]

As for continuity between language and nonlinguistic neural mechanisms, we find it ironic that arguments that are touted as being "biological" do not take even the most elementary steps to distinguish between analogy and homology. Lieberman's claim that syntactic rules must be retooled motor programs, a putative case of pre-adaptation, is a good example. It may be right, but there is no reason to believe it. Lieberman's evidence is only that motor programs are hierarchically organized and serially ordered, and so is syntax. But hierarchical organization characterizes many neural systems, perhaps any system, living or nonliving, that we would want to call complex (Simon, 1969). And an organism that lives in real time is going to need a variety of perceptual, motor, and central mechanisms that keep track of serial order. Hierarchy and seriality are so useful that for all we know they may have evolved many times in neural systems (Bickerton, 1984, 1986, also makes this point). To distinguish true homology from mere analogy it is necessary to find some unique derived nonadaptive character shared by the relevant systems, for example, some quirk of grammar that can be seen in another system. Not only has no such shared character been shown, but the dissimilarities between syntax and motor control are rather striking. Motor control is a game of inches, so its control programs must have open continuous parameters for time and space at every level of organization. Syntax has no such analogue parameters. A far better case could be made that grammar exploited mechanisms originally used for the conceptualization of topology and antagonistic forces (Jackendoff, 1983; Pinker, 1989b; Talmy, 1983, 1988), but that is another story.

6. Conclusion

As we warned, the thrust of this paper has been entirely conventional. All we have argued is that human language, like other specialized biological systems, evolved by natural selection. Our conclusion is based on two facts that we would think would be entirely uncontroversial: language shows signs of complex design for the communication of propositional structures, and the only explanation for the origin of organs with complex design is the process of natural selection. Although distinguished scientists from a wide variety of fields and ideologies have tried to cast doubt on an orthodox Darwinian account of the evolution of a biological specialization for grammar, upon close examination none of the arguments is compelling.

But we hope we have done more than try and set the record straight. Skepticism about the possibility of saying anything of scientific value about language evolution has a long history, beginning in the prohibition against discussing the topic by the Société de Linguistique de Paris in 1866 and culminating in the encyclopedic volume edited by Harnad, Steklis, and Lancaster (1976) that pitted a few daring speculators against an army of doubters. A suspicious attitude is not entirely unwarranted when one reads about The Age of Modifiers, *Pithecanthropus alalus* ("Ape-man without speech"), and the Heave-ho theory. But such skepticism should not lead to equally unsupported assertions about the necessity of spandrels and saltations.

A major problem among even the more responsible attempts to speculate about the origins of language has been that they ignore the wealth of specific knowledge about the structure of grammar discovered during the past 30 years. As a result language competence has been equated with cognitive development, leading to confusions between the evolution of language and the evolution of thought, or has been expediently equated with activities that leave tangible remnants, such as tool manufacture, art, and conquest.

We think there is a wealth of respectable new scientific information relevant to the evolution of language that has never been properly synthesized. The computational theory of mind, generative grammar, articulatory and acoustic phonetics, developmental psycholinguistics, and the study of dynamics of diachronic change could profitably be combined with recent molecular, archeological, and comparative neuroanatomical discoveries and with strategic modeling of evolution using insights from evolutionary theory and anthropology (see, e.g., Bickerton, 1981; Brandon and Hornstein, 1986; Barkow, Cosmides, and Tooby, 1992; Hurford, 1989a, 1989b; Tooby & DeVore, 1987; Hinton and Nowlan, 1987). It is certain there many questions about the evolution of language that we will never answer. But we are optimistic that there are insights to be gained, if only the problems are properly posed.

Acknowledgements

This paper has been greatly influenced by discussions with Leda Cosmides and John Tooby. We also thank Ned Block, Susan Carey, Noam Chomsky, Leda Cosmides, Robert Freidin, Jane Grimshaw, James Hurford, Massimo Piattelli-Palmarini, Alan Prince, Jerry Samet, Donald Symons, John Tooby, and several BBS reviewers for their helpful comments on earlier drafts. Needless to say all deficiencies and errors are ours. Preparation of this paper was supported by NIH Grant HD 18381; the second author was supported by a Surdna Predoctoral Fellowship.

Notes

1. For example, he says that "Language must surely confer enormous selective advantages" (Chomsky, 1980: 239; see also Chomsky, 1975:252), and argues that,

   > ...suppose that someone proposes a principle which says: The form of a language is such-and-such because having that form permits a function to be fulfilled—a proposal of this sort would be appropriate at the level of evolution (of the species, or of language), not at the level of acquisition of language by an individual. (Chomsky, 1977: 86-87)

2. Interestingly, Dennett (1983) argues that Gould and Lewontin's critique is remarkably similar in logic to critiques of another large-scale theory, the representational theory of mind in cognitive science, by behaviorists. Dennett sees common flaws in the critiques: both fail to account for cases of adaptive complexity that are not direct consequences of any law of physics, and both apply the criterion of falsifiability in too literal-minded a way.

3. Note also that historical change in languages occurs very rapidly by biological standards. Wang (1976) points out, for example, that one cycle of the process whereby a language alternates between reliance on word order and reliance on affixation typically takes a thousand years. A hominid population evolving language could be exposed to the full range of linguistic diversity during a single tick of the evolutionary clock, even if no single generation was faced with all humanly possible structures.

4. We thank John Tooby for pointing this out to us.

References

Alexander, R. (1987) Paper presented at the conference "The origin and dispersal of modern humans," Corpus Christi College, Cambridge, England, March 22–26. *Reported in Science* 236: 668–669.

Ayala, F. (1983) Microevolution and macroevolution. In: *Evolution from molecules to man*, ed., D. S. Bendall. Cambridge University Press.

Axelrod, R. & Hamilton, W. D. (1981) The evolution of cooperation. *Science 211*:1390–1396.

Barkow, J., Cosmides, L., & Tooby, J. ed. (1992) *The adapted mind*. Oxford University Press.

Bates, E. (1976) *Language and context: studies in the acquisition of pragmatics*. Academic Press.

Bates, E., Thal, D, & Marchman, V. (1989) Symbols and syntax: A Darwinian approach to language development. In: *The Biological foundations of language development*, eds. N. Krasnegor, D. Rumbaugh, M. Studdert-Kennedy, & R. Schiefelbusch. Oxford University Press.

Bendall, D. S., ed. (1983) *Evolution from molecules to men*. Cambridge University Press.

Berwick, R. C. & Weinberg, A. S. (1984) *The grammatical basis of linguistic performance*. MIT Press.

Berwick, R. C. & Wexler, K. (1987). Parsing efficiency, binding, c-command, and learnability. In: *Studies in the acquisition of anaphora*, ed. B. Lust. Reidel.

Bever, T. G. (1970) The cognitive basis for linguistic structures. In: *Cognition and the development of language*, ed. J. R. Hayes. Wiley.

Bever, T.G., Carrithers, C., Cowart, W., & Townsend, D.J. (1989). Language processing and familial handedness. In A. Galaburda (Ed.), *From neurons to reading*. Cambridge, MA: MIT Press.

Bickerton, D. (1981) *The roots of language*. Karoma.

Bickerton, D. (1984) The language bioprogram hypothesis. *Behavioral and Brain Sciences* 7:173–212.

Bickerton, D. (1986) More than nature needs? A reply to Premack. *Cognition* 23:73–79.

Bloom, P. (1989). Nominals in child language. Unpublished manuscript, Department of Brain and Cognitive Sciences, MIT.

Bloom, P. (1990) Syntactic distinctions in child language. *Journal of Child Language, 17*, 343–355.

Bolinger, D. (1980) *Language: the loaded weapon*. New York: Longman.

Brandon, R. N. & Hornstein, N. (1986) From icons to symbols: Some speculations on the origin of language. *Biology and Philosophy 1*:169–189.

Bresnan, J. (1982) Control and complementation. In: *The mental representation of grammatical relations*, ed., J. Bresnan. MIT Press.

Bresnan, J. & Kaplan, R. M. (1982) Grammars as mental representations of language. In: *The mental representation of grammatical relations*, ed., J. Bresnan. MIT Press.

Brown, R. & Hanlon, C. (1970) Derivational complexity and order of acquisition in child speech. In: *Cognition and the development of language*, ed., J. R. Hayes. Wiley.

Bybee, J. (1985) *Morphology: A study of the relation between meaning and form*. Benjamins.

Chomsky, N. (1965) *Aspects of the theory of syntax*. MIT Press.

Chomsky, N. (1972) Language and mind. Harcourt, Brace, and World. (Extended edition).

Chomsky, N. (1975) *Reflections on language*. Pantheon.

Chomsky, N. (1980) *Rules and representations*. Columbia University Press.

Chomsky, N. (1981) *Lectures on government and binding*. Foris.

Chomsky, N. (1982a) *Noam Chomsky on the generative enterprise: A discussion with Riny Junybregts and Henk van Riemsdijk*. Foris.

Chomsky, N. (1982b) Discussion of Putnam's comments. In: *Language and learning: The debate between Jean Piaget and Noam Chomsky*, ed. M. Piattelli-Palmarini. Harvard University Press.

Chomsky, N. (1986) *Knowledge of language: Its nature, origin, and use*. Praeger.

Chomsky, N. (1988a) *Language and problems of knowledge: The Managua lectures*. MIT Press.

Chomsky, N. (1988b) Prospects for the study of language and mind. Paper presented at the conference "Linguistics and cognitive science: Problems and mysteries," University of Tel Aviv, April.

Chomsky, N. & Lasnik, H. (1977) Filters and control. *Linguistic Inquiry* 8:425–504.

Clutton-Brock, T. H. (1983) Selection in relation to sex. In: *Evolution from molecules to men*, ed. D. S. Bendall. Cambridge University Press.

Comrie, B. (1981) *Language universals and linguistic typology: Syntax and morphology*. Basil Blackwell.

Cosmides, L. (1989) The logic of social exchange: Has natural selection shaped how humans reason? Studies with the Wason selection task. *Cognition* 31:187–276.

Cosmides, L. & Tooby, J. (1989) Evolutionary psychology and the generation of culture, Part II. Case study: A computational theory of social exchange. *Ethology and Sociobiology* 10: 51–97.

Cummins, R. (1984) Functional analysis. In: *Conceptual issues in evolutionary biology*, ed., E. Sober. MIT Press.

Darwin, C. (1859) *On the origin of species*. Reprinted by Harvard University Press, 1964.

Dawkins, R. (1976) *The selfish gene*. Oxford University Press.

Dawkins, R. (1982) *The extended phenotype: The gene as the unit of selection*. Freeman.

Dawkins, R. (1983) Universal Darwinism. In: *Evolution from molecules to man*, ed., D. S. Bendall. Cambridge University Press.

Dawkins, R. (1986) *The blind watchmaker: Why the evidence of evolution reveals a universe without design*. Norton.

Dennett, D. C. (1983) Intentional systems in cognitive ethology: The 'Panglossian Paradigm' defended. *Behavioral and Brain Sciences* 6:343–390.

Dodd, J. & Jessell, T. M. (1988) Axon guidance and the patterning of neuronal projections in vertebrates. *Science* 242:692–699.

Eldredge N., & Gould, S. J. (1972). Punctuated equilibria: An alternative to phyletic gradualism. In: *Models in Paleobiology*, ed., T. J. M. Schopf. Freeman.

Ekman, P., & Friesen, W. V. (1975) *Unmasking the face*. Prentice Hall.

Etcoff, N. L. (1986) The neuropsychology of emotional expression. In: *Advances in Clinical Neuropsychology*, Volume 3, eds., G. Goldstein & R. E. Tarter. Plenum.

Falk, D. (1983) Cerebral cortices of East African early hominids. *Science* 221: 1072–1074.

Fisher, R. A. (1930) *The genetical theory of natural selection*. Clarendon Press.

Fodor, J. (1975) *The language of thought*. Thomas Crowell.

Fodor, J. (1983) *The modularity of mind*. MIT Press.

Fodor, J. (1987) *Psychosemantics*. MIT Press.

Frazier, L., Clifton, C., & Randall, J. (1983) Filling gaps: decision principles and structure in sentence comprehension. *Cognition* 13: 187–222.

Freidin, R. (1978) Cyclicity and the theory of grammar. *Linguistic Inquiry* 9: 519–549.

Freidin, R. & Quicoli, C. (1989) Zero-stimulation for parameter setting. *Behavioral and Brain Sciences* 12: 338–339.

Freyd, J. J. (1983) Shareability: The social psychology of epistemology. *Cognitive Science* 7:191–210.

Gazdar, G., Klein, E., Pullum, G, & Sag, I. A. (1985) *Generalized phrase structure syntax*. Harvard University Press.

Geschwind, N. (1980) Some comments on the neurology of language. In: *Biological studies of mental processes*, ed., D. Caplan. MIT Press.

Gopnik, M. (1990a) A featureless grammar in a dysphasic child. *Language Acquisition*.

Gopnik, M. (1990b) Genetic dysphasia and feature blindness. *Nature*, accepted pending revisions.

Gould, S. J. (1977a) Darwin's untimely burial. In: *Ever since Darwin: Reflections on natural history*, ed., S. J. Gould. Norton.

Gould, S. J. (1977b) Problems of perfection, or how can a clam mount a fish on its rear end. In: *Ever since Darwin: Reflections on natural history*, ed., S. J. Gould. Norton.

Gould, S. J. (1979) Panselectionist pitfalls in Parker & Gibson's model of the evolution of intelligence. *The Behavioral and Brain Sciences* 2:385–386.

Gould, S. J. (1980) Is a new and general theory of evolution emerging? *Paleobiology* 6:119–130.

Gould, S. J. (1981) Return of the hopeful monster. In: *The Panda's Thumb: More reflections on natural history*, ed. S. J. Gould. Norton.

Gould, S. J. (1987a) The limits of adaptation: Is language a spandrel of the human brain? Paper presented to the Cognitive Science Seminar, Center for Cognitive Science, MIT, October.

Gould, S. J. (1987b) Integrity and Mr. Rifkin. In: *An urchin in the storm: Essays about books and ideas*, ed., S. J. Gould. Norton.

Gould, S. J. (1989) Evolutionary considerations. Paper presented to the McDonnell Foundation conference "Selection vs. Instruction," Venice, May 22-27, 1989.

Gould, S. J., & Eldredge, N. (1977) Punctuated equilibria: The tempo and mode of evolution reconsidered. *Paleobiology* 3:115–151.

Gould, S. J., & Lewontin, R. C. (1979) The spandrels of San Marco and the Panglossian program: A critique of the adaptationist programme. *Proceedings of the Royal Society of London* 205:281–288,

Gould, S. J. & Piattelli-Palmarini, M. (1987) *Evolution and cognition*. Course taught at Harvard University.

Gould, S. J., & Vrba, E. S. (1982) Exaptation—a missing term in the science of form. *Paleobiology* 8:4–15.

Greenfield, P. (1987) *Departmental colloquium, Department of Psychology*, Harvard University.

Greenfield, P. & Smith, J. (1976) *The structure of communication in early language development*. Academic Press.

Greenberg, J. H., ed. (1966) *Universals of language*. MIT Press.

Greenberg, J. H., Ferguson, C. A. & Moravcsik, E. A., eds. (1978) *Universals of human language 4 vols*. Stanford University Press.

Haldane, J. B. S. (1927). A mathematical theory of natural and artificial selection. Part V. Selection and mutation. *Proceedings of the Cambridge Philosophical Society* 23:838–844.

Hamilton, W. D. (1964) The genetical evolution of social behavior, I & II. *Journal of Theoretical Biology* 104:451–471.

Harnad, S. R., Steklis, H. S., & Lancaster, J., eds. (1976) *Origin and evolution of language and speech*. Annals of the New York Academy of Sciences 280.

Harrelson, A. L. and Goodman, C. S. (1988) Growth cone guidance in insects: Fasciclin II is a member of the immunoglobulin superfamily. *Science* 242:700–708.

Hawkins, J. ed. (1988). *Explaining language universals*. Basil Blackwell.

Hawkins, J. & Cutler, A. (1988) Psycholinguistic factors in morphological asymmetry. In: *Explaining language universals*, ed. J. Hawkins. Basil Blackwell.

Hinton, G. E. & Nowlan, S. J. (1987). How learning can guide evolution. *Complex systems*, 1:495–502.

Hurford, J. R. (1989a) Biological evolution of the Saussurean sign as a component of the language acquisition device. *Lingua* 77:187–222.

Hurford, J. R. (1989b) The evolution of the critical period for language acquisition. Unpublished manuscript. Linguistics Department, University of Edinburgh.

Isaac, F. J. (1983) Aspects of human evolution. In: *Evolution from molecules to men*, ed., D. S. Bendall. Cambridge University Press.

Jackendoff, R. (1977) *X-bar syntax: A study of phrase structure*. MIT Press.

Jackendoff, R. (1983) *Semantics and cognition*. MIT Press.

Jackendoff, R. (1990) *Semantic structures*. MIT Press.

Jacob, F. (1977) Evolution and tinkering. *Science* 196:1161–1166.

Kaplan, & Bresnan, J. (1982) Lexical Functional Grammar: A formal system for grammatical representations. In: *The mental representation of grammatical relations*, ed., J. Bresnan. MIT Press.

Keenan, E. O. (1976) Towards a universal definition of "subject." In: *Subject and Topic*, ed., C. Li. Academic Press.

Keil, F. C. (1979). *Semantic and conceptual development*. Harvard University Press.

King, M. & Wilson, A. (1975) Evolution at two levels in humans and chimpanzees. *Science 188*:107–116.

Kingsolver, J. G., & Koehl, M. A. R. (1985) Aerodynamics, thermoregulation, and the evolution of insect wings: Differential scaling and evolutionary change. *Evolution, 39*:488–504.

Kiparsky, P. (1976). Historical linguistics and the origin of language. In: *Origin and evolution of language and speech*, ed., Harnad, S. R., Steklis, H. S., & Lancaster, J. Annals of the New York Academy of Sciences 280.

Kitcher, P. (1985) *Vaulting ambition: Sociobiology and the quest for human nature*. MIT Press.

Konner, M. (1982) *The tangled wing: Biological constraints on the human spirit*. Harper.

Kuno, S. (1973) Constraints on internal clauses and sentential subjects. *Linguistic Inquiry 4*:363–385.

Kuno, S. (1974) The position of relative clauses and conjunctions. *Linguistic Inquiry 5*:117–136.

Lachter, J. & Bever, T. G. (1988) The relation between linguistic structure and associative theories of language learning—a constructive critique of some connectionist learning models. *Cognition 28*: 195–247.

Lenneberg, E. H. (1964) A biological perspective on language. In: *New directions in the study of language*, ed. E. H. Lenneberg. MIT Press.

Lenneberg, E. H. (1967) *Biological foundations of language*. Wiley.

Lewontin, R. (1978) Adaptation. *Scientific American 239*:157–169.

Liberman, A. M., Cooper, F. S., Shankweiler, D. P., & Studdert-Kennedy, M. (1967). Perception of the speech code. *Psychological Review 74*:431–461.

Liberman, A. M. & Mattingly, I. G. (1989) A specialization for speech perception. *Science 243*:489–496.

Lieberman, P. (1976). Interactive models for evolution: neural mechanisms, anatomy, and behavior. In: *Origin and evolution of language and speech*, ed., Harnad, S. R., Steklis, H. S., & Lancaster, J. Annals of the New York Academy of Sciences 280.

Lieberman, P. (1984) *The biology and evolution of language*. Harvard University Press.

Lieberman, P. (1989) Some biological constraints on universal grammar and learnability. In: *The teachability of language*, eds. M. Rice & R. L. Schiefelbusch. Paul H. Brookes.

Ludlow, C. L & Cooper, J. A. (1983) Genetic aspects of speech and language disorders: Current status and future directions. In: *Genetic aspects of speech and language disorders*, ed. Ludlow, C. L & Cooper, J. A. Academic Press.

Miyamoto, M. M., Slightom, J. L., & Goodman, M. (1987) Phylogenetic relations of humans and African apes from DNA sequences in the psi eta-globin region. *Science 238*:369–373.

Maratsos, M. (1983) Some current issues in the study of the acquisition of grammar. In: *Carmichael's Manual of Child Psychology*, 4th ed., ed. P. Mussen. Wiley.

Maratsos, M. (1989) Innateness and plasticity in language acquisition. In: *The teachability of language*, eds. M. Rice & R. L. Schiefelbusch. Paul H. Brookes.

Maynard Smith, J. (1974) The theory of games and the evolution of animal conflicts. *Journal of Theoretical Biology 47*:209–221.

Maynard Smith, J. (1984) Optimization theory in evolution. In: *Conceptual issues in evolutionary biology*, ed. E. Sober. MIT Press.

Mayr, E. (1982) *The growth of biological thought*. Harvard University Press.

Mayr, E. (1983). How to carry out the adaptationist program? *The American Naturalist, 121*:324–334.

Mehler, J. (1985). Review of P. Lieberman's "The Biology and Evolution of Language." *Journal of the Acoustic Society of America 80*:1558–1560.

Morgan, J. L. (1986) *From simple input to complex grammar*. Cambridge, MA: MIT Press.

Morgan, J. & Travis (1989). Limits on negative information in language input. *Journal of Child Language, 16, 531–552.*.

Newport, E. L. & Meier, R. P. (1985) The acquisition of American sign language. In *The cross-linguistic study of language acquisition*. Volume 1: The data, ed., D. I. Slobin. Erlbaum.

Petitto, L. (1987) On the autonomy of language and gesture: Evidence from the acquisition of personal pronouns in American Sign Language. *Cognition* 27:1–52.

Piattelli-Palmarini, M. (1989) Evolution, selection, and cognition: From "learning" to parameter setting in biology and the study of language, *Cognition* 31:1–44.

Pinker, S. (1979) Formal models of language learning. *Cognition* 7:217–283.

Pinker, S. (1984). *Language learnability and language development*. Harvard University Press.

Pinker, S. (1989a). Language acquisition. In: *Foundations of cognitive science*, ed. M. I. Posner. MIT Press.

Pinker, S. (1989b). *Learnability and cognition: The acquisition of argument structure*. MIT Press.

Pinker, S. & Prince, A. (1988) On language and connectionism: Analysis of a Parallel Distributed Processing model of language acquisition. *Cognition* 28:73–193.

Pinker, S. & Prince, A. (1989) *The nature of human concepts: Evidence from an unusual source.* Unpublished manuscript, MIT.

Premack, D. (1985) 'Gavagai!' or the future history of the animal language controversy. *Cognition* 19:207–296.

Premack, D. (1986) Pangloss to Cyrano de Bergerac: "nonsense, it's perfect!" *Cognition* 23:81–88.

Reichenbach, H. (1947). *Elements of symbolic logic*. Macmillan.

Ridley, M. (1986). *The problems of evolution*. Oxford University Press.

Rose, M. (1980) The mental arms race amplifier. *Human Ecology* 8:285–293.

Rozin, P. (1976) The evolution of intelligence and access to the cognitive unconscious. In: *Progress in psychobiology and physiological psychology*, eds., L. Sprague & A. N. Epstein. Academic Press.

Samuels, M. L. (1972) *Linguistic evolution*. Cambridge University Press.

Saussure, F. de, (1959) *Course in general linguistics*. McGraw-Hill.

Seidenberg, M. S. (1986) Evidence from the great apes concerning the biological bases of language. In: *Language learning and concept acquisition: Foundational issues*, eds. W. Demopoulos & A. Marras. Ablex.

Seidenberg, M. S., & Petitto, L. A. (1979) Signing behavior in apes: A critical review. *Cognition* 7:177–215.

Seidenberg, M. S., & Petitto, L. A. (1987) Communication, symbolic communication, and language: Comment on Savage-Rumbaugh, McDonald, Sevcik, Hopkins, and Rupert (1986), *Journal of Experimental Psychology: General* 116:279–287.

Shepard, R. (1986) Evolution of a mesh between principles of the mind and regularities of the world. In: *The latest on the best: Essays on optimization and evolution*, ed. J. Dupré. MIT Press.

Shopen, T., ed. (1985) *Language typology and syntactic description*. 3 vols. Cambridge University Press.

Simon, H. A. (1969) The architecture of complexity. In: *The sciences of the artificial*, H. Simon. MIT Press.

Skinner, B. F. (1957) *Verbal Behavior*. Appleton.

Slobin, D. (1977) Language change in childhood and in history. In: *Language learning and thought*, ed. J. Macnamara. Academic Press.

Sober, E. (1984) *The nature of selection*. MIT Press.

Smolensky, P. (1988) The proper treatment of connectionism. *Behavioral and Brain Sciences* 11:1–74.

Stebbins, G. L. (1982) *Darwin to DNA, molecules to humanity*. Freeman.

Stebbins, G. L., & Ayala, F. J. (1981) Is a new evolutionary synthesis necessary? *Science* 213:967–971.

Steele, S., Akmajian, A., Demers, R., Jelinek, E., Kitagawa, C., Oehrle, R., and Wasow, T. (1981) *An encyclopedia of AUX: A study of cross-linguistic equivalence*. MIT Press.

Stringer, C. B. & Andrews, P. (1988) Genetic and fossil evidence for the origin of modern humans. *Science* 239:1263–1268.

Symons, D. (1979) *The evolution of human sexuality*. Oxford University Press.

Talmy, L. (1983) How language structures space. In: *Spatial orientation: Theory, research, and application*, ed. H. Pick and L. Acredolo. Plenum.

Talmy, L. (1988) Force dynamics in language and cognition. *Cognitive Science* 12:49–100.

Tobias, P. V. (1981) The emergence of man in Africa and beyond. *Philosophical Transactions of the Royal Society of London B 292*: 43–56.

Tooby, J., & Cosmides, L. (1990) On the universality of human nature and the uniqueness of the individual: The role of genetics and adaptation. *Journal of Personality.*

Tooby, J., and DeVore, I. (1987) The reconstruction of hominid evolution through strategic modeling. In: *The evolution of human behavior: Primate models,* ed., W. G. Kinzey. SUNY Press.

Travis, L. (1984) *Parameters and effects of word order variation.* Ph.D. dissertation, MIT.

Trivers, R. L. (1971) The evolution of reciprocal altruism. *Quarterly Review of Biology 46*:35–57.

Trivers, R. L. (1974) Parent-offspring conflict. *American Zoologist 14*:249–264.

Tversky, A. & Kahneman, D. (1981) The framing of decisions and the psychology of choice. *Science 211*:453–458.

Wang, W. S-Y. (1976) Language change. In: *Origin and evolution of language and speech,* ed., Harnad, S. R., Steklis, H. S., & Lancaster, J. Annals of the New York Academy of Sciences 280.

Wexler, K. & Culicover, P. (1980) *Formal principles of language acquisition.* MIT Press.

Wexler, K. & Manzini, R. (1984) Parameters and learnability in binding theory. In: *Parameter Setting,* eds. T. Roeper & E. Williams, Reidel.

Williams, G. C. (1966) *Adaptation and natural selection: A critique of some current evolutionary thought.* Princeton University Press.

Zubrow, E. (1987) Paper presented at the conference "The origin and dispersal of modern humans: Behavioral and biological perspectives," University of Cambridge, England, March 22-27. *Reported in Science 237*:1290–1291.

6

The Acquisition of Argument
Structure

For almost ten years I was obsessed with solving a paradox in language acquisition. It begun with a linguistic puzzle: Why do sentences such as He poured water into the glass *and* He filled the glass with water *sound OK, but seemingly similar sentences such as* He poured the glass with water *and* He filled water into the glass *sound odd? The puzzle was complicated by a fact about children's environment—that they are not systematically corrected when they make speech errors—and a fact about their behavior—that they do not confine themselves to the constructions they hear from their parents. It forced me to confront foundational questions about language and cognition: When and how do children generalize? What is the rationale behind apparent quirks of language? How is language related to thought? And why does children's language seem different from that of adults? The effort to tie these ideas together in a way that would resolve the paradox resulted in my second academic book,* Learnability and Cognition: The Acquisition of Argument Structure *(1989), which was reprinted with a new preface in 2013.*

Writing a big book on a seemingly small topic made me feel like Alice stumbling down a rabbit hole and finding a phantasmagoric underworld. I found that the only way to explain how children master contrasting verbs like fill *and* pour *was to probe the human concepts of causation, space, time, matter, and purpose. It seemed to me that the syntax of verbs revealed the stuff of thought, an idea I pursued in my 2007 book* The Stuff of Thought: Language as a Window into Human Nature. *The chapter reprinted here is a self-contained explanation of the paradox and of the resulting theory which inspired those two books.*

1. Introduction: Argument Structure

A major topic in understanding language and language acquisition is lexical argument structure, that is, the information attached to verbs in the mental lexicon that allows the speaker to express who did what to whom. Verbs are choosy about which arguments they can appear with, as the following sentences, and their verbs' dictionary entries, show.

The dormouse dined.
*The dormouse dined something.
dine: NP$_{agent}$ ___

The dormouse devoured something.
*The dormouse devoured.
devour: ___ NP$_{theme}$

The dormouse ate something.
The dormouse ate.
eat: ___ NP$_{theme}$
eat: ___

The Mad Hatter put the dormouse into the teapot.
*The Mad Hatter put the dormouse.
*The Mad Hatter put into the teapot.
*The Mad Hatter put.
put: ___ NP$_{theme}$ PP$_{location}$

The verbs *dine, devour,* and *eat,* though semantically similar, have different argument structures. *Dine* is intransitive, and must appear with an agent subject before it but with nothing after it. *Devour* is transitive, and must appear with an agent subject and with an object playing the semantic role of "theme," the entity whose state or condition is the focus of the sentence. *Eat* has both transitive and intransitive frames. And *put* takes a third kind of argument structure: agent, theme, and location arguments must all appear. Thus the verb largely determines the structure of the clause, and to understand language acquisition, it is important to understand how children learn the argument structures of verbs.

2. A Learnability Paradox

Georgia Green (1974) and C. L. Baker (1979) have pointed out a paradox in the acquisition of argument structure. Many verbs can encode their arguments in several, basically synonymous ways. This is shown in the following examples, in which the relevant arguments are labeled with their general and specific semantic roles ("content" and "container" are particular types of "theme" and "goal").

John loaded hay onto the wagon. ("content locative")
          theme   goal
          content   container

John loaded the wagon with hay. ("container locative")
        goal   theme
        container   content

Sally splashed water onto the wall.
Sally splashed the wall with water.

Biff stuffed breadcrumbs into the turkey.
Biff stuffed the turkey with breadcrumbs.

Since children, to learn an infinite language in a finite childhood, must be able to generalize beyond what they hear, they should construct a rule such that allows them to take a verb that they hear in one structure (e.g., *I brushed paint onto the wood*) and predict that it can appear in the related structure (*I brushed the wood with paint*). Such a "locative" rule might look something like this:

V: NP$_{agent}$ ___ NP$_{content}$ *into/onto* NP$_{container}$ $\rightarrow$
V: NP$_{agent}$ ___ NP$_{container}$ *with* NP$_{content}$

Unfortunately, some verbs stand as exceptions to the pattern: *Amy poured water onto the glass* is a natural sentence of English, but when its entry for *pour* is fed into the locative rule, the output is *˙Amy poured the glass with water,* which sounds odd to adult ears. But how could this happen if speakers have a rule that automatically creates the second structure from the first? Similarly, if the rule were to run in the opposite direction, it would take the grammatical form *Carol filled the glass with water* and generate the ungrammatical *˙Carol filled water into the glass.*

In general, this kind of learnability paradox appears in any area of language in which there are both generalizations and exceptions, so its solution is of general interest in understanding the logic of language learning.

All of the simple solutions that come to mind fail to work (see Pinker 1989 for a review). One is that children are conservative: they actually do not coin productive rules at all, but only use verbs in the argument structures that they hear their parents use them in. This is false: children utter sentences that must be the output of a productive, non-imitative mechanism. Some examples from children's spontaneous speech (Bowerman 1982; Gropen, Pinker, Hollander, and Goldberg 1991a)) include:

I filled the grain up.
And fill the little sugars up in the bowl.
Can I fill some salt into the bear?
I'm going to cover a screen over me.
Feel your hand to that.
She's gonna pinch it on my foot.
Look, Mom, I'm gonna pour it with water.
I don't want it because I spilled it of orange juice.

This is confirmed in experiments. Gropen et al. (1991a) found that more than half of the 2- to 6-year-old children they tested described pictures (e.g., of a woman filling a glass) using ungrammatical phrases like *fill water into the glass.*

A second incorrect hypothesis is that children are corrected or receive reliable feedback from their parents when they make such errors, and use them to mark exceptional verbs in their mental lexicons. This, too, is almost surely false (Brown and Hanlon 1970; Pinker 1989; Grimshaw and Pinker 1989; Morgan and Travis 1989; Marcus 1993; Bowerman 1988). Parents neither selectively correct nor selectively miscomprehend their children's ungrammatical sentences. Though it has been suggested that subtle statistical patterns in other parental reactions might differentiate ungrammatical from grammatical sentences, it seems highly unlikely that such feedback could be of much use in unlearning locative errors, since they are too infrequent to allow aggregation of significant differences in parental feedback types, they differ in direction from parent to parent, and they occur far later than the ages at which they would be needed. Indeed, such feedback may not even exist; much of the claimed evidence for it is based on statistical artifacts (Marcus 1993).

A third possibility is that there is some simple semantic criterion that differentiates the alternating and non-alternating verbs. But this, too, seems unlikely: *splash, pour,* and *fill* all involve an agent causing the motion of a non-solid content to some surface or container. But *splash* alternates, *pour* takes only the content-locative argument structure, and *fill* takes only the container-locative argument structure.

The fact that all the straightforward solutions to this simple problem fail suggests that we must be in ignorance of some deep and far-ranging principles about the nature of argument structure, how it is related to verb meanings, how verb meanings are mentally represented, how meanings and argument structures are acquired, and what causes children to overgeneralize argument structure alternations. I have presented a detailed exploration of these problems, and an integrated set of theories capable of solving this learnability paradox, in Pinker (1989). In this paper I review the nature of this theory, and experimental research in support of it that has been reported more recently.

3. A Theory of Argument Structure Alternations

The key to the solution to the problem is the insight that alternations like the locative involve not one but two rules (Rappaport and Levin 1985). First, there is a "lexical semantic rule," effecting a change on the verb's meaning:

V_1: "X causes Y to go to Z" $\rightarrow$
V_2: "X changes the state of Z by means of causing Y to go to Z"

Thus the version of *load* that underlies *load hay onto the wagon* means roughly "cause hay to go onto the wagon"; the lexical semantic rule would change it to a new version with the same stem but with a subtly different meaning: "cause the wagon to be full of hay." The second part of the alternation consists of the application of a universal set of "linking rules" which map certain kinds of semantic arguments onto syntactic roles. Specifically, agents are mapped onto the subject role, and entities that are caused to undergo a change are mapped onto the object role. Crucially, a caused-to-change entity can change either its *location* or its *state*; in either case, the linking rule "entity-caused-to-change → object" applies. There are six empirical facts supporting this general theory.

First, the theory predicts that the verbs in the two sentences should not be completely synonymous. This has long been known to be true, a phenomenon sometimes called the "holism effect" (see Pinker 1989; Gropen, Pinker, Hollander, and Goldberg 1991b for reviews): *Chuck loaded hay onto the wagon* can mean that the wagon can be partly empty; *Chuck loaded the wagon with hay* implies that it is full. This is predicted if only the second sentence means that the wagon has changed state, and being full of something, as opposed to just containing some of something, is easily construed as a state change.

Second, the theory explains why the sentences are perceived as *almost* synonymous. If *load hay onto the wagon* means "cause hay to go onto the wagon," and *load the wagon with hay* means "cause the wagon to be full by causing hay to go onto the wagon," then the semantic representation of the second sentence actually contains the semantic representation of the first sentence as a proper part. This large overlap in mental representations accounts for the sense of similarity in meaning.

Third, the theory explains why the two alternating structures have the syntactic forms that they do (as opposed to arbitrary substitutions of prepositions or subject and object roles). The single linking rule "entity-caused-to-change → object," when applied to a verb meaning "cause hay to change location," makes the *hay* (content) argument the object; the same rule, when applied to a verb meaning "cause wagon to change state," makes the *wagon* (container argument) the object.

Fourth, and most relevant to the paradox, it explains why not all verbs undergo the alternation. If the locative rule creates a verb containing the meaning "cause to change state," then only those verbs whose intrinsic meanings specify some causation of state change fit the rule and are liable to undergo it. Though events involving *pouring, filling,* and *stuffing* all tend to involve situations in which motion occurs with respect to a container, that does not mean that the mental dictionary definitions of the verbs are parallel. What has to be true of a situation in order for it to be an example of *pouring*? Roughly, the substance must move downward in a cohesive stream; this is what contrasts *pouring* with, say, *dripping* or *showering*. But *pour* does not specify the change of state of any container or surface to which the substance moves: one can pour water into a glass, beside a glass, onto the ground, and so on. Since a *manner* of motion (downward stream) is specified by the verb, the *fact* of motion must be specified, and this tells us that the verb means "cause to go" and hence the moving entity is mapped onto the object role. *Spill, drip,* and *shake* involve similar semantic constraints, and as predicted, they can appear only in the content-locative argument structure.

In contrast, for an event to be an example of *filling,* the container must change from being not full to being full; a few drops of water in a glass are not enough to fill it. But *fill* does not specify the particular manner in which the filling substance gets there: one can fill a glass by pouring water into it, by dripping water into it, or by dipping a glass into a bathtub. Since a *kind* of state change (fullness) is specified by the verb, the *fact* of state change must be specified, and this tells us that the verb means "cause to change" and hence the changing entity (the container) is mapped onto the object role. *Cover, saturate,* and *stop up* involve similar semantic constraints, and as predicted, they can appear only in the content-locative argument structure.

Finally, consider the alternating *stuff,* which can alternate between *Mary stuffed mail into the sack* and *Mary stuffed the sack with mail.* In order for an action to be an instance of *stuffing,* it cannot be the case (e.g.) that Mary simply dropped letters into the sack until it was full. In fact, it wouldn't count as *stuffing* even if Mary had wadded up a few letters before dropping them in. Instead, the mail must be forced into the sack *because* the sack is being filled to a point where its remaining capacity is too small, or just barely big enough, relative to the amount of mail that is being forced in. The semantic representation of *stuff* jointly constrains the change of location that the content undergoes *and* the change of state that the container undergoes. That is why the object of *stuff* can be linked either to the content or to the container; that is, it alternates. Other alternators also denote changes or effects simultaneously specified in terms of content and container: for *brush* and *dab,* force is applied pushing the content against the container; for *load,* the insertion of a kind of contents specific to the container enables the container to act in a designated way (e.g., a camera, or a gun).

Fifth, if one proposes that the linking rules are universal, then the theory predicts that the effects reviewed above should be found in a variety of constructions in a variety of languages, and this seems to be true (see Pinker 1989 and Gropen et al. 1991a for reviews). Both the same kinds of verbs that alternate in English, and the holistic interpretation accompanying the container-object form, can be found in the locative alternations of a variety of languages, including many that are genetically and areally distinct from English. Furthermore the theory can be seen to apply to constructions other than locative forms across languages. Verbs in which an animate entity (an 'agent') brings about a direct effect on another entity (a 'patient'), such as verbs of causation of change of position (e.g., causative *slide*) or state (e.g., causative *melt*), or verbs of ingestion (e.g., *eat*), are almost invariably transitive across languages, with patients as grammatical objects. Furthermore, the holism effect accompanies the interpretation of grammatical objects quite generally; similar semantic shifts can be seen in the difference between *Kurt climbed the mountain* and *Kurt climbed up the mountain,* only the first implying that the entire mountain has been scaled, and in a variety of other constructions.

Sixth, the general theory has been supported in a set of experiments reported in Gropen et al. (1991b). Children aged 3;4-9;4 and adults were taught made-up verbs, presented in a neutral syntactic context (*this is mooping*). The verbs all referred to a transfer of items to a surface or container. Subjects were tested on their willingness to use either the moving items (content), or the surface (container), as the verb's object when describing the events. In one condition, items were moved in a particular manner; for example, a cloth zig-zagged over to an unchanging sponge, or a sack of pennies hopped onto a platform. In that case, people were likely to express the moving items as the verb's object, as in *you're pilking the sponge.* In another condition, a surface changed state as the result of the motion; for example, a cloth changed color when a sponge was moved onto it (via a litmus reaction), or a platform sagged when a sack of pennies was placed on it. In that case, people were more likely to express the *surface* as the object, as in *you're pilking the cloth.* We also demonstrated the holism effect: people said *you're pilking pegs* when a pegboard was partly filled, and *you're pilking the pegboard* when it was completely filled. This confirms that speakers are not confined to mapping moving entities onto the grammatical object; when a stationary entity undergoes a state change as the result of a motion, it can be represented as the main affected argument and thereby linked to the grammatical object instead.

There is an outstanding problem, however, in predicting alternating and non-alternating verbs with precision, and solving the problem requires introducing an additional extra premise. The problem is that although it is a *necessary* condition for alternation that a verb have a meaning compatible with the semantic change effected by a rule, it is not a *sufficient* condition. Some verbs, for example, are compatible with causation of a change of state of a container but still do not undergo the alternation. For example, *splash* and *splatter* alternate, but *drip* and *dribble* do not ('I dripped/ dribbled the floor with paint). But there is no a priori rationale for saying that splashing involves causing a wall to be covered with paint in a way that dribbling does not cause a floor to be covered with paint. Similarly, *brush* and *smear* alternate between content- and container-locative forms, but semantically similar *pour* and *spill* do not.

The solution is that a language allows only some kinds of verbs to specify change of state of a container in their semantic representations, while not allowing other, cognitively similar verbs, to do so. That is, the actual alternating verbs in a language are licensed by fine-grained subclasses of semantically and morphophonologically similar verbs, and the speaker must actually consult these subclass definitions before permitting a verb to alternate (Levin 1985; Rappaport and Levin 1985; Levin and Rappaport Hovav 1991). For example, verbs of simultaneous contact and motion, where the agent pushes the content against the container and moves it, all undergo the locative alternation (*brush, daub, rub, slather, smear, smudge, spread, streak*). In addition, verbs of imparting force, causing the ballistic motion of the substance in some direction, all alternate (*inject, spatter, splash, splatter, spray, squirt, sprinkle*), as do verbs of overfilling (*cram, crowd, jam, stuff, wad*). But other subclasses of verbs, defined by equally narrow criteria, do not alternate. For example, if motion is caused not by an agent imparting force in some direction to a substance, but by the agent merely enabling gravity to cause the motion of the object (*dribble, drip, drizzle, dump, ladle, pour, shake, slosh, spill*), the verb may *not* alternate. Similarly, if an agent attaches an object to a surface using some mediating object, like a staple or glue, the verb may not alternate, such as ˙*He stapled the board with posters*. Other such verbs of mediated attachment, all non-alternating, include *pin, fasten, tape, attach, nail, glue, paste*, and *stick*.

We can call the general locative rule, the one that converts "cause to go" verbs to "cause to change" verbs, a *broad-range* rule. A broad-range rule, however, may not be used directly by a speaker to extend a verb from one alternation to another. Instead, the broad-range rules merely constrain a set of what we may call *narrow-range* rules. A narrow-range rule is stated so as to apply to a narrow subclass. One of the narrow-range rules for the locative alternation, then, converts a verb meaning "impart force to a substance causing it to move ballistically in the direction of a surface" to a verb meaning "cause a surface to be covered by a substance by means of imparting force to the substance causing it to move ballistically to the surface." Only the narrow-range rules may be applied automatically to a verb in one argument structure to derive the alternative argument structure.

Why some subclasses within the range of a broad-range rule are allowed to alternate, but others are not, is not completely arbitrary. The semantics of grammatical objects generally requires them to be interpretable as inherently or directly affected by the action specified by the verb. This "directness effect" is well-known from the study of the causative alternation: *Bill caused the glass to break* can mean that Bill startled Mary, who was putting it away, but *Bill broke the glass* implies that Bill physically manipulated the glass in some way. The generalization is that those subclasses whose meanings are more easily construed as "directly" acting or impinging on a surface are more likely to have narrow-range rules allowing them to alternate. For example, the surface is more directly affected in brushing (where force is being applied to the surface), splashing (where the force aims the substance in the direction of the surface), and stuffing (where the caused motion has to overcome the resistance of the container) than in *pouring* (where it is gravity that is allowed to cause the motion, rather than the motion being caused by the agent) or in fastening (where some mediating object or substance comes between an moveable object and the surface it is attached to).

4. Extension of the Theory to the Dative Alternation

Another nice feature of the theory is that it is easily extendible to other grammatical alternations. These include the causative alternation (*The water boiled/He boiled the water* versus *The light glowed/˙He glowed the light*), the "conative" alternation (*He cut the bread/He cut at the bread* versus *He broke the bread/*He broke at the bread*), and with some modifications, the passive (*The Mafia owns many cars/Many cars are owned by the Mafia* versus *The Mafia has many cars/*Many cars are had by the Mafia*).

The dative alternation, in particular, presents the same kind of paradox, and submits to the same kind of theory, as the locative does (see Pinker 1989; Gropen, Pinker, Hollander, Goldberg, and Wilson 1989 for a full presentation). The dative involves a set of alternating verbs:

> John gave a dish to Sam. (a prepositional dative)
> John gave Sam a dish. (a double-object dative)
>
> John told a joke to Mary.
> John told Mary a joke.
>
> John baked a cake for Mary.
> John baked Mary a cake.

These verbs would seem to inspire a dative rule:

> $\text{V: NP}_{\text{agent}} \underline{\quad} \text{NP}_{\text{theme}} \text{ } to/for \text{ NP}_{\text{goal/beneficiary}} \rightarrow$
> $\text{V: NP}_{\text{agent}} \underline{\quad} \text{NP}_{\text{goal/beneficiary}} \text{NP}_{\text{theme}}$

But, there are semantically similar verbs which, puzzlingly, do not alternate:

> John drove the car to Chicago.
> *John drove Chicago the car.
>
> John painted the house for Mary.
> *John painted Mary the house.
>
> John donated a painting to the museum.
> *John donated the museum a painting.

As in the case of the locative alternation, there is evidence that children do not memorize verbs' argument structures faithfully from parental sentences but extend them productively. The evidence comes both from errors in children's spontaneous speech and from experiments (Mazurkewich and White 1984; Bowerman 1988; Gropen et al. 1989). Speech errors include:

> I'll brush him his hair.
> Pick me up all these things.
> Mummy, open Hadwen the door.
> I said her no.
> Don't say me that or you'll make me cry.
> Button me the rest.

You put me the bread and butter.
I do what my horsie says me to do.
Put Eva the yukky one first.
How come you're putting me that kind of juice?
I gon' put me all dese rubber bands on.
You finished me lots of rings.
Mommy, fix me my tiger.
Jay said me no.
Don't say me that.
You ate me my cracker.
You're taking me too long to wait.

Gropen et al. (1989) taught children novel words in prepositional dative sentences, as in "I'm pilking the X to the Y." They found that about half of the 5- to 8-year-olds they tested were willing to extend it to the double-object argument structure, saying "I'm pilking the Y the X."

The key to solving the problem is identical to the one we used for the locative verbs, and was first proposed by Georgia Green (1974). The dative rule is really two rules. One is a lexical semantic rule changing a verb's semantic representation:

V_1: "X causes Y to go to Z" →
V_2: "X causes Z to have Y"

Syntactic argument structures are projected from the lexicosemantic structures via linking rules. There are two that we have already used for the dative: agents are subjects; "affected" entities (entities directly caused to change) are objects. Another linking rule is needed for the argument playing the role of the second object (*the book* in *give John the book*). It links the "possession" to the second object.

The advantages of the theory are identical to those we saw for the dative. First, it correctly predicts that the two versions of the dative alternation are not exactly synonymous. A subtle difference in the two has often been noted in the linguistics literature (see Pinker 1989 for a review). *Bonnie taught Spanish to the students* is noncommittal about what the students took away; she may have taught her heart out without the students having learned a thing. But *Bonnie taught the students Spanish* suggests that the student now know (in some sense, "have") Spanish. Similarly, *Biff threw the ball to her* is compatible with ball flying over her head or her having dropped it. But *Biff threw her the ball* suggests that she caught it, hence now has it. This follows from a semantic representation for the double object that means "cause Z to have Y," not merely "cause Y to go to Z."

Second, the theory accounts for the obvious similarity of meaning between the alternants: if X causes Y to go to Z, and Z is animate, then Z usually has

X. Hence the meaning of the prepositional object form generally entails that of the double-object form.

Third, it accounts for the kind of change of syntactic form we see in the alternation. A single linking rule, mapping the caused-to-change entity onto the object position, predicts the two structures from their semantics. In the form meaning "cause the book to change location," the *book* is the object; in the form meaning "cause John to gain possession," *John* is the object.

Fourth, it accounts for the verbwise choosiness of the alternation. If the dative rule creates a verb containing the meaning 'cause to possess', then only those verbs whose intrinsic meanings are compatible with the notion of causation of possession will combine with the rule to yield sensible meanings. For example, for something to be an example of driving, a vehicle must go somewhere under the control of an agent, but the goal of the motion (e.g., New York City) does not possess anything, as it is generally inanimate. So the verb *drive* can only be about causing to go, not causing to have. Reasonably enough, *drive* does not alternate: *drive the car to New York* is possible, *drive New York the car* is not.

In contrast, for some event to be an example of passing, it is both true that a thing has to go somewhere, and that the goal of motion has to possess something. Both a possession change and a location change are specified, and either is eligible for construal as the affected entity, hence mappable onto object position. Indeed, one can *pass the book to John* or *pass John the book*.

Finally, there are cases where one can cause someone to have something without causing something to go to someone. Consider the idiom *give X an idea,* meaning "inspire," as in *John's hat gave her an idea.* To inspire means to cause someone to have an idea, but the causal entity—John's hat, in this case—does not have the idea itself. So it is not an example of causing an idea to go to someone. Since only causing-to-have, not causing-to-go, is specified, only the double-object form should be grammatical, and that is indeed the case: *?John's hat gave an idea to her.* Of course, a common reading of the idiom implies "communicate," which sense is interpretable both as "causing an idea to go to" and as "causing to have an idea," and this sense of the verb does alternate: *John gave an idea to her/gave her an idea.*

Fifth, the dative alternation can be identified on syntactic grounds in a variety of unrelated languages by the presence of two grammatical objects, and when it is, it takes verbs with the same general kinds of meanings as one sees in English.

Sixth, there are several experimental demonstrations that children and adults are sensitive to the semantics of the dative alternation when generalizing it to new verbs. Gropen et al. (1989) had adult subjects learn new verbs by reading them in prepositional object structures (involving both *to* and *for*) in paragraphs like the following:

> Sue, who had wanted the deed to the house for twenty years, was very
> excited when her lawyer called with the good news. Her lawyer told her

that Bob, the current owner, was ready to begin tonkation, the formal (and only legal) process by which she could obtain the house from him. After Bob had finally tonked the house to Sue, she tonked her duplex to Francis.

Ned, a young but upcoming inventor, was eager to spring his latest idea on the unsuspecting world. He thought he'd begin with his neighbor, Cindy, by offering to do her ceiling with his new pell. It is a profound understatement to say that Cindy was displeased after Ned had pelled the ceiling for her.

The subjects then were asked to rate the naturalness of double-object sentences containing the verb, like *Bill tonked Rob the car* and *Ned pelled Cindy the ceiling*. We found that when the verb involved a change of possession, as in the first paragraph, the ratings were far higher than they were when the verb involved no possession change, as in the second paragraph. Similarly, in Gropen et al.'s (1989) experiment teaching dative verbs to children, the children uttered double objects more often when the goal of the motion was animate (e.g., a tiger doll, or the child herself), hence a potential possessor, than when the goal was inanimate (e.g., a book or plate).

And as in the case of the locative alternation, the theory as stated so far is not quite adequate. Change of possession is a necessary condition for the dative alternation, and hence can be part of a broad-range rule that indicates what must be true of all the verbs that undergo the alternation. But change of possession is not a sufficient condition; some verbs that are easily construable as involving a change of possession do not alternate. For example, although *give* and *pass* alternate, similar *donate* and *transfer* do not. Although the verbs of communication *tell* and *write* alternate (*tell me a story*), the verbs of communication *shout, whisper,* and *say* do not (*whisper me a story*). Although the verbs of motion *throw, flip, kick, bring* and *take* alternate (*Guy flipped him the puck*), the verbs of motion *pull, carry,* and *lift* do not (*He lifted me the box*). Although the verbs of creation *make* and *build* alternate (*She built me a house*), the verbs of creation *create* and *design* do not (*She designed me a house*). Although *buy* and *get* alternate (*Get me another one*), *choose* and *select* do not (*Choose me another one*). One can *bake her a cake* or *sew her a dress,* but one cannot *heat her a cake* or *mend her a dress.*

The solution is the same. Speakers may not apply the broad-range rule directly; they must apply one of a set of narrow-range rules embraced by it. The narrow-range rules allow only some kinds of verbs to be extended so as to encode causation of change of possession; other, cognitively similar verbs, may not be so extended. The subclasses that come with narrow-range dative alternation rules include the following:

Giving: *give, pass, send, hand*
Future having: *offer, promise, bequeath, leave, refer*

Caused Autonomous Motion: *throw, toss, flip, slap, kick, poke, fling, shoot, blast*
Direction of Accompanied Motion: *take, bring*
Fact of Communication/Type of Message: *tell, show, ask, teach, pose, write*
Creation: *bake, make, build, cook, sew, knit*
Obtaining: *get, buy, find, steal, order, win*

The subclasses that do not come with narrow-range rules include these fairly closely related ones:

Manner of Accompanied Motion: *carry, pull, push, shlep, lift, lower, haul*
Fulfilling/Deserving: *credit, reward, entrust, honor, supply, furnish*
Manner of Speaking: *shout, scream, murmur, whisper, shriek, yodel, yell*
Choosing: *choose, pick, select, favor, indicate, prefer, designate*

In the case of the dative, the narrow subclasses are defined by a second kind of of criterion. Some subclasses are restricted to the native (non-Latinate) vocabulary of English, which generally corresponds to monomorphemic verbs consisting of a single metrical foot. This accounts for contrasts like the following:

give vs. *˙donate*
tell vs. *˙inform*
throw vs. *˙propel*
make vs. *˙create*
get vs. *˙obtain*

We have shown that adults are sensitive to the morphophonological constraint. In Gropen et al.'s (1989) experiment, adults rated double-object sentences with monosyllabic verbs, like *tonk, norp, moop,* and *pell* higher than double-object sentences with polysyllabic multimorphemic verbs like *calimod, orgulate, repetrine,* and *dorfinize.* Children, too, were more likely to utter double-object sentences with the novel verbs *moop* and *keat* than with the novel verbs *orgulate* and *calimode.* In none of these cases did we observe a difference for the same verbs in prepositional object sentences.

5. How Are the Argument Structure Rules Learned?

Now that we have some understanding of the kinds of rules that allow productive generalization of verbs from one argument structure to a related one, we can ask how children acquire those rules, and why they sometimes seem to flout them. Learning that a language has a given alternation is relatively straightforward for a child equipped to encode verbs in terms of their argument structures at all. The child hears parents say *spray water onto the wall* and *spray the wall with water, load hay onto the wagon* and *load the wagon with hay,* and can conclude that some verbs that appear in the content-locative structure can also appear in the container-locative structure (see Pinker 1984: ch. 8). The problem is how the child mentally encodes this generalization in a form that allows it to be applied only to those verbs, like *splash,* that alternate, not to the verbs, like *fill,* that do not alternate.

Recall that there are two kinds of restrictions to learn. One consists of the broad-range constraints, or necessary conditions for an alternation, such as that the locative requires a state change of the container, or that the dative requires a possession change. It is possible that these constraints are not acquired at all. Say the language acquisition mechanisms of children are incapable of couching alternations as single syntactic rules, like this one:

$$\text{NP}_{\text{agent}} \text{ V NP}_{\text{content}} \; onto\text{-NP}_{\text{container}} \rightarrow$$
$$\text{NP}_{\text{agent}} \text{ V NP}_{\text{container}} \; with\text{-NP}_{\text{content}}$$

Instead, they are equipped to formulate such generalizations as lexical semantic rules that reassign which argument is construed as the affected one. Moreover, the linking rules that map these arguments onto syntactic positions could simply be part of the language acquisition mechanism, that is, innate. There is some evidence for this suggestion.

First, as mentioned, the broad-range constraints on alternations (like the dative and locative) are very widespread across languages (see Pinker 1989 for a review), and may be universal. Linking rules, too, appear to be largely universal (Pinker 1989).

Second, children never violate the broad-range semantic constraints in their spontaneous speech errors (Pinker 1989; Bowerman 1982, 1988). That is, they are never seduced by false generalizations based on the purely syntactic arrangement of arguments accompanying a verb. Errors like the following have never been recorded from the voluminous records of children's spontaneous speech that have given us the errors noted earlier:

I followed him into the room./*I followed the room with him.
The fairy turned the frog into a prince./*The fairy turned the prince with a frog.
Jimmy drove the car to the top./*Jimmy drove the top the car.
Jane planted the trees for six hours./*Jane planted six hours the trees.

Third, in the experiments we have reported (Gropen et al. 1989, 1991b; Pinker, Lebeaux, and Frost 1987; Pinker 1989), children obey the broad-range constraints at the youngest age we can test them, and show little if any improvement with age.

The second kind of constraint for children to learn are those defining the narrow-range subclasses, or sufficient conditions for an alternation, such as that the locative alternation may apply to verbs of imparted force or that the dative alternation may apply to verbs of creation. These constraints are not universal, and must be learned.

To explain such learning, it is necessary to work out the precise semantic representations of the dozens of subclasses, and hundreds of verbs, that define the narrow-range rules. An entire chapter of Pinker (1989: ch. 5) is devoted to motivating these representations. The key discovery is that verbs' meaning representations contain two kinds of semantic symbols. One kind consists of a small set of universal basic notions involving causation, force, the topology of paths and places, possession, and certain coarse properties of objects like humanness, solidity, and extendedness in one or more dimensions. These symbols include 'cause', 'go', 'act', 'have', 'path', 'manner', 'means', 'surface', certain object features, and a time-line representation. The other kind consists of a much larger set of features that are idiosyncratic to particular verbs in particular languages, such as particular manners (e.g., leaping versus striding) and particular kinds of substances (e.g., buttering versus oiling). Thus for a verb like *to butter*, which means something like "cause to be covered by a butterlike substance," the basic symbols include "cause to be covered by a substance," and the idiosyncratic symbol is "butterlike."

In general, the basic symbols appear to be *grammatically relevant*, in that they can be encoded in closed-class functional morphemes in a variety of languages (e.g., pronouns, aspect inflections, causative morphemes). And importantly, these are the features that delineate syntactically cohesive subclasses of verbs with regard to argument structure alternations. This provides a relatively simple theory of learning (worked out in chapter 6 of Pinker 1989). Say children generalize alternating verbs very narrowly, paying close attention to the grammatically-relevant versus idiosyncratic components of a verb's semantic representation. That is, when they hear a verb alternating, they form a narrow-range rule that captures all the grammatically-relevant features of that verb's semantic representation, and they substitute a variable for any idiosyncratic features. This would automatically allow them to generalize only to new verbs that are in the same subclass. That is, when hearing *throw the doll to me* and *throw me the doll*, they would generalize automatically from *kick the doll to me* to *kick me the doll*, because *throw* and *kick* are identical in their grammatically-relevant semantics (roughly, "instantaneously impart force to an object causing it to move autonomously"), and differ only in their idiosyncratic semantics (release from hands versus contact with foot). But they would not generalize to *lift me the box* because *lift* differs from *throw* in several grammatically-relevant features, primarily temporal/aspectual and causal ones (lifting is extended in time, not instantaneous, and the motion is caused by the agent throughout its duration, rather than being autonomous). Children would learn the narrow-range rules one at a time, as they hear their parents use a verb that has some new combination of grammatically-relevant notions in its semantic representation. Finally, children would also restrict narrow-range rules to apply to verbs in the same salient morphophonological class as the ones they have heard alternating. This is how they would restrict the dative alternation in English, say, to verbs of the native vocabulary class.

There is some evidence that children confine their productivity to verbs that are semantically similar to those they have heard alternate (Pinker 1989: ch. 7). First, children's errors are rare; the default is conservativism. In one analysis (Gropen et al. 1989), we found that 95 percent of children's double-object sentences contained verbs that were used in the double-object construction by that child's parents. Second, in experiments, children produce double-object sentences more often when they have heard the verb in the double-object form than when they must generate it productively. Similar patterns of conservatism were found for the passive (Pinker, Lebeaux, and Frost 1987). Third, Gropen et al. (1989) were puzzled by the difficulty their young experimental subjects had in extending the double-object construction to verbs of motion. It turns out that double-object dative constructions with verbs of motion (e.g., *throw me the ball*) are quite uncommon in parental speech to children. When children in later experiments in the series were first given examples of *give* or *pass* in the double-object form referring to motion, we found they were much more likely to use new verbs of motion in the double-object form.

6. Why Do Children's Argument Structure Errors Come and Go?

There is a final piece to the puzzle. I have suggested that children make argument-structure errors only with regard to the narrow-range subclasses; they never violate the boundaries of the broad-range classes. And I have suggested that even these errors are uncommon. So why do children make errors at all? And what makes them stop? Recall that this was one of the phenomena that defined the learnability paradox.

I have found that most, if not all, of children's errors come from two sources, both compatible with the psychological mechanisms proposed so far. One is that children do not learn verbs' meanings instantaneously (probably because they cannot; Gentner 1982; Gleitman 1990; Pinker 1989, 1994). Recall that according to the theory, children and adults project verbs' syntactic argument structures from their semantic representations via linking rules. This implies that if a child has an incorrect semantic representation for a verb, either over a sustained period of time because learning is not complete, or momentarily, because of memory retrieval failure, the syntax of the verb should be malformed as well. As the child fine-tunes the verb's meaning by observing it used in a variety of situations (Pinker 1989, 1994), the syntax should fall into line automatically.

A clear example of this process is the verb *fill*. There is evidence that children have trouble in general learning the change-of-state components of a verb's meaning; they are much more attentive to the manner of motion it specifies (Gentner 1978). Say children misconstrued *fill* as meaning "cause X to move to Y by means of pouring," or even "cause Y to become full by means of pouring," rather than "cause Y to become full." The linking rule that maps affected entities to the object position would automatically generate the syntactic error *fill water into the glass*. Gropen et al. (1991a) ran experiments that provided several kinds of evidence for this explanation of the errors. Adults and 2½- to 8-year-old children were shown two series of pictures, one showing a woman pouring water into a pitcher but it ending up not full, the other showing a woman allowing water to drip from a faucet, filling a pitcher. They were asked to choose which picture showed "filling." Adults, of course, chose the picture with the dripping water and full pitcher. But many children systematically chose the picture with pouring water and a part-empty pitcher (and similar pictures and verbs showing a typical manner but lacking the state change required of the verb by adults). This is exactly the kind of semantic error that the theory predicts would underlie syntactic errors like *fill water into the pitcher*. In a separate task, susceptibility to the *syntactic* errors was measured, by asking the children to describe pictures. Many children made such errors, and interestingly, there was a statistical tendency for the children who thought that *fill* meant *pour* or *fill by pouring* to say *fill water into X*, exactly as predicted. As children learn the true meaning of *fill* by hearing adults use it in contexts like dripping, bailing, or leaving glasses on windowsills during a rainstorm, the syntactic errors should disappear automatically.

The second source of children's errors is one for which we my not need an explanation of how they outgrow it, because in fact they may never outgrow it. Maybe children occasionally use broad-range rules productively, ignoring the constraints of narrow-range rules, as one-shot innovations that they realize are ungrammatical, and do not retain as incorrect entries in their mental lexicons. There are two bits of evidence for this suggestion. The first is that children often seem to be cognizant of the narrow-range constraints, even while they occasionally flout them in their own speech. For example, Bowerman has shown that children can spontaneously correct their own errors in overgeneralizing the causative alternation:

> I have to be—have it up!
> And go—put it like that.
> She won't sit me—let me sit next to her.
> I'm not going to pick up the Cheerios that I fall—that I drop on the floor.

They also correct such errors in other children—even at stages at which they, hypocritically, are making such errors themselves. For example:

> [Sister: Will you learn me how to read that book?]
> "Learn" you? What does she mean, "learn" you?
> [Sister: Christy, you fell me into the car!]
> You *fell* me into the car!! HA HA HA!!!

Moreover, the same phenomenon can be seen in adults. Adults occasionally extend verbs to new argument structures that fall within a broad-range class but outside a narrow-range subclass, presumably to fill some temporary communicative gap. But when confronted with these usages later, the same adults will often judge them as marginal or even ungrammatical. Here are some examples I have gathered of adult innovations in the dative and locative constructions:

> They filed him with charges.
> They and a lot of other public figures were bestowed yesterday with the 1987 Bozo awards.
> He squeezed them [fish filets] with lemon juice.
> Drizzle them [apple slices] with fresh lemon juice.
> Take a little of the mixture at a time and fill it into the zucchini.
> I'm just going to rinse some water now.
> She pierced needles under her fingernails.
>
> Sun donated them a bunch of computers.
> I returned her the books.
> Can you explain me language breakdown?
> An intriguing down side to the three-hour ceremonies...was the snub extended Michael Jackson.
> Even if he dribbles me in one subject a year...
> When you go I'm going to preach you a great funeral.
> She didn't have to snap me about it.
> We'll credit you back the full purchase price.
> If you'll indulge me just two in-jokes.

Minor differences in children and adult's lexical gaps, together with somewhat different pragmatic and discourse sensibilities, could account for why some of the children's errors like *button me the rest* sound childlike (when they do at all). Otherwise (and apart from the systematic semantic errors discussed above), children are just like adults. Grammaticality and generalizability are not all-or-none for either group. Somewhere between the clearly generalizable verbs (falling within the narrow-range subclasses) and the non-generalizable verbs (outside the broad-range classes) lies a gray area in which verbs can occasionally be used in a construction, but not with unequivocal confidence that the extension is a natural part of the language.

7. Summary

The theory outlined and defended in this paper (see Pinker 1989 for a more detailed presentation) can be summed up simply. There is a paradox in the acquisition of argument structure: languages contain generalizations that children should and do exploit, but the generalizations have lexical exceptions to them, and children cannot count on being corrected if they overgeneralize. The paradox, I suggest, is explained by attributing to speakers certain semantic and morphological *criteria* that distinguish generalizable, nongeneralizable, and partially generalizable verbs. The broad boundaries of generalization (which are never violated) come from the grammatical nature of argument structure alternations: they are interactions between *lexical semantic rules,* that subtly change a verb's meaning, and *linking rules,* that map meanings onto syntactic argument structures. Linking rules seem to be universal and inviolable in development. Lexical semantic structures, or meaning representations, are composed of grammatically-relevant parts and idiosyncratic parts. The former define the narrow boundaries of generalization. Children's errors do not violate the fundamentals of this system; they either come from temporarily incorrect representations of a verb's meaning, or from temporary ungrammatical innovations of a sort that adults make as well.

Acknowledgments

I thank Yukio Otsu for making possible the visit to Japan and the symposium during which this paper was presented, and Jess Gropen, for collaborating on the experiments described herein. The research reported in this paper was supported by NIH Grant HD 18381 and NSF Grant BNS 91-09766.

References

Baker, Carl L. (1979) "Syntactic Theory and the Projection Problem," *Linguistic Inquiry 10,* 533–581.

Bowerman, Melissa (1982) "Reorganizational Processes in Lexical and Syntactic Development," *Language Acquisition: The State of the Art,* ed. by Eric Wanner and Lila R. Gleitman, 319–346, Cambridge University Press, New York.

Bowerman, Melissa (1988) "The 'No Negative Evidence' Problem: How Do Children Avoid Constructing an Overly General Grammar?" *Explaining Language Universals,* ed. by John A. Hawkins, 73–101, Blackwell, Oxford.

Brown, Roger and Camille Hanlon (1970) "Derivational Complexity and Order of Acquisition in Child Speech," *Cognition and the Development of Language,* ed. by John R. Hayes, 11–53, Wiley, New York.

Gentner, Dedre (1978) "On Relational Meaning: The Acquisition of Verb Meaning," *Child Development 49*, 988–998.

Gentner, Dedre (1982) "Why Nouns Are Learned before Verbs: Linguistic Relativity vs. Natural Partitioning," *Language Development 2: Language, Thought, and Culture*, ed. by Stan A. Kuczaj II, 301–334, Lawrence Erlbaum Associates, Hillsdale, NJ.

Gleitman, Lila R. (1990) "The Structural Sources of Verb Meaning," *Language Acquisition 1*, 3–55.

Green, Georgia M. (1974) *Semantics and Syntactic Regularity*, Indiana University Press, Bloomington, Indiana.

Grimshaw, Jane and Steven Pinker (1989) "Positive and Negative Evidence in Language Acquisition (Commentary on David Lightfoot's 'The Child's Trigger Experience: Degree-0 Learnability')," *Behavioral and Brain Sciences 12*, 341.

Gropen, Jess, Steven Pinker, Michelle Hollander, Richard Goldberg, and Ronald Wilson (1989) "The Learnability and Acquisition of the Dative Alternation in English," *Language 65*, 203–257.

Gropen, Jess, Steven Pinker, Michelle Hollander, and Richard Goldberg (1991a) "Syntax and Semantics in the Acquisition of Locative Verbs," *Journal of Child Language 18*, 115–151.

Gropen, Jess, Steven Pinker, Michelle Hollander, and Richard Goldberg (1991b) "Affectedness and Direct Objects: The Role of Lexical Semantics in the Acquisition of Verb Argument Structure," *Cognition 41*, 153–195.

Levin, Beth (1985) "Lexical Semantics in Review: An Introduction," *Lexicon Project Working Papers 1: Lexical Semantics in Review*, ed. by Beth Levin, MIT Center for Cognitive Science, Cambridge, MA.

Levin, Beth and Malka Rappaport Hovav (1991) "Wiping the Slate Clean: A Lexical Semantic Exploration," *Cognition 41*, 123–151.

Marcus, Gary F. (1993) "Negative Evidence in Language Acquisition," to appear in *Cognition*.

Mazurkewich, Irene and Lydia White (1984) "The Acquisition of the Dative Alternation: Unlearning Overgeneralizations," *Cognition 16*, 261–283.

Morgan, James L. and Lisa Travis (1989) "Limits on Negative Information on Language Learning," *Journal of Child Language 16*, 531–552.

Pinker, Steven (1984) *Language Learnability and Language Development*, Harvard University Press, Cambridge, MA.

Pinker, Steven (1989) *Learnability and Cognition: The Acquisition of Argument Structure*, MIT Press, Cambridge, MA.

Pinker, Steven (1994) "How Could a Child Use Verb Syntax to Learn Verb Semantics," *Lingua, 92*, 377–410..

Pinker, Steven, David S. Lebeaux, and Loren Ann Frost (1987) "Productivity and Constraints in the Acquisition of the Passive," *Cognition 26*, 195–267.

Rappaport, Malka and Beth Levin (1985) "A Case Study in Lexical Analysis: The Locative Alternation," ms., MIT Center for Cognitive Science.

7

The Nature of Human Concepts

Evidence from an Unusual Source

with A L A N   P R I N C E

This article grew out of a moment of astonishment that overcame me as I was working with Alan Prince on the analysis of the neural-network model of children's acquisition of the English past tense. Irregular past-tense forms are mostly idiosyncratic. For example, the past tense of sing is sang, but the past tense of string is strung, and the past tense of bring is brought. Yet they fall into clusters of similar verbs that have all the hallmarks of Ludwig Wittgenstein's "family resemblance" categories, in which the various exemplars, like the members of a family, have partial and overlapping traits in common but no single trait that runs through the entire family. String-strung, fling-flung, and cling-clung, for example, end in the velar nasal consonant ng. Stick-stuck and dig-dug end in a consonant that is velar (produced with the soft palate) but not nasal (hummed through the nose), while swim-swum and begin-begun end in a consonant that is nasal but not velar. Why should families of verbs behave like families of people, and like other conceptual categories such as tools, vegetables, and vehicles, which also share partially overlapping features rather than submitting to a neat definition? Conversely, why do regular verbs like walk-walked, stay-stayed, and explain-explained uniformly obey a simple rule ("add –ed"), similar to the way in which arithmetic categories (like "even number"), genealogical categories (like "mother"), and legal categories (like "senator") can be precisely defined by a rule?

A key to the mystery, I thought, was another quirk of the irregular verbs. If we use their spelling as a guide to the way that words used to be pronounced, then some of the irregular families used to be more rule-governed than they are today. Take the family which includes grow-grew, blow-blew, throw-threw, fly-flew, draw-drew, and know-knew. All begin with a cluster of two consonants except the last, know—but its spelling, originating at a time when the k was pronounced, show that it used to obey the rule, but at some point had fallen off the wagon, leaving us with the messy family resemblance category we find today. History turns rule-governed categories into fuzzy ones.

This struck me as a stunning phenomenon, rich with insights about the nature of categories in the world and concepts in the human mind. It has struck no one else that way. As far as I know this article has attracted zero citations (except by me), and the summary of it that served as the climax of my 1999 book Words and Rules: The Ingredients of Language *proved to be just as uninteresting to the world. In this collection I'm going to try one last time.*

This paper is about an extensive parallel we have discovered between a part of language and a part of cognition, and about the possibility that the parallel is not a coincidence. The parallel involves the difference between a *classical category* and a *prototype* or *family resemblance category,* a topic of controversy for many years in cognitive psychology, philosophy, linguistics, and artificial intelligence.

Classical categories are defined by necessary and sufficient criteria, and membership in them is all-or-none. Examples include squares, grandmothers, odd numbers, and the vertebrate class *Aves.* Family Resemblance categories differ from classical categories in a number of ways:

- They *lack necessary and sufficient conditions* for membership. For example, the category "chair" includes objects that have legs and that lack them (e.g. beanbag chairs), and objects that can be sat upon and that cannot (e.g. delicate museum pieces).
- They have *graded degrees of membership.* A robin is a better example of the family resemblance category "bird" than an eagle is; and a penguin a worse example.
- The category can be summarized by an ideal member or *prototype,* sometimes but not always an actual exemplar of the category. The more similar other members are to the prototype, the "better" examples they are. The sparrow, which is used to illustrate the entry for "bird" in many dictionaries, might be a prototype of the bird category.
- There can be *unclear cases*—objects which may or may not be members of the category at all. One example is the fossil genus *Archaeopteryx,* characterized by one paleontologist as "a piss-poor reptile, and not very much of a bird" (Konner, 1982). Garlic is an unclear example of the category "vegetable," as is ketchup, as we see in the famous controversy that followed the proposal of the Reagan administration that ketchup be classified as a vegetable in meeting nutritional guidelines for school lunch menus.
- They often display a *family resemblance* structure (Wittgenstein, 1953).[1] The members of a family of people generally do not have a single feature in common. Instead, a pool of features such as hair color, mouth shape, and nose size is shared by various sets of family members. Similarly, the members of family resemblance categories have different features that run through different subsets: green color is shared by spinach, celery, and broccoli, but not carrots or cauliflower; stems and bunches of florets are shared by broccoli and cauliflower but not carrots.

- Good members tend to have *characteristic nondefining features.* For example, gray hair and a domestic lifestyle characterize many grandmothers, but someone can be a grandmother without possessing either property, such as Elizabeth Taylor.

Evidence for Family Resemblance Categories

Human concepts pick out categories of objects; what kind of category do they pick out? There is a large body of evidence, summarized in Smith and Medin (1981) and Rosch (1972, 1977, 1988), that has been taken to show that human concepts correspond to family resemblance categories.

First, semanticists and philosophers have generally failed in their attempts to find necessary and sufficient conditions for most natural concepts that are labeled by words (see Fodor, Garrett, Walker, and Parkes, 1980). Second, psychologists have found that subjects can give ratings of the goodness of membership of a list of exemplars with respect to a category that are reliable and in close agreement with one another. Similarly, there is good agreement about prototypes and unclear cases. Third, these judgments are not unanalyzable gut feelings but can be predicted in a systematic way using a feature calculus, in which the features possessed by a given exemplar (assessed independently, for example, by asking subjects to list the attributes of the object) are compared with those possessed by the other members of the category. Fourth, judgments of goodness of membership have strong effects on performance in various psychological tasks. For example, people can verify that prototypical members are members of a category faster and more accurately than they do peripheral members, and when asked to recall instances of a category, they name prototypical members first. Fifth, developmental psychologists have found that children often learn the names for prototypical exemplars of a category before learning other exemplars, and apply superordinate terms such as *bird* to its prototypical members first. Sixth, linguists have found that certain adverbials called *hedges* are sensitive to prototypicality: one can say that a sparrow, but not a penguin, is a bird *par excellence,* and that a penguin, but not a sparrow, is *technically* or *strictly speaking* a bird.

Evidence against Family Resemblance Categories

On the other hand, there is also evidence that certain aspects of human concepts do not correspond to family resemblance categories. Some of the empirical effects that have been interpreted as demonstrating family resemblance classes also occur for categories that people clearly treat as being classical. Armstrong, Gleitman, and Gleitman (1983) have found that subjects show a great deal of agreement with one another in rating the degree of membership of exemplars of categories like "female" and "odd number." For example, they agree that a mother is a better example of a female than a comedienne is, and that 13 is a better example of an odd number than 23. Similarly, Armstrong et al. found that people take less time and are more accurate at deciding that 13 is an odd number than that 23 is, and that a mother is a female than that a comedienne is. Since these subjects surely knew that 'female' and 'odd number' in reality have sharp boundaries and all-or-none membership (and Armstrong et al. discovered, in an independent questionnaire, that their subjects believed as such), it calls into question whether the analogous results that Rosch and others obtained for 'bird' or 'tool' really tell us anything about people's representations of those concepts.

Moreover, most judgments of membership in a family resemblance category based on characteristic features are highly corrigible when people are asked to engage in careful reasoning about it. For some purposes people are willing to consider a penguin as a full-fledged bird and Elizabeth Taylor a full-fledged grandmother. In fact characteristic non-defining features can be quickly abandoned, even by young children. Children say that three-legged dogs are dogs, that raccoons with stripes painted down their backs are raccoons, not skunks (Rey, 1983; Armstrong et al., 1983; Keil, 1989).

Similar demonstrations with adults have shown that inference is often not driven by the similarity criteria that define family resemblance categories (see Murphy, 1993; Medin, 1989; Kelly, 1992; Smith, Langston, & Nisbett, 1992; Rips, 1989; Rey, 1983). For example, when people are asked which two out of three belong together—white hair, gray hair, black hair—they say that "black" is the odd hair out, because aging hair turns gray then white. But when asked about a white cloud, a gray cloud, and a black cloud, they say that "white" is the odd cloud out, because gray and black clouds give rain. In another experiment, subjects were asked whether a three-inch disk is more similar to a quarter or a pizza, and whether it is more likely to *be* a quarter or a pizza. Most said it is more similar to a quarter but more likely to be a pizza, presumably because quarters have to be standardized but pizzas can vary. Most people, upon being presented with a centipede, a caterpillar that looks like it, and a butterfly that the caterpillar turns into, feel that the caterpillar and butterfly are "the same animal," but the caterpillar and centipede are not, despite appearances to the contrary.

Possible Resolutions

There are several possible resolutions of this conflicting evidence.

First, human concepts could basically pick out family resemblance categories. Classical categories would be special cases or artifacts resulting from explicit instruction, such as in formal schooling.

Alternatively, human concepts could basically pick out classical categories. Family resemblance categories would be artifacts of experimental tasks asking subjects for graded judgments or asking them to make categorization decisions under time pressure.

A third, compromise position would say that human concepts correspond to both classical and family resemblance categories. Classical categories are the "core" of the concept, used for reasoning. Family resemblance categories are "identification procedures" or "stereotypes," used for identification of category exemplars on the basis of available perceptual information, or for rapid approximate reasoning.

Although most theorists have tended toward compromise positions, something close to the mainly-family-resemblance view can be found in Lakoff (1987), Rosch (1978), and Smith, Medin, and Rips (1984); something close to the mainly-classical view can be found in Rey (1983), Fodor (1981), and Armstrong et al. (1983), and tentative proposals favoring the core-plus-identification-procedure compromise can be found in Smith and Medin (1981), Armstrong et al. (1983), and Osherson and Smith (1981).

This leads to several open questions. (1) Is one type of category psychologically real, the other an artifact or special case? (2) If both are psychologically real, can they be distinguished by function (e.g., reasoning versus categorization)? (3) If both are psychologically real, are they handled by the same kind of computational architecture? (4) If either or both are psychologically real, do they correspond to ontological categories? Rey (1983) stresses the importance of distinguishing the metaphysical problem of what kinds of categories the world contains (as characterized by the best current scientific characterization of that aspect of the world), and the epistemological or psychological question of what kinds of categories people use to understand the world. That is, are classical (or family resemblance) categories incorrectly imposed by people on the world because of limitations of the way the mind works, or is there some sense in which the world contains classical (or family resemblance) categories, which people can accurately represent as such, presumably because the mind evolved to grasp aspects of the world accurately?

We will attempt to shed light on these questions by examining an unusual source of evidence: English past tense forms.

An Unexpected Test Case: English Past Tense Forms

English verbs come in two types: those that have regular past tense forms, and those that have irregular past tense forms. Consider them as two categories: "regular verbs," such as *walk/walked, talk/talked, jog/jogged, pat/patted, kiss/kissed,* and *play/played,* and "irregular verbs," such as *hit/hit, go/went, sleep/slept, make/made, ring/rang, bring/brought, stink/stunk,* and *fly/flew.*

In fact the irregular verbs are not a single class but a set of subclasses, which can be subdivided according to the kind of change that the stem undergoes to form the past tense (see Pinker and Prince, 1988, for a full list). Here are some examples:

- Lax the Vowel: *bleed, breed, feed, lead, mislead, read, speed, plead, meet, hide, slide, bite, light, shoot*
- Lax the Vowel, Add a *-t*: *lose, deal, feel, kneel, mean, dream, creep, keep, leap, sleep, sweep, weep, leave*
- Change the Rhyme to *-ought*: *buy, bring, catch, fight, seek, teach, think*
- Change *i* to *-a* or *u*: *ring, sing, spring, drink, shrink, sink, stink, swim, begin, cling, fling, sling, sting, string, swing, wring, stick, dig, win, spin, stink, slink, run, hang, strike, sneak*
- Change the Vowel to *u*: *blow, grow, know, throw, draw, withdraw, fly, slay*

Let us consider some properties of the irregular subclasses.

Properties of the Irregular Subclasses

1. CHARACTERISTIC NONDEFINING FEATURES

The irregular subclasses tend to be characterized by phonological properties other than those that are strictly necessary to define the change from stem to past form. Consider the subclass that changes an *o* vowel to *u*. *blow, grow, know, throw, draw, withdraw, fly, slay*. In principle, any verb with an *o* or similar vowel could be included in the subclass. In fact, all the verbs in the subclass end in a vowel, usually a diphthong, and most begin with a consonant cluster.

Similarly, the subclass that changes *ay* to *aw*—*bind, find, grind, wind*—could include any verb with the vowel *ay*, but in fact, all the verbs happen to end in *-nd*. The subclass that changes a final *d* to *t*—*bend, send, spend, lend, rend, build*—could include any word ending in *d*, but in fact, most of the verbs rhyme with *-end*. Finally, the subclass that changes the vowel *e* to *U*—*take, mistake, forsake, shake*—could include any word with an *e*, but in fact all the verbs rhyme with *-ake* and begin with a coronal consonant.

Note that the characteristic nondefining features are arbitrary, not lawful, with respect to the sound pattern of English. No rule of phonology excludes *loon* as the past tense of *loan* or *choud* as the past of *chide*.

2. FAMILY RESEMBLANCE

Irregular subclasses display a family resemblance structure (Bybee and Slobin, 1982a; Bybee and Moder, 1983). Consider the subclass that changes an *I* to an ʌ Most of the verbs end with velar nasal consonant: *shrink, sink, stink, cling, fling, sling, sting, string, swing, wring, slink*. Some end in a consonant that is velar but not nasal: *stick, dig, sneak, strike*. Others end in a vowel that is nasal but not velar: *win, spin, swim, begin*.

Similarly, within the subclass that changes a final diphthong to *u*, some begin with a consonant-sonorant cluster, and contain the diphthong *ow: blow, grow, throw*. But one member, *know*, contains the *ow* diphthong, but does not begin with a consonant cluster. Others begin with a consonant cluster, but have a different diphthong or no diphthong: *draw, withdraw, fly, slay*.

3. PROTOTYPICALITY

Bybee and Moder (1983) point out that for many of the subclasses one can characterize a prototype, based on the kinds of characteristic phonological properties that go into defining the family resemblance structure. According to Bybee and Moder, the prototype of the *ing* —> *ung* subclass is:

S C C i [velar nasal]

where 'C' stands for a consonant. This prototype is maximally similar to the most members of the existing subclass, but more interestingly, it predicts subjects' generalization of the *I* —> ʌ change to novel verbs. Bybee and Moder asked subjects to rate how natural a variety of putative past tense forms sounded for each of a set of nonce stems. The independent variable was the similarity of the stem to the prototype listed above. They found that subjects were extremely likely to accept the vowel change for stems like *spling, strink*, and *skring*, which match the schema for the prototype exactly. They were only slightly less willing to accept *struck* and *skrum* as the past of *strick* and *skrim*, which differ from the prototype in one feature. Somewhat lower in acceptability were *spruv* for *spriv*, and similar past forms for *sking, smig, pling* and *krink*. *Glick, krin, plim, shink* were even less likely to admit of the vowel change, and *trib, vin*, and *sid*, the forms furthest from the prototype, were the least acceptable of all. The results have been replicated by Prasada and Pinker (1993), and with analogous German forms by Marcus, Brinkmann, Clahsen, Wiese, & Pinker (1995).

4. GRADED GOODNESS-OF-MEMBERSHIP

Within most of the subclasses, there are some verbs that clearly accept the irregular past tense form, but others, usually of low but nonzero frequency, for which the specified past tense form is less than fully acceptable, being accompanied by a sense of unusualness or stiltedness. Below we contrast, for a variety of subclasses, some "good examples" of the past tense form with "poor examples" of the same kinds of forms. Intuitions vary from person to person for the "poor" examples, as is true for nonprototypical exemplars of conceptual categories; the perceptions of "poorness" we report here are true for most of the speakers of American English we have consulted, and are documented quantitatively by Ullman (1993):

(1)

Good Examples	Poor Examples
hit, split	spit, forbid
bled, fed	pled, sped
burnt, bent	learnt, lent, rent
dealt, felt, meant	knelt, dreamt
froze, spoke	wove, hove
got, forgot	begot, trod
wrote, drove, rode	dove, strove, smote, strode

5. UNCLEAR CASES

For some verbs associated with a subclass, the mandated past tense form is so poor in people's judgment that it is unclear whether the verb can be said to belong to the subclass at all. Sometimes these are verbs are restricted to idioms, clichés, or other specialized usages. For example, the expression *forgo the pleasure of,* as in *You will excuse me if I forgo the pleasure of reading your paper until it's published,* sounds fairly natural. Because the verb has a transparent morphological decomposition as [*for* + *go*], the form *forgoed* is clearly unacceptable, but the irregular past tense form, as in *Last night I forwent the pleasure of grading student papers,* is decidedly peculiar if not outright ungrammatical (this intuition has been corroborated by ratings from subject in an unpublished study by Michael Ullman and me). Likewise, the sentence *the Vietnam War is rending the fabric of American society* is a natural-sounding cliché, but ?*The Vietnam War rent the fabric of American society* is distinctly less natural. One occasionally hears the idiom *That conclusion does not sit well with me,* but many people balk at *That conclusion has not sat well with many people. That dress really becomes you* is a natural English sentence; *When you were ten pounds lighter, that dress really became you* is almost unintelligible.

In other cases grammatical phenomena conspire to make the past tense form of a verb extremely rare. The transitive verb *stand* meaning "to tolerate" is fairly common, but because it is usually used as the complement of a negated auxiliary, as in *She can't stand him,* the verb is almost always heard in its stem form. In constructions where the past is allowed to reveal itself, the verb sounds odd: compare *I don't know how she stands him* with ?*I don't know how she stood him;* similarly, *I don't know how she bears it* versus ?*I don't know how she bore it.*

Conclusions about the Irregular Subclasses

Subclasses of irregular verbs in English have characteristic nondefining features, family resemblance structures, prototypes, gradations of goodness of membership, and unclear or fuzzy cases. Since these are exactly the properties that define family resemblance categories, we conclude, in agreement with Bybee and Moder (1983), that the irregular subclasses are family resemblance categories.

This is a surprising conclusion. Linguistic rules are traditionally thought of as paradigm case of categorical, all-or-none operations, and might be thought to correspond to classical categories if anything did. The fact that entities subject to grammatical operations can have a clear family resemblance structure thus has far-ranging implications for some theorists. For example, for Rumelhart and McClelland (1986) this phenomenon is part of their argument for a radically new approach to studying language, based on a computational architecture in which rules play no causal role. For Lakoff (1987), it is part of a call for a radically new way of understanding human cognition in general.

It seems clear that at least one kind of linguistic object, English irregular past tenses, fall into family resemblance categories. An important question at this point is: Do all linguistic objects fall into family resemblance categories?

Properties of the Regular Class

More specifically, we might ask, do English *regular* verbs fall into family resemblance categories? One answer, favored by Bybee (Bybee and Moder, 1983; Bybee, 1991) and by Rumelhart and McClelland (1986) is "yes": the regular class just has more members, and more general characteristic features. Let us examine this possibility.

A Confounding Factor: The Blocking Principle

The regular and irregular classes interact in a specific way, and it is necessary to take account of this interaction so that the properties of the irregular subclasses do not confound our examination of the properties of the regular class. The interaction is governed by what has been called the Blocking Principle (Aronoff, 1976) and the Unique Entry Principle (Pinker, 1984): if a verb has an irregular past tense form, its regular form is pre-empted or "blocked." Thus the fact that *go* has an irregular past *went* not only allows us to talk of past instances of going using *went,* but it prevents us from using *goed.* The verb *glow,* in contrast, does not have an irregular past *glew,* so its regular past *glowed* is not blocked.

We saw in a previous section how some irregular past forms are "fuzzy" or marginal in their grammaticality. As a result of Blocking, these gradations of goodness can cause the appearance of complementary gradations of goodness of the corresponding regular. Thus because *pled* is a marginal past tense form for *plead* but one that we nonetheless recognize, the regular form *pleaded guilty* sounds fairly good but for some speakers may be tinged with a bit of uncertainty. Conversely, *wept* is a fairly good past tense form of *weep*, though not maximally natural (compare, for example, *kept* for *keep*). As a result *??weeped* does not sound terribly good, though it is not perceived as being completely ungrammatical either (compare *keeped*). This effect has been documented by Michael Ullman (1993; see also Pinker, 1991 and Pinker & Prince, 1994) who asked subjects to rate the naturalness of irregular and regularized past tense forms for 40 verbs whose irregular pasts were somewhat fuzzy in goodness. The two sets of ratings were consistently negatively correlated.

What we now try to do is put aside this tradeoff due to blocking and assess whether the regular class has family resemblance-category properties independent of those of the irregular subclasses with which it competes.

1. INDEPENDENCE OF THE PHONOLOGY OF THE STEM

The first salient property of the regular class is that it has no sensitivity to the phonological properties of its stems. As a result, it has no phonologically characterized prototype, gradations of membership, or characteristic features.

First, the phonological conditions that govern the irregular subclasses can be entirely flouted by regular verbs. In the extreme case, homophones can have different past tense forms: *ring/rang* versus *wring/wrung, hang/hung* (suspend) versus *hang/hanged* (execute), *lie/lay* (recline) versus *lie/lied* (fib), *fit/fit* (what a shirt does) versus *fit/fitted* (what a tailor does). More generally, there are regular counterexamples to the membership criteria for each of the irregular subclasses:

(2)

shut/shut/	jut/jutted
bleed/bled	need/needed
bend/bent	mend/mended
sleep/slept	seep/seeped
sell/sold	yell/yelled
freeze/froze	seize/seized
grow/grew	glow/glowed
take/took	fake/faked
stink/stunk	blink/blinked
ring/rang	ring/ringed

This shows that the phonologically defined fuzzy boundaries of the irregular subclasses do not create complementary phonological fuzzy boundaries of the regular classes. The effect of the Blocking Principle is that specific irregular *words* block their corresponding regulars. Though most of those words come from regions of phonological space whose neighbors are also often irregular, those regions do not define complementary fuzzy holes in the space from which the regulars are excluded; a regular form can occupy any point in that space whatsoever.

Moreover, it is not just that there already exist regular verbs in the language that live in irregular phonological neighborhoods Regular class can *add* members that violate *any* irregular membership criteria. The reason has been spelled out by Kiparsky (1982a,b), Pinker and Prince (1988, 1992), Kim, Pinker, Prince, & Prasada (1991), Kim, Marcus, Pinker, Hollander, & Coppola (1994). Irregular forms are verb roots, not verbs. Not all verbs have verb roots: a verb that is intuitively derived from a noun (e.g. *to nail*) has a noun root. A noun or an adjective cannot be marked in the lexicon has having an "irregular past," because nouns and adjectives do not have past tense forms at all; the notion makes no sense. Therefore, a verb created out of a noun or adjective cannot have an irregular past either. All such verbs are regular, regardless of their phonological properties:

(3)

> He braked the car suddenly. ≠ broke
> He flied out to center field. ≠ flew
> He ringed the city with artillery. *rang
> Martina 2-setted Chris. *2-set
> He sleighed down the hill. *slew
> He de-flea'd his dog. *de-fled
> He spitted the pig. *spat
> He righted the boat. *rote
> He high-sticked the goalie. *high-stuck
> He grandstanded to the crowd. *grandstood.

This makes it possible, in principle, for any sound sequence whatsoever to become a regular verb. There is a lexical rule in English that converts a name into a verb prefixed with *out*, as in *Reagan has finally out-Nixoned Nixon*. Like all verbs derived from non-verbs, it is regular. Since any linguistically-possible sound can be someone's name, any linguistically possible sound can be a regular verb, allowing there to be regular homophones for any irregular. For example:

(4)

> Mary out-Sally-Rided Sally Ride.
> *Mary out-Sally-Rode Sally Ride.
> In grim notoriety, Alcatraz out-Sing-Singed Sing-Sing.
> *In grim notoriety, Alcatraz out-Sing-Sang Sing-Sing.

This effect has been demonstrated experimentally with several kinds of participants. Kim et al. (1991) asked subjects to rate the regular and irregular past tense forms of a set of verbs which were either derived from nouns that were homophonous with an irregular verb or were derived directly from the irregular verbs. For verbs with noun roots, the regular form was given higher ratings; for verbs with verb roots, the irregular form was given higher ratings. Similar effects have been demonstrated in non-college-educated subjects (Kim et al., 1991), children (Kim et al., 1994), and German-speaking adults (Marcus et al., 1995).

Perfectly natural-sounding regular past tense forms exist not only when the verb root is similar to an irregular but when it is dissimilar to existing regular roots, and hence lacks a prototype that would serve as the source of an analogical generalization. Prasada and Pinker (1993) replicated Bybee and Moder's (1983) study but also presented novel *regular* words of differing similarity to existing English regular words. For example, *plip* is close to one of the prototypes for regular verbs in English, because it rhymes with *slip, flip, trip, nip, sip, clip, dip, grip, strip, tip, whip,* and *zip,* whereas *smaig* rhymes with no existing verb root, and *ploamph* is not even phonologically well-formed in English. Nonetheless people rated the prototypical and peripheral forms as sounding equally natural (relative to their stems), and produced the prototypical and peripheral forms with the same probability when they had to produce them.

2. NO PROTOTYPES, GRADATION OF MEMBERSHIP, OR UNCLEAR CASES CAUSED BY LOW FREQUENCY OR RESTRICTED CONTEXTS

Unlike irregular past tense forms, regular past tense forms do not suffer in well-formedness on account of frequency, familiarity, idiomaticity, frozenness, or restricted syntactic contexts. Pinker and Prince (1988) noted that though the verb *perambulate* may be of low frequency, it is no worse-sounding in its past tense form than it is in its stem form; there is no feeling that *perambulated* is a worse past tense form of *perambulate* than *walked* is of *walk.* In fact, a verb can be of essentially zero frequency and still have a regular past tense form that is judged as no worse than the verb itself. Though *fleech, fleer,* and *anastomose* are unknown to most speakers, speakers judge *fleeched, fleered,* and *anastomosed* to be perfectly good as the past tense forms of those verbs. These observations have been confirmed experimentally by Ullman (1993), in a study in which people judged the naturalness of hundreds of verbs and their past tense forms. Subjects' ratings of regular pasts correlate highly with their ratings of the corresponding stems, but not with the frequency of the past form (partialing out stem rating). In contrast, ratings of irregular pasts correlate less strongly with their stem ratings but significantly with past frequency, partialing out stem rating.

Unlike irregular verbs, when a regular verb gets trapped in a frozen or restricted expression, putting it into the past tense makes it no worse. For example, the verb *eke* is seldom used outside contexts such as *She ekes out a living,* but *She eked out a living,* unlike *forwent the pleasure of,* does not suffer because of it. Similarly: *He crooked his finger; She stinted no effort; I broached the subject with him; The news augured well for his chances.* The regular verb *to afford,* like the irregular verb *to stand,* usually occurs as a complement to *can't,* but when liberated from this context its past tense form is perfectly natural: *I don't know how she afforded it.* Similarly, both *She doesn't suffer fools gladly* and *She never suffered fools gladly* are acceptable.

The phenomena discussed in this section and the preceding one show why the apparent gradedness of acceptability of regular forms like *pleaded* or *weeped* can be localized to the gradedness of the corresponding irregulars, thanks to the effects of the Blocking principle, and are not inherent to the regular verbs per se. The gradedness of certain irregulars generally comes from low frequency combined with similarity to the prototypes of their subclasses (Ullman, 1993). But for regular verbs that do not compete with specific irregular roots, there is no complementary landscape of acceptability defined by phonology and frequency; all are equally good.

3. DEFAULT STRUCTURE

As we have seen, the regular past tense alternation can apply regardless of the stem's phonological properties, verb-root versus non-verb-root status, frequency, listedness (familiarity), and range of contexts. It seems that regular verbs are a *default* class. The category of regular verbs in a sense has no properties; it is an epiphenomenon of the scope of application of the regular rule.

Conclusions about the Regular Class

These phenomena invite the following conclusion: The class of regular verbs in English is a classical category. Its necessary and sufficient conditions are simply the conditions of application of the regular rule within English grammar. Those conditions for membership can be stated simply: a member must be a verb, unless it has an irregular root.

Psychological Implications

We have shown that by the standard criteria the irregular subclasses are prototype or family resemblance categories, and the regular class is a classical category. If we take this conclusion seriously, it has several immediate implications.

Psychological Reality

First, both family resemblance categories and classical categories can be psychologically real and natural. Classical categories need not be the product of explicit instruction or formal schooling: the regular past tense alternation does not have to be taught, and indeed every child learns it and begins to use it productively in the third year of life (Marcus, Pinker, Ullman, Hollander, Rosen, & Xu, 1992). The fact that children apply the regular alternation even to high-frequency irregular stems such as *come* and *go*, which they also use with their correct irregular pasts much of the time, suggests that children in some way appreciate the inherently universal range of the regular rule. And like adults, they apply the regular suffix to regular verbs regardless of the degree of the verbs' similarity to other regular verbs (Marcus et al., 1992), and to irregular-sounding verbs that are derived from nouns and adjectives (Kim et al., 1994). Gordon (1985) and Stromswold (1990) have shown that children as young as three make qualitative distinctions between regular and irregular plural nouns related to their different formal roles within the grammar, without the benefit of implicit or explicit teaching inputs (see Marcus et al., 1992, and Kim et al., 1994 for discussion).

The regularization-through-derivation effect (*flied out, high-sticked*) provides particularly compelling evidence that classical categories do not have to be the product of rules that are explicitly formulated and deliberately transmitted. The use of the regular rule as a default operation, applying to any derived verb regardless of its phonology, is a grass-roots phenomenon whose subtleties are better appreciated at an unconscious level by the person in the street than by those charged with formulating prescriptive rules. Kim et al. (1991) found that non-college-educated subjects showed the effect strongly, and in the recent history of English and other languages there are documented cases in which the language has accommodated such regularizations in the face of explicit opposition from editors and prescriptive grammarians. For example, Mencken (1936) notes that the verb *to joy-ride*, which first attained popularity in the 1920's, was usually given the past tense form *joy-rided,* as we would predict given its obvious derivation from the noun *a joy-ride.* Prescriptive grammarians unsuccessfully tried to encourage *joy-rode* in its place. Similarly, Kim et al. (1994) showed that children display the effect despite the fact that most have rarely or ever heard regularized past tense forms for irregular-sounding verbs in the speech of adults.

On the other side, family resemblance categories are not necessarily artifacts of reaction time studies or rating studies, as Fodor (1981) and Armstrong et al. (1983) have suggested. Children generalize family resemblance patterns of irregular subclasses to inappropriate regular and irregular verbs in their spontaneous speech, as in *brang* for *brought* and *bote* for *bit*, and their generalizations appear to be sensitive to the frequency and family resemblance structure of the subclasses (Xu & Pinker, 1995; Bybee and Slobin, 1982a; Rumelhart and McClelland, 1986; Pinker & Prince, 1988). The irregular subclass structure also affects dialectal variation and historical change in adult speech (Bybee and Slobin, 1982b; Mencken, 1936; Prasada & Pinker, 1993) with new irregular forms occasionally entering the language if their stems are sufficient similar to existing irregular stems.

Psychological Function

A further corollary is that classical categories and family resemblance categories do not have to have different psychological functions such as careful versus casual reasoning, or reasoning versus categorization of exemplars. What is perhaps most striking about the contrast between the regular and irregular verbs is that the two kinds of entities live side-by-side in people's heads, serving the same function within the grammar as a whole: regular and irregular verbs play indistinguishable roles in the syntax and semantics of tense in English. There is no construction, for example, in which a regular but not an irregular verb can be inserted or vice-versa, and no systematic difference in the temporal relationships semantically encoded in the past tense forms of regular and irregular verbs.

More specifically, it is difficult to make sense of the notion that family resemblance categories are the product of a set of identification procedures used to classify exemplars as belonging to core categories with a more classical structure. The suggestion that "irregulars are used in perceptually categorizing members of the regular class" is uninterpretable. The irregulars are a class of words that display one kind of category structure; the regulars do not display it.

Underlying Psychological Mechanism

Though classical and family resemblance categories, in the case of the past tense, do not differ in psychological function (what they are used for), they do differ in psychological structure (which mental processes give rise to them).

As we have seen, the classical category consisting of regular verbs is defined completely and implicitly by the nature of a rule in the context of a formal system, in this case, a rule within English grammar which applies to any word bearing the part-of-speech symbol "verb," unless it has an irregular root. The category is not a generalization or summary over a set of exemplars; indeed, it is blind to the properties of the exemplars that fall into the category. It falls out of the combinatorial rule system that allows humans to communicate propositions (including novel, unusual, or abstract propositions) by building complex words, phrases, and sentences in which the meaning of the whole is determinable by the meanings of the parts and the way in which they are combined.

Family resemblance categories, in contrast, are generalizations of patterns of property correlations within a set of memorized exemplars. Consequently, factors that affect human memory affect the composition of the irregular class. A well-known example is word frequency. Irregular verbs tend to be higher in frequency than regular verbs (Ullman, 1993; Marcus et al., 1995), and if an irregular verb's frequency declines historically, it is liable to become regular (Hooper, 1976; Bybee and Slobin, 1982b; Bybee, 1985). Presumably this is because irregulars are essentially memorized. To memorize an item one has to hear it; if opportunities for hearing an item are few, its irregular form cannot be acquired and the regular rule can apply as the default. This is also presumably the cause of the fuzziness of the past tenses of irregular verbs that are used mainly in nonpast forms, such as *forgo* or the idiomatic meanings of *stand* or *become.*

A related account could help explain the genesis of the family resemblance structure of the irregular verbs. Rosch and Mervis (1975) found that people find lists of strings that display family resemblance structures easier to remember than lists of strings with arbitrary patterns of similarity. Just as frequency affects the memorizability, and hence composition, of the irregular subclasses, so might family resemblance structure. The current subclasses may have emerged from a Darwinian process in which the irregular verbs that survived the generation-to-generation memorization cycle were those that could be grouped into easy-to-remember family resemblance clusters.

In sum, the properties of the regular and irregular classes of verbs in English show that both classical categories and family resemblance categories can be psychologically real, easily and naturally acquired, and not subject to a division of labor by function along the lines of reasoning-versus-identification of exemplars. Rather, they differ because they are the products of two different kinds of mental processes: a formal rule system, and a memorized, partially-structured list of exemplars. We now point out two less obvious conclusions. Classical and prototype categories are suited to different kinds of computational architectures, and the mental mechanisms giving rise to classical and family resemblance categories are suited to representing inherently different kinds of entities in the world. Finally, we return to human conceptual categories like "bird" and "mother," seeing whether we can gain insight by generalizing our findings about classical and prototype categories.

Computational Architecture

The acquisition of English past tense morphology has recently been implemented in a computer simulation model by Rumelhart and McClelland (1986). The architecture of the simulation, its behavior, and its fidelity to human data have been discussed in detail (Pinker & Prince, 1988, 1992; Lachter and Bever, 1988; Sproat, 1992; Prasada & Pinker, 1993; Marcus et al., 1992, 1995).

The RM model makes use of a device called a "pattern associator." This device is paradigmatic of Parallel Distributed Processing (PDP) or Connectionist architectures that are currently a central topic of debate in cognitive science (Rumelhart & McClelland, 1986; McClelland & Rumelhart, 1986; Pinker & Mehler, 1988).

Two properties of pattern associators are crucial in understanding their behavior: items are represented by their properties, and statistical contingencies between every input property and every output property across a set of items are recorded and superimposed.

Before being applied to the case of learning past tense forms, pattern associators had been studied in detail, including their ability to learn and identify members of conceptual categories (McClelland & Rumelhart, 1985) and they are known to do certain things well. They can often reproduce a set of associations in a training set, and generalize to new cases based on their similarity to existing ones. They are sensitive to input pattern frequencies in ways similar to humans. Furthermore they reproduce many of the effects displayed by people when dealing with family resemblance categories. McClelland & Rumelhart (1985) and Whittlesea (1989) have devised pattern associators that are fed sequences of data concerning properties of a set of nonlinguistic objects. They found that the models do fairly well at duplicating the effects of frequency, prototypicality, family resemblance, gradations of membership, and the influence of particular exemplars on human classification times and error rates. Since such effects are known to be related to co-occurrence frequencies among objects' features (Smith & Medin, 1981), this is not surprising.

Thanks to these abilities, the pattern associator that Rumelhart and McClelland applied to learning past tense forms handled the irregular verbs with some success. The model was fed a set of 420 verbs (each one presented as a pair consisting of its stem and its past form), including 84 irregular verbs, about 200 times each. Following this training it was able to approximate the past tense forms for all of them given only the stem as input. Furthermore, it was able to generalize to new irregular verbs by analogy to similar ones in the training set, such as *bid* for *bid, clung* for *cling,* and *wept* for *weep.* In addition, it showed a tendency to extend some of the subregular alternations to regular verbs based on their similarity to irregulars, such as *kid* for *kid* and *slept* for *slip,* showing a sensitivity to the family resemblance structure of the irregular subclasses. Finally, its tendencies to overgeneralize the regular *d* ending to the various irregular subclasses is in rough accord with children's tendencies to do so, which in turn is based on the frequency and consistency of the vowel changes that the verbs within each subclass undergo (Pinker & Prince, 1988; Sproat, 1992).[2]

However, pattern associators do not seem to perform as well for other kinds of mappings. In particular, they are deficient in handling regular verbs. For one thing, the model's uniform structure, in which regulars and irregulars are handled by a single associative mechanism, provides no explanation for why the regular class has such different properties from the irregular classes; it falsely predicts that the regular class should just be a larger and more general prototype subclass.

Moreover, the pattern associator fails to acquire the regulars properly. Pinker & Prince (1988) pointed out that the model is prone to *blending.* Competing statistical regularities in which a stem participates do not block each other, they get superimposed. For example, the model produced erroneous forms in which an irregular vowel change was combined with the regular ending, as in *sepped* as the past of *sip* or *browned* for *brown*. It would often blend the *t* and *id* variants of the regular past tense form, producing *stepted* for *step* or *typted* for *type*. Sometimes the blends were quite odd, such as *membled* for *mailed* or *toureder* for *tour*.

Furthermore, Pinker & Prince noted that in contrast to the default nature of the regular rule, the RM model failed to produce any past form at all for certain verbs, such as *jump, pump, glare,* and *trail*. Presumably this was because the model could not treat the regular ending as an operation that was capable of applying to any stem whatsoever, regardless of its properties; the ending was simply associated with the features of the regular stems encountered in the input. If a new verb happened to lie in a region of phonological space in which no verbs had previously been supplied in the training set (e.g. *jump* and *pump*, with their unusual word-final consonant cluster), no coherent set of output features was strongly enough associated with the active input features, and no response above the background noise could be produced. Pinker & Prince's diagnosis was tested by Prasada and Pinker (1993) who presented typical-sounding and unusual-sounding verbs to the trained network. For the unusual-sounding items, it produced odd blends and chimeras such as *smairf-sprurice, trilb-treelilt, smeej-leefloag,* and *frilg-freezled*.

The model is also inconsistent with developmental evidence. Children first use many irregulars properly when they use them in a past tense form at all (e.g. *broke*), then begin to overregularize them occasionally (producing both *broke* and *breaked*) before the overregularizations drop out years later. Since pattern associators are driven by pattern frequency, the only way the RM model could be made to duplicate this sequence was first to expose it to a small number of high-frequency verbs, most of them irregular, presented a few times each, followed by a large number of medium-frequency verbs, most of them regular, presented many times each. Only when the model was swamped with exemplars of the regular pattern did it begin to overregularize verbs it had previously handled properly. However, the onset of overregularization in children is not caused by a sudden shift in the proportion of regular verbs in the speech they hear from their parents: the proportion remains largely unchanged before, during, and after the point at which they begin to overregularize (Pinker & Prince, 1988; Slobin, 1971; Marcus et al., 1992). Nor is it caused by a rapid increase in the proportion of verbs in their vocabulary that is regular; the percentage of children's vocabulary that is regular increases quickly when they are not overregularizing, and increases more slowly when they are overregularizing (Marcus et al., 1992).

The results support the traditional explanation of overregularization, which appeals not to frequency but to different internal mechanisms: children at first memorize irregular and regular pasts, then they discover that a regularity holds between many regular stems and their past forms, and create a rule which they apply across the board, including instances in which a memorized irregular form does not come to mind quickly enough. The rule is available to fill the gap, resulting in an overregularization. Consistent with this interpretation, Marcus et al. (1992) found that children begin to overregularize at the age at which they first start using *regular* forms consistently in the past tense; that, presumably, is the point at which the regular rule has been acquired. As mentioned, the fact that the regular rule is applied even to high-frequency irregular stems, which remain high in frequency in children's input throughout development, shows that children treat the regular rule as having an unlimited range.

Proponents of connectionist models of language have offered two kinds of counterarguments, but both are inadequate. One is that the RM model was a two-layer perceptron, and that three-layer models, which have a hidden layer whose weights are trained by error-back-propagation, perform much better (see, e.g., Plunkett & Marchman, 1991, 1993; MacWhinney & Leinbach, 1992). However, Sproat (1992), Prasada & Pinker (1993), and Marcus (1995) have shown that hidden-layer models have the same problems as the original RM model. The other reply is that the effects of regularity in English come from the fact that regular verbs are in the majority in English, fostering the broadest generalization. The German language presents a crucial comparison. Marcus et al. (1995) reviewed the grammar and vocabulary statistics of German, and documented that the participle *-t* and plural *-s* are found in a *minority* of words in the language, compared to irregular alternatives, but nonetheless apply in exactly the "default" circumstances where access to memorized verbs or their sounds fails, including novel, unusual-sounding, and derived words (i.e., the *flied-out* examples have exact analogues in German). The findings were verified in two experiments eliciting ratings of novel German words from German adults. The cross-linguistic comparison suggests that default suffixation is not explicable in terms of numerous regular words reinforcing a pattern in associative memory, but in terms of a memory-independent, symbol-concatenating mental operation.

In sum, pattern associators handle irregular subclasses reasonably well, but handle the regular class poorly, both in terms of computational ability and psychological fidelity. We suggest that this is a symptom of the relative suitability of this architecture to handle family resemblance and classical categories in general. The reasons, we suggest, are straightforward:

- Classical categories are the product of formal rules.
- Formal rules apply to objects regardless of their content (that is what "formal rule" means).
- Pattern associators soak up patterns of correlation among objects' contents— that is what they are designed to do.
- Therefore, pattern associators are not suited to handling classical categories.

We conclude that the brain contains some kind of non-associative architecture, used in language, and presumably elsewhere.

Epistemological Categories versus Ontological Categories

Rey (1983) has pointed out that even if people can be shown to use prototype (or classical) categories, it doesn't mean that the world contains prototype (or classical) categories—that is, that the lawful generalizations of how the world works, as captured by the best scientific description, make reference to one kind of category or the other. That raises a question: if there is a psychological distinction between the representation of prototype and classical categories, is it because these representations accurately reflect different kinds of categories in the world? Or does the human system of categorization arise from some limitation or quirk of our neurological apparatus which does necessarily correspond to the lawful groupings in the world?

The question of what kinds of categories are in the mind and what kinds of categories are in the world are related. If the mind evolved to allow us to grasp and make predictions about the world, the mental system that forms conceptual categories should be built around implicit assumptions about the kinds of categories that that the world contains, in the same way that a visual algorithm for recovering structure from motion might presuppose a world with rigid objects and might work best in situations where the assumption is satisfied.

Because the English past tense system shows classical and family resemblance categories, but must have a very different ontology from that underlying concepts of tools, vegetables, animals, and other entities that ordinarily compose conceptual categories, an analysis of the source of classical and family resemblance categories in the past tense system may help us to identify the distinctive conditions in which these two kinds of categories arise.

Where Do the Properties of the Regular and Irregular Classes Come From?

The properties of the regular class are simply products of the regular rule. From any speaker's perspective, the class exists "in the world" in the sense that other speakers of the language possess the rule and use it in speaking and understanding. This in turn comes from the basic requirement for parity in any communicative system. Language can function only if the rule system that generates forms is shared by a community of speakers. Thus one person's use of a past tense rule (or any rule) in production presupposes that the same rule is in the head of the listener and that it will be used to interpret the produced form. Similarly, the use of a rule in comprehension presupposes that the speaker used it in programming his speech. So the answer to the question "What class of entities in the world is picked out by a rule-generated class, such as the regular verbs?" is: "The class of entities that can be generated by a replica of that rule in other speakers' minds."

For the irregulars, the issue is more complex. Of course, irregulars, like regulars, are usable only because they are shared by other speakers. But unlike the case of regulars, where the rule is so simple and efficient that it naturally fits into a grammar shared by all members of a community, the composition of the irregular class is so seemingly illogical that one must ask how other speakers came to possess it to begin with.

In a previous section we alluded to a Darwinian metaphor in the struggle for survival among verbs in the memories of the speakers whose learning in turn shapes the input to the current generation. Even though each generation reproduces the previous generation's irregulars with high accuracy, changes occasionally creep in. These changes result in both convergent evolution, in which new members are attracted to existing subclasses, and divergent evolution, in which old members drift away.

Convergent evolution toward certain attractor states may take place when certain regular verbs are attracted into an irregular class because of their high similarity to existing irregulars, as is happening today with *sneak-snuck* (cf. *stick-stuck, string-strung,* etc.). If some of these occasional forgettings and analogies get fixed in a language community in a contagion-like process (see Cavalli-Svorza and Feldman, 1981) and accumulate across generations, classes of verbs with a family resemblance structure can arise. The past tense forms *quit* and *knelt,* for example, are fairly recent additions to the language, and are presumably irregular because of their similarity to verbs like *hit* and *feel.* This process can be seen even more clearly in the more rapid process of dialect formation in smaller communities, where forms such as *bring-brang, slide-slud,* and *drag-drug* are common (see Mencken, 1936).

In the history of English, divergence has been an even more prominent trend. In Old English, there were seven "strong" past tense classes, in which the vowel of the stem was altered, and three "weak" classes, in which a suffix containing *d* was added, which sometimes caused a modification of the stem vowel for phonological reasons. Most of the modern irregulars derived from verbs in the strong classes. The modern regular rule, and most of the irregulars that end in *t* or *d* such as *meant* and *made,* evolved from the weak classes. The Old English strong classes had themselves evolved out of classes that can be traced back to Proto-Germanic, and before that, to Proto-Indo-European. Many scholars believe that the proto-Indo-European classes were defined by regular rules: the number and type of segments following the vowel within the stem determined the kind of change the vowel underwent (Johnson, 1986; Bever and Langendoen, 1963; Prokosch, 1939; Campbell, 1959). By the time of Old English the patterns are more complicated, but they were still more pervasive and productive and tolerated fewer arbitrary exceptions than the alternations in the modern English irregular subclasses. That is, many stems that are now regular but fit the characteristic pattern of an irregular subclass in fact used to undergo the irregular change: *deem/dempt, lean/leant, chide/chid, seem/sempt, believe/beleft, greet/gret, heat/het, bite/bote, slide/slode, abide/abode, fare/fore, help/holp,* and many others. Furthermore, there was a moderate degree of productivity within the classes (Johnson, 1986).

Beginning in the Middle English period, there was an even greater decline in the productivity and systematicity of the past tense subclasses, with the exception of one of the weak suffixing processes. The main causes were the huge influx of new words from Latin and French that needed a general, condition-free past tense operation, and the widespread shifts in vowel pronunciation that obscured regularities in the vowel-change operations. The weak suffixing operation was already being used in Old English for verbs derived from nouns, which did not fit the sound patterns defining the strong classes of verbs, so their extension to borrowed words was natural (see Marcus et al., 1995 for further discussion).

In sum, there has been a marded trend in the history of English since the Proto-Indo-European period for the strong classes, originally defined by phonological properties of their stems, to become lists of items to be learned individually. This had an interesting consequence. Originally, lists would have been relatively homogeneous, owing to their once having been generated by rule-like operations. But then, a variety of unrelated processes, operating on individual items, destroyed the homogeneity of the classes. Here are some examples:

Phonological Change: *Blow, grow, throw, know, draw, fly, slay* all begin with a consonant-sonorant cluster except for *know*. The reason that *know* is exceptional leaps from the page in the way it is spelled. As it was originally pronounced, with an initial *k*, it did fit the pattern; when syllable-initial *kn* mutated to *n* within the sound pattern of the language as a whole, *know* was left stranded as an exception within its subclass.

Morphological Category Collapse: In Old English, past tenses were distinguished by person and number. For example, *sing* had a paradigm which we can simplify as follows:

(5)

	Singular	**Plural**
1st	*sang*	*sung*
2nd	*sung*	*sung*
3rd	*sang*	*sung*

When the number distinctions collapsed, each verb had to pick a form for its past tense, as if playing musical chairs. Different verbs made different choices; hence we have *sing/sang/sung* alongside *sling/slung/slung*. The contrast between *freeze/froze* and *cleave/cleft* has a similar cause.

Attrition: Earlier, the class in which *t* changed to *d* had the following members; *bend, lend, send, spend, blend, wend, rend, shend, build, geld, gild, gird* (Bybee & Slobin, 1982b). The class is succinctly characterized as containing a vowel followed by a sonorant followed by *d*. In modern American English, the verbs *geld, gird, gild, wend, rend* and *shend* are now obsolete or obscure. The residue of the class has five members, four rhyming with *end* and one with *ild*. Although logically it still can be characterized as ending in a vowel-sonorant-*d* cluster, the presence of regular verbs ending in *eld* and *ird,* and the highly specific nature of the rhyme with *end,* makes it more natural to represent the class as containing verbs that rhyme with *end* but with one exception.

We conclude that a class of items that originally is homogeneous on account of its being generated by a rule can acquire a family resemblance structure by divergent evolution once the rule ceases to operate and the effects of unrelated processes acting on individual members accumulates through history. Superimposed on these patterns is a convergent process in which the accumulated effects of the analogizing and forgetting tendencies of previous generations of learners cause partly similar forms to accrete onto an existing class. Thus a learner in a single generation is confronted with family resemblance structures as products of these divergent and convergent historical processes, and these structures can be said to exist in the world independent of his or her psychology.

Implications for Conceptual Categories

Do the discoveries about classical and family resemblance categories in past-tense forms offer insight into the role of classical and family resemblance categories in the domain of conceptual categories like birds and mothers? The best way to begin to answer this question is to consider what conceptual categories are for.

The Function of Conceptual Categories: Inference of Unobserved Properties

No two objects are exactly alike. So why do we use conceptual categories? Why don't we treat every object as the unique individual that it is? And why do we form the categories we do? Why lump together salmon, minnow, and sharks, as opposed to sharks, leaves, and spaghetti? These are elementary questions, but possible answers to them have not informed research on conceptual categories as much as would be desirable. Often it is suggested that people need categories to reduce memory or processing load, but given that the cortex has on the order of a trillion synapses and that long term memory is often characterized as "infinite," the suggestion carries little force. Furthermore for many categories (e.g., months, baseball teams, one's friends) both the category and every individual member of it are stored in memory. Rey (1983) provides a list of the main functions that concepts are supposed to perform. They include the stability of concepts at different times in a given individual or at the same time for different individuals, and the ability of a concept to serve as the basis for a word's meaning, the basis for things to belong to categories in the world, and the basis for people to know which things belong to which categories. But none of the functions had anything to do with why we form conceptual categories at all, or why some categories in the world are natural bases for concepts and others unnatural.

Bobick (1987), Shepard (1987), and Anderson (1990) have attempted to reverse-engineer human conceptual categories. They have independently proposed that categories are useful because they allow us to infer objects' unobserved properties from their observed properties (see also Rosch, 1978, and Quine, 1969.) Though we being cannot know *everything* about an object, we can observe *some* things. The observed properties allow us to assign the object to a category, and the structure of the category then allows us to infer the values of the objects' unobserved properties. Categories at different levels of a hierarchy (e.g., cocker spaniels, dogs, mammals, vertebrates, animals, living things) are useful because they allow a variety of tradeoffs between the ease of categorization and the power of the licensed inference. For low-level, specific categories, one has to know a lot about the object to know that it belongs in the category, but one can then infer many unobserved aspects of the object. For high-level, general categories, one need know only a few properties of an object to know it belongs to the category, but one can infer only a few of its unobserved properties once it is thus categorized.

To be concrete: knowing that Peter is a cottontail, we can predict that he grows, breathes, moves, was suckled, inhabits open country or woodland clearings, spreads tularemia, and can contract myxomatosis. If we knew only that that he was a mammal, the list would include only growing, breathing, moving, and being suckled. If we knew only that he was an animal, it would shrink to growing, breathing, and moving. On the other hand, it's much harder to tag Peter as a cottontail than as a mammal or an animal. To tag him as a mammal we need only notice that he is furry and moving, but to tag him as a cottontail we have to notice that he is long-eared, shorttailed, long-hind-legged, and has white on the underside of his tail. To identify *very* specific categories we have to examine so many properties that there would be few left to predict. Most of our everyday categories are somewhere in the middle: "rabbit," not mammal or cottontail; "car," not vehicle or Ford Tempo; "chair," not furniture or Barcalounger. They represent a compromise between how hard it is to identify the category and how much good the category does. These compromises correspond to Rosch's (1978) notion of the "basic level" of a category.

We can get away with inductive leaps based on categories only because the world works in certain ways. Objects are not randomly distributed through the multidimensional space of properties that humans are interested in; they cluster in regions of co-occurring properties that Bobick calls "natural modes" and Shepard calls "consequential regions." These modes are the result of the laws of form and function that govern the processes that create and preserve objects. For example, the laws of geometry dictate that objects formed out of multiple parts have concavities at the part boundaries. The laws of physics dictate that objects denser than water will be found on lake bottoms rather than lake surfaces. Laws of physics and biology dictate that objects that move quickly through fluid media have streamlined shapes, and bigger objects tend to have thicker legs. Knowing some of the coordinates of an object in property space, the existence of natural modes allows us to infer (at least probabilistically) some of its unknown coordinates.

Classical Categories: Inferences within Idealized Lawful Systems

All this raises the question of what kinds of regularities in the world generate natural modes that humans can exploit by forming concepts. In the most general sense, regularities in the world are the result of scientific and mathematical laws (e.g., of physics, geometry, physiology). Given a suitable idealization of the world, such laws can be captured in formal systems. By "formal system" we mean a symbol manipulation scheme, consisting of a set of propositions and a set of inference rules that apply to the propositions by virtue of their form alone, so that any knowledge not explicitly stated in the propositions cannot affect the inferences made within it. Formal systems, we suggest, are the contexts in which classical categories are defined. Therefore, under whatever idealization of the world a set of scientific or mathematical laws applies, the world contains classical categories. For example, when the texture, material, thickness, and microscopically ragged edges of real-world objects are provisionally ignored, some can be idealized as plane geometry figures. Under this idealization, objects with two equal sides can be assigned to the category "isosceles triangle." Once the object is assigned to that category, one can make the inference that it also has two equal angles, among other things. Frictionless planes, ideal gases, randomly interbreeding local populations, and uniform communities of undistractable speaker-hearers are other idealizations under which regularities in the behavior of objects can be captured in formal systems. A smart organism could use formal systems as idealizations of the world to infer unknown properties from known ones. In the psychology of categorization, no less than in the history of science, idealization or selective *ignoring* of salient correlational structure is crucial to apprehending causal laws.

We suggest, then, that wherever classical categories are to be found in human cognition, they will be part of a mentally represented formal system allowing deductions to be made. Given the function of concepts, why else would one bother to assign an object to a classical category? What is unnaturalabout the categories taught in traditional experiments in concept formation, such as "red square with two borders" (see, e.g., Hull, 1920; Bruner, Goodnow, & Austin, 1956; Hunt, 1962), is not that the categories have sharp boundaries or necessary and sufficient conditions, but that the categories are not part of a system allowing interesting inferences to be drawn—they are unnatural because they are literally useless.

Though one tends to think of formal systems as the province of systematic education in modern societies, there are a variety of kinds of formal systems capturing inference-supporting regularities that could be accessible to people, including those in preindustrial and preagricultural societies. For example, bodies of folk science need not resemble their counterparts in modern scientific systems, but they can reproduce some of their visible predictions with alternative means. Mathematical intuitions too are incorporated into many other systems of common knowledge. Here are some examples:

- Arithmetic, with classical categories like "a set of 3 objects," supporting inferences like "cannot be divided into two equal parts," independent of the properties of objects that can be grouped into threes.
- Geometry, with classical categories like "circle," supporting inferences like "all points equidistant from the center" or "circumference is a constant multiple of diameter," regardless of whether previously encountered circles are sections of tree trunks or drawings in sand.
- Logic, with classical categories like "disjunctive proposition," supporting inferences like "is true if its second part is true" or "is false if the negations of both its parts are true."
- Folk biology, with classical categories like "toad of kind x." which support inferences like "extract of mouth gland when dried is poisonous," regardless of its similarities to nonpoisonous toads or its dissimilarities to other poisonous toads.
- Folk physiology, with the famous all-or-none category "pregnant," supporting the inferences "female," "nonvirgin," and "future mother," regardless of weight or body shape.

In addition, the world of humans contains other humans, and there is reason to expect mentally represented formal systems to arise which govern the conduct of humans with one another. Given the fuzziness and experience-dependent individual variation inherent to family resemblance categories, it is not surprising that conflicts of interest between individuals will often be resolved by reasoning within systems that have a classical structure, allowing all-or-none decisions whose basis can be agreed to by all parties. There is a rationale to assigning drinking privileges to people after their twenty-first birthday, arbitrary though that is, rather than attempting to ascertain the maturity of each individual when he or she asks for a drink. Furthermore, Freyd (1983) and Smolensky (1988) have suggested that certain kinds of socially transmitted knowledge are likely to assume the form of discrete symbol systems because of constraints on the channels of communication with which they must be communicated between individuals and transmitted between generations. It is not hard to identify formal systems involved in social interactions which define classical categories:

- Kinship, with classical categories like "grandmother of X," supporting inferences like "may be the mother of X's uncle or aunt" or "is the daughter of one of X's great-grandparents," regardless of hair color or propensity to bake muffins.
- Sociopolitical structure, with classical categories like "president" or "chief," supporting inferences like "decisions on entering wars are carried out," regardless of physical strength, height, sex, and so on.
- Law, with classical categories like "felon," supporting inferences like "cannot hold public office," regardless of presence or absence of a sinister appearance, social class, and so on.
- Language, with the category "verb," supporting the inference "has a past tense form suffixed with *d* unless it has an irregular root," regardless of its phonological properties.

It is unlikely to be a coincidence that humans uniquely and nearly universally have language, counting systems, folk science, kinship systems, music, and law. As we have seen, classical categories deriving from formal systems require a neural architecture that is capable of ignoring the statistical microstructure of the properties of the exemplars of a category that an individual has encountered. One can speculate that the development of a non-associative neural architecture suitable to formal systems was a critical event in the evolution of human intelligence.

Family Resemblance Categories: Inferences within Historically-Related Similarity Clusters

In a previous section we showed that learners of English are presented with a family resemblance structure and must cope with it if they are to speak the same language as their parents. Are there cases where learners of conceptual categories are similarly forced to cope with a family resemblance structure in nature if they are to be able to make inferences about it? Many people have noted similarities between linguistic and biological evolution (see, e.g. Cavalli-Sforza & Feldman, 1981), and there is a particularly compelling analogy in the formation of family resemblance categories in the evolution of biological taxa.

It is generally believed that a novel species evolves from a small interbreeding population occupying a local, relatively homogeneous environment. Through natural selection, the organisms become adapted to the local environment, with the adaptive traits spreading through the population via sexual reproduction. As a result the population assumes a morphology that is relatively uniform—since selection acts to reduce variation (Sober, 1984; Ridley, 1986)—and predictable in part from engineering considerations to the extent that the organism's niche and selection pressures can be identified (Hutchinson, 1959; Williams, 1966; Dawkins, 1986).

Subsequent geographic dispersal can cause the members of the ancestral population to form reproductively isolated subgroups. They are no longer homogenized by interbreeding, and no longer subject to the same set of selection pressures imposed by a local environment. In the first generation following dispersal, the species is still homogeneous. Then, a set of distinct processes destroys the homogeneity of class: genetic drift, local geographic and climatic changes imposing new selection pressures, adaptive radiations following entry into empty environments, and local extinctions. As a result, the descendants of the ancestral species form a family resemblance category—the category of "birds," for example. Robins, penguins, and ostriches share many features (e.g. feathers) because of their common ancestry from a single population adapted to flying, while differing because of independent processes applying to different members of that population through history.

This suggests that as in the case of irregular past tense subclasses, the family resemblance structure of many biological taxa comes from the world, not just the minds of those learning about them. Note that such family resemblance structures are not always identical with classically-defined categories, and may be indispensable even in the best scientific theories. Many traditional biological taxa are somewhat arbitrary, serving as useful summaries of similar kinds of organisms. There are, to be sure, some biological categories that are well defined, including species (a population of interbreeding organisms sharing a common genepool), and monophyletic groups or clades (all the descendants of a common ancestor also belonging to the category). But many important biological taxa are neither. For example, fish comprise thousands of species, including coelocanths and trout. But the most recent common ancestor of coelocanths and trout is also an ancestor of mammals. Therefore no branch of the genealogical tree of organisms corresponds to all and only fish; trout and coelocanths are grouped together and distinguished from mammals by virtue of their many shared properties. To some biologists this is reason to deny the scientific significance of the category altogether, but most probably agree with the sentiment captured by Gould when he writes: "A coelocanth looks like a fish, tastes like a fish, acts like a fish, and therefore—in some legitimate sense beyond hidebound tradition—*is* a fish" (Gould, 1983; p. 363). In other words, biologists often recognize a category that is characterized as a cluster of co-occurring properties. Indeed some taxonomists have tried to characterize taxa using clustering algorithms that use criteria similar to those thought to lead to the formation of prototype conceptual categories in humans (see Ridley, 1986; Bobick, 1987).

Thus we have seen two examples of family resemblance categories that exist in the world, and that have the same genesis: a law-governed process creating a relatively homogeneous class, followed by a cessation of the influence of the process and the operation of independent historical causes that heterogenize the class, though not to such an extent that the inter-member similarities are obliterated entirely. Since objects can escape the direct influence of laws while retaining some of their effects, a smart organism cannot count on always being able to capture the world's regularities in formal systems. For example, no observer knowing only the United States Constitution would be able to explain why presidents are always wealthy white Christian males. Similarly, presumably no observer, not even a scientist equipped with a knowledge of physiology and ecology, would be able to explain why penguins have feathers, like robins, rather than fur, like seals. Instead, it will often be best simply to record the interpredictive contingencies among objects' properties and use them to infer unknown properties from known ones. Thus a smart observer can record the contingencies among feathers, wings, egg-laying, beaks, and so on, to note that the world contains a set of objects in which these properties cluster, and to use the presence of one subset of properties to infer the likely presence of others.

Just as irregular subclasses were shaped both by divergent and convergent historical processes, in the domain of conceptual categories there is a convergent process that can cause objects to cluster around natural modes even if the objects are not linked as descendants of a more homogeneous ancestral population. For example, there is no genealogical account of chairs that parallels the ones we give for languages or species. The similarities among chairs are caused solely by a convergent process, in which a set of properties repeatedly arises because it is particularly stable and adaptive in a given kind of environment. As a result, several historically unrelated groups of organisms evolve to attain that set. Examples include nonhomologous organs such as the eyes of mammals and of cephalopods, the wings of bats and of birds, and polyphyletic groups such as cactuslike plants (which have independently evolved succulent leaves, spines, and corrugated stems as adaptations to desert climates in several parts of the world). As in the case of divergent evolution, we are left with a mixture of shared and distinct properties that are respectively caused by law-governed adaptation and historical accident, though here the influences are temporally reversed. For example, although vertebrate and cephalopod eyes are strikingly similar, in vertebrates the photoreceptors point away from the light source and incoming light has to pass through the optic nerve fibers, whereas in cephalopods the photoreceptors point toward the light in a more sensible arrangement. The difference is thought to have arisen from the different evolutionary starting points defined by the ancestors to the two groups, presumably relating to differences in the embryological processes that lay down optic and neural tissue. Artifacts such as chairs develop via a similar process; for a chair to be useful, it must have a shape and material that is suited to the function of being stable and accessible (Winston,

Binford, Katz, & Lowry, 1983), but it is also influenced by myriad historical factors such as style, available materials, and ease of manufacture with contemporary technology. Social stereotypes, arising from the many historical accidents that cause certain kinds of people to assume certain roles, are yet another example.

We might expect family resemblance categories to be formed whenever there is a correlational structure in the properties that people attend to among sets of objects they care about, and that the world will contain opportunities for such clusters to form wherever there are laws that cause properties to be visibly correlated and historical contingencies that cause the correlations to be less than perfect—which is to say, almost everywhere.

Interactions between Classical and Family Resemblance Categories

The referents of many words, such as *bird* and *grandmother,* appear to have properties of both classical and family resemblance categories. How are these two systems to be reconciled? We suggest that people have parallel mental systems, one that records the correlational structure among sets of similar objects, and another that sets up systems of idealized laws.

In general we might expect family resemblance categories to be more accessible to observers than classical categories. Most objects in the world are cluttered by the effects of the myriad historical processes that led to their creation and preservation, obscuring any underlying laws. In the lucky cases when people are able to see these laws peeking through the clutter and try to capture them in idealized systems, the elements of these systems partly coincide with members of family resemblance clusters that are independently identified by simple observation of similar exemplars, and languages generally assign the same verbal label to both. This is what leads to the ambiguity of *A penguin is a perfectly good bird,* one of whose readings is true, the other false. It also leads to such paradoxes as Armstrong et al.'s subjects' asserting both that odd numbers form an all-or-none category and that 13 is a better example of that category than 23 is.

The human tendency to induce categories from clusters of similar objects they have encountered, to construct formal systems of rules applying to ideal objects, and to link entities of the two kinds with each other is probably the root of many apparent paradoxes in the study of concepts and often within the conceptual systems themselves. For example, exactly this duality can be found in the legal system in the distinction between reasoning by constitutionality and by precedent. Legal questions are commonly resolved by appealing to precedents, with more similar prior decisions carrying more weight. However when the constitutionality of a current decision is at issue, only a restricted set of principles is relevant, and similarity to earlier cases must be ignored.

Conclusion

It may be surprising to see so many parallels drawn between two phenomena that seem to be in such different domains. We are not claiming that past tense forms and conceptual categories are alike in all essential respects or that they are generated by a single cognitive system. But widespread similarities in remote domains makes the case for *some* common underlying principles compelling. English past tense forms come in two versions that are identical in function and at first glance only differ in size and degree of uniformity. On closer examination they turn out to represent two distinct systems that correspond point for point with classical and family resemblance categories, respectively. Moreover the two systems are linked with distinct psychological faculties, developmental courses, real world causes, and computational architectures. A fundamental distinction must lie at the heart of this duality. Specifically, we suggest, human concepts can correspond to classical categories or to family resemblance categories. Classical categories are defined by formal rules and allow us to make inferences within idealized law-governed systems. Family resemblance categories are defined by correlations among features in sets of similar memorized exemplars, and allow us to make inferences about the observable products of history.

Acknowledgments

The order of authors is arbitrary. We thank Ned Block, Paul Bloom, Ray Jackendoff, and Ed Smith for comments. This paper was prepared while the first author was a visitor at the MRC Cognitive Development Unit, University of London, and was supported by NIH grant HD 13831.

Notes

1. Note that the term means only "a pattern of resemblance such as one sees in a family"; it does not imply literal genealogical links.
2. There are also problems with the model's treatment of these phenomena; see Pinker and Prince (1988); Lachter and Bever (1988), and Sproat (1992).

References

Anderson, J. R. (1990). *The adaptive character of thought.* Hillsdale, NJ: Erlbaum.

Armstrong, S. L., Gleitman, L. R. & Gleitman, H. (1983) What some concepts might not be. *Cognition, 13,* 263–308.

Aronoff, M. (1976). *Word formation in generative grammar.* Cambridge, MA: MIT Press.

Bever, T. & Langendoen, T. (1963) (a) The formal justification and linguistic role of variables in phonology. (b) The description of the Indo-European E/O ablaut. (c) The E/O ablaut in Old English. *RLE Quarterly Progress Report* (summer). Cambridge, MA: MIT Research Laboratory of Electronics.

Bobick, A. (1987). *Natural object categorization.* Unpublished doctoral dissertation, Department of Brain and Cognitive Sciences, MIT.

Bruner, J. S., Goodnow, J. & Austin, G. (1956). *A study of thinking.* New York: Wiley.

Bybee, J. L. (1985). *Morphology.* Philadelphia: Benjamins.

Bybee, J. L. (1991). Natural morphology: The organization of paradigms and language acquisition. In: T. Huebner and C. Ferguson (Eds.), *Crosscurrents in Second Language Acquisition and Linguistic Theories.* Amsterdam: Benjamins. 67–92.

Bybee, J. L. & Moder, C. L. (1983). Morphological classes as natural categories. *Language, 59,* 251–270.

Bybee, J. L. & Slobin, D. I. (1982a). Rules and schemes in the development and use of the English past tense. *Language, 58,* 265–289.

Bybee, J. L. & Slobin, D. I. (1982b). Why small children cannot change language on their own: Suggestions from the English past tense. In A. Ahlqvist (Ed.), *Papers from the 5th Internation Conference on Historical Linguistics. (Current Issues in Linguistic Theory Vol. 21, Amsterdam Studies in the theory and history of linguistic science IV.)* Philadelphia/ Amsterdam: John Benjamins.

Campbell, A. (1959). *Old English Grammar.* Oxford: Oxford University Press.

Cavalli-Sforza, L. L. Feldman. M. W. (1981). *Cultural transmission and evolution: A quantitative approach.* Princeton, NJ: Princeton University Press.

Curme, G. (1935). *A Grammar of the English Language II.* Boston: Barnes & Noble.

Dawkins, R. (1986) *The blind watchmaker.* New York: Norton.

Ervin, S. (1964). Imitation and structural change in children's language. In E. Lenneberg (Ed.), *New directions in the study of language.* Cambridge, MA: MIT Press.

Fodor, J. A. (1981). The present status of the innateness controversy. In J.A. Fodor, *Representations.* Cambridge, Mass.: MIT Press.

Fodor, J. A., Garrett, M. F., Walker, E. C. T., and Parkes, C. H. (1980). Against definitions. *Cognition, 8:* 263–267.

Freyd, J. J. (1983). Shareability: The social psychology of epistemology. *Cognitive Science, 7,* 191–210.

Gelman, S. A. & Markman, E. (1987). Young children's inductions from natural kinds: The role of categories and appearances. *Child Development, 58,* 1532–1540.

Gelman, S., A., Coley, J. D. & Gottfried, G. M. (1994). Essentialist beliefs in children: The acquisition of concepts and theories. In L. A. Hirschfeld & S. Gelman (Eds.), *Mapping the mind: Domain specificity in cognition and culture.* New York: Cambridge University Press.

Gordon, P. (1985). Level-ordering in lexical development. *Cognition, 21,* 73–93.

Gould, S. J. (1983). What, if anything, is a zebra? In S. J. Gould, *Hen's teeth and horses toes.* New York: Norton.

Hooper, J. B. (1976). *Introduction to natural generative phonology.* New York: Academic Press.

Hull, C. L. (1920). Quantitative aspects of the evolution of concepts. *Psychological Monographs, 28,* Whole No. 213.

Hunt, E. (1962). *Concept learning: An information processing problem.* New York: Wiley.

Hutchinson, G. E. (1959). Homage to Santa Rosalia, or why are there so many kinds of animals. *American Naturalist, 93,* 145–159.

Jespersen, O. (1942). *A modern English grammar on historical principles, VI.* Reprinted 1961: London: George Allen & Unwin Ltd.

Johnson, K. (1986). Fragmentation of strong verb ablaut in Old English. *Ohio State University Working Papers in Linguistics 34:* 108–122.

Keil, F. C. (1989). *Concepts, kinds, and cognitive development.* Cambridge, MA: MIT Press.

Kelly, M. H. (1992). Darwin and psychological theories of classification. *Evolution and Cognition, 2,* 79–97.

Kim, J. J., MARCUS, G. F., PINKER, S., HOLLANDER, M., & COPPOLA, M. (1994). Sensitivity of children's inflection to morphological structure. *Journal of Child Language, 21,* 173–209.

Kim, J. J., Pinker, S., Prince, A. & Prasada, S. (1991). Why no more mortal has ever flown out to center field. *Cognitive Science, 15*, 173–218.

Kiparsky, P. (1982a). From cyclical to lexical phonology. In H. van der Hulst, & N. Smith (Eds.), *The structure of phonological representations.* Dordrecht, Netherlands: Foris.

Kiparsky, P. (1982b). Lexical phonology and morphology. In I. S. Yang (Ed.), *Linguistics in the morning calm.* Seoul: Hansin, pp. 3–91.

Konner, M. (1982). *The tangled wing.* New York: Harper and Row.

Kuczaj, S. A. (1977). The acquisition of regular and irregular past tense forms. *Journal of Verbal Learning and Verbal Behavior, 16*, 589–600.

Kuczaj, S. A. (1978). Children's judgments of grammatical and ungrammatical irregular past tense verbs. *Child Development, 49*, 319–326.

Kuczaj, S. A. (1981). More on children's initial failure to relate specific acquisitions. *Journal of Child Language, 8*, 485–487.

Lachter, J. & Bever, T. G. (1988). The relation between linguistic structure and associative theories of language learning—A constructive critique of some connectionist learning models. *Cognition, 28*: 195.

Lakoff, G. (1987). *Women, fire, and dangerous things: What categories reveal about the mind.* Chicago: University of Chicago Press.

Macwhinney, B. & Leinbach, J. (1991). Implementations are not conceptualizations: Revising the verb learning model. *Cognition, 40*, 121–157.

Marcus, G. F. (1995). The acquisition of inflection in children and multilayered connectionist networks. *Cognition, 56*, 271–279.

Marcus, G. F., Brinkmann, U., Clahsen, H., Wiese, R. & Pinker, S. (1995). German inflection: The exception that proves the rule. *Cognitive Psychology, 29*, 189–256.

Marcus, G., Pinker, S., Ullman, M., Hollander, M., Rosen, T. J. & Xu, F. (1992). *Overregularization in language acquisition. Monographs of the Society for Research in Child Development, 57* (4, Serial No. 228).

Maynard Smith, J. (1986). *The problems of biology.* Oxford: Oxford University Press.

Mayr, E. (1982). *The growth of biological thought.* Cambridge, MA: Harvard University Press.

Mcclelland, J. L. & Rumelhart, D. E. (1985). Distributed memory and the representation of general and specific information. *Journal of Experimental Psychology: General, 114*, 159–188.

Mcclelland, J. L., Rumelhart, D. E. & The PDP Research Group. (1986). *Parallel distributed processing: Explorations in the microstructure of cognition. Volume 2: Psychological and biological models.* Cambridge, MA: Bradford Books/MIT Press.

Medin, D. L. (1989). Concepts and conceptual structure. *American Psychologist, 44*, 1469–1481.

Mencken, H. (1936). *The American Language.* New York: Knopf.

Murphy, G. L. (1993). A rational theory of concepts. In G. H. Bower (Ed.), *The psychology of learning and motivation. Vol. 29.* New York: Academic Press.

Osherson, D. N. & Smith, E. E. (1981). On the adequacy of prototype theory as a theory of concepts. *Cognition, 15*, 35–58.

Pinker, S. (1984). *Language learnability and language development.* Cambridge, Mass.: Harvard University Press.

Pinker, S. (1991) Rules of language. *Science, 253*, 530–535.

Pinker, S. & Mehler, J. (Eds.) (1988). *Connections and symbols.* Cambridge, MA: MIT Press/Bradford Books.

Pinker, S. & Prince, A. (1994). Regular and irregular morphology and the psychological status of rules of grammar. In S. D. Lima, R. L., Corrigan, & G. K. Iverson (Eds.), *The reality of linguistic rules.* Philadelphia: John Benjamins.

Pinker, S. and Prince, A. (1988). On language and connectionism: Analysis of a Parallel Distributed Processing model of language acquisition. *Cognition, 28*: 73–193.

Plunkett, K. & Marchman, V. (1991). U-shaped learning and frequency effects in a multi-layered perceptron: Implications for child language acquisition. *Cognition, 38*, 43–102.

Plunkett, K. & Marchman, V. (1993). From rote learning to system building. *Cognition, 48*, 21–69.

Prasada, S. & Pinker, S. (1993). Generalizations of regular and irregular morphology. *Language and Cognitive Processes, 8,* 1–56.

Prokosch, E. (1939). *A comparative Germanic grammar.* Philadelphia: Linguistic Society of America.

Quine, W. V. O. (1969). Natural kinds. In W. V. O. Quine, *Natural kinds and other essays.* New York: Columbia University Press.

Rey, G. (1983). Concepts and stereotypes. *Cognition, 15,* 237–262.

Ridley, M. (1986). *The problems of evolution.* Oxford: Oxford University Press.

Rips, L. J. (1989). Similarity, typicality, and categorization. In S. Vosniadou & A. Ortony (Eds.), *Similarity and analogical reasoning.* New York: Cambridge University Press.

Rosch, E. (1973). On the internal structure of perceptual and semantic categories. In T. E. Moore (Ed.), *Cognitive development and the acquisition of language.* New York: Academic Press.

Rosch, E. (1978). Principles of categorization. In E. Rosch & B. B. Lloyd (Eds.), *Cognition and categorization.* Hillsdale, NJ: Erlbaum.

Rosch, E. (1988). Coherences and categorization: A historical view. In F. Kessel (Ed.), *The development of language and of language researchers: Papers presented to Roger Brown.* Hillsdale, NJ: Erlbaum.

Rosch, E. & Mervis, C. B. (1975). Family resemblances: Studies in the internal representation of categories. *Cognitive Psychology, 7,* 573–605.

Rumelhart, D. E. & Mcclelland, J. L. (1986). On learning the past tenses of English verbs. In J. L. McClelland, D. E. Rumelhart & The PDP Research Group, *Parallel distributed processing: Explorations in the micro-structure of cognition. Volume 2: Psychological and biological models.* Cambridge, MA: Bradford Books/MIT Press.

Shepard, R. N. (1987). Toward a universal law of generalization for psychological science. *Science,* 237, 1317–1323.

Slobin, D. I. (1971). On the learning of morphological rules: A reply to Palermo and Eberhart. In D.I. Slobin (Ed.), *The ontogenesis of grammar: A theoretical symposium.* New York: Academic Press.

Smith, E. E. & Medin, D. L. (1981). *Categories and concepts.* Cambridge, MA: Harvard University Press.

Smith, E. E., Langston, C. & Nisbett, R. (1992). The case for rules in reasoning. *Cognitive Science,* 16, 1–40.

Smith, E. E., Medin, D. L. and Rips, L. J. (1984). A psychological approach to concepts: Comments on Rey's "Concepts and Stereotypes." *Cognition, 17,* 265–274.

Sober, E. (1984). *The nature of selection.* Cambridge, MA: MIT Press.

Sproat, R. (1992). *Morphology and computation.* Cambridge, MA: MIT Press.

Stromswold, K. J. (1990). Learnability and the acquisition of auxiliaries. Doctoral Dissertation, Department of Brain and Cognitive Sciences, MIT.

Ullman, M. (1993). The computation and neural localization of inflectional morphology. Unpublished doctoral dissertation, Dept. of Brain & Cognitive Sciences, MIT.

Whittlesea, B. W. A. (1989). Selective attention, variable processing, and distributed representation: Preserving particular experiences of general structures. In R.G. Morris (Ed.), *Parallel Distributed Processing: Implications for psychology and neuroscience.* New York: Oxford University Press.

Williams, G. C. (1966). *Adaptation and natural selection: A critique of some current evolutionary thought.* Princeton: Princeton University Press.

Winston, P. H., Binford, T. O., Katz, B. & Lowry, M. (1983). Learning physical descriptions from functional definitions, examples, and precedents. MIT Artificial Intelligence Laboratory Memo 679.

Wittgenstein, L. (1953). *Philosophical investigations.* New York: Macmillan.

Xu, F. & Pinker, S. (1995). Weird past tense forms. *Journal of Child Language, 22,* 531–556.

8

Why Nature and Nurture Won't Go Away

This paper, published in the house journal of the American Academy of Arts and Sciences, put forward the main idea in my 2002 book The Blank Slate: The Modern Denial of Human Nature, *together with my response to some of the major criticism leveled at it. It takes aim at an attitude that I call holistic interactionism. This is the attitude that nature and nurture are so inextricably intertwined with each other that it is vulgar and unseemly to try to disentangle them—in particular, to specify the innate motives and learning mechanisms which do the interacting with the environment. Though many commentators, including not a few scientists, tout holistic interactionism as a sophisticated and nuanced way to understand the nature-nurture debate, I argue that it is a dodge: a way to evade fundamental scientific problems because of their moral, emotional, and political baggage.*

When Richard Mulcaster referred in 1581 to "that treasure...bestowed on them by nature, to be bettered in them by nurture," he gave the world a euphonious name for an opposition that has been debated ever since. People's beliefs about the relative importance of heredity and environment affect their opinions on an astonishing range of topics. Do adolescents engage in violence because of the way their parents treated them early in life? Are people inherently aggressive and selfish, calling for a market economy and a strong police, or could they become peaceable and cooperative, allowing the state to wither and a spontaneous socialism to blossom? Is there a universal aesthetic that allows great art to transcend time and place, or are people's tastes determined by their era and culture? With so much seemingly at stake in so many fields, it is no surprise that debates over nature and nurture evoke more rancor than just about any issue in the world of ideas.

During much of the twentieth century, a common position in this debate was to deny that human nature existed at all—to aver, with José Ortega y Gasset, that "Man has no nature; what he has is history." The doctrine that the mind is a blank slate was not only a cornerstone of behaviorism in psychology and social constructionism in the social sciences, but also extended widely into mainstream intellectual life.[1]

Part of the blank slate's appeal came from the realization that many differences among people in different classes and ethnic groups that formerly were thought to reflect innate disparities in talent or temperament could vanish through immigration, social mobility, and cultural change. But another part of its appeal was political and moral. If nothing in the mind is innate, then differences among races, sexes, and classes can never be innate, making the blank slate the ultimate safeguard against racism, sexism, and class prejudice. Also, the doctrine ruled out the possibility that ignoble traits such as greed, prejudice, and aggression spring from human nature, and thus held out the hope of unlimited social progress.

Though human nature has been debated for as long as people have pondered their condition, it was inevitable that the debate would be transformed by the recent efflorescence of the sciences of mind, brain, genes, and evolution. One outcome has been to make the doctrine of the blank slate untenable.[2] No one, of course, can deny the importance of learning and culture in all aspects of human life. But cognitive science has shown that there must be complex innate mechanisms for learning and culture to be possible in the first place. Evolutionary psychology has documented hundreds of universals that cut across the world's cultures, and has shown that many psychological traits (such as our taste for fatty foods, social status, and risky sexual liaisons) are better adapted to the evolutionary demands of an ancestral environment than to the actual demands of the current environment. Developmental psychology has shown that infants have a precocious grasp of objects, intentions, numbers, faces, tools, and language. Behavioral genetics has shown that temperament emerges early in life and remains fairly constant throughout the life span, that much of the variation among people within a culture comes from differences in genes, and that in some cases particular genes can be tied to aspects of cognition, language, and personality. Neuroscience has shown that the genome contains a rich tool kit of growth factors, axon guidance molecules, and cell adhesion molecules that help structure the brain during development, as well as mechanisms of plasticity that make learning possible.

These discoveries not only have shown that the innate organization of the brain cannot be ignored, but have also helped to reframe our very conception of nature and nurture.

Nature and nurture, of course, are not alternatives. Learning itself must be accomplished by innate circuitry, and what is innate is not a set of rigid instructions for behavior but rather programs that take in information from the senses and give rise to new thoughts and actions. Language is a paradigm case: though particular languages such as Japanese and Yoruba are not innate, the capacity to acquire languages is a uniquely human talent. And once acquired, a language is not a fixed list of sentences, but a combinatorial algorithm allowing an infinite number of new thoughts to be expressed.

Moreover, because the mind is a complex system composed of many interacting parts, it makes no sense to ask whether humans are selfish or generous or nasty or noble across the board. Rather, they are driven by competing motives elicited in different circumstances. And if genes affect behavior, it is not by tugging on the muscles directly, but by their intricate effects on the circuitry of a growing brain.

Finally, questions of what people innately have in common must be distinguished from questions of how races, sexes, or individuals innately differ. Evolutionary biology gives reasons to believe that there are systematic species-wide universals, circumscribed ways in which the sexes differ, random quantitative variation among individuals, and few if any differences among races and ethnic groups.[3]

This reframing of human nature also offers a rational way to address the political and moral fears of human nature.[4] Political equality, for example, does not hinge on a dogma that people are innately indistinguishable, but on a commitment to treat them as individuals in spheres such as education and the criminal justice system. Social progress does not require that the mind be free of ignoble motives, only that it have other motives (such as the emotion of empathy and cognitive faculties that can learn from history) that can counteract them.

By now most scientists reject both the nineteenth-century doctrine that biology is destiny and the twentieth-century doctrine that the mind is a blank slate. At the same time, many express a discomfort with any attempt to characterize the innate organization that the mind does have (even in service of a better understanding of learning). Instead, there is a widespread desire that the whole issue would somehow just go away. A common position on nature and nurture among contemporary scientists can be summarized as follows:

> No one today believes that the mind is a blank slate; to refute such a belief is to tip over a straw man. All behavior is the product of an inextricable interaction between heredity and environment during development, so the answer to all nature-nurture questions is "some of each." If people only recognized this truism, the political recriminations could be avoided. Moreover, modern biology has made the very distinction between nature and nurture obsolete. Since a given set of genes can have different effects in different environments, there may always be an environment in which a supposed effect of the genes can be reversed or canceled; therefore the genes impose no significant constraints on behavior. Indeed, genes are expressed in response to environmental signals, so it is meaningless to try to distinguish genes and environments; doing so only gets in the way of productive research.

The attitude is often marked by words like 'interactionist,' 'developmentalist,' 'dialectic,' 'constructivist,' and 'epigenetic,' and is typically accompanied by a diagram with the labels 'genes,' 'behavior,' 'prenatal environment,' 'biochemical environment,' 'family environment,' 'school environment,' 'cultural environment,' and 'socioeconomic environment,' and arrows pointing from every label to every other label.

This doctrine, which I will call holistic interactionism, has considerable appeal. It is based on some unexceptionable points, such as that nature and nurture are not mutually exclusive, that genes cannot cause behavior directly, and that the direction of causation can go both ways (for example, school can make you smarter, and smart people are most engaged by schooling). It has a veneer of moderation, of conceptual sophistication, and of biological up-to-dateness. And as John Tooby and Leda Cosmides have put it, it promises "safe conduct across the politicized minefield of modern academic life."[5]

But the very things that make holistic interactionism so appealing should also make us wary of it. No matter how complex an interaction is, it can be understood only by identifying the components and how they interact. Holistic interactionism can stand in the way of such understanding by dismissing any attempt to disentangle heredity and environment as uncouth. As Dan Dennett has satirized the attitude: "Surely 'everyone knows' that the nature-nurture debate was resolved long ago, and neither side wins since everything-is-a-mixture-of-both-and-it's-all-very-compl icated, so let's think of something else, right?"

In the following pages I will analyze the tenets of holistic interactionism one by one and show that they are not as reasonable or as obvious as they first appear.

"No one believes in the extreme nurture position that the mind is a blank slate." Whether or not this is true among scientists, it is far from true in the rest of intellectual life. The prominent anthropologist Ashley Montagu, summing up a common understanding in twentieth-century social science, wrote in 1973 that "With the exception of the instinctoid reactions in infants to sudden withdrawals of support and to sudden loud noises, the human being is entirely instinctless.... Man is man because he has no instincts, because everything he is and has become he has learned...from his culture, from the man-made part of the environment, from other human beings."[6] Postmodernism and social constructionism, which dominate many of the humanities, vigorously assert that human emotions, conceptual categories, and patterns of behavior (such as those characterizing men and women or homosexuals and heterosexuals) are social constructions. Even many humanists who are not postmodernists insist biology can provide no insight into human mind and behavior. The critic Louis Menand, for instance, recently wrote that "every aspect of life has a biological foundation in exactly the same sense, which is that unless it was biologically possible it wouldn't exist. After that, it's up for grabs."[7]

Nor is a belief in the blank slate absent among prominent scientists. Richard Lewontin, Leon Kamin, and Steven Rose, in a book entitled *Not in Our Genes*, asserted that "the only sensible thing to say about human nature is that it is 'in' that nature to construct its own history."[8] Stephen Jay Gould wrote that the "brain [is] capable of a full range of behaviors and predisposed to none."[9] Anne Fausto-Sterling expressed a common view of the origin of sex differences: "The key biological fact is that boys and girls have different genitalia, and it is this biological difference that leads adults to interact differently with different babies whom we conveniently color-code in pink or blue to make it unnecessary to go peering into their diapers for information about gender."[10]

These opinions spill into research and policy. Much of the scientific consensus on parenting, for example, is based on studies that find a correlation between the behavior of parents and the behavior of children. Parents who spank have children who are more violent; authoritative parents (neither too permissive nor too punitive) have well-behaved children; parents who talk more to their children have children with better language skills. Virtually everyone concludes that the behavior of the parent causes the outcomes in the child. The possibility that the correlations may arise from shared genes is usually not even mentioned, let alone tested.[11]

Other examples abound. Many scientific organizations have endorsed the slogan "violence is learned behavior," and even biologically oriented scientists tend to treat violence as a public health problem like malnutrition or infectious disease. Unmentioned is the possibility that the strategic use of violence could have been selected for in human evolution, as it has been in the evolution of other primate species.[12] Gender differences in the professions, such as that the proportion of mechanical engineers who are women is less than 50 percent, are attributed entirely to prejudice and hidden barriers. The possibility that, on average, women might be less interested than men in people-free pursuits is similarly unspeakable.[13] The point is not that we know that evolution or genetics are relevant to explaining these phenomena, but that the very possibility is often treated as an unmentionable taboo rather than as a testable hypothesis.

"For every question about nature and nurture, the correct answer is 'some of each.'" Not true. Why do people in England speak English and people in Japan speak Japanese? The 'reasonable compromise' would be that the people in England have genes that make it easier to learn English and the people in Japan have genes that make it easier to learn Japanese, but that both groups must be exposed to a language to acquire it at all. This compromise is, of course, not reasonable but false, as we see when children exposed to a given language acquire it equally quickly regardless of their racial ancestry. Though people may be genetically predisposed to learn language, they are not genetically predisposed, even in part, to learn a particular language; the explanation for why people in different countries speak differently is 100 percent environmental.

Sometimes the opposite extreme turns out to be correct. Psychiatrists commonly used to blame psychopathology on mothers. Autism was caused by 'refrigerator mothers' who did not emotionally engage their children, schizophrenia by mothers who put their children in double binds. Today we know that autism and schizophrenia are highly heritable, and though they are not completely determined by genes, the other plausible contributors (such as toxins, pathogens, and developmental accidents) have nothing to do with how parents treat their children. Mothers don't deserve some of the blame if their children have these disorders, as a nature-nurture compromise would imply. They deserve none of it.

"If people recognized that every aspect of behavior involves a combination of nature and nurture, the political disputes would evaporate." Certainly many psychologists strive for an innocuous middle ground. Consider this quotation:

> If the reader is now convinced that either the genetic or environmental explanation has won out to the exclusion of the other, we have not done a sufficiently good job of presenting one side or the other. It seems highly likely to us that both genes and environment have something to do with this issue.

This appears to be a reasonable interactionist compromise that could not possibly incite controversy. But in fact it comes from one of the most incendiary books of the 1990s, Richard Herrnstein and Charles Murray's *The Bell Curve*. In this passage, Herrnstein and Murray summed up their argument that the difference in average IQ scores between American blacks and American whites has both genetic and environmental causes. A "some-of-each" position did not protect them from accusations of racism and comparisons to Nazis. Nor, of course, did it establish their position was correct: as with the language a person speaks, the black-white average IQ gap could be 100 percent environmental. The point is that in this and many other domains of psychology, the possibility that heredity has any explanatory role at all is still inflammatory.

"The effects of genes depend crucially on the environment, so heredity imposes no constraints on behavior." Two examples are commonly used to illustrate the point: different strains of corn may grow to different heights when equally irrigated, but a plant from the taller strain might end up shorter if it is deprived of water; and children with phenylketonuria (PKU), an inherited disorder resulting in retardation, can end up normal if given a diet low in the amino acid phenylalanine.

There is an aspect of this statement that indeed is worth stressing. Genes do not determine behavior like the punched paper roll of a player piano. Environmental interventions—from education and psychotherapy to historical changes in attitudes and political systems—can significantly affect human affairs. Also worth stressing is that genes and environments may interact in the statistician's sense, namely, that the effects of one can be exposed, multiplied, or reversed by the effects of the other, rather than merely summed with them. Two recent studies have identified single genes that are respectively associated with violence and depression, but have also shown that their effects are manifested only with particular histories of stressful experience.[14]

At the same time, it is misleading to invoke environment dependence to deny the importance of understanding the effects of genes. To begin with, it is simply not true that any gene can have any effect in some environment, with the implication that we can always design an environment to produce whatever outcome we value. Though some genetic effects may be nullified in certain environments, not all of them are: studies that measure both genetic and environmental similarity (such as adoption designs, where correlations with adoptive and biological parents can be compared) show numerous main effects of personality, intelligence, and behavior across a range of environmental variation. This is true even for the poster child of environmental mitigation, PKU. Though a low-phenylalanine diet does prevent severe mental retardation, it does not, as is ubiquitously claimed, render the person 'perfectly normal.' PKU children have mean IQs in the 80s and 90s and are impaired in tasks that depend on the prefrontal region of the cerebral cortex.[15]

Also, the mere existence of *some* environment that can reverse the expected effects of genes is almost meaningless. Just because extreme environments can disrupt a trait does not mean that the ordinary range of environments will modulate that trait, nor does it mean that the environment can explain the nature of the trait. Though unirrigated corn plants may shrivel, they won't grow arbitrarily high when given ever-increasing amounts of water. Nor does their dependence on water explain why they bear ears of corn as opposed to tomatoes or pinecones. Chinese foot-binding is an environmental manipulation that can radically affect the shape of the foot, but it would be misleading to deny that the anatomy of the human foot is in an important sense specified by the genes, or to attribute it in equal parts to heredity and environment. The point is not merely rhetorical. The fact that kittens' visual systems show abnormalities when their eyelids are sewn shut in a critical period of development does not imply (as was believed in the 1990s) that playing Mozart to babies or hanging colorful mobiles in their cribs will increase their intelligence.[16]

In short, the existence of environmental mitigations doesn't make the effects of the genes inconsequential. On the contrary, the genes specify what kinds of environmental manipulations will have what kinds of effects and with what costs. This is true at every level, from the expression of the genes themselves (as I will discuss below) to large-scale attempts at social change. The totalitarian Marxist states of the twentieth century often succeeded at modifying behavior, but at the cost of massive coercion, owing in part to mistaken assumptions about how easily human motives would respond to changed circumstances.[17]

Conversely, many kinds of genuine social progress succeeded by engaging specific aspects of human nature. Peter Singer observes that normal humans in all societies manifest a sense of sympathy: an ability to treat the interests of others as comparable to their own.[18] Unfortunately, the size of the moral circle in which sympathy is extended is a free parameter. By default, people sympathize only with members of their own family, clan, or village, and treat anyone outside this circle as less than human. But under certain circumstances the circle can expand to other clans, tribes, races, or even species. An important way to understand moral progress, then, is to specify the triggers that prompt people to expand or contract their moral circles. It has been argued that the circle may be expanded to include people to whom one is bound by networks of reciprocal trade and interdependence,[19] and that it may be contracted to exclude people who are seen in degrading circumstances.[20] In each case, an understanding of nonobvious aspects of human nature reveals possible levers for humane social change.

"Genes are affected by their environments, and learning requires the expression of genes, so the nature-nurture distinction is meaningless." It is, of course, in the very nature of genes that they are not turned on all the time but are expressed and regulated by a variety of signals. These signals in turn may be triggered by a variety of inputs, including temperature, hormones, the molecular environment, and neural activity.[21] Among the environmentally sensitive gene-expression effects are those that make learning itself possible. Skills and memories are stored as physical changes at the synapse, and these changes require the expression of genes in response to patterns of neural activity.

These causal chains do not, however, render the nature-nurture distinction obsolete. What they do is force us to rethink the casual equation of 'nature' with genes and of 'nurture' with everything beyond the genes. Biologists have noted that the word 'gene' accumulated several meanings during the twentieth century.[22] These include a unit of heredity, a specification of a part, a cause of a disease, a template for protein synthesis, a trigger of development, and a target of natural selection.

It is misleading, then, to equate the prescientific concept of human nature with 'the genes' and leave it at that, with the implication that environment-dependent gene activity proves that human nature is indefinitely modifiable by experience. Human nature is related to genes in the sense of of units of heredity, development, and evolution, particularly those units that exert a systematic and lasting effect on the wiring and chemistry of the brain. This is distinct from the most common use of the term 'gene' in molecular biology, namely, in reference to stretches of DNA that code for a protein. Some aspects of human nature may be specified in information carriers other than protein templates, including the cytoplasm, noncoding regions of the genome that affect gene expression, properties of genes other than their sequence (such as how they are imprinted), and cross-generationally consistent aspects of the maternal environment that the genome has been shaped by natural selection to expect. Conversely, many genes direct the synthesis of proteins necessary for everyday metabolic function (such as wound repair, digestion, and memory formation) without embodying the traditional notion of human nature.

The various concepts of 'environment,' too, have to be refined. In most nature-nurture debates, 'environment' refers in practice to aspects of the world that make up the perceptual input to the person and over which other humans have some control. This encompasses, for example, parental rewards and punishments, early enrichment, role models, education, laws, peer influence, culture, and social attitudes. It is misleading to blur 'environment' in the sense of the psychologically salient environment of the person with 'environment' in the sense of the chemical milieu of a chromosome or cell, especially when that milieu itself consists of the products of other genes and thus corresponds more closely to the traditional notion of heredity. There are still other senses of 'environment,' such as nutrition and environmental toxins. The point is not that one sense is primary, but that one should seek to distinguish each sense and characterize its effects precisely.

A final reason that the environment dependence of the genes does not vitiate the concept of human nature is that an environment can affect the organism in very different ways. Some aspects of the perceptual environment are "instructive" in the technical sense that their effects are predictable by information contained in the input. Given a child who is equipped to learn words in the first place, the content of her vocabulary is predictable from the words spoken to her. Given an adult equipped to understand contingencies, the spot where he will park his car will depend on where the No Parking signs are posted. But other aspects of the environment, namely, those that affect the genes directly rather than affecting the brain through the senses, trigger genetically specified if-then contingencies which do not preserve information in the trigger itself. Such contingencies are pervasive in biological development, where many genes produce transcription factors and other molecules that set off cascades of expression of other genes. A good example is the Pax6 gene, which produces a protein that triggers the expression of twenty-five hundred other genes, resulting in the formation of the eye. Highly specific genetic responses can also occur when the organism interacts with its social environment, as when a change of social status in a male cichlid fish triggers the expression of more than fifty genes, which in turn alter its size, aggressiveness, and stress response.[23] These are reminders both that innate organization cannot be equated with a lack of sensitivity to the environment, and that responses to the environment are often not specified by the stimulus but by the nature of the organism.

"Framing problems in terms of nature and nurture prevents us from understanding human development and making new discoveries." On the contrary, some of the most provocative discoveries in twentieth-century psychology would have been impossible if there had not been a concerted effort to distinguish nature and nurture in human development.

For many decades psychologists have looked for the causes of individual differences in cognitive ability (as measured by IQ tests, school and job performance, and indices of brain activity) and in personality (as measured by questionnaires, ratings, psychiatric evaluations, and tallies of behavior such as divorce and crime). The conventional wisdom has been that such traits are strongly influenced by parenting practices and role models. But recall that this belief is based on flawed correlational studies that compare parents and children but forget to control for genetic relatedness.

Behavioral geneticists have remedied those flaws with studies of twins and adoptees, and have discovered that in fact virtually all behavioral traits are partly (though never completely) heritable.[24] That is, some of the variation among individual people within a culture must be attributed to differences in their genes. The conclusion follows from repeated discoveries that identical twins reared apart (who share their genes but not their family environment) are highly similar; that ordinary identical twins (who share their environment and all their genes) are more similar than fraternal twins (who share their environment but only half their variable genes); and that biological siblings (who share their environment and half their variable genes) are more similar than adoptive siblings (who share their environment but none of their variable genes). These studies have been replicated in large samples from several countries, and have ruled out the most common alternative explanations (such as selective placement of identical twins in similar adoptive homes). Of course, concrete behavioral traits that patently depend on content provided by the home or culture—which language one speaks, which religion one practices, which political party one supports—are not heritable at all. But traits that reflect the underlying talents and temperaments—how proficient with language a person is, how religious, how liberal or conservative—*are* partially heritable. So genes play a role in making people different from their neighbors, and their environments play an equally important role.

At this point it is tempting to conclude that people are shaped both by genes and by family upbringing: how their parents treated them and what kind of home they grew up in. But the conclusion is unwarranted. Behavioral genetics allows one to distinguish two very different ways in which people's environments might affect them. The *shared* environment is what impinges on a person and his or her siblings alike: their parents, home life, and neighborhood. The *unique* environment is everything else: anything that happens to a person that does not necessarily happen to that person's siblings.

Remarkably, most studies of intelligence, personality, and behavior turn up few or no effects of the shared environment—often to the surprise of the researchers themselves, who thought it was obvious that nongenetic variation had to come from the family.[25] First, adult siblings are about equally correlated whether they grew up together or apart. Second, adoptive siblings, when tested as adults, are generally no more similar than two people from the same culture chosen at random. And third, identical twins are no more similar than one would expect from the effects of their shared genes. Setting aside cases of extreme neglect or abuse, whatever experiences siblings share by growing up in the same home in a given culture make little or no difference to the kind of people they turn into. Specific skills like reading and playing a musical instrument, of course, can be imparted by parents, and parents obviously affect their children's happiness and the quality of family life.

But they don't seem to determine their children's intellects, tastes, and personalities in the long run.

The discovery that the shared family environment has little to no lasting effect on personality and intelligence comes as a shock to the traditional wisdom that "as the twig is bent, so grows the branch." It casts doubt on forms of psychotherapy that seek the roots of an adult's dysfunction in the family environment, on theories that attribute adolescents' alcoholism, smoking, and delinquency to how they were treated in early childhood, and on the philosophy of parenting experts that parental micromanagement is the key to a well-adjusted child. The findings are so counterintuitive that one might doubt the behavioral genetic research that led to them, but they are corroborated by other data.[26] Children of immigrants end up with the language, accent, and mores of their peers, not of their parents. Wide variations in child-rearing practices—day-care versus stay-at-home mothers, single versus multiple caregivers, same-sex versus different-sex parents—have little lasting effect when other variables are controlled. Birth order and only-child status also have few effects on behavior outside the home.[27] And an extensive study testing the possibility that children might be shaped by *unique* aspects of how their parents treat them (as opposed to ways in which parents treat all their children alike) showed that differences in parenting within a family are effects, not causes, of differences among the children.[28]

The discovery of the limits of family influence is not just a debunking exercise, but opens up important new questions. The finding that much of the variance in personality, intelligence, and behavior comes neither from the genes nor from the family environment raises the question of where it does come from. Judith Rich Harris has argued that the phenomena known as socialization—acquiring the skills and values needed to thrive in a given culture—take place in the peer group rather than the family. Though children are not prewired with cultural skills, they also are not indiscriminately shaped by their environment. One aspect of human nature directs children to figure out what is valued in their peer group—the social milieu in which they will eventually compete for status and mates—rather than to surrender to their parents' attempts to shape them.

Acknowledging this feature of human nature in turn raises questions about how the relevant environments, in this case peer cultures, arise and perpetuate themselves. Does a peer culture trickle down from adult culture? Does it originate from high-status individuals or groups and then proliferate along peer networks? Does it emerge haphazardly in different forms, some of which entrench themselves when they reach a tipping point of popularity?

A revised understanding of how children socialize themselves has practical implications as well. Teen alcoholism and smoking might be better addressed by understanding how these activities become status symbols in peer groups than by urging parents to talk more to their adolescents (as current advertisements, sponsored by beer and tobacco companies, insist). A major determinant of success in school might be whether classes fission into peer groups with different status criteria, in particular whether success in school is treated as admirable or as a sign of selling out.[29]

The development of personality—a person's emotional and behavioral idiosyncrasies—poses a set of puzzles distinct from those raised by the process of socialization. Identical twins growing up in the same home share their genes, their parents, their siblings, their peer groups, and their culture. Though they are highly similar, they are far from indistinguishable: by most measures, correlations in their traits are in the neighborhood of 0.5. Peer influence cannot explain the differences, because identical twins largely share their peer groups. Instead, the unexplained variance in personality throws a spotlight on the role of sheer chance in development: random differences in prenatal blood supply and exposure to toxins, pathogens, hormones, and antibodies; random differences in the growth or adhesion of axons in the developing brain; random events in experience; random differences in how a stochastically functioning brain reacts to the same events in experience. Both popular and scientific explanations of behavior, accustomed to invoking genes, parents, and society, seldom acknowledge the enormous role that unpredictable factors must play in the development of an individual.

If chance in development is to explain the less-than-perfect similarity of identical twins, it also highlights an interesting property of development in general. One can imagine a developmental process in which millions of small chance events cancel one another out, leaving no difference in the resulting organism. One can imagine a different process in which a chance event could disrupt development entirely. Neither of these happens to identical twins. Their differences are detectable both in psychological testing and in everyday life, yet both are (usually) healthy human beings. The development of organisms must use complex feedback loops rather than prespecified blueprints. Random events can divert the trajectories of growth, but the trajectories are confined within an envelope of functioning designs for the species.

These profound questions are not about nature versus nurture. They are about nurture versus nurture: about what, precisely, are the nongenetic causes of personality and intelligence. But the puzzles would never have come to light if researchers had not first taken measures to factor out the influence of nature, by showing that correlations between parents and children cannot glibly be attributed to parenting but might be attributable to shared genes. That was the first step that led them to measure the possible effects of parenting empirically, rather than simply assuming that parents had to be all-powerful. The everything-affects-everything diagram turns out to be not sophisticated but dogmatic. The arrows emanating from 'parents,' 'siblings,' and 'the home' are testable hypotheses, not obvious truisms, and the tests might surprise us both by the arrows that shouldn't be there and by the labels and arrows we may have forgotten.

The human brain has been called the most complex object in the known universe. No doubt hypotheses that pit nature against nurture as a dichotomy or that correlate genes or environment with behavior without looking at the intervening brain will turn out to be simplistic or wrong. But that complexity does not mean we should fuzz up the issues by saying that it's all just too complicated to think about, or that some hypotheses should be treated a priori as obviously true, obviously false, or too dangerous to mention. As with inflation, cancer, and global warming, we have no choice but to try to disentangle the multiple causes.[30]

Notes

1. Carl N. Degler, *In Search of Human Nature: The Decline and Revival of Darwinism in American Social Thought* (New York: Oxford University Press, 1991); Steven Pinker, *The Blank Slate: The Modern Denial of Human Nature* (New York: Viking, 2002); Robin Fox, *The Search for Society: Quest for a Biosocial Science and Morality* (New Brunswick, N.J.: Rutgers University Press, 1989); Eric M. Gander, *On Our Minds: How Evolutionary Psychology Is Reshaping the Nature-Versus-Nurture Debate* (Baltimore: Johns Hopkins University Press, 2003); John Tooby and Leda Cosmides, "The Psychological Foundations of Culture," in *The Adapted Mind: Evolutionary Psychology and the Generation of Culture*, ed. Jerome H. Barkow, Leda Cosmides, and John Tooby (New York: Oxford University Press, 1992).

2. Pinker, *The Blank Slate*; Gary F. Marcus, *The Birth of the Mind: How a Tiny Number of Genes Creates the Complexities of Human Thought* (New York: Basic Books, 2004); Matt Ridley, *Nature Via Nurture: Genes, Experience, and What Makes Us Human* (London: Fourth Estate, 2003); Robert Plomin, Michael J. Owen, and Peter McGuffin, "The Genetic Basis of Complex Human Behaviors," *Science* 264 (1994): 1733–1739.

3. John Tooby and Leda Cosmides, "On the Universality of Human Nature and the Uniqueness of the Individual: The Role of Genetics and Adaptation," *Journal of Personality* 58 (1990): 17–67.

4. Pinker, *The Blank Slate*.

5. Tooby and Cosmides, "The Psychological Foundations of Culture."

6. Ashley Montagu, ed., *Man and Aggression* 2nd ed. (New York: Oxford University Press, 1973).

7. Louis Menand, "What Comes Naturally," *The New Yorker* 25 November 2002.

8. R. C. Lewontin, Steven Rose, and Leon J. Kamin, *Not in Our Genes: Biology, Ideology, and Human Nature* (New York: Pantheon Books, 1984).

9. Stephen Jay Gould, "Biological Potential vs. Biological Determinism," in *Ever Since Darwin: Reflections in Natural History*, ed. Stephen Jay Gould (New York: Norton, 1977).

10. Anne Fausto-Sterling, *Myths of Gender: Biological Theories about Women and Men* (New York: Basic Books, 1985).

11. David C. Rowe, *The Limits of Family Influence: Genes, Experience, and Behavior* (New York: Guilford Press, 1994); Judith Rich Harris, *The Nurture Assumption: Why Children Turn Out the Way They Do* (New York: Free Press, 1998).

12. Martin Daly and Margo Wilson, *Homicide* (New York: A. de Gruyter, 1988).

13. David Lubinski and Camilla Benbow, "Gender Differences in Abilities and Preferences Among the Gifted: Implications for the Math-Science Pipeline," *Current Directions in Psychological Science* 1 (1992): 61–66.

14. Avshalom Caspi, Karen Sugden, Terrie E. Moffitt, Alan Taylor, and Ian W. Craig, "Influence of Life Stress on Depression: Moderation by a Polymorphism in the 5-htt Gene," *Science* (2003): 386–389; Avshalom Caspi, Joseph McClay, Terrie E. Moffitt, Jonathan Mill, Judy Martin, and Ian W. Craig, "Evidence that the Cycle of Violence in Maltreated Children Depends on Genotype," *Science* 297 (2002): 727–742.

15. Adele Diamond, "A Model System for Studying the Role of Dopamine in the Prefrontal Cortex during Early Development in Humans: Early and Continuously Treated Phenylketonuria,"

in *Handbook of Developmental Cognitive Neuroscience*, ed. Charles A. Nelson and Monica Luciana (Cambridge, Mass.: MIT Press, 2001).

16. John T. Bruer, *The Myth of the First Three Years: A New Understanding of Early Brain Development and Lifelong Learning* (New York: Free Press, 1999).

17. Jonathan Glover, *Humanity: A Moral History of the Twentieth Century* (London: J. Cape, 1999); Peter Singer, *A Darwinian Left: Politics, Evolution, and Cooperation* (London: Weidenfeld & Nicolson, 1999).

18. Peter Singer, *The Expanding Circle: Ethics and Sociobiology* (New York: Farrar, Straus & Giroux, 1981).

19. Robert Wright, *NonZero: The Logic of Human Destiny* (New York: Pantheon Books, 2000).

20. Glover, *Humanity*; Philip G. Zimbardo, Christina Maslach, and Craig Haney, in *Obedience to Authority: Current Perspectives on the Milgram Paradigm*, ed. Thomas Blass (Mahwah, N.J.: Lawrence Erlbaum Associates, 2000).

21. Marcus, *The Birth of the Mind*; Ridley, *Nature Via Nurture*.

22. Ridley, *Nature Via Nurture*; Richard Dawkins, *The Extended Phenotype: The Gene as the Unit of Selection* (San Francisco: W. H. Freeman & Company, 1982); Seymour Benzer, "The Elementary Units of Heredity," in *A Symposium on the Chemical Basis of Heredity*, ed. William D. McElroy and Bentley Glass (Baltimore: Johns Hopkins Press, 1957).

23. Russell Fernald, "How Does Behavior Change the Brain? Multiple Methods to Answer Old Questions," *Integrative Comparative Biology* 43 (2003): 771–779.

24. Plomin, Owen, and McGuffin, "The Genetic Basis of Complex Human Behaviors"; Eric Turkheimer, "Three Laws of Behavior Genetics and What They Mean," *Current Directions in Psychological Science* 9 (5) (2000): 160–164; Thomas J. Bouchard, Jr., "Genetic and Environmental Influences on Intelligence and Special Mental Abilities," *Human Biology* 70 (1998): 257–259.

25. Rowe, *The Limits of Family Influence*; Harris, *The Nurture Assumption*; Turkheimer, "Three Laws of Behavior Genetics"; Robert Plomin and Denise Daniels, "Why Are Children in the Same Family So Different from One Another?" *Behavioral and Brain Sciences* 10 (1987): 1–60.

26. Harris, *The Nurture Assumption*.

27. Ibid.; Judith Rich Harris, "Context-Specific Learning, Personality, and Birth Order," *Current Directions in Psychological Science* 9 (2000): 174–177; Jeremy Freese, Brian Powell, and Lala Carr Steelman, "Rebel Without a Cause or Effect: Birth Order and Social Attitudes," *American Sociological Review* 64 (1999): 207–231.

28. David Reiss, Jenae M. Neiderhiser, E. Mavis Hetherington, and Robert Plomin, *The Relationship Code: Deciphering Genetic and Social Influences on Adolescent Development* (Cambridge, Mass.: Harvard University Press, 2000).

29. Harris, *The Nurture Assumption*.

30. The writing of this paper was supported by NIH Grant HD-18381. I thank Helena Cronin, Jonathan Haidt, Judith Rich Harris, and Matt Ridley for comments on an earlier draft.

9

The Faculty of Language: What's Special about It?

with RAY JACKENDOFF

Noam Chomsky was one of my major intellectual influences, and many reviewers have assumed that I was his student or disciple. I did take two courses from him, one as a graduate student at Harvard, another as a postdoctoral fellow at MIT, and we were colleagues at MIT for twenty-one years (he in the Department of Linguistics and Philosophy, me in the Department of Brain and Cognitive Sciences). Some of my deepest convictions as a cognitive scientist come from his early writings: that language and higher cognition are forms of mental computation over structured, symbolic representations; that the mind is not a homogeneous mass but is organized into specialized systems, including language and its major components; that the human child is innately prepared, among other things, for the demands of acquiring a language.

Yet I have always kept a certain distance from Chomsky's specific theories of language and from the worshipful academic cult that surrounds him. I find the technical apparatus of his theories to be far too complicated and abstruse, motivated more by Chomsky's personal conception of what a theory of language should look like than by the actual phenomena of language. I am more persuaded by the theories advanced by Joan Bresnan (a former student of Chomsky's, and my postdoctoral adviser) and Ray Jackendoff (another former student of his, and the architect of the theory of semantics I adopted in Learnability and Cognition, The Stuff of Thought, *and chapter 6 in this collection).*

And as my paper with Paul Bloom (chapter 5 in this collection) shows, I also do not share Chomsky's hostility to natural selection as part of the explanation of why language is the way it is. Perhaps not coincidentally, my politics also differ from Chomsky's left-wing anarcho-syndicalism, ultimately because we have different conceptions of human nature. To put it crudely, Chomsky is a Rousseauean, I am a Hobbesian; see my books The Blank Slate *and* The Better Angels of Our Nature *for a discussion that is less crude.*

Chomsky is also famous for implementing an academic version of the ideal of continuous revolution. Every decade or so he tears down his own theory and builds a new one on a foundation of different assumptions. With the latest version, the misleadingly named

Minimalist Program, the enterprise has finally jumped the shark, or so Jackendoff and I argue in this paper. We respond to a famous 2002 Science article by Chomsky and the biologists Marc Hauser and Tecumseh Fitch in which Chomsky revised his theory of what is unique about human language (whittling it down to the computational process of recursion) and reiterated his skepticism that language is a Darwinian adaptation which evolved gradually by natural selection. In our reply, Jackendoff and I argue that Chomsky gave away the store (in part because of his commitments to the Minimalist Program), and that language is a complex human adaptation, which evolved through a number of modifications of perceptual, motor, and central computational systems.

1. The Issue of What Is Special to Language

The most fundamental question in the study of the human language faculty is its place in the natural world: what kind of biological system it is, and how it relates to other systems in our own species and others. This question embraces a number of more specific ones (Osherson & Wasow, 1976). The first is which aspects of the faculty are learned from environmental input and which aspects arise from the innate design of the brain (including the ability to learn the learned parts). To take a clear example, the fact that a canine pet is called *dog* in English but *chien* in French is learned, but the fact that words can be learned at all hinges on the predisposition of children to interpret the noises made by others as meaningful signals.

A second question is what parts of a person's language ability (learned or built-in) are specific to language and what parts belong to more general abilities. Words, for example, are specifically a part of language, but the use of the lungs and the vocal cords, although necessary for spoken language, are not limited to language. The answers to this question will often not be dichotomous. The vocal tract, for example, is clearly not exclusively used for language, yet in the course of human evolution it may have been tuned to subserve language at the expense of other functions such as breathing and swallowing.

A third question is which aspects of the language capacity are uniquely human, and which are shared with other groups of animals, either homologously, by inheritance from a common ancestor, or analogously, by adaptation to a common function. This dimension cuts across the others. The system of sound distinctions found in human languages is both specific to language and uniquely human (partly because of the unique anatomy of the human vocal tract). The sensitive period for learning language may be specific to certain aspects of language, but it has analogues in developmental phenomena throughout the animal kingdom, most notably bird song. The capacity for forming concepts is necessary for language, as it provides the system of meaning that language expresses, but it is not specific to language: it is also used in reasoning about the world. And since other primates engage in such reasoning, it is not uniquely human (though parts of it may be).

As with the first two questions, answers will seldom be dichotomous. They will often specify mixtures of shared and unique attributes, reflecting the evolutionary process in which an ancestral primate design was retained, modified, augmented, or lost in the human lineage.

Answers to this question have clear implications for the evolution of language. If the language faculty has many features that are specific to language itself, it would suggest that the faculty was a target of natural selection. But if represents a minor extension of capacities that existed in the ancestral primate lineage, it could be the result of a chance mutation that became fixed in the species through drift or other non-adaptive evolutionary mechanisms (Pinker & Bloom, 1990).

Ina recent article in *Science*, Hauser, Chomsky, and Fitch (2002) offer a hypothesis about what is special about language, with reflections on its evolutionary genesis. The article (henceforth HCF) has attracted much attention both in the popular press (Kenneally, 2003; Wade, 2003) and among other language scientists. HCF differentiate (as we do) between aspects of language that are special to language (the "Narrow Language Faculty" or FLN) and the faculty of language in its entirety, including parts that are shared with other psychological abilities (the "Broad Language Faculty" or FLB). The abstract of HCF makes the very strong proposal that the narrow language faculty "only includes recursion and is the only uniquely human component of the faculty of language." (Recursion refers to a procedure that calls itself, or to a constituent that contains a constituent of the same kind.)[1] In the article itself, the starkness of this hypothesis is mitigated only slightly. The authors suggest that "most, if not all, of FLB is based on mechanisms shared with non-human animals....In contrast, we suggest that FLN—the computational mechanism of recursion—is recently evolved and unique to our species" (p. 1573). Similarly (p. 1573), "We propose in this hypothesis that FLN comprises only the core computational mechanisms of recursion as they appear in narrow syntax and the mappings to the interfaces" (i.e. the interfaces with mechanisms of speech perception, speech production, conceptual knowledge, and intentions).[2]

Inother words, HCF are suggesting that recursion is the mechanism responsible for everything that distinguishes language both from other human capacities and from the capacities of animals. (These assertions are largely independent: there may be parts of the narrow language faculty other than recursion even if the narrow faculty is the only part that is uniquely human; and the narrow faculty might consist only of recursion even if parts of the broad faculty are uniquely human as well.) The authors go on to speculate that the recursion mechanism, defining what is special about language, may not even have evolved for language itself but for other cognitive abilities such as navigation, number, or social relationships.

HCF's hypothesis appears to be a radical departure from Chomsky's earlier position that language is a complex ability for which the human brain, and only the human brain, is specialized:

A human language is a system of remarkable complexity. To come to know a human language would be an extraordinary intellectual achievement for a creature not specifically designed to accomplish this task. A normal child acquires this knowledge on relatively slight exposure and without specific training. He can then quite effortlessly make use of an intricate structure of specific rules and guiding principles to convey his thoughts and feelings to others, arousing in them novel ideas and subtle perceptions and judgments. (Chomsky, 1975, p. 4)

Similarly, Chomsky's frequent use of the terms "language faculty" and "mental organ"[3] underscore his belief that language is distinct from other cognitive abilities, and therefore distinct from the abilities of species that share those abilities but lack the ability to acquire languages. For example:

It would be surprising indeed if we were to find that the principles governing [linguistic] phenomena are operative in other cognitive systems, although there might be certain loose analogies, perhaps in terms of figure and ground, or properties of memory, as we see when the relevant principles are made explicit. Such examples illustrate ... that there is good reason to suppose that the functioning of the language faculty is guided by special principles specific to this domain ... (Chomsky, 1980, p. 44)

Indeed, the position that very little is special to language, and that the special bits are minor modifications of other cognitive processes, is one that Chomsky's strongest critics have counterposed to his for years. Not surprisingly, many have viewed the *Science* paper as a major recantation (e.g. Goldberg, 2003).

The HCF paper presents us with an opportunity to reexamine the question of what is special about language. As HCF note (p. 1572), the two of us have advanced a position rather different from theirs, namely that the language faculty, like other biological systems showing signs of complex adaptive design (Dawkins, 1986; Williams, 1966), is a system of co-adapted traits that evolved by natural selection (Jackendoff, 1992, 1994, 2002; Pinker, 1994b, 2003; Pinker & Bloom, 1990). Specifically, the language faculty evolved in the human lineage for the communication of complex propositions. HCF contrast this idea with their recursion-only hypothesis, which "has the interesting effect of nullifying the argument from design, and thus rendering the status of FLN as an adaptation open to question" (p. 1573).

In this paper we analyze HCF's recursion-only hypothesis, and conclude that it is hard to sustain. We will show that there is considerably more of language that is special, though still, we think, a plausible product of the processes of evolution. We will assess the key bodies of evidence, coming to a different reading from HCF's, and then consider how they arrived at their position.

Despite our disagreements over the recursion-only hypothesis, there is much in the paper with which we are sympathetic. We agree that it is conceptually useful to distinguish between the language faculty in its broad and narrow sense, to dissect the broad language faculty into sensorimotor, conceptual, and grammatical components, and to differentiate among the issues of shared versus unique abilities, gradual versus saltational evolution, and continuity versus change of evolutionary function. The rigorous laboratory study of possible homologues and analogues of aspects of language in other species is a hallmark of the research programs of Hauser and Fitch, and we agree that they promise major advances in our understanding of the evolution of language. Our disagreement specifically centers on the hypothesis that recursion is the only aspect of language that is special to it, that it evolved for functions other than language, and that this nullifies "the argument from design" that sees language as an adaptation.

The claims of HCF are carefully hedged, and the authors could argue that they are not actually advocating the recursion-only hypothesis but merely suggesting that it be entertained or speculating that it may turn out to be correct in the long run. We are not so much interested in pinning down who believes what as in accepting HCF's invitation to take the hypothesis itself seriously.

2. What's Special: A Brief Examination of the Evidence

We organize our discussion in line with HCF, distinguishing the conceptual, sensorimotor, and specifically linguistic aspects of the language faculty in turn.

2.1. CONCEPTUAL STRUCTURE

Let us begin with the messages that language expresses: mental representations in the form of conceptual structure (or, as HCF put it, outputs of the "conceptual–intentional system"). The primate literature, incisively analyzed in HCF, gives us good reason to believe that some of the foundations of the human conceptual system are present in other primates, such as the major subsystems dealing with spatial, causal, and social reasoning. If chimpanzees could talk, they would have things to talk about that we would recognize.

HCF also argue that some aspects of the human conceptual system, such as Theory of Mind (intuitive psychology) and parts of intuitive physics, are absent in monkeys, and questionable or at best rudimentary in chimpanzees. They are special to humans, though not special to language. We add that many other conceptual systems, though not yet systematically studied in non-human primates, are conspicuous in human verbal interactions while being hard to discern in any aspect of primates' naturalistic behavior. They include essences (a major component of intuitive biology and chemistry), ownership, multi-part tools, fatherhood, romantic love, and most moral and deontic concepts. It is possible that these abilities, like Theory of Mind, are absent or discernable only in rudimentary form in other primates. These too would be uniquely human aspects of the language faculty in its broad sense, but would be part of a system for non-linguistic reasoning about the world rather than for language itself.

In addition, there are domains of human concepts which are probably unlearnable without language (Jackendoff, 1996). For example, the notion of a "week" depends on counting time periods that cannot all be perceived at once; we doubt that such a concept could be developed or learned without the mediation of language. More striking is the possibility that numbers themselves (beyond those that can be subitized) are parasitic on language—that they depend on learning the sequence of number words, the syntax of number phrases, or both (Bloom, 1994a; Wiese, 2004) (though see Grinstead, MacSwan, Curtiss, & Gelman, 1997, 2004, for a contrary view). Vast domains of human understanding, including the supernatural and sacred, the specifics of folk and formal science, human-specific kinship systems (such as the distinction between cross- and parallel cousins), and formal social roles (such as "justice of the peace" and "treasurer"), can be acquired only with the help of language.[4] The overall picture is that there is a substrate of conceptual structure in chimps, overlain by some uniquely human but not necessarily language-based subsystems, in turn overlain by subsystems that depend on the pre-existence of linguistic expression. So here we more or less concur with HCF, while recognizing a more ramified situation.

2.2. SPEECH PERCEPTION

HCF implicitly reject Alvin Liberman's hypothesis that "Speech is Special" (SiS). According to SiS, speech recognition is a mode of perception that is distinct from our inherited primate auditory analyzers in being adapted to recover the articulatory intentions of a human speaker (Liberman, 1985, 1991; Liberman, Cooper, Shankweiler, & Studdert-Kennedy, 1967; Liberman & Mattingly, 1989). One of the first kinds of evidence adduced for SiS, dating to the 1950s, was the existence of categorical phoneme perception (Liberman et al., 1967), in which pairs of phonemes differing in say, voicing (e.g. p and b) are discriminated more accurately than pairs of stimuli separated by the same physical difference (in this case, in voice-onset time) but falling into the same phonemic category (both voiced, or both unvoiced). This particular bit of evidence for human uniqueness was deflated in the 1970s by findings that chinchillas make similar discriminations (Kuhl & Miller, 1975). HCF cite this as evidence against SiS, together with three other findings: that certain animals can make auditory distinctions based on formant frequency, that tamarin monkeys can learn to discriminate the gross rhythms of different languages, and that monkeys can perceive formants in their own species' vocalizations.

These phenomena suggest that at least some aspects of the ability to perceive speech were present long before the advent of language. Of course, some version of this conclusion is unavoidable: human ancestors began with a primate auditory system, adapted to perform complex analyses of the auditory world, and it is inconceivable that a system for speech perception in humans could have begun de novo. HCF go further and suggest that there have been *no* evolutionary changes to the mammalian auditory system for the function of speech perception in humans. They suggest that this null hypothesis has withstood all attempts to reject it. We are not so sure.

Most experiments testing the perception of human speech by non-human animals have them discriminate pairs of speech sounds, often after extensive operant conditioning (supervised learning). It is not surprising that some animals can do so, or even that their perceptual boundaries resemble those of humans, since auditory analyzers suited for non-speech distinctions might suffice to discriminate among speech sounds, even if the analyzers humans use are different (Trout, 2001, 2003b). For example, a mammalian circuit that uses onset asynchrony to distinguish two overlapping auditory events from a single event with a complex timbre might be sufficient to discriminate voiced from unvoiced consonants (Bregman & Pinker, 1978). But humans do not just make one-bit discriminations between pairs of phonemes. Rather, they can process a continuous, information-rich stream of speech. In doing so, they rapidly distinguish individual words from tens of thousands of distracters despite the absence of acoustic cues for phoneme and word boundaries, while compensating in real time for the distortions introduced by coarticulation and by variations in the age, sex, accent, identity, and emotional state of the speaker. And all of this is accomplished by children as a product of unsupervised learning. A monkey's ability to be trained to discriminate pairs of phonemes provides little evidence that its auditory system would be up to the task accomplished by humans. It would be extraordinarily difficult at present to conduct experiments that fairly compared a primate's ability to a human's, fully testing the null hypothesis.

Moreover, there is considerable evidence that *has* cast doubt on the null hypothesis (Anderson, 2004; Liberman, 1985, 1991; Remez, 1989, 1994; Trout, 2001, 2003b). First, speech and sound are phenomenologically different: under certain conditions, a given sound can be perceived simultaneously as part of a syllable and as a non-speechlike chirp (Liberman & Mattingly, 1989), or a stretch of sound can be heard to flip qualitatively between speech and non-speech (Remez, Pardo, Piorkowski, & Rubin, 2001).

Second, in humans the perception of speech dissociates in a number of ways from the perception of auditory events (the latter presumably using the analyzers we share with other primates). Neuroimaging and brain-damage studies suggest that partly distinct sets of brain areas subserve speech and non-speech sounds (Hickok & Poeppel, 2000; Poeppel, 2001; Trout, 2001; Vouloumanos, Kiehl, Werker, & Liddle, 2001). A clear example is pure word deafness, in which a neurological patient has lost the ability to analyze speech while recognizing other environmental sounds (Hickok & Poeppel, 2000; Poeppel, 2001). Cases of amusia and auditory agnosia, in which patients can understand speech yet fail to appreciate music or recognize environmental sounds (Peretz, Gagnon, & Bouchard, 1998; Poeppel, 2001), show that speech and non-speech perception in fact doubly dissociate.

Third, many of the complex hallmarks of speech perception appear early in infancy (Eimas & Miller, 1992; Miller & Eimas, 1983). Recent studies suggest that young infants, including neonates, prefer speech sounds to non-speech sounds with similar spectral and temporal properties. These include sounds that would have been indistinguishable in the womb, so the preference cannot be explained by learning in utero (Vouloumanos & Werker, 2004a,b). Moreover, neonates' sensitivity to speech appears to depend on the parts of the brain that subserve language in adults: a recent study using optical tomography showed that left-hemisphere temporal regions of the brains of newborns responded more to normal speech than to spectrally similar reversed speech (Peña et al., 2003).

Fourth, comparisons among primates turn up significant differences between their abilities to perceive speech and our abilities. For example, monkeys fail to categorize consonants according to place of articulation using formant transitions alone (Sinnott & Williamson, 1999). They discriminate /ra/ from /la/ at a different boundary from the one salient to humans (Sinnott & Brown, 1997). They fail to segregate the initial consonant from the vowel when compensating for syllable length in discriminating phonemes (Sinnott, Brown, & Borneman, 1998). They fail to trade off the duration of the silent gap with the formant transition in perceiving stop consonants within consonant clusters (Sinnott & Saporita, 2000). They fail to show the asymmetrical "magnet effect" that characterizes infants' discrimination of speech sounds varying in acoustic similarity to prototype vowels (Kuhl, 1991). And their subjective similarity spaces among vowels (measured by discrimination reaction times analyzed by multidimensional scaling) is very different from that of humans (Sinnott, Brown, Malik, & Kressley, 1997). Chimpanzees, too, have a subjective similarity space for vowels that differs from humans', and, like macaques, have difficulty discriminating vowel pairs differing in advancement or frontness (Kojima & Kiritani, 1989). Quail (Trout, 2003a)[5] and budgerigars (Dooling & Brown, 1990) that have been trained to discriminate human speech sounds also show patterns of discrimination and generalization that differ from those of humans. A recent review of research on speech perception in humans, chinchillas, budgerigars, and quail showed that the phoneme boundaries for humans and animals differed in more than a third of the studies (Sinnott, 1998). These findings must be qualified by the fact that human speech perception necessarily reflects the effects of experience listening to a specific language, and it is difficult to equate such experience between humans and other animals. Nonetheless, if findings of similarities between humans and animals trained on human speech contrasts are taken as evidence that primate audition is a sufficient basis for human speech perception, findings of differences following such training must be taken as weakening such a conclusion.

2.3. SPEECH PRODUCTION

Turning to the articulatory side of speech, HCF cite two arguments against evolutionary adaptation for language in the human lineage. One is that some birds and primates produce formants (time-varying acoustic energy bands) in their vocalizations by manipulating the supralaryngeal vocal tract, a talent formerly thought to be uniquely human. Nonetheless, by all accounts such manipulations represent a minuscule fraction of the intricate gestures of lips, velum, larynx, and tip, body, and root of the tongue executed by speakers of all human languages (Browman & Goldstein, 1992; Hauser, 1996). Non-human primates are also notoriously resistant to training of their vocalizations (Hauser, 1996), and as HCF themselves note, they show no ability to learn vocalizations through imitation. HCF try to downplay the difference between humans and primates by pointing out that vocal imitation is not uniquely human. But this is irrelevant to the question of whether vocal imitation evolved for language in the human lineage. The other species that evolved comparable talents, namely certain birds and porpoises, are not ancestral to humans, and must have evolved their talents independently of what took place in human evolution.

Other evidence, not mentioned by HCF, also suggests that vocal production has been adapted for speech in humans. In comparison with extant apes and pre-*sapiens* hominids, modern humans have an enlarged region of the spinal cord responsible for the voluntary control over breathing required by speech production (MacLarnon & Hewitt, 1999).[6] Humans also display greater cortical control over articulation and breathing, compared with the largely subcortical control found in other primates (Deacon, 1997). And as Darwin noted, the innate vocal babbling of human infants is one of the clearest signs that "man has an instinctive tendency to speak."

To reconcile the recursion-only hypothesis with the fact that vocal learning and imitation are distinctively human (among primates), HCF refer to a "capacity for vocal imitation" and assign it to the "broad language faculty" which subsumes non-language-specific abilities. But this is questionable. Humans are not notably talented at vocal imitation in general, only at imitating speech sounds (and perhaps melodies). For example, most humans lack the ability (found in some birds) to convincingly reproduce environmental sounds. Even the ability to convincingly imitate a foreign or regional accent is the exception rather than the rule among human adults, and adults are notoriously poor at imitating the phonetics of a second language. Thus "capacity for vocal imitation" in humans might better be described as a capacity to learn to produce speech, contradicting the idea that grammatical recursion is the only human-specific and language-specific component of the language faculty.

HCF's second argument against human adaptations for speech production is the discovery that the descended human larynx (which allows a large space of discriminable vowels, while compromising other functions) can be found in certain other mammalian species, where it may have evolved to exaggerate perceived size. HCF note that while a descended larynx "undoubtedly plays an important role in speech production in modern humans, it need not have first evolved for this function" but may be an example of "preadaptation" (in which a trait originally was selected for a function other than the one it currently serves). But this suggestion, even if correct, does not speak to the issue of whether the human vocal tract was evolutionarily shaped to subserve human language. Modifications of function are ubiquitous in natural selection (for example, primate hands, bear paws, and bat wings are adaptations that evolved by natural selection from the fins of fish), so the fact that a trait was initially shaped by selection for one function does not imply that it was not subsequently shaped by selection for another function. Thus even if the larynx originally descended to exaggerate size, that says nothing about whether its current anatomical position was subsequently maintained, extended, or altered by selection pressures to enhance speech.

Moreover, evidence that the larynx was recently adapted for speech is stronger than evidence that it was originally adapted for size exaggeration. The human larynx is permanently descended in women, children, and infants past the age of 3 months (Lieberman, 1984), all of whom speak or are learning to speak, and none of whom, in comparison with adult males engaged in intrasexual competition, had much evolutionary incentive to exaggerate size if doing so would incur costs in other functions. Compare this with a related trait that is clearly adapted to size exaggeration in intrasexual competition, namely lowered vocal fundamental frequency. This trait, as expected, is specifically found in males of reproductive age. Moreover, even with its descended larynx, the human supralaryngeal vocal tract is no longer than what would be expected for a primate of our size, because the human oral cavity has shortened in evolution owing to the fact that humans, unlike chimpanzees, lack snouts (Lieberman, 2003). This further suggests that the vocal tract was not primarily shaped for size exaggeration. Finally, the descended larynx is part of a suite of vocal-tract modifications in human evolution, including changes in the shape of the tongue and jaw, that expand the space of discriminable speech sounds despite compromises in other organic functions, such as breathing, chewing, and swallowing (Lieberman, 1984, 2003). These other aspects of vocal tract anatomy are not addressed by HCF.

2.4. PHONOLOGY

Having the potential to articulate speech sounds—that is, having a vocal tract of the right shape and controllable in the right ways—is not the same as being able to produce the sounds of a language. The articulatory commands sent to the vocal tract to produce speech are organized in distinctive ways. Speech segments are drawn from a finite repertoire of phonemes, each defined by a set of discrete articulatory or acoustic feature values such as voicing, place of articulation, and mode of onset and release. Speech segments are concatenated into patterned rhythmic constituents such as syllables, feet, and prosodic phrases, upon which are superimposed systematic patterns of stress and pitch. The composition of the segments can then be modified in rule-governed ways according to their contexts (as in the three pronunciations of the past-tense suffix in *walked, jogged,* and *patted*). Languages differ in their repertoire of speech segments, their repertoire of syllable and intonation patterns, and in constraints, local and non-local, on how one sound can affect the pronunciation of others. This system of patterns and constraints is the subject matter of phonology.

The set of phonological structures of a language forms a "discrete infinity," a property which, in the case of syntax, HCF identify as one of the hallmarks of language. Just as every language has an unlimited number of syntactic structures built from a finite collection of morphemes, every language has an unlimited number of phonological structures built from a finite repertoire of phonetic segments. One can always concatenate segments into longer and longer well-formed phonological sequences (whether meaningful or not). We note that the segmental and syllabic aspect of phonological structure, though discretely infinite and hierarchically structured, is not technically recursive. Recursion consists of embedding a constituent in a constituent of the same type, for example, a relative clause inside a relative clause (*a book that was written by the novelist you met last night*), which automatically confers the ability to do so ad libitum (e.g. *a book [that was written by the novelist [you met on the night [that we decided to buy the boat [that you liked so much]]]]*). This does not exist in phonological structure: a syllable, for instance, cannot be embedded in another syllable. Full syllables can only be concatenated, an operation that does not require a pointer stack or equivalent apparatus necessary to implement true recursion.[7]

Is phonological structure specific to language, or does it serve other more general purposes? Hierarchical and featural organization of gestures characterize other domains of motor control, such as manual manipulation. However, the kinds of constituents, the principles of combination, and the nature of the adjustment processes in phonology appear to be specific to language. And unlike motor programs, phonological structure is a level of representation that is crucially used both in perception and production.[8] Moreover, every language contains a set of partly arbitrary, learned conventions which permit certain kinds of articulatory shortcuts but prohibit others (that is why there are different accents), rather than being real-time adjustments to ease articulation or clarity.

Rhythmic organization similar to that of higher levels of phonological structure appears in music, but with somewhat different implementation. The two rhythmic components might be homologous the way fingers and toes are; hybrids of the two appear in poetry, song, and chant (Jackendoff, 1989; Lerdahl & Jackendoff, 1983). We do not know of other human capacities that have been shown to reflect this formal organization, though it is an interesting open question.

Is phonology uniquely human? It appears that some of the combinatorial properties of phonology have analogues in some species of birdsong, and perhaps in some cetacean song, but not in any primates; if so, they would have to have evolved separately in humans. The rhythmic properties of language and music may well be unique to humans: informal observations suggest that no other primate can easily be trained to move to an auditory beat, as in marching, dancing, tapping the feet, or clapping the hands (Brown, Merker, & Wallin, 2000, p. 12). This is surely one of the most elementary characteristics of the human rhythmic response, and one that is displayed spontaneously by young children. And the rule-governed recombination of a repertoire of tones, which appears in music, tone languages, and more subtly in intonation contours of language, is as far as we know unparalleled elsewhere among primates. So overall, major characteristics of phonology are specific to language (or to language and music), uniquely human, discretely infinite, and not recursive. Thus phonology represents a major counterexample to the recursion-only hypothesis.

We note that there are good adaptive reasons for a distinct level of combinatorial phonological structure to have evolved as part of the language faculty. As noted as early as Hockett (1960), "duality of patterning"—the existence of two levels of rule-governed combinatorial structure, one combining meaningless sounds into morphemes, the other combining meaningful morphemes into words and phrases—is a universal design feature of human language. A combinatorial sound system is a solution to the problem of encoding a large number of concepts (tens of thousands) into a far smaller number of discriminable speech sounds (dozens). A fixed inventory of sounds, when combined into strings, can multiply out to encode a large number of words, without requiring listeners to make finer and finer analogue discriminations among physically similar sounds. Recently Nowak and his collaborators have borne out this speculation in computer simulations of language evolution (Nowak & Krakauer, 1999).

Phonological adjustment rules also have an intelligible rationale. Phonologists have long noted that many of them act to smooth out articulation or enhance discriminability. Since these two requirements are often at cross-purposes (slurred speech is easy to produce but hard to discriminate; exaggerated enunciation vice-versa), a fixed set of rules delineating which adjustments are mandated within a speech community may act in service of the "parity" requirement of language (Liberman & Mattingly, 1989; Slobin, 1977), namely that the code be usable both by speakers and hearers.

Whether or not these hypotheses about the adaptive function of phonology are correct, it is undeniable that phonology constitutes a distinct level of organization of all human languages. Surprisingly, HCF make no mention of phonology, only of perception and articulation.

2.5. WORDS

We now come to an aspect of language that is utterly essential to it: the word. In the minimal case, a word is an arbitrary association of a chunk of phonology and a chunk of conceptual structure, stored in speakers' long-term memory (the lexicon). Some words, such as *hello, ouch, yes,* and *allakazam,* do not combine with other words (other than trivially, as in direct quotes). But most words (as well as smaller morphemes such as affixes) can combine into complex words such as compounds (e.g. *armchair*) and other derived forms (e.g. *squeezability*) according to principles of the component of language called morphology. Morphology, together with syntax, constitutes the classical domain of recursion à la HCF.

As acknowledged by HCF in passing, words have several properties that appear to be uniquely human. The first is that there are so many of them—50,000 in a garden-variety speaker's lexicon, more than 100 times the most extravagant claims for vocabulary in language-trained apes or in natural primate call systems (Wallman, 1992). The second is the range and precision of concepts that words express, from concrete to abstract (*lily, joist, telephone, bargain, glacial, abstract, from, any*). Third, they all have to be learned. This certainly requires proficiency at vocal imitation, as HCF note. But it also requires a prodigious ability to construct the proper meaning on the basis of linguistic and nonlinguistic context. Children come into their second year of life expecting the noises other people make to be used symbolically; much of the job of learning language is figuring out what concepts (or sets of things in the world, depending on your view of semantics) these noises are symbols for.

HCF observe that "the rate at which children build the lexicon is so massively different from non-human primates that one must entertain the possibility of an independently evolved mechanism." They also observe that "unlike the best animal examples of putatively referential signals, most of the words of human language are not associated with specific functions" (1576) and may be "detached from the here and now," another feature of words that may be "uniquely human." These suggestions, however, contradict their claim that the narrow language faculty "only includes recursion and is the only uniquely human component of the faculty of language." They reconcile the contradiction by retaining the idea that the narrow language faculty includes only recursion but weakening the idea that only the narrow language faculty is uniquely human; specifically, they relegate word leaning to the broad language faculty. They do so by suggesting that word learning is not specific to language, citing the hypothesis, which they attribute to Bloom (1999) and Markson and Bloom (1997) that "human children may use domain-general mechanisms to acquire and recall words." Actually, while Markson and Bloom did argue against a dedicated system for learning words, they did not conclude that words are acquired by a *domain-general* mechanism. Rather, they argued that word-learning is accomplished by the child's Theory of Mind, a mechanism specific to the domain of intuitive psychology, possibly unique to humans.

In any case, the conclusion that there are no mechanisms of learning or representation specific to words may be premature. The experiment by Markson and Bloom cited by HCF showed that children display similar levels of recognition memory after a single exposure to either a new word or a new fact (e.g. "My uncle gave it to me"). But on any reasonable account, words and facts are stored using the same kinds of neural mechanisms responsible for storage, retention, and forgetting. A demonstration that word learning and fact learning have this property in common does not prove they have all their properties in common.

Markson and Bloom's case that word learning can be reduced to a Theory of Mind mechanism is most tenable for the basic act of learning that a noun is the label for a perceptible object. But words are not just names for things (see Bloom, 1999). They also are marked for a syntactic category (verb, preposition, and so on), for obligatory grammatically encoded arguments (agent, theme, path, and so on), and for selection restrictions on the syntactic properties of their complements (e.g. whether each one is headed by a preposition, a finite verb, or a non-finite verb). This information, which is partly idiosyncratic to each word and therefore must be stored in the lexicon, critically governs how the word enters into the recursive components of grammar (morphology and syntax); it cannot be identified with the conceptual database that makes up general world knowledge.

Moreover, functional morphemes such as articles, auxiliaries, and affixes are also part of the lexicon (since each involves a pairing between a sound and some other information, both of which are specific to the particular language), yet the information they encode (case, agreement, finiteness, voice, and so on) is continuous with the information encoded by syntax. Such words are not used, and presumably could not be acquired, in isolation from some syntactic context. And as functional morphemes go, so go verbs, since verbs encode similar kinds of grammatical and semantic information (Gentner, 1981; Pinker, 1989; Talmy, 1985), have similarly close linguistic, psychological, and neurological ties to syntax (Gentner, 1981; Pinker, 1989; Shapiro, Pascual-Leone, Mottaghy, Gangitano, & Caramazza, 2001), and, at least in part, require syntactic analysis to be acquired (Gleitman, 1990; Pinker, 1994a). So other than the process of acquiring the names for salient things, it is hard to see how words can be carved away from the narrow language faculty and relegated to a generic mechanism that learns facts from people's intentions.

Even in the case of learning nouns, there are reasons to suspect that children treat facts and words in different ways. These different ways reflect the hallmarks of words that distinguish them from other kinds of factual knowledge. One is that words are bidirectional and arbitrary ("Saussurean") signs: a child, upon hearing a word used by a speaker, can conclude that other speakers in the community, and the child himself or herself, may use the word with the same meaning and expect to be understood (Hurford, 1989). This is one of the assumptions that allows babies to use words upon exposure to them, as opposed to needing to have their vocal output shaped or reinforced by parental feedback. Diesendruck and Markson (2001) (see also Au & Glusman, 1990) showed that young children tacitly assume that speakers share a code. If one speaker labels a novel object as a *mep* out of earshot of a second speaker, and the second speaker then asks about a *jop*, the children interpret the second speaker as referring to a different object. Presumably it is because they attributed common knowledge of a name (*mep*) to that speaker, even though they had never witnessed that speaker learning the name. In contrast, if one speaker mentions a *fact* about an object (e.g. "my sister gave it to me") out of earshot of a second speaker, and the second speaker then asks about an object characterized by another fact (e.g. "dogs like to play with it"), they do not interpret the second speaker as referring to a different object. Presumably this is because they do not attribute common knowledge of facts to the members of a speech community the way they do with words. Somewhat to their surprise, Diesendruck and Markson conclude, "Interestingly, the present findings lend indirect support to the idea that in some respects, word learning *is* special" (p. 639).

Another hallmark of words is that their meanings are defined not just by the relation of the word to a concept but by the relation of the word to other words in the lexicon, forming organized sets such as superordinates, antonyms, meronyms (parts), and avoiding true synonyms (Clark, 1993; Deacon, 1997; Miller, 1991; Miller & Fellbaum, 1991). Behrend and collaborators (Behrend, Scofield, & Kleinknecht, 2001; Scofield & Behrend, 2003), refining a phenomenon discovered by Markman (1989), showed that two-year-old children assign a novel word to an object they are unfamiliar with rather than to one they are familiar with (presumably a consequence of an avoidance of synonymy), but they show no such effect for novel facts.

Another distinctive feature about words is that (with the exception of proper names, which in many regards are more like phrases than words; see Bloom, 1994b) they are generic, referring to kinds of objects and events rather than specific objects and events (di Sciullo & Williams, 1987). Waxman and Booth (2001), and Behrend et al. (2001) showed that children generalize a newly learned noun to other objects of the same kind, but do not generalize a newly learned fact (e.g. "my uncle gave it to me") to other objects of the same kind. Similarly, Gelman and Heyman (1999) showed that children assume that a person labeled with the word *carrot-eater* has a taste for carrots, whereas one described as eating carrots (a fact about the person) merely ate them at least once.

Our assessment of the situation is that words, as shared, organized linkages of phonological, conceptual, and grammatical structures, are a distinctive language-specific part of human knowledge. The child appears to come to social situations anticipating that the noises made by other humans are made up of words, and this makes the learning of words different in several regards from the learning of facts. Moreover, a good portion of people's knowledge of words (especially verbs and functional morphemes) consists of exactly the kind of information that is manipulated by recursive syntax, the component held to make up the narrow language faculty. This makes it difficult to hold that the capacity to represent and learn words is part of a general knowledge system that evolved independently of the demands of language.

2.6. SYNTAX

We finally turn to syntactic structure, the principles by which words and morphemes are concatenated into sentences. In our view, syntax functions in the overall system of language as a regulator: it helps determine how the meanings of words are combined into the meanings of phrases and sentences. Every linguist recognizes that (on the surface, at least), syntax employs at least four combinatorial devices. The first collects words hierarchically into syntactic phrases, where syntactic phrases correspond (in prototypical cases) to constituents of meaning. (For example, word strings such as *Dr Ruth discussed sex with Dick Cavett* are ambiguous because their words can be grouped into phrases in two different ways). This is the recursive component referred to by HCF. The second orders words or phrases within a phrase, for example, by specifying that the verb of a sentence falls in a certain position such as second, or that the phrase serving as the topic comes first. Most languages of the world are not as strict about word order as English, and often the operative principles of phrase order concern topic and focus, a fairly marginal issue in English grammar. A third major syntactic device is agreement, whereby verbs or adjectives are marked with inflections that correspond to the number, person, grammatical gender, or other classificatory features of syntactically related nouns. The fourth is case-marking, whereby noun phrases are marked with inflections (nominative, accusative, and so on) depending on the grammatical role of the phrase with respect to a verb, preposition, or another noun.

Different languages rely on these mechanisms to different extents to convey who did what to whom, what is where, and other semantic relations. English relies heavily on order and constituency, but has vestigial agreement and no case except on pronouns. The Australian language Warlpiri has virtually free word order and an exuberant system of case and agreement; Russian and Classical Latin are not far behind. Many languages use the systems redundantly, for instance German, with its rich gender and case systems, moderate use of agreement, and fairly strong constraints on phrase order.

And this barely scratches the surface. Languages are full of devices like pronouns and articles, which help signal which information the speaker expects to be old or new to the hearer; quantifiers, tense and aspect markers, complementizers, and auxiliaries, which express temporal and logical relations; restrictive and appositive modification (as in relative clauses); and grammatical distinctions among questions, imperatives, statements, and other kinds of illocutionary force, signaled by phrase order, morphology, or intonation. A final important device is long-distance dependency, which can relate a question word or relative pronoun to a distant verb, as in *Which theory did you expect Fred to think Melvin had disproven last week?*, where *which theory* is understood as the object of *disprove*.

Is all this specific to language? It seems likely, given that it is specialized machinery for regulating the relation of sound and meaning. What other human or non-human ability could it serve? Yet aside from phrase structure (in which a noun phrase, for example, can contain a noun phrase, or a sentence can contain a sentence) and perhaps long-distance dependencies,[9] none of it involves recursion per se. A case marker may not contain another instance of a case marker; an article may not contain an article; a pronoun may not contain a pronoun, and so on for auxiliaries, tense features, and so on. HCF cite none of these devices as part of language, although each weakens the hypothesis that the narrow language faculty consists only of recursion.

Indeed, at least one language seems to rely entirely on these devices, forgoing use of the recursive power of syntax entirely. Based on 30 years of fieldwork on the Amazonian language Pirahã, Everett (2004) claims that this language lacks any evidence of recursion. All semantic relations conveyed by clausal or NP embedding in more familiar languages, such as conditionality, intention, relative clauses, reports of speech and mental states, and recursive possession (*my father's brother's uncle*), are conveyed in Pirahã by means of monoclausal constructions connected paratactically (i.e. without embedding). However, Pirahã very clearly has phonology, morphology, syntax, and sentences, and is undoubtedly a human language, qualitatively different from anything found in animals.

HCF do discuss the ability to learn linearly ordered recursive phrase structure. In a clever experiment, Fitch and Hauser (2004) showed that unlike humans, tamarins cannot learn the simple recursive language A^nB^n (all sequences consisting of n instances of the symbol A followed by n instances of the symbol B; such a language can be generated by the recursive rule $S \rightarrow A(S)B$). But the relevance of this result to HCF's argument is unclear. Although human languages are recursive, and A^nB^n is recursive, A^nB^n is not a possible human language. No natural language construction has such phrases, which violate the X-bar principles that have long been at the heart of the mainstream theory of Universal Grammar (Chomsky, 1972).[10] If the conclusion is that human syntactic competence consists only of an ability to learn recursive languages (which embrace all kinds of formal systems, including computer programming languages, mathematical notation, the set of all palindromes, and an infinity of others), the fact that actual human languages are a minuscule and well-defined subset of recursive languages is unexplained.

2.7. SUMMARY OF EVIDENCE ON THE RECURSION-ONLY HYPOTHESIS

The state of the evidence for HCF's hypothesis that only recursion is special to language is as follows:

- Conceptual structure: HCF plausibly suggest that human conceptual structure partly overlaps with that of other primates and partly incorporates newly evolved capacities.

- Speech perception. HCF suggest it is simply generic primate auditory perception. But the tasks given to monkeys are not comparable to the feats of human speech perception, and most of Liberman's evidence for the Speech-is-Special hypothesis, and more recent experimental demonstrations of human–monkey differences in speech perception, are not discussed.
- Speech production. HCF's recursion-only hypothesis implies no selection for speech production in the human lineage. But control of the supralaryngeal vocal tract is incomparably more complex in human language than in other primate vocalizations. Vocal imitation and vocal learning are uniquely human among primates (talents that are consistently manifested only in speech). And syllabic babbling emerges spontaneously in human infants. HCF further suggest that the distinctively human anatomy of the vocal tract may have been selected for size exaggeration rather than speech. Yet the evidence for the former in humans is weak, and does not account for the distinctive anatomy of the supralaryngeal parts of the vocal tract.
- Phonology. Not discussed by HCF.
- Lexicon. HCF discuss two ways in which words are a distinctively human ability, possibly unique to our species. But they assign words to the broad language faculty, which is shared by other human cognitive faculties, without discussing the ways in which words appear to be tailored to language—namely that they consist in part (sometimes in large part) of grammatical information, and that they are bidirectional, shared, organized, and generic in reference, features that are experimentally demonstrable in young children's learning of words.
- Morphology: Not discussed by HCF.
- Syntax: Case, agreement, pronouns, predicate-argument structure, topic, focus, auxiliaries, question markers, and so on, are not discussed by HCF. Recursion is said to be human-specific, but no distinction is made between arbitrary recursive mathematical systems and the particular kinds of recursive phrase structure found in human languages.

We conclude that the empirical case for the recursion-only hypothesis is extremely weak.

2.8. SOME GENETIC EVIDENCE

Recent findings from genetics cast even stronger doubt on the recursion-only hypothesis. There is a rare inherited impairment of language and speech caused by a dominant allele of a single gene, FOXP2 (Lai, Fisher, Hurst, Vargha-Khadem, & Monaco, 2001). The gene has been sequenced and subjected to comparative analyses, which show that the normal version of the gene is universal in the human population, that it diverged from the primate homologue subsequent to the evolutionary split between humans and chimpanzees, and that it was a target of natural selection rather than a product of genetic drift or other stochastic evolutionary processes (Enard et al., 2002). The phenotype is complex and not completely characterized, but it is generally agreed that sufferers have deficits in articulation, production, comprehension, and judgments in a variety of domains of grammar, together with difficulties in producing sequences of orofacial movements (Bishop, 2002; Gopnik & Crago, 1991; Ullman & Gopnik, 1999; Vargha-Khadem, Watkins, Alcock, Fletcher, & Passingham, 1995). The possibility that the affected people are impaired only in recursion is a non-starter. These findings refute the hypothesis that the only evolutionary change for language in the human lineage was one that grafted syntactic recursion onto unchanged primate input–output abilities and enhanced learning of facts. Instead they support the notion that language evolved piecemeal in the human lineage under the influence of natural selection, with the selected genes having pleiotropic effects that incrementally improved multiple components.

FOXP2, moreover, is just the most precisely identified of a number of genetic loci that cause impairments of language, or related impairments such as stuttering and dyslexia (Dale et al., 1998; Stromswold, 2001; The SLI Consortium, 2002; van der Lely, Rosen, & McClelland, 1998). None of these impairments knock out or compromise recursion alone. Even in the realm of speech perception, genetic evidence may point to adaptation for language. A recent comparison of the genomes of mice, chimpanzees, and humans turned up a number of genes that are expressed in the development of the auditory system and that have undergone positive selection in the human lineage (Clark et al., 2003). Since speech is the main feature that differentiates the natural auditory environments of humans and of chimpanzees, the authors speculate that these evolutionary changes were in the service of enhanced perception of speech.

As more genes with effects on speech and language are identified, sequenced, and compared across individuals and species, additional tests contrasting the language-as-adaptation hypothesis with the recursion-only hypothesis will be available. The latter predicts heritable impairments that completely or partially knock out recursion but leave people with abilities in speech perception and speech production comparable to those of chimpanzees. Our reading of the literature on language impairment is that this prediction is unlikely to be true.

3. The Minimalist Program as a Rationale for the Recursion-Only Hypothesis

Given the disparity between the recursion-only hypothesis and the facts of language, together with its disparity from Chomsky's earlier commitment to complexity and modularity, one might wonder what motivated the hypothesis. We believe that it arises from Chomsky's current overall approach to the language faculty, the

Minimalist Program (MP) (Chomsky, 1995, 2000a,b; Lasnik, 2002). This is a decade-long attempt at a unified theory for language, based on the following vision. Since language is a mapping between sounds and meanings, only representations of sound (Phonetic Form) and representations of meaning (Logical Form) are truly indispensable. Other than these representations, whose existence is, in Chomsky's terminology, a "virtual conceptual necessity," all other linguistic structures and the principles applying to them, being conceptually unnecessary, should be eliminated. These include the long-prominent deep structure (or d-structure) and surface structure (s-structure). The minutiae of linguistic phenomena should instead be explained by details of words (which uncontroversially are specific to a particular language and must be learned) and certain principles of "economy" that apply to the mapping between meaning and sound. In this way, the core of language may be characterized as an optimal or "perfect system," containing only what is conceptually necessary. The messy complexity of linguistic phenomena comes from the need to interface with the systems for sounds and concepts, which necessarily embody the complexity of human thoughts and speech organs.

Since language combines words into hierarchical tree structures, it is necessary for the language faculty to include, at a minimum, an operation for combining items. In the Minimalist Program this mechanism, called *Merge,* recursively joins two elements (words or phrases) into a binary tree bearing the label of one of them. The Minimalist commitment to bare necessity leads to the conjecture that Merge is the *only* element necessary to create the system of language. The vast number of logical possibilities for constructing erroneous derivations using Merge are kept in check by several principles of economy, which dictate, for example, that certain operations are to be executed later rather than earlier in a derivation, that local relations among elements are to be preferred to longer-distance ones, or that simple operations are to be preferred to more complex ones.

The Minimalist Program appears to be parsimonious and elegant, eschewing the baroque mechanisms and principles that emerged in previous incarnations of generative grammar such as the Extended Standard Theory and Government-Binding Theory (Chomsky, 1972, 1981). And the implications for the evolution of language are clear. If language per se does not consist of very much, then not much had to evolve for us to get it: Merge would be the only thing that had to be added to the pre-existing auditory, vocal, and conceptual systems. This modification could even have been effected by a single genetic change that became fixed in the population through drift or other random processes. Therefore invoking natural selection to explain the adaptive complexity of language (analogously to the way it is invoked to explain the adaptive complexity of the vertebrate eye or echolocation in bats) is no longer necessary (Boeckx & Piatelli-Palmarini, 2005; Hornstein, 2002; Piatelli-Palmarini & Uriagereka, 2004). Indeed, HCF themselves point out the connection between the recursion-only hypothesis and the Minimalist Program:

Recent work on FLN suggests the possibility that at least the narrow-syntactic component satisfies conditions of highly efficient computation to an extent previously unsuspected.... [T]he generative processes of the language system may provide a near-optimal solution that satisfies the interface conditions to FLB. Many of the details of language that are the traditional focus of linguistic study... may represent by-products of this solution, generated automatically by neural/computational constraints and the structure of FLB-components that lie outside of FLN.

The major difficulty with the Minimalist Program, as Chomsky (2000b, p. 124) himself admits, is that "All the phenomena of language appear to refute it." He reassures the reader immediately by adding, "...just as the phenomena of the world appeared to refute the Copernican thesis. The question is whether this is a real refutation." There follows an extended discussion of how science is always deciding which evidence is relevant and which to discard. The general point is unexceptionable, but it offers few grounds for confidence that the *particular* theory under discussion is correct. After all, any theory can be rescued from falsification if one chooses to ignore enough inconvenient phenomena (see also Newmeyer, 2003). The Minimalist Program, in Chomsky's original conception, chooses to ignore:

- all the phenomena of phonology.
- most or all the phenomena of derivational morphology, such as compounds and complex inflected forms.[11]
- most of the phenomena of inflectional morphology: the leading theory in the Chomskyan framework, Halle and Marantz's Distributive Morphology, does not naturally conform to the principles of Minimalism (Halle & Marantz, 1993), and considerable work must be done to reconcile them.
- many basic phrase structures, such as those involved in modification.[12]
- many phenomena of phrase and word order, such as topic and focus, figure and ground, and effects of adjacency and linearity.[13] There is also no account of free word order phenomena, characteristic of many languages of the world.
- the source and nature of lexical entries, which do considerable work in the theory (defining phrase structures, triggering movement), and which therefore are far more abstract and language-specific than mere sound-meaning pairings.
- the connection of the grammar to processing (a difficulty shared with previous versions of Chomskyan theory).
- the connection of the grammar to acquisition, especially how the child can identify the numerous abstract features and configurations that are specific to languages but have no perceptible correlate (see Culicover, 1999; Pinker, 1984, 1987).

In fact, most of the technical accomplishments of the preceding 25 years of research in the Chomskyan paradigm must be torn down, and proposals from long-abandoned 1950s-era formulations and from long-criticized 1970s-era rivals must be rehabilitated (Pullum, 1996).[14]

We do not disagree with Chomsky that a new theory should be cut some slack if it promises advances in parsimony or explanatory power. But in practice, the elegance, economy, and conceptual necessity claimed for Minimalism turn out not to be so obvious. For instance, when Chomsky says that Minimalism does without deep and surface structures, he means only that these structures are not singled out as representations to which constraints such as the Projection Principle or Case Filter apply. The theory still posits that the derivation of every sentence involves a sequence of abstract syntactic trees, related by movement operations or their equivalent. These trees, moreover, are anything but minimal. They contain full branching structures for just about every morpheme (including articles and complementizers), for inflectional features like "tense" and "agreement," and for numerous empty nodes which morphemes are destined to move to or be coindexed with. For example, in the version of Chomsky (1995), a sentence like *John saw Mary* has a tree with six levels of embedding, four traces (the result of four movement operations), and five alternative derivations that need to be compared to ensure that one of the economy requirements has been satisfied (Johnson & Lappin, 1997). Moreover, the lexicon is not just a conceptually necessary list of sound-meaning pairings for identifiable words: it is packed with abstract morphemes and features (such as the "strength" of agreement) whose main rationale is to trigger the right syntactic phenomena, thereby offloading work from the syntactic component and preserving its "minimalist" nature.

Just as Minimalist syntax is far from minimalist, the "principles of economy" that regulate these derivations are not particularly economical. As noted by several critics (Johnson & Lappin, 1997, 1999; Lappin, Levine, & Johnson, 2000; Newmeyer, 2003; Pullum, 1996), these are not independently motivated by least-action principles of physics, resource limitations in cognitive information processing, or mechanical symbol- or step-counting in some formal notation (any of which might, in some sense, come "for free"). Rather, they are a mixture of metaphors involving speed, ease, cost, and need, and anthropomorphic traits such as "greed," "procrastination," and "last resort." Insofar as their desired effects on linguistic structures are clear at all, those effects must be explicitly stipulated, and would have to be spelled out as complicated conditions on operations in any explicit implementation. (That is, they are not derivable mathematically from deeper principles in the way that principles of naive physics like "water finds its own level" are derivable from principles of energy minimization). Moreover, implementing the conditions requires the processor to choose an optimal derivation from among a set of possibilities, a requirement which is computationally far more complex than the implementations of other extant theories of grammar, where conditions may be checked locally against information available at each step within a single derivation (Johnson & Lappin, 1997, 1999).[15]

To be fair, recent work on Minimalism has tried to fill in the gaps and address the problems of Chomsky's original formulations. Yet it is just as clear that such work should not be taken as empirically vindicating Minimalist hypotheses about the empirical nature of language, but rather as carrying out a mandate to implement this vision of Chomsky's. We share the bemusement of Lappin et al. (2000) who write, "What is altogether mysterious from a purely scientific point of view is the rapidity with which a substantial number of investigators, who had significant research commitments in the Government-Binding framework, have abandoned that framework and much of its conceptual inventory, virtually overnight. In its place they have adopted an approach which, as far as we can tell, is in no way superior with respect to either predictive capabilities or explanatory power" (p. 667). Most of the work has consisted of reformulations to meet theory-internal desiderata rather than empirical tests of competing hypotheses, and such simplifications as have been achieved have been at the expense of relegating an increasing number of phenomena to unknown "interface phenomena." The numerous critical analyses of Minimalism which have appeared in the literature (Johnson & Lappin, 1997, 1999; Lappin et al., 2000; Newmeyer, 2003; Postal, 2004; Pullum, 1996; Rochemont & Culicover, 1997; Seuren, 2004) differ considerably in politeness but are remarkably similar in substance.

The conjectural status of Minimalism has been emphasized not just by critics but by the practitioners themselves. Koopman (2000, p. 2), has written that Minimalism "led to relatively few new insights in our understanding of phenomena in the first half of the nineties. This is probably because it did not generate new analytical tools, and thus failed to generate novel ways of looking at well-known paradigms or expand and solve old problems, an essential ingredient for progress to be made at this point" (p. 2). Lasnik's recent tutorial (Lasnik, 2002) concedes that after more than a dozen years, "Minimalism is as yet still just an 'approach', a conjecture about how language works ('perfectly') and a general program for exploring and developing the conjecture" (p. 436). An enthusiastic exposition by Boeckx and Hornstein (2007) includes a caveat (attributed to Chomsky) that "The only note of caution worth bearing in mind is that the Minimalist Program may be premature" (p. 18).

We conclude that on both empirical and theoretical grounds, the Minimalist Program is a very long shot. This is not to say that we believe all of generative grammar should be abandoned. Indeed, we have both written passionate expositions of the overall program, defending core assumptions such as that language is a combinatorial, productive, and partly innate mental system (Jackendoff, 1994, 2002; Pinker, 1994b). But it is necessary to evaluate what aspects of the current mainstream version of generative grammar to keep and what to replace (see (Culicover & Jackendoff, 2005; Jackendoff, 2002), for assessments).

Returning to our main question of what is special about language: Behind HCF's claim that the only aspect of language that is special is recursion lies a presumption that the Minimalist Program is ultimately going to be vindicated. The linguistic phenomena they ignore, listed in Section 2, are among the phenomena also set aside in the overall vision of the MP, listed in this section. Given the empirical status of MP, it seems shaky at best to presume it or its variants when drawing conclusions about the evolution of language.

4. Language, Communication, and Evolution

The intuition that Minimalism reduces the amount of linguistic machinery that had to evolve is not HCF's only argument against the possibility that natural selection was a crucial cause of the evolution of the language faculty. They touch on three other themes that comprise an overall vision of what language is like. These are:

- Language is not "for" communication and may even be badly designed for communication (thus "nullifying the argument from design").
- Language is an "optimal" or "perfect" mapping between sound and meaning, and in this perfection it is unlike other biological systems.
- The narrow language faculty was not selected for language but originated in some other cognitive ability.

These hypotheses challenge a more conventional evolutionary vision of language, according to which the language faculty evolved gradually in response to the adaptive value of more precise and efficient communication in a knowledge-using, socially interdependent lifestyle (Nowak & Komarova, 2001; Nowak & Krakauer, 1999; Nowak, Plotkin, & Jansen, 2000; Pinker, 1994b, 2003; Pinker & Bloom, 1990; Tooby & DeVore, 1987). Gradual emergence implies that later stages had to build on earlier ones in the contingent fashion characteristic of natural selection, resulting in a system that is better than what existed before but not necessarily optimal on first principles (Bickerton, 1990; Givon, 1995; Jackendoff, 2002). We consider HCF's assertions about the function of language in turn.

4.1. LANGUAGE IS BADLY DESIGNED FOR COMMUNICATION

The operative quote from HCF is this:

> The question is whether particular components of the functioning of FLN are adaptations for language, specifically acted upon by natural selection—or, even more broadly, whether FLN evolved for reasons other than communication. (1574)

This passage is an allusion to a position that Chomsky has developed at greater length in other writings:

> ...language is not properly regarded as a system of communication. It is a system for expressing thought, something quite different. It can of course be used for communication, as can anything people do—manner of walking or style of clothes or hair, for example. But in any useful sense of the term, communication is not the function of language, and may even be of no unique significance for understanding the functions and nature of language. (Chomsky, 2000b, p. 75)
>
> Language design as such appears to be in many respects "dysfunctional," yielding properties that are not well adapted to the function language is called upon to perform....What we seem to discover are some intriguing and unexpected features of language design...[which are] unusual among biological systems of the natural world. (Chomsky, 1995, p. 162)

These claims are, to say the least, surprising. At least since the story of the Tower of Babel, everyone who has reflected on language has noted its vast communicative power and indispensable role in human life. Humans can use language to convey everything from gossip, recipes, hunting techniques, and reciprocal promises to theories of the origin of the universe and the immortality of the soul. This enormous expressive power clearly meshes with two of the other zoologically unusual features of *Homo sapiens*: a reliance on acquired know-how and a high degree of cooperation among non-kin (Pinker, 1997; Tooby & DeVore, 1987). Moreover, the design of language—a mapping between meaning and sound—is precisely what one would expect in a system that evolved for the communication of propositions. We cannot convey recipes, hunting techniques, gossip, or reciprocal promises by "manner of walking or style of clothes or hair," because these forms of behavior lack grammatical devices that allow propositions to be encoded in a recoverable way in details of the behavior. Though Chomsky denies the truism that language is "properly regarded as a system for communication," he provides no compelling reasons to doubt it, nor does he explain what a communication system would have to look like for it to be more "usable" or less "dysfunctional" than human languages.

Chomsky's positive argument that language is not "for" communication is that "language use is largely to oneself: 'inner speech' for adults, monologue for children" (Chomsky, 2000b, p. 77). HCF make the point indirectly in the passage quoted above. In part, they are distancing themselves from claims that language is a homologue of primate calls, a point with which we agree. But in order to make this point, one need not deny that language is for communication, or claim that it could just as easily be thought of as being for inner speech.

For one thing, the fragmentary snatches of inner speech that run through a person's mind are likely to be quite different from the well-formed sentences that motivate Chomsky's theories of linguistic competence. Other than in preparation for speaking and writing, interior monologues do not seem to consist of fully grammatical sequences of words complete with functional morphemes, such as *The teachers asked what attitudes about each other the students had noticed*, but rather of snatches of incomplete phrases. Whatever mechanism underlies inner speech—presumably the phonological loop that makes up a major component of working memory—it is not the subject matter of any familiar theory of grammatical competence.

Moreover, the key question in characterizing a biological function is not what a trait is typically *used* for but what it is *designed* for, in the biologist's sense—namely, which putative function can predict the features that the trait possesses. For all we know, hands might be used more often in fidgeting than grasping, but that would not make fidgeting the biological function of the hand. The reason is that hands have improbable anatomical features that are necessary for grasping but not for fidgeting. By similar logic, a system for "talking to oneself" would not need phonology or phonetics tuned to the properties of the human vocal tract, it would not need linear order or case or agreement, and it would not need mechanisms for topic and focus, all of which presuppose that information has to be coded into a serial, perceptible signal for the benefit of listeners who currently lack the information and have to integrate it piecemeal with what they know. After all, when one part of the brain is "talking to" another part, it does not have to encode the information into a serial format suitable for the vocal-acoustic channel; such communication takes place via massively parallel transmission. The visual system, for example, does not have to encode the retinal image into something like an ordered sequence of phonemes in order to communicate with the hippocampus or frontal lobes.

Indeed, if language were not designed for communication, the key tenet of Minimalism—that language consists of a mapping from meaning to sound—would not be a "virtual conceptual necessity," as Chomsky has repeatedly asserted, but an inexplicable coincidence. The only way to make sense of the fact that humans are equipped with a way to map between meaning and vocally produced sound is that it allows one person to get a meaning into a second person's head by making a sound with his or her vocal tract.

We note in addition that the innate aspect of the language faculty is for *learning* language from the community, not for *inventing* language. One cannot have inner speech without having words, and words above all are learned. (To be sure, people invent new words from time to time, but this is not the major source of their vocabulary). Moreover, the fact that the inner speech of deaf signers consists of signs rather than sounds follows from the assumption that inner language is based on learned outer language. If inner speech were primary, this too would be an unexplained coincidence. Turning to cases in which languages *are* invented, we find that Nicaraguan Sign Language, for example, arose in the context of a community seeking communication (Senghas & Coppola, 2001). Similarly, isolated deaf children who create home signs do so in the context of communication with others. We are unaware of cases in which deaf individuals develop a complex vocabulary and grammar just to talk to themselves. And without exception, other linguistic isolates do not develop speech at all (Pinker, 1994b).

This is not to deny that inner speech enhances thought (Jackendoff, 1996), and that this enhancement has been a major influence on the growth of civilization. But given that inner speech depends on having outer speech, acquired in a communicative situation, we are inclined to think that if anything is a by-product (or "spandrel") here, it is inner speech. The primary adaptation is communication, with enhanced thought as an additional benefit.

4.2. LANGUAGE IS "PERFECT"

Next let us consider the conjecture, central to the Minimalist Program, that language, though dysfunctional for communication, is a "perfect" or "optimal" mapping between sound and meaning, such that its form is structurally inevitable given what it has to bridge. As HCF express it, "FLN may approximate a kind of 'optimal solution' to the problem of linking the sensory-motor and conceptual–intentional systems" (1574). This conjecture is not easy to evaluate, because nothing is "perfect" or "optimal" across the board but only with respect to some desideratum. Let us consider the criteria that Chomsky defends in other recent writings.

Language is (mostly) like invented formal symbol systems. In one place, Chomsky explains his criterion for perfection as follows: "A good guiding intuition about imperfection is to compare natural languages with invented 'languages', invented symbolic systems. When you see differences, you have a suspicion that you are looking at something that is a prima facie imperfection" (Chomsky, 2000b, p. 109). This, however, assumes that invented symbolic systems are designed to satisfy the same desiderata as human language. But there is little reason to believe this. Human languages, unlike invented symbolic systems, must be used in real time and by agents with limitations of knowledge and computational capacity. Languages develop spontaneously in a community subject to the vagaries of history, rather than being stipulated by formal arbiters. And they must be induced by exposure to examples rather than being applied in explicit conformity with published standards. Any of these differences could explain why human languages might differ from invented symbolic systems, quite apart from matters of "imperfection."

In other places, Chomsky's notion of a "perfect" symbolic system involves intuitions about certain kinds of economy in the mapping between meaning and sound (for example, no meaningless grammatical elements left in Logical Form, short derivations preferred to long ones, and movement rules operating after phonological Spell-Out rather than before). Yet as we have noted, judged by other criteria that might be thought to characterize well-designed symbolic systems, language (as seen through the Minimalist lens) is anything but optimal. It appears to be computationally inefficient, because the processor must evaluate multiple possible derivations for entire sentences or at local choice points (Johnson & Lappin, 1997, 1999, chap. 3). And it is far from optimal in terms of parsimony of structure, given that Minimalist tree structures are packed with abstract and empty elements, in fact typically more of these than there are words.

Moreover, even by Chomsky's own criteria, language is full of "apparent imperfections," which he sees as challenges to be overcome by future research in the Minimalist framework. (Presumably such research will show them to be exigencies imposed by the semantic and phonological interfaces.) Agreement and case are called "apparent imperfections," rather than basic design features of language (Chomsky, 2000b, p. 111); their virtues in free word order languages are ignored. Another "imperfection" is the fact that phrases are sometimes moved from their canonical positions, as in questions or passives. Calling this an "imperfection" ignores the fact (which Chomsky elsewhere notes) that movement allows sentences to use some aspects of word order to convey topic and focus while others convey who did what to whom (Chomsky, 2000a, p. 13). The principle that functional systems must trade off conflicting demands is absent from such reasoning; it is as if the "perfect" car is defined to be one that goes as fast as possible, and the tradeoffs against weight, braking, steering, safety, gas mileage, and cost are "apparent imperfections." Even more egregiously, "the whole phonological system looks like a huge imperfection, it has every bad property you can think of" (Chomsky, 2000b, p. 118). And "even the fact that there is more than one language is a kind of imperfection." (Chomsky, 2000b, p. 109). Quite so: there are thousands of different solutions to the problem of mapping from sound to meaning, and they cannot *all* be optimal.

Perhaps "optimal" is meant to refer to the general style of derivational solution. But, as we noted, languages use four different devices for conveying semantic relations: phrase structure, linear order, agreement, and case, often deployed redundantly. In this sense language is reminiscent of other cognitive systems such as depth perception, where multiple mechanisms compute the same output—the relative distance of objects in the visual field—in some situations redundantly and in some not. It looks as if evolution has found several solutions that ordinarily reinforce each other, with some predominating over others in special circumstances; in the case of language, the balance among them shifts depending on the language's history, the sentence's context, or both. If so, case and agreement are not "imperfections" at all, just alternative mechanisms to the same end as phrase order and hierarchy.

We conclude that the overall claim that language is "perfect" or "optimal" is a personal vision of how language ought to be characterized rather than an empirical discovery about the way language is. As such it cannot be used to motivate assertions about how language evolved.

Language exists in the only possible form that is usable. One might ask what the relevance of the possible "perfection" of language is to its evolution. The idea seems to be that nothing less than a perfect system would be in the least bit usable, so if the current language faculty is perfect, one could not explain its evolution in terms of incremental modification of earlier designs. Thus Chomsky (2000b, p. 58) asks "how closely human language approaches an optimal solution to design conditions that the system must meet to be usable at all." This echoes an earlier suggestion that "In the case of such systems as language or wings it is not easy even to imagine a course of selection that might have given rise to them. A rudimentary wing, for example, is not "useful" for motion but is more of an impediment. Why then should the organ develop in the early stages of evolution?" (Chomsky, 1988, p. 167).

The "What good is five percent of a wing?" argument has long been raised by creationists, and in every case has been answered by showing that intermediary structures in fact are useful (Dawkins, 1986; Pennock, 2000). In the case of language, pidgins are a key source of evidence. They are mappings of phonological structure to meaning that lack fixed word order, case, and agreement. They also lack subordinate clauses, which are the standard mark of recursion, and possibly lack phrase structure altogether. Yet they definitely are usable, though not as reliably as fully developed language. Bickerton (1990), Givon (1995), and Jackendoff (2002) suggest that modern language is a tuning up of evolutionary earlier systems resembling pidgins. The four major syntactic mechanisms for encoding meaning can be thought of as incremental improvements, each of which makes the system more reliable. There is a progression of functionality, not a dichotomy between one system that is "perfect" and other systems that are "not usable at all."

Language is non-redundant. Chomsky does adduce one criterion for "perfection" that is explicit and hence easier to evaluate, namely that language is not redundant:

> The general conclusion . . . is that language is designed as a system that is "beautiful" but in general unusable. It is designed for elegance, not for use, though with features that enable to it to be used sufficiently for the purposes of normal life. . . . Insofar as this is true, the system is elegant, but badly designed for use. Typically, biological systems are not like that at all. They are highly redundant, for reasons that have a plausible functional account. . . . Why language should be so different from other biological systems is a problem, possibly even a mystery. (Chomsky, 1991)

The assertion that language displays little or no redundancy is puzzling. With regard to the speech waveform, one can high-pass, low-pass, or band-pass speech at various cutoffs, discarding non-overlapping pools of information, yet leave the speech perfectly intelligible; telephones would not work without this property (Green, 1976). With regard to recovering the meaning of words and sentences, one can rxmxve thx vxwxls, rexove exery xecoxd xonxonaxt, order the scramble words the of, or omit functional morpheme, and still retain partial (and sometimes total) intelligibility (Miller, 1967).[16] With regard to encoding meanings into words and sentences, there are several ways to do so, one can accomplish the task by multiple methods, and more than one means is available.

Chomsky occasionally has alluded to the alleged non-redundancy of lexical storage in memory: "Consider the way an item is represented in the lexicon, with no redundancy, including just what is not predictable by rule" (Chomsky, 2000b, p. 118). Chomsky has embraced this claim (which he attributes to Bloomfield, 1933, p. 274) at least since *Aspects of the Theory of Syntax* (Chomsky, 1965, p. 214); the idea is that one should factor language into a set of rules which capture all redundancies and an irreducible residue that is stored in memory. But the idea appears to be less an empirical discovery than a methodological dictum, according to which characterizations of language are to be stated in as compressed a form as possible. Psycholinguistic experiments have uncovered numerous instances in which redundant information is stored in memory. For instance, although regularly inflected items can be constructed by rule, at least some regular forms can be shown to be stored redundantly with their stems (Baayen, Schreuder, de Jong, & Krott, 2002; Pinker, 1999, chap. 5; Ullman, 1999).

But even at the level of linguistic theory proper (without considering experiments), lexical entries appear to be significantly redundant. What would a truly non-redundant language look like? Presumably it would consist only of Saussurean, arbitrary lexical items like *red* and *coat* and rules that create compositional structures on demand, like *a red coat*, obviating the need for storage. But consider exocentric compounds (discussed in Jackendoff, 1997). Part of one's linguistic knowledge is that a *redcoat* is a British soldier of the 1770s who wore a red coat, a *yellowjacket* is a kind of wasp with a yellow "jacket," a *redhead* is a person with reddish hair, and a *blackhead* is a pimple with a black "head." The general rule for such Adjective–Noun compounds is that they have meanings of the form 'X with a Y that is Z', where Y is the meaning of the noun, Z the meaning of the adjective, and X has to be learned item by item. The *red* in the lexical entry for *redcoat* is clearly redundant with the lexical entry for *red* which combines freely with noun phrases: they are pronounced the same, both are adjectives, and both refer to colors in the same range. Likewise for two uses of *coat*. Moreover, speakers recognize that the word *redcoat* is not an arbitrary string of English phonemes but refers to someone who characteristically wore a red coat (that is, *redcoat* is not perceived as an arbitrary, non-redundant, sound-meaning pairing like *soldier*). At the same time, the word cannot be composed out of *red* and *coat* by a general compounding rule, because speakers also recognize that a *redcoat* is not just anyone attired in a rufous outergarment but specifically a late eighteenth-century British soldier. Similarly, speakers know that a *redhead* specifically has red *hair*, rather than a totally red head. This irreducible redundancy is widespread in human languages, such as in idioms, semi-productive derivational morphology, and families of irregular forms (Jackendoff,

1997; Pinker, 1999). If the claim that the lexicon is non-redundant has any empirical content (rather than being the mathematical truism that a redundant representation can always be compressed and then reconstituted by an algorithm), the facts of English would seem to refute it.

Chomsky's claim that the putative non-redundancy of language poses a "mystery" for modern biology is part of a larger claim that current biology must be revamped to accommodate the findings of Minimalist linguistics:

> Any progress toward this goal [showing that language is a "perfect system"] will deepen a problem for the biological sciences that is far from trivial: how can a system such as language arise in the mind/brain, or for that matter, in the organic world, in which one seems not to find anything like the basic properties of human language? That problem has sometimes been posed as a crisis for the cognitive sciences. The concerns are appropriate, but their locus is misplaced; they are primarily a problem for biology and the brain sciences, which, as currently understood, do not provide any basis for what appear to be fairly well established conclusions about language. (Chomsky, 1995, pp. 1–2)

Given the relative rigor and cumulativeness of biology and linguistics, this strikes us as somewhat presumptuous (especially since the Minimalist Program is "still just an 'approach,'" "a conjecture about how language works").[17] There is a simpler resolution of the apparent incompatibility between biology and Minimalism, namely that Chomsky's recent claims about language have it backwards. Rather than being useless but perfect, language is useful but imperfect, just like other biological systems.

4.3. THE NARROW FACULTY LANGUAGE FACULTY EVOLVED FOR REASONS OTHER THAN LANGUAGE

HCF speculate that recursion, which they identify as the defining characteristic of the narrow language faculty, may have "evolved for reasons other than language." Specifically, recursion could have evolved in other animals "to solve other computational problems such as navigation, number quantification, or social relationships," in a module that was "impenetrable with respect to other systems. During evolution, the modular and highly-domain-specific system of recursion may have become penetrable and domain-general. This opened the way for humans, perhaps uniquely, to apply the power of recursion to other problems" (HCF, 1578).

We note that the suggestion that recursion evolved for navigation (or other cognitive domains) rather than language, like the earlier suggestion that the vocal tract evolved for size exaggeration rather than speech, assumes a false dichotomy: that if a system originally underwent selection for one function, it did not undergo subsequent selection for some other function. Just as forelimbs originally were selected for stability in water and subsequently were selected for flight, legged locomotion, or grasping, certain circuitry could have been shaped by selection for (say) navigation and subsequently have been *re*shaped by selection for language.

But even if we allow for the possibility of selection before, during, and after a change of function, the suggestion that the system for linguistic recursion is a minor modification of a system for navigation is questionable. Although Chomsky frequently characterizes linguistic recursion as "discrete infinity," the two principal navigation systems documented in non-human animals (Gallistel, 1990) show no such property. Dead reckoning is infinite but not discrete; recognition of landmarks is discrete but not infinite.

As for recursion in language evolving out of recursion in number cognition, if this involves co-opting at all (see Grinstead et al., 1997, 2004, for doubts), the proposed direction in HCF's hypothesis would appear to be backwards (Bloom, 1994a; Dehaene, Spelke, Pinel, Stanescu, & Tsivkin, 1999; Wiese, 2004). Recursive language is a human universal or near-universal, emerging reliably and spontaneously in ontogeny. But recursive number cognition is not. The majority of human cultures, like all animal species, do not have recursive number systems (or at least did not until recent incursions of Western civilization), but instead quantify objects using a system for estimating analogue amounts and a system for categorizing a finite number of small numerosities (Dehaene, 1997; Wiese, 2004). Those that have developed recursive number systems in their cultural history may have exapted them from the recursive properties of language, rather than vice-versa.

We do agree with HCF that recursion is not unique to language. Indeed, the only reason language *needs* to be recursive is because its function is to express recursive *thoughts*. If there weren't any recursive thoughts, the means of expression would not need recursion either. So here we join HCF in inviting detailed formal study of animal cognition and other human capacities to ascertain which abilities require recursive mental representations and which do not. Plausible candidates include music (Lerdahl and Jackendoff, 1983), social cognition (touched on in Jackendoff, 1992, 2007), visual decomposition of objects into parts (Marr, 1982), and the formulation of complex action sequences (Badler et al., 1999; Jackendoff, 2007 ; Miller, Galanter, & Pribram, 1960; Schank and Abelson, 1975).

Here the problem is not a paucity of candidates for evolutionary antecedents but a surfeit. As Herbert Simon has pointed out (Simon, 1969), probably all complex systems are characterized by hierarchical organization. So if "recursion" is identified with hierarchical decomposition and used as a criterion for identifying some pre-existing cognitive function as a source for exaptation to language, speculations can proliferate unconstrained.

We also wish to point out that language is not just any old recursive system but embodies at least four additional design constraints. First, its recursive products are temporally sequenced, unlike those of social cognition or visual decomposition. Second, syntactic trees have a characteristic structure, in which each constituent contains a distinguished member, the head, which determines the category and semantic referent of the constituent, and around which the other elements are grouped as arguments and modifiers (this is the basis of the X-bar theory of phrase structure). Third, syntax is not just a recursive representational system externalized. It maps multi-directionally (in production and comprehension) *among* systems: recursive semantic representations, recursive communicative intentions, and hierarchical phonological signals. Fourth, the details of the recursive structures are largely arbitrary and learned, conforming to the words and constructions of the linguistic community, rather than being dictated by immediate real-world constraints such as how a scene is put together or which sequence of actions is physically capable of effecting a goal. As such, language is unlikely to be just a straightforward exaptation of a single pre-existing recursive system such as visual cognition, motor control, or social relationships. Rather, it appears to be a kind of interface or connective tissue among partly pre-existing recursive systems, mapping among them in an evolutionarily novel manner.

In sum, we find HCF's case that language is not an adaptation for communication unconvincing. The argument that presupposes the Minimalist Program to conclude that language is too simple to require invoking natural selection is circular, because this is a desideratum that the MP hopes to fulfill (in the teeth of much counterevidence), rather than a discovery it has established. The argument that language is no better designed for communication than hair styles is belied by the enormously greater expressive power of language and the fact that this power is enabled by the grammatical machinery that makes language so unusual. The argument that language is designed for interior monologues rather than communication fails to explain why languages map meaning onto sounds and why they must be learned from a social context. The argument that language is "perfect" or "optimal" has never been stated clearly, and is, by Chomsky's own admission, apparently refuted by many "imperfections." The argument that language is not redundant is false in every domain in which it can be evaluated. Finally, the suggestion that the recursive power of language arose as a simple co-opting of recursion in other cognitive systems such as navigation or number encounters numerous problems: that navigation is not discretely infinite; that recursive number cognition is parasitic on language rather than vice-versa; and that language maps *among* recursive systems rather than being a straightforward externalization of a single recursive system.

The alternative in which language is an adaptation for the communication of knowledge and intentions faces none of these problems. It is consistent with behavioral and genetic evidence that language shows multiple signs of partial specialization for this task rather than grafting one component (recursion) onto a completely unchanged primate base. It is based on defensible conclusions about the nature of language established by existing linguistic research rather than a promissory program that is admittedly incompatible with the facts. It does not require tendentious claims such as that language is non-redundant, perfect, unsuited for communication, or designed for beauty rather than use. It meshes with other features of human psychology that make our species unusual in the animal kingdom, namely a reliance on acquired technological know-how and extensive cooperation among non-kin. And it does not imply that linguistics poses a crisis for biology but rather helps bring them into consilience.

Acknowledgments

We thank Stephen Anderson, Paul Bloom, Susan Carey, Andrew Carstairs-McCarthy, Matt Cartmill, Noam Chomsky, Barbara Citko, Peter Culicover, Dan Dennett, Tecumseh Fitch, Randy Gallistel, David Geary, Tim German, Henry Gleitman, Lila Gleitman, Adele Goldberg, Marc Hauser, Greg Hickok, David Kemmerer, Patricia Kuhl, Shalom Lappin, Philip Lieberman, Alec Marantz, Martin Nowak, Paul Postal, Robert Provine, Robert Remez, Ben Shenoy, Elizabeth Spelke, Lynn Stein, J. D. Trout, Athena Vouloumanos, and Cognition referees for helpful comments and discussion. Supported by NIH grants HD 18381 (Pinker) and DC 03660 (Jackendoff).

Notes

1. Theoretical computer scientists often distinguish between *tail recursion* and *true recursion*. Roughly, in tail recursion, a procedure invokes another instance of itself as a final step (or, in the context of language, a constituent contains an identical kind of constituent at its periphery). In true recursion, a procedure invokes an instance of itself in mid-computation and then must resume the original procedure from where it left off (or a constituent has an identical kind of constituent embedded inside it). True recursion requires a computational device with a stack of pointers (or an equivalent mechanism) to keep track of where to return after an embedded procedure has been executed. Tail recursion can be mimicked (at least in input–output behavior or "weak generative capacity") by a computational device that implements simple iteration, where one instance of a procedure can be completed and forgotten by the time the next instance has begun. Tail recursion, nonetheless, cannot be mimicked by iteration when it comes to computations that require more than duplicating input–output behavior ("strong generative capacity"), such as inferences that depend on the grouping and labeling of constituents.
2. It is possible to parse this sentence as saying that FLN consists of recursion *and, in addition,* the mappings to the interfaces, rather than recursion *as it appears* in the mappings to the interfaces. But this interpretation is more strained, and is inconsistent with the preceding two quotations, which simply identify the narrow language faculty with recursion.
3. "We may usefully think of the language faculty, the number faculty, and others, as 'mental organs,' analogous to the heart or the visual system or the system of motor coordination and planning" (Chomsky, 1980, p. 39).
4. We leave open whether such concepts are simply impossible without language or whether they are within the expressive power of the conceptual system but require language as a crutch to attain them. They certainly cannot be shared via ostension, so in either case language is necessary for their cultural transmission.
5. R. Remez, commenting in this reference on the work of Kluender (1994), notes that Kluender's trained quail failed to distinguish labial and palatal phonemes. He also suggests that the quail's ability to distinguish other place-of-articulation distinctions may hinge on

their detecting the salient apical bursts that initiate stop consonants rather than the formant transitions that suffice for such discriminations in humans.

6. The fact that *Homo erectus* had a spinal cord like that of other primates rules out an alternative hypothesis in which the change was an adaptation to bipedal locomotion.

7. Syllables can sometimes be expanded by limited addition of non-syllabic material; the word *lengths*, for example, is in some theories analyzed as having syllabic structure along the line of $[_{Syl} [_{Syl}$ length$]$ s$]$ (Halle & Vergnaud, 1980). But there are no syllables built out of the combination of two or more full syllables, which is the crucial case for true recursion.

8. The existence in monkeys of mirror-neurons (Rizolatti, Fadiga, Gallese, & Fogassi, 1996), which are active both in the execution and the sight of particular actions, suggests that some kind of representation shared by perception and production antedates the evolution of language in humans. However, the information coded by such neurons appears to be different from phonological representations in two ways. First, they are specific to the semantic goal of an action (e.g. obtaining an object), rather than its physical topography, whereas phonology is concerned with configurations for articulation. Second, as noted by HCF, they do not support transfer from perception to production, since the ability to imitate is rudimentary or absent in monkeys, whereas humans learn to articulate speech sounds based on what they hear.

9. Long-distance dependency can involve dependencies extending into recursively embedded structures, and on some accounts involves recursive movement of the fronted phrase up through the phrase structure tree.

10. Also unclear is whether the human subjects who learned these artificial languages did so by using the strong generative capacity of an $A^n B^n$ grammar. Each stimulus consisted of a sequence of nonsense syllables spoken by a female voice followed by an equal number of syllables spoken by a male voice. Phonological content was irrelevant, and the learning could have been accomplished by counting from the first syllable of each subsequence (*high: 1–2–3; low: 1–2–3*). This differs from the kind of analysis mandated by a grammar of recursively embedded phrases, namely [*high*–[*high*–[*high*–*low*]–*low*]–*low*].

11. "I have said nothing about other major components of the theory of word formation: compound forms, agglutinative structures, and much more" (Chomsky, 1995, p. 241).

12. "We still have no good phrase structure theory for such simple matters as attributive adjectives, relative clauses, and adjuncts of many different types" (Chomsky, 1995, p. 382, n. 22).

13. "I am sweeping under the rug questions of considerable significance, notably, questions about what in the earlier framework were called "surface effects" on interpretation. These are manifold, including topic-focus and theme-rheme structures, figure-ground properties, effects of adjacency and linearity, and many others" (Chomsky, 1995, p. 220).

14. "The minimalist program seeks to show that everything that has been accounted for in terms of [deep and surface structure] has been misdescribed . . . that means the projection principle, binding theory, Case theory, the chain condition, and so on" (Chomsky, 2000a, p. 10).

15. Johnson and Lappin (1999) show that the "principles of economy" are problematic not just in Chomsky's original formulation in which entire derivations are compared, but for subsequent proposals based on "local economy" in which principles are evaluated at individual steps in a derivation.

16. The following text has recently been circulating over the Internet: "Acocdrnig to an elgnsih unviesitry sutdy the oredr of letetrs in a wrod dosen't mttaer, the olny thnig thta's iopmrantt is that the frsit and lsat ltteer of eevry word is in the crcreot ptoision. The rset can be jmbueld and one is stlil able to raed the txet wiohtut dclftfuiiy."

17. We concur that language does raise challenges for neurobiology, in particular, how neural networks can implement the kinds of computation found in language and the parts of cognition it interfaces with, especially the recursive concatenation of symbols and instantiation of variables (Jackendoff, 2002, chap. 3; Marcus, 2001; Pinker, 1997, chap. 2). However, Chomsky's quotation refers specifically to the claim that "language is something like a 'perfect system'" (p. 1).

References

Anderson, S. R. (2004). *Dr. Dolittle's delusion: animal communication, linguistics, and the uniqueness of human language.* New Haven: Yale University Press.

Au, T. K., & Glusman, M. (1990). The principle of mutual exclusivity in word learning: to honor or not to honor. *Child Development, 61,* 1474–1490.

Baayen, H., Schreuder, R., de Jong, N., & Krott, A. (2002). Dutch inflection: the rules that prove the exception. In S. Nooteboom, F. Weerman, & F. Wijnen (Eds.), *Storage and computation in the language faculty.* Boston: Kluwer, 61–92.

Badler, N. I., Bindinganavale, R., Allbeck, J., Schuler, W., Zhao, L., Lee, S., et al. (1999). *Parameterized action representation and natural instructions for dynamic behavior modification of embodied agents.* American Association for Artificial Intelligence.

Behrend, D. A., Scofield, J., & Kleinknecht, E. E. (2001). Beyond fast mapping: young children's extensions of novel words and novel facts. *Developmental Psychology, 37*(5), 698–705.

Bickerton, D. (1990). *Language and species.* Chicago: University of Chicago Press.

Bishop, D. V. M. (2002). Putting language genes in perspective. *Trends in Genetics, 18,* 57–59.

Bloom, P. (1994a). Generativity within language and other cognitive domains. *Cognition, 51,* 177–189.

Bloom, P. (1994b). Possible names: the role of syntax-semantics mappings in the acquisition of nominals. *Lingua, 92,* 297–329.

Bloom, P. (1999). *How children learn the meanings of words.* Cambridge, MA: MIT Press.

Bloomfield, L. (1933). *Language.* New York: Holt.

Boeckx, C., & Hornstein, N. (2007). The varying aims of linguistic theory. In J. Franck, & J. Bricmont (Eds.), *Cahier Chomsky.* Paris L'Herne.

Boeckx, C., & Piatteli-Palmarini, M. (2005). Language as a natural object; linguistics as a natural science. *Linguistic Review, 22,* 447–466

Bregman, A. S., & Pinker, S. (1978). Auditory streaming and the building of timbre. *Canadian Journal of Psychology, 32,* 19–31.

Browman, C. P., & Goldstein, L. F. (1992). Articulatory phonology: an overview. *Phonetica, 49,* 155–180.

Brown, S., Merker, B., & Wallin, N. (2000). An introduction to evolutionary musicology. In N. Wallin, B. Merker, & S. Brown (Eds.), *The origins of music.* Cambridge, MA: MIT Press.

Chomsky, N. (1965). *Aspects of the theory of syntax.* Cambridge, MA: MIT Press.

Chomsky, N. (1972). *Studies on semantics in generative grammar.* The Hague: Mouton.

Chomsky, N. (1975). *Reflections on language.* New York: Pantheon.

Chomsky, N. (1980). *Rules and representations.* New York: Columbia University Press.

Chomsky, N. (1981). *Lectures on government and binding.* Dordrecht, Netherlands: Foris.

Chomsky, N. (1988). *Language and problems of knowledge: the Managua lectures.* Cambridge, MA: MIT Press.

Chomsky, N. (1991). Linguistics and cognitive science: problems and mysteries. In A. Kasher (Ed.), *The Chomskyan turn.* Cambridge, MA: Blackwell.

Chomsky, N. (1995). *The minimalist program.* Cambridge, MA: MIT Press.

Chomsky, N. (2000a). *New horizons in the study of language and mind.* New York: Cambridge University Press.

Chomsky, N. (2000b). *On nature and language.* New York: Cambridge University Press.

Clark, E. V. (1993). *The lexicon in acquisition.* New York: Cambridge University Press.

Clark, A. G., Glanowski, S., Nielsen, R., Thomas, P. D., Kejariwal, A., Todd, M. A., et al. (2003). Inferring nonneutral evolution from human-chimp-mouse orthologous gene trios. *Science, 302*(5652), 1960–1963.

Culicover, P. W. (1999). *Syntactic nuts: hard cases, syntactic theory, and language acquisition.* New York: Oxford University Press.

Culicover, P. W., & Jackendoff, R. (2005). *Simpler syntax.* New York: Oxford University Press.

Dale, P. S., Simonoff, E., Bishop, D. V. M., Eley, T. C., Oliver, B., Price, T. S., Purcell, S., Stevenson, J., & Plomin, R. (1998). Genetic influence on language delay in two-year-old children. *Nature Neuroscience, 1*(4), 324–328.

Dawkins, R. (1986). *The blind watchmaker: why the evidence of evolution reveals a universe without design.* New York: Norton.

Deacon, T. (1997). *The symbolic species: the coevolution of language and the brain.* New York: Norton.

Dehaene, S. (1997). *The number sense: how the mind creates mathematics.* New York: Oxford University Press.

Dehaene, S., Spelke, L., Pinel, P., Stanescu, R., & Tsivkin, S. (1999). Sources of mathematical thinking: behavioral and brain-imaging evidence. *Science, 284,* 970–974.

Diesendruck, G., & Markson, L. (2001). Children's avoidance of lexical overlap: a pragmatic account. *Developmental Psychology, 37,* 630–644.

di Sciullo, A. M., & Williams, E. (1987). *On the definition of word.* Cambridge, MA: MIT Press.

Dooling, R. J., & Brown, S. D. (1990). Speech perception by budgerigars (*Melopsittacus undulatus*): spoken vowels. *Perception and Psychophysics, 47,* 568–574.

Eimas, P. D., & Miller, J. L. (1992). Organization in the perception of speech by young infants. *Psychological Science, 3*(6), 340–345.

Enard, W., Przeworski, M., Fisher, S. E., Lai, C. S., Wiebe, V., Kitano, T., Monaco, A. P., & Paabo, S. (2002). Molecular evolution of *FOXP2*, a gene involved in speech and language. *Nature, 418,* 869–872.

Everett, D. (2004). *Cultural constraints on grammar and cognition in Pirahã: another look at the design features of human language.* Unpublished manuscript, University of Manchester, http://lings.ln.man.ac.uk/info/staff/DE/cultgram.pdf.

Fitch, W. T., & Hauser, M. D. (2004). Computational constraints on syntactic processing in nonhuman primates. *Science, 303,* 377–380.

Gallistel, C. R. (1990). *The organization of learning.* Cambridge, MA: MIT Press.

Gelman, S. A., & Heyman, G. D. (1999). Carrot-eaters and creature-believers: the effects of lexicalization on children's inferences about social categories. *Psychological Science, 10*(6), 489–493.

Gentner, D. (1981). Some interesting differences between verbs and nouns. *Cognition and Brain Theory, 4,* 161–178.

Givon, T. (1995). *Functionalism and grammar.* Philadelphia: John Benjamins.

Gleitman, L. R. (1990). The structural sources of verb meaning. *Language Acquisition, 1,* 3–55.

Goldberg, A. (2003). Constructions: a new theoretical approach to language. *Trends in Cognitive Sciences, 7*(5), 219–224.

Gopnik, M., & Crago, M. (1991). Familial aggregation of a developmental language disorder. *Cognition, 39,* 1–50.

Green, D. M. (1976). *An introduction to hearing.* Hillsdale, NJ: Erlbaum.

Grinstead, J., MacSwan, J., Curtiss, S., & Gelman, R. (1997). *The independence of language and number.* Paper presented at the Twenty-Second Boston University Conference on Language Development.

Grinstead, J., MacSwan, J., Curtiss, S., & Gelman, R. (2004). *The independence of language and number.* Unpublished manuscript, University of Iowa, Cedar Fall, IA.

Halle, M., & Marantz, A. (1993). Distributed morphology and the pieces of inflection. In K. Hale, & S. J. Keyser (Eds.), *The view from building 20: essays in honor of Sylvain Bromberger.* Cambridge, MA: MIT Press.

Halle, M., & Vergnaud, J.-R. (1980). Three-dimensional phonology. *Journal of Linguistic Research, 1,* 83–105.

Hauser, M. D. (1996). *The evolution of communication.* Cambridge, MA: MIT Press.

Hauser, M. D., Chomsky, N., & Fitch, W. T. (2002). The faculty of language: what is it, who has it, and how did it evolve? *Science, 298,* 1569–1579.

Hickok, G., & Poeppel, D. (2000). Towards a functional neuroanatomy of speech perception. *Trends in Cognitive Sciences, 4*(4), 131–138.

Hockett, C. F. (1960). The origin of speech. *Scientific American, 203,* 88–111.

Hornstein, N. (2002). *The minimalist program and the evolution of language.* Paper presented at the "The structure of the innate mind," AHRB Project on Innateness and the Structure of the Mind, Baltimore.

Hurford, J. R. (1989). Biological evolution of the Saussurean sign as a component of the language acquisition device. *Lingua, 77,* 187–222.

Jackendoff, R. (1989). A comparison of rhythmic structures in music and language. In P. Kiparsky, & G. Youmans (Eds.), *Phonetics and phonology (Vol. 1).* New York: Academic Press.

Jackendoff, R. (1992). *Languages of the mind.* Cambridge, MA: MIT Press.

Jackendoff, R. (1994). *Patterns in the mind: language and human nature.* New York: Basic Books.

Jackendoff, R. (1996). How language helps us think. *Pragmatics and Cognition, 4,* 1–34.

Jackendoff, R. (1997). *The architecture of the language faculty.* Cambridge, MA: MIT Press.

Jackendoff, R. (2002). *Foundations of language: brain, meaning, grammar, evolution.* New York: Oxford University Press.

Jackendoff, R. (2007). *Language, culture, consciousness: essays on mental structure.* Cambridge, MA: MIT Press.

Johnson, D., & Lappin, S. (1997). A critique of the Minimalist program. *Linguistics and Philosophy, 20,* 273–333.

Johnson, D., & Lappin, S. (1999). *Local constraints vs. economy.* Stanford, CA: CSLI Publications.

Kenneally, C. (2003). The human factor. *Boston globe,* Jan. 5, 2003 (pp. D1–D3).

Kluender, K. (1994). Speech perception as a tractable problem in cognitive science. In M. Gernsbacher (Ed.), *Handbook of psycholinguistics.* San Diego: Academic Press.

Kojima, S., & Kiritani, S. (1989). Vocal-auditory functions in the chimpanzee: vowel perception. *International Journal of Primatology, 10,* 199–213.

Koopman, H. (2000). *The syntax of specifiers and heads.* New York: Routledge.

Kuhl, P. K. (1991). Human adults and human infants show a "perceptual magnet effect" for the prototypes of speech categories, monkeys do not. *Perception and Psychophysics, 50*(2), 93–107.

Kuhl, P. K., & Miller, J. D. (1975). Speech perception by the chinchilla: voiced-voiceless distinction in alveolar plosive consonants. *Science, 190,* 69–72.

Lai, C. S. L., Fisher, S. E., Hurst, J. A., Vargha-Khadem, F., & Monaco, A. P. (2001). A novel forkhead-domain gene is mutated in a severe speech and language disorder. *Nature, 413,* 519–523.

Lappin, S., Levine, R. D., & Johnson, D. (2000). The structure of unscientific revolutions. *Natural Language and Linguistic Theory, 18,* 665–671.

Lasnik, H. (2002). The minimalist program in syntax. *Trends in Cognitive Sciences, 6*(10), 432–437.

Lerdahl, F., & Jackendoff, R. (1983). *A generative theory of tonal music.* Cambridge, MA: MIT Press.

Liberman, A. M. (1985). The motor theory of speech perception revised. *Cognition, 21,* 1–36.

Liberman, A. M. (1991). Afterthoughts on modularity and the motor theory. In I. G. Mattingly, & M. Studdert-Kennedy (Eds.), *Modularity and the motor theory of speech perception.* Mahwah, NJ: Erlbaum.

Liberman, A. M., Cooper, F. S., Shankweiler, D. P., & Studdert-Kennedy, M. (1967). Perception of the speech code. *Psychological Review, 74,* 431–461.

Liberman, A. M., & Mattingly, I. G. (1989). A specialization for speech perception. *Science, 243,* 489–494.

Lieberman, P. (1984). *The biology and evolution of language.* Cambridge, MA: Harvard University Press.

Lieberman, P. (2003). Motor control, speech, and the evolution of language. In M. Christiansen, & S. Kirby (Eds.), *Language evolution: states of the art.* New York: Oxford University Press.

MacLarnon, A., & Hewitt, G. (1999). The evolution of human speech: the role of enhanced breathing control. *American Journal of Physical Anthropology, 109,* 341–363.

Marcus, G. F. (2001). *The algebraic mind: reflections on connectionism and cognitive science.* Cambridge, MA: MIT Press.

Markman, E. (1989). *Categorization and naming in children: problems of induction.* Cambridge, MA: MIT Press.

Markson, L., & Bloom, P. (1997). Evidence against a dedicated system for word learning in children. *Nature*, *385*, 813–815.

Marr, D. (1982). *Vision*. San Francisco: W.H. Freeman.

Miller, G. A. (1967). The psycholinguists. In G. A. Miller (Ed.), *The Psychology of communication*. London: Penguin Books.

Miller, G. A. (1991). *The science of words*. New York: W.H. Freeman.

Miller, G. A., & Fellbaum, C. (1991). Semantic networks of English. *Cognition*, *41*(1–3), 197–229.

Miller, G. A., Galanter, E., & Pribram, K. H. (1960). *Plans and the structure of behavior*. New York: Adams-Bannister-Cox.

Miller, J. L., & Eimas, P. D. (1983). Studies on the categorization of speech by infants. *Cognition*, *13*(2), 135–165.

Newmeyer, F. J. (2003). Review article: Chomsky, "On nature and language"; Anderson and Lightfoot, "The language organ"; Bichakjian, "Language in a Darwinian perspective." *Language*, *79*(3), 583–599.

Nowak, M. A., & Komarova, N. L. (2001). Towards an evolutionary theory of language. *Trends in Cognitive Sciences*, *5*(7), 288–295.

Nowak, M. A., & Krakauer, D. C. (1999). The evolution of language. *Proceedings of the National Academy of Science USA*, *96*, 8028–8033.

Nowak, M. A., Plotkin, J. B., & Jansen, V. A. (2000). The evolution of syntactic communication. *Nature*, *404*, 495–498.

Osherson, D. N., & Wasow, T. (1976). Task-specificity and species-specificity in the study of language: a methodological note. *Cognition*, *4*, 203–214.

Peña, M., Maki, A., Kovacic, D., Dehaene-Lambertz, G., Kiozumi, H., Bouquet, F., et al. (2003). Sounds and silence: an optical tomography study of language recognition at birth. *Proceedings of the National Academy of Science USA*, *100*(20), 11702–11705.

Pennock, R. T. (2000). *Tower of Babel: the evidence against the new creationism*. Cambridge, MA: MIT Press.

Peretz, I., Gagnon, L., & Bouchard, B. (1998). Music and emotion: perceptual determinants, immediacy, and isolation after brain damage. *Cognition*, *68*, 111–141.

Piatelli-Palmarini, M., & Uriagereka, J. (2004). The immune syntax: the evolution of the language virus. In L. Jenkins (Ed.), *Variation and universals in biolinguistics*. Oxford: Elsevier.

Pinker, S. (1984). *Language learnability and language development*. Cambridge, MA: Harvard University Press.

Pinker, S. (1987). The bootstrapping problem in language acquisition. In B. MacWhinney (Ed.), *Mechanisms of language acquisition*. Hillsdale, NJ: Erlbaum.

Pinker, S. (1989). *Learnability and cognition: the acquisition of argument structure*. Cambridge, Mass: MIT Press.

Pinker, S. (1994a). How could a child use verb syntax to learn verb semantics? *Lingua*, *92*, 377–410.

Pinker, S. (1994b). *The language instinct*. New York: HarperCollins.

Pinker, S. (1997). *How the mind works*. New York: Norton.

Pinker, S. (1999). *Words and rules: the ingredients of language*. New York: HarperCollins.

Pinker, S. (2003). Language as an adaptation to the cognitive niche. In M. Christiansen, & S. Kirby (Eds.), *Language evolution: states of the art*. New York: Oxford University Press.

Pinker, S., & Bloom, P. (1990). Natural language and natural selection. *Behavioral and Brain Sciences*, *13*, 707–784.

Poeppel, D. (2001). Pure word deafness and the bilateral processing of the speech code. *Cognitive Science*, *21*(5), 679–693.

Postal, P. M. (2004). *Skeptical linguistic essays*. New York: Oxford University Press.

Pullum, G. K. (1996). Nostalgic views from building 20. *Journal of Linguistics*, *32*, 137–147.

Remez, R. E. (1989). When the objects of perception are spoken. *Ecological Psychology*, *1*(2), 161–180.

Remez, R. E. (1994). A guide to research on the perception of speech. *Handbook of psycholinguistics*. New York: Academic Press, 145–172.

Remez, R. E., Pardo, J. S., Piorkowski, R. L., & Rubin, P. E. (2001). On the bistability of sine wave analogues of speech. *Psychological Science, 12*(1), 24–29.

Rizolatti, G., Fadiga, L., Gallese, V., & Fogassi, L. (1996). Premotor cortex and the recognition of motor actions. *Cognitive Brain Research, 3,* 131–141.

Rochemont, M. S., & Culicover, P. W. (1997). Deriving dependent right adjuncts in English. In D. Beerman, D. LeBlanc, & H. Van Riemsdijk (Eds.), *Rightward movement.* Amsterdam: John Benjamins.

Schank, R., & Abelson, R. (1975). *Scripts, plans, goals, and knowledge.* Mahwah, NJ: Erlbaum.

Scofield, J., & Behrend, D. A. (2003). *Two-year-olds differentially disambiguate novel words and facts.* Unpublished manuscript, University of Arizona.

Senghas, A., & Coppola, M. (2001). Children creating language: how Nicaraguan sign language acquired a spatial grammar. *Psychological Science, 12,* 323–328.

Seuren, P. (2004). *Chomsky's minimalism.* New York: Oxford University Press.

Shapiro, K. A., Pascual-Leone, A., Mottaghy, F. M., Gangitano, M., & Caramazza, A. (2001). Grammatical distinctions in the left frontal cortex. *Journal of Cognitive Neuroscience, 13*(6), 713–720.

Simon, H. A. (1969). The architecture of complexity. In H. A. Simon (Ed.), *The sciences of the artificial.* Cambridge, Mass: MIT Press.

Sinnott, J. M. (1998). Comparative phoneme boundaries. *Current Topics in Acoustical Research, 2,* 135–138.

Sinnott, J. M., & Brown, C. H. (1997). Perception of the American English liquid /ra-la/ contrast by humans and monkeys. *Journal of the Acoustical Society of America, 102*(1), 588–602.

Sinnott, J. M., Brown, C. H., & Borneman, M. A. (1998). Effects of syllable duration on stop-glide identification in syllable-initial and syllable-final position by humans and monkeys. *Perception and Psychophysics, 60*(6), 1032–1043.

Sinnott, J. M., Brown, C. H., Malik, W. T., & Kressley, R. A. (1997). A multidimensional scaling analysis of vowel discrimination in humans and monkeys. *Perception and Psychophysics, 59*(8), 1214–1224.

Sinnott, J. M., & Saporita, T. A. (2000). Differences in American English, Spanish, and monkey perception of the say-stay trading relation. *Perception and Psychophysics, 62*(6), 1312–1319.

Sinnott, J. M., & Williamson, T. L. (1999). Can macaques perceive place of articulation from formant transition information? *Journal of the Acoustical Society of America, 106*(2), 929–937.

Slobin, D. I. (1977). Language change in childhood and in history. In J. Macnamara (Ed.), *Language learning and thought.* New York: Academic Press.

Stromswold, K. (2001). The heritability of language: a review and meta-analysis of twin and adoption studies. *Language, 77,* 647–723.

Talmy, L. (1985). Lexicalization patterns: semantic structure in lexical forms. In T. Shopen (Ed.), *Language typology and syntactic description. (Vol. III).* New York: Cambridge University Press.

The SLI Consortium. (2002). A genomewide scan identifies two novel loci involved in specific language impairment. *American Journal of Human Genetics, 70,* 384–398.

Tooby, J., & DeVore, I. (1987). The reconstruction of hominid evolution through strategic modeling. In W. G. Kinzey (Ed.), *The evolution of human behavior: primate models.* Albany, NY: SUNY Press.

Trout, J. D. (2001). The biological basis of speech: what to infer from talking to the animals. *Psychological Review, 108*(3), 523–549.

Trout, J. D. (2003a). *The biological basis of speech: talking to the animals and listening to the evidence.* http://www.columbia.edu/~remez/27apr03.pdf

Trout, J. D. (2003b). Biological specializations for speech: what can the animals tell us? *Current Directions in Psychological Science, 12*(5), 155–159.

Ullman, M. T. (1999). Acceptability ratings of regular and irregular past-tense forms: evidence for a dual-system model of language from word frequency and phonological neighborhood effects. *Language and Cognitive Processes, 14,* 47–67.

Ullman, M. T., & Gopnik, M. (1999). Inflectional morphology in a family with inherited specific language impairment. *Applied Psycholinguistics, 20,* 51–117.

Van der Lely, H. K. J., Rosen, S., & McClelland, A. (1998). Evidence for a grammar-specific deficit in children. *Current Biology, 8,* 1253–1258.

Vargha-Khadem, F., Watkins, K., Alcock, K., Fletcher, P., & Passingham, R. (1995). Praxic and non-verbal cognitive deficits in a large family with a genetically transmitted speech and language disorder. *Proceedings of the National Academy of Sciences USA, 92,* 930–933.

Vouloumanos, A., Kiehl, K. A., Werker, J. F., & Liddle, P. F. (2001). Detection of sounds in the auditory stream: event-related fMRI evidence for differential activation to speech and nonspeech. *Journal of Cognitive Neuroscience, 13*(7), 994–1005.

Vouloumanos, A., & Werker, J. F. (2004a). *A neonatal bias for speech that is independent of experience.* Paper presented at the Fourteenth Biennial International Conference on Infant Studies, Chicago.

Vouloumanos, A., & Werker, J. F. (2004b). Tuned to the signal: the privileged status of speech for young infants. *Developmental Science, 7,* 270–276.

Wade, N. (2003). Early voices: the leap to language. *New York Times,* July 15, D1–D3.

Wallman, J. (1992). *Aping language.* New York: Cambridge University Press.

Waxman, S., & Booth, A. (2001). On the insufficiency of domain-general accounts of word-learning: a reply to Bloom and Markson. *Cognition, 78,* 277–279.

Wiese, H. (2004). *Numbers, language, and the human mind.* New York: Cambridge University Press.

Williams, G. C. (1966). *Adaptation and natural selection: a critique of some current evolutionary thought.* Princeton, NJ: Princeton University Press.

10

So How *Does* the Mind Work?

The philosopher Jerry Fodor was a teacher of mine in graduate school, a colleague at MIT for three years, and a major influence on my thinking. I have profited greatly from his lucid explications of the computational theory of mind, of the logic of innateness in cognition, and of the theory that the human mind is a modular system.

We also have our disagreements, to put it mildly. In The Stuff of Thought *I took on his notorious hypothesis that the human mind is innately equipped with 50,000 concepts, including "doorknob," "trombone," and "carburetor," a hypothesis which follows from Fodor's factually incorrect premise (or so I argue) that the mental representation of word meanings are atomic, that is, not decomposable into more elementary semantic concepts such as "cause" and "move." And the title of his 2000 book* The Mind Doesn't Work That Way *alludes to the title of my 1997 book* How the Mind Works. *This essay is my reply to Fodor, and defends ideas about the computational theory of mind, the modularity of mind, and the evolution of mind that are very different from Fodor's.*

In 2000 Jerry Fodor published a book called *The Mind Doesn't Work That Way* (hereafter: *TMDWTW*). The way that the mind doesn't work, according to Fodor, is the way that I said the mind does work in my book *How the Mind Works* (*HTMW*).[1] This essay is a response to Fodor, and one might think its title might be *Yes, It Does!* But for reasons that will soon become clear, a more fitting title might be *No One Ever Said It Did.*

Fodor calls the theory in *How the Mind Works* the New Synthesis. It combines the key idea of the cognitive revolution of the 1950s and 1960s—that the mind is a computational system—with the key idea of the new evolutionary biology of the 1960s and 1970s—that signs of design in the natural world are products of the natural selection of replicating entities, namely genes. This synthesis, sometimes known

Supported by NIH grant HD 18381. I thank Clark Barrett, Arthur Charlesworth, Helena Cronin, Dan Dennett, Rebecca Goldstein, and John Tooby for invaluable comments.

as evolutionary psychology, often incorporates a third idea, namely that the mind is not a single entity but is composed of a number of faculties specialized for solving different adaptive problems. In sum, the mind is a system of organs of computation that enabled our ancestors to survive and reproduce in the physical and social worlds in which our species spent most of its evolutionary history.

Readers who are familiar with Fodor's contributions to cognitive science but who have not read *TMDWTW* might be puzzled to learn that Fodor begs to differ so categorically. The first major theme of *HTMW* is computation, and Fodor, more than anyone, has defended what he calls the computational theory of mind: that thinking is a form of computation. The second major theme is specialization, and Fodor's most influential book is called *The Modularity of Mind,* a defense of the idea that the mind is composed of distinct faculties rather than a single general-purpose learning device or intelligent algorithm. The third theme is evolution, the source of innate biological structure, and Fodor, like many evolutionary psychologists, is willing to posit far more innate structure than is commonly accepted in contemporary philosophy and psychology. So it is surprising that Fodor insists that *HTMW* is wrong, wrong, wrong. Fodor and I must disagree on how the concepts of computation, faculty psychology (specialization), and innate biological organization should be applied to explaining the mind. This essay will be organized accordingly.

The Concept of Computation in *How the Mind Works*

According to *HTMW* (pp. 24–27; chap. 2), mental life consists of information-processing or computation. Beliefs are a kind of information, thinking a kind of computation, and emotions, motives, and desires are a kind of feedback mechanism in which an agent senses the difference between a current state and goal state and executes operations designed to reduce the difference. 'Computation' in this context does not refer to what a commercially available digital computer does but to a more generic notion of mechanical rationality, a concept that Fodor himself has done much to elucidate (Fodor, 1968; 1975; 1981; 1994).

In this conception, a computational system is one in which knowledge and goals are represented as patterns in bits of matter ('representations'). The system is designed in such a way that one representation causes another to come into existence; *and* these changes mirror the laws of some normatively valid system like logic, statistics, or laws of cause and effect in the world. The design of the system thus ensures that if the old representations were accurate, the new ones are accurate as well. Deriving new accurate beliefs from old ones in pursuit of a goal is not a bad definition of 'intelligence', so a principal advantage of the computational theory of mind (CTM) is that it explains how a hunk of matter (a brain or a computer) can be intelligent.

CTM has other selling points. It bridges the world of mind and matter, dissolving the ancient paradox of how seemingly ethereal entities like reasons, intentions, meanings, and beliefs can interact with the physical world. It motivates the science of cognitive psychology, in which experimenters characterize the mind's information structures and processes (arrays for images, tree structures for sentences, networks for long-term memory, and so on). Since computational systems can have complex conditions, loops, branches, and filters which result in subtle, situationally appropriate behavior, the CTM allows the mind to be characterized as a kind of biological mechanism without calling to mind the knee-jerk reflexes and coarse drives and imperatives that have made people recoil from the very idea. Finally, mental life—internal representations and processes—appears to be more lawful and universal than overt behavior, which can vary with circumstances. This claim also lies behind Chomsky's idea that there is a single Universal Grammar that applies to all the world's languages despite their differences in overt words and constructions. Much of *HTMW* extends this idea to other areas of human psychology, such as the emotions, social and sexual relations, and humor.

Fodor, as I have acknowledged, deserves credit for capturing the sense of 'computation' in which it can sensibly be said that the mind is a kind of computer. That sense—in which a system's state transitions map onto logical relationships, or, as Fodor often puts it, the components of the system have both causal and semantic properties—says nothing about binary digits, program counters, register operations, stored programs, or any of the other particulars of the machines that process our email or compute our taxes and which are improbable characterizations of a human brain. The beauty of Fodor's original formulation is that it embraces a variety of systems that we might call 'computational', including ones that perform parallel computation, analogue computation (as in slide rules and adding machines), and fuzzy computation (in which graded physical variables represent the degree to which something is true, or the probability that something is true, and the physical transitions are designed to mirror operations in probability theory or fuzzy logic rather than in classical logic). Any adequate characterization of the concept of 'computation' should embrace these possibilities. After all, the term *digital computer* is not redundant, and the terms *analogue computer* and *parallel computer* are not self-contradictory.

At the same time, the computational theory of mind is by no means empty or necessary. It can be distinguished from the traditional belief that intelligence comes from an immaterial substance, the soul. It differs from the claim that intelligence is made possible only by specific biochemical properties of neural tissue. It differs from the assertion that mental life can be understood only in terms of first-person present-tense subjective experience. And it differs from the claim that intelligence can be understood only by considering what mental states refer to in the world, or by examining the incarnate person embedded in a physical and social context. Fodor emphasizes the idea that the representations in a computational system are *syntactic*: they are composed of parts in some arrangement, and the causal mechanisms of the system are sensitive to the identity and arrangement of those parts rather than to what they refer to in the world.

The Concept of Specialization in *How the Mind Works*

HTMW does not try to account for all of human behavior using a few general-purpose principles such as a large brain, culture, language, socialization, learning, complexity, self-organization, or neural-network dynamics. Rather, the mind is said to embrace subsystems dedicated to particular kinds of reasoning or goals (pp. 27–31). Our intelligence, for example, consists of faculties dedicated to reasoning about space, number, probability, logic, physical objects, living things, artifacts, and minds. Our affective repertoire comprises emotions pertaining to the physical world, such as fear and disgust, and emotions pertaining to the social and moral worlds, such as trust, sympathy, gratitude, guilt, anger, and humor. Our social relationships are organized by distinct psychologies applied to our children, parents, siblings, other kin, mates, sex partners, friends, enemies, rivals, trading partners, and strangers. We are also equipped with communicative interfaces, most prominently language, gesture, vocal calls, and facial expressions.

The intended analogy is to the body, which is composed of systems divided into organs assembled from tissues built out of cells. Our 'organs of computation', therefore, are not like discrete chips laid out on a board with a few solder tracks connecting them. Just as some kinds of tissue, like the epithelium, are used (with modifications) in many organs, and some organs, like the blood and the skin, interact with the rest of the body across an extensive interface, some kinds of specialized thoughts and emotions may serve as constituents that are combined into different assemblies. The concept of an artifact, for example—an object fashioned by an intelligent agent to bring about a goal—combines the concept of an object from intuitive physics with the concept of a goal from intuitive psychology. The psychology of sibling relations embraces the emotion of affection (also directed toward mates and friends), an extra feeling of solidarity triggered by perceived kinship, and a version of disgust pinned to the thought of having sexual relations with the sibling.

This kind of faculty psychology has numerous advantages. It is consistent with models of cognitive faculties such as language, spatial cognition, and audition that require specialized machinery (nouns and verbs, allocentric and egocentric frames of reference, and pitch and timbre, respectively). It is supported by the existence of neurological and genetic disorders that target these faculties unevenly, such as a difficulty in recognizing faces (and facelike shapes) but not other objects, or a difficulty in reasoning about minds but not about objects or pictures. Finally, a faculty psychology is necessary to account for many of the complex but systematic patterns in human thought and emotion. The fact that we love our siblings but don't want to have sex with them, and may want to have sex with attractive strangers without necessarily loving them, is inexplicable by a theory of social psychology that doesn't distinguish among kinds of human relationships but appeals only to global drives like 'positive affect'.

The Appeal to Evolution in *How the Mind Works*

Evolution is the third key idea in *HTMW* (pp. 21–24; chap. 3). The organs of computation that make up the human mind are not tailored to solve arbitrary computational problems but only those that increased the reproductive chances of our ancestors living as foragers in pre-state societies.

One advantage of invoking evolution is that it provides psychology with explanatory adequacy. It helps account for *why* we have the specializations we do: why children learn spoken language instinctively but written language only with instruction and effort, why the system for recalling memories satisfies many of the specifications of an optimal information-retrieval system, why our preferred sexual partners are nonsiblings who show signs of health and fertility. More generally, it explains why the human psyche has specific features that could not be predicted from the mere proposition that the brain engages in computation.

Evolutionary psychology also helps to explain many instances of error, irrationality, and illusion—why we gamble, eat junk food, fall for visual illusions, obsess over celebrities, and fear snakes and heights more than hair dryers near bathtubs or driving without a seatbelt. The nature of the explanation is that there can be a mismatch between the ancestral environment to which our minds are evolutionarily adapted and the current environment in which we find ourselves.

The most general attraction of a synthesis between cognitive science and evolutionary psychology is that it continues the process of the unification of putatively incommensurable metaphysical realms that has been the major thrust of science for four centuries (Tooby and Cosmides, 1992; Wilson, 1998). Newton united the sublunary and superlunary spheres, Lyell united the formative past and static present, Wöhler united living tissue and nonliving chemistry, and Darwin, Mendel, and Watson and Crick united seeming teleological design in organisms with ordinary processes of forward causation. In the same way, the idea that the human mind is an evolved computer aims to bridge the last major chasm in human knowledge, that between matter and mind, biology and culture, nature and society, the natural sciences and the humanities. This consilience promises not only a more parsimonious metaphysics but greater depth and explanatory power for the disciplines that study the mind and its products. Hypotheses about psychological function cannot be conjured up by whim but must be compatible with evolutionary biology and in some cases may be deduced from it.

I turn now to how each of these themes is treated in Fodor's critique of *HTMW*.

The Concept of Computation in *The Mind Doesn't Work that Way*

In *TMDWTW*, Fodor argues that he never meant that *all* of the mind could be explained as a kind of computation. On the contrary, there is a key thing that a human mind can do but which a computational system cannot do. I will discuss this allegedly special human feat soon, but the debate cannot proceed if *HTMW* and *TMDWTW* don't mean the same thing by the word 'computation'.

And they don't. In *TMDWTW*, Fodor departs from the generic characterization of computation in his previous writings and assumes a far more specific and far less psychologically plausible version. He now defines the Computational Theory of Mind as 'whether the architecture of (human) cognition is interestingly like the architecture of Turing's kind of computer' (p. 105, note 3). Similarly, he evaluates the idea that 'cognitive architecture is Classical Turing architecture; that is, that the mind is interestingly like a Turing machine' (p. 30).[2]

A Turing Machine is a design for a hypothetical computer that Alan Turing found convenient to use in his proof that partial recursive functions could be computed by formally specified mechanical systems. It consists of a control unit and an infinite tape divided into squares which can be imprinted with any of a fixed number of symbols. The tape serves as the machine's input, output, and working memory; the control unit can 'look at' one square at a time. The control unit can be in a finite number of states, and is governed by a finite transition network which senses the machine's state and the visible symbol on the tape, and in response can change state, print or erase a symbol, and move the tape one square to the left or right. A Turing machine can compute any partial recursive function, any grammar composed of rewrite rules, and, it is commonly thought, anything that can be computed by any other physically realizable machine that works on discrete symbols and that arrives at an answer in a finite number of steps.

No one has ever built a Turing Machine (other than for pedagogical purposes) because it is maddeningly difficult to program and stupefyingly inefficient to run. It was invented only as a convenient mathematical construction, not as a prototype for a workable computer, and certainly not as a model of the functioning of the human mind. No one has ever taken seriously the idea that 'cognitive architecture is Classical Turing architecture', so the central premise of *TMDWTW*—that a Turing Machine is unsuited to solve a certain kind of problem that the human mind easily solves—is not relevant to anything. It is certainly not relevant to *HTMW*, which took pains to differentiate Turing Machines and current digital computers from the generic notion of computation (pp. 26–27, 64–69).

It's hard to credit that Fodor takes seriously the idea that the human memory is like a tape divided into squares, even for the domains (like language parsing) in which he believes that CTM is true. Could Fodor have something more abstract in mind, notwithstanding his explicit references to computational architecture? He does bring up the weaker idea that 'the mind is Turing-equivalent' (p. 105, note 3; see also p. 33), and that 'minds are "input-output equivalent" to Turing machines' (p. 30). But no one would defend this version of the Computational Theory of Mind either. The class of functions computable by Turing machines includes every computer program you would ever have reason to think of (calculating the digits of *pi,* organizing a company's payroll), and countless ones that one would never have reason to think of. In the domain that Fodor considers most amenable to computational analyses, language, it is axiomatic among linguists that the set of possible human languages is vastly smaller than the set of languages generable by Turing machines. If it weren't, characterizing Universal Grammar would be trivial, and languages would be unlearnable (Pinker, 1979). So Turing-Machine equivalence is as red a herring as Turing-Machine architecture.

In one place Fodor adumbrates what he means by properties of computational architecture that are 'interestingly like' Turing Machines. He attributes to Turing a version of CTM in which 'mental processes are operations defined on syntactically structured mental representations that are much like sentences' (p. 4). This characterization of CTM is also puzzling. For one thing, Turing machines *aren't,* by design, sensitive to the structure of representations: they can 'see' only a single symbol at a time, and at best can be programmed to *emulate* systems that are sensitive to structure. Nor did Turing himself say anything about structured or sentence-like representations.[3] One could, in principle, program a Turing machine to emulate a structure-sensitive architecture, but then one could program a Turing machine to emulate a connectionist architecture as well (with the analogue values approximated to some arbitrary degree of precision). As for real computers, they avail themselves of many representational formats, most of which are not particularly like sentences (relational databases, image files, recursive list structures, and so on). And with the possible exception of Chomsky's 'Logical Form' and other representations of the semantically relevant information in syntax, computational models of the human mind rarely posit 'mental representations that are much like sentences'. Consider, for example, visible-surface arrays (a.k.a. 2½–D sketches), semantic networks, mental models, phrase-structure rules, and analogue imagery representations.

At times Fodor invokes a still weaker ('minimal') form of CTM, namely that 'the role of a mental representation in cognitive processes supervenes on some syntactic fact or other' (p. 29), that is, that mental representations affect cognitive processing by virtue of the identity and arrangement of the symbols composing them. He refers to a system of this sort as having 'classical' computational architecture (e.g., p. 31), contrasts it with connectionist and associationist alternatives (which are sensitive only to collections of features and lack syntactic organization), and grants it the computational power of Turing machines (p. 30). In an abstruse and disorganized discussion, (pp. 28–33), Fodor seems to contrast minimal-CTM with his strong, Turing-machine-architecture-CTM in the following way. Turing machines can process only local information, such as the information inside a proposition, and hence are unable to respond to global properties of the total set of propositions, such as whether they are collectively parsimonious, or whether they are mutually relevant or consistent. A minimal-CTM computer, in contrast, can process an arbitrarily large set of propositions at once, including propositions that help determine whether the remaining propositions satisfy some global property. Fodor warns the reader that in order to do this, a minimal-CTM computer would have to swallow implausibly large databases in one bite, perhaps the entirety of the system's knowledge.

In all these characterizations, Fodor describes a computational system at a level close to what hackers call 'bare metal': the elementary information-processing operations built directly into the hardware. This leads to his repeated emphasis on how myopic and inflexible computational systems are, an emphasis that, we shall see, he compares unfavorably to the human mind. Nowhere does Fodor acknowledge that real computers overlay the bare metal with many layers of software that endow them with more global reach and more flexible powers, and that it is this 'virtual machine', the one visible to programmers and users, that specifies the system's powers in practice. An obvious example is an internet search engine, which repeatedly examines pages on the World Wide Web and constructs a database capturing which words are found in which documents and which documents are linked to which other documents. By processing this database, instead of the entire Web directly, the search engine can respond to global properties, such as which page on the Web is likely to be most relevant to a search query. A person who learned about the nature of computation from *TMDWTW* would have no idea that computers might be capable of such a feat.

Just as curiously, Fodor says nothing about the computational architectures that have been proposed as actual models of the *mind*. There is no mention in *TMDWTW* of production systems, semantic networks, knowledge representation languages, unification systems, dynamic binding networks, massively parallel architectures, and hybrid connectionist-symbolic systems. All of these are 'computational' in Fodor's original, generic sense (that is, they contain symbols that have both semantic and causal properties), and all of them are syntactic (rather than connectionist or associationist) in that at least some of their operation depends on the internal relations among the elements in their representations. Yet they do not work like Turing Machines or the variants that Fodor presents as the essence of the computational theory of mind, and Fodor does not refer to them in his discussion. As we shall see, this is a key omission.

Fodor on the Limits of Computational Psychology

Fodor believes he has identified a feat that human minds can do but that Turing machines and their kin cannot do.[4] He calls this feat 'abduction', 'globality', the 'frame problem', and 'inference to the best explanation'.

Frustratingly, Fodor never gives a clear definition of what he means by abduction, nor does he work through an example that lays bare exactly how a computational system (Turing machine or other) fails to do something that humans easily do. He often seems to use 'abduction' and its relatives to embrace any really hard problem about cognition, as if the real title of the book was *We Don't Understand Everything About the Mind Yet*. But Fodor's general idea is that when people solve a problem they have an uncanny ability to bring to bear on it just the information that is most relevant to it. Moreover, people can absorb the implications of some new fact or conclusion, and can be sensitive to the overall parsimony and consistency of a belief system, without exhaustively searching the contents of memory and testing the implications of a fact against everything they know.

Fodor asserts that abduction is beyond the abilities of a classical computational system, because such a system can only apply rules to circumscribed strings according to local conditions of matching and mismatching symbols. This may suffice to parse a sentence using a set of grammatical rules, or to derive a conclusion from a set of premises using modus ponens. But it does not allow the system to revise a belief that is an indirect implication of an entire set of beliefs. In those cases there is no simple 'if-then' rule that cranks such implications out.

Fodor offers an example from common-sense reasoning. A reasoning system implemented on a classical computer would depart from human reasoning, he claims, in the following scenario:

> The thought that there will be no wind tomorrow significantly complicates your arrangements if you had intended to sail to Chicago, but not if your plan was to fly, drive, or walk there. But, of course, the syntax of the mental representation that expresses the thought *no wind tomorrow* is the same whichever plan you add it to. The long and short of it is: The complexity of a thought is not intrinsic: it depends on the context. (p. 26)

The example is quite unconvincing. Even the stupidest reasoning system would be programmed to test for wind conditions before sailing, and branch to an appropriate course of action depending on the outcome, but not run that test before driving or walking. Perhaps realizing this, Fodor spends most of his time on examples from the history of science. He ventures, for example, that a classical computer cannot understand that in Newtonian mechanics heavier objects don't necessarily fall faster, nor that in modern chemistry metals need not be solid. Fodor mentions the names W. V. O. Quine and Pierre Duhem without explanation; presumably it is an allusion to their arguments that the entire set of one's beliefs form an interconnected whole, and that the only criterion for justifying a *particular* belief is its effect on the coherence and simplicity of the entire *system* of beliefs. One's definition of art, for example, might depend on assumptions about the universality of art across human cultures, which may depend on the antiquity of artistic creation in human prehistory, which may depend on radiocarbon dating of cave paintings. So a revision in physicists' understanding of the process of radioactive decay could alter our definition of art, despite the fact that any explicit set of canons for physics would say nothing about art or vice versa.

Fodor's argument, then, is that there is an unbridgeable chasm between the feats of human abduction and the powers of computational systems. It is a crisis for cognitive science, not just for *HTMW*: 'I'm inclined to think that Chicken Little got it right. Abduction really is a terrible problem for cognitive science, one that is unlikely to be solved by any kind of theory we have heard of so far' (p. 41). Inverting the paper-ending cliché, Fodor suggests that in this area, *less* research needs to be done. 'Do nothing about abduction', he advises; 'Wait until someone has a good idea' (p. 52). Until that day, cognitive scientists should concentrate on parts of the mind in which global interactions with knowledge are minimal, such as vision, speech, and syntactic parsing.

Problems with Fodor's Critique of Computational Psychology

But Fodor's supposed chasm can be narrowed from both sides. Let's begin with the human mind's powers of abduction. Fodor's reliance on examples from the history of science to illustrate the inimitable feats of cognition has an obvious problem: the two work in very different ways. A given scientific inference is accomplished by a community of thousands of scientists, who work over centuries, use sophisticated mathematical and technological tools, pool their results in journals and conferences, and filter out false conclusions through empirical hypothesis-testing and peer criticism. And their accomplishments are appreciated in hindsight through histories written by the victors, with the false starts edited out (the phlogiston, the N-rays, the Lamarckism, the cold fusion). A common-sense inference, in contrast, is accomplished by a single brain working in seconds, doing its best with what it has, and scrutinized by cognitive scientists in real time, errors and all. Granted that several millennia of Western science have given us non-obvious truths involving circuitous connections among ideas, but why should theories of a single human mind be held to the same standard? Would a typical person, working alone and unprompted, abduce that in modern chemistry, solidity is not a necessary property of metals, or that planetary regression complicates geocentric theory? This is far from obvious.

Fodor briefly concedes that this is a problem for his argument. As he notes, one could argue that 'the apparent nonlocality of quotidian cognitive processes is somehow an illusion… *Scientific* inference may really sometimes be abductive; but then, science is social, whereas quotidian cognition, of the kind psychologists care about, is carried out in single heads. Psychology isn't, after all, philosophy of science writ small' (p. 52). Quite so. And here is how he replies to this objection: 'It strikes me as wildly implausible that the structure of human cognition changed radically a few hundred years ago' (p. 53). This is not an excerpt or a summary of Fodor's reply; it is the totality of his reply. And it is a startling non sequitur. The problem for Fodor's argument is not the difference between how the mind works today and how the mind worked a few hundred years ago. It's the difference between how a single human mind works and how the entire edifice of Western science works.

The gap between minds and computational models can be narrowed from the other side as well. Fodor argues that cognitive science is utterly clueless about how to address the problems he lumps together as abduction. 'The substantive problem is to understand, even to a first approximation, *what sort* of architecture cognitive science ought to switch to insofar as the goal is to accommodate abduction. As far as I know, however, nobody has the slightest idea' (p. 47). As a particularly damning indictment, he writes, 'The frame problem doesn't [even] make it into the index of Pinker's...book' (p. 42). As a matter of fact, the frame problem *is* in the index of *HTMW* (p. 639, fourth entry). And contra Fodor, cognitive scientists do have the slightest idea of what sort of cognitive architecture, at least to a first approximation, might explain abductive inference.

Recall that Fodor's touchstone for the abduction problem is Quine's analysis of the interconnectedness of knowledge. Quine (1960) wrote:

> The totality of our so-called knowledge or beliefs, from the most casual matters of geography and history to the profoundest laws of atomic physics or even of pure mathematics and logic, is a man-made fabric which impinges on experience only along the edges. Or, to change the figure, total science is like a field of force whose boundary conditions are experience. (p. 42)

Quine's metaphors of a fabric and a force field, with constraints along their edges that propagate across their surface, are reminiscent of the kind of computational system sometimes known as soap-film or soap-bubble models and which cognitive scientists call constraint satisfaction networks (Attneave, 1982; Marr and Poggio, 1976; Rumelhart et al., 1986; Waltz, 1975). The key idea is that a global property (in the soap film example, minimal area of a curved surface) can emerge without a master plan through numerous local interactions among the constituents (in this case, surface tension among neighboring molecules). In *HTMW* (pp. 103–109; see also pp. 233–236, 242–255) I presented an example (see figure 10.1, originally from Feldman and Ballard, 1982) of soap-film computation in a constraint network that settles on a global 3-D shape defined by locally ambiguous 2-D contours, in this case those of a Necker cube. The units represent possible interpretations of local features. The interpretations that are mutually consistent in a single 3-D object excite each other (arrows) while the ones that are inconsistent inhibit each other (dots)

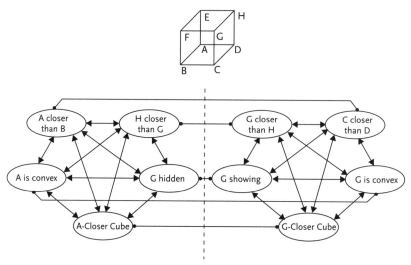

Figure 10.1 Soap-film computation for a Necker cube (adapted from Feldman and Ballard, 1982)

More generally, a constraint satisfaction network consists of a large number of representations of possible states of affairs (the nodes) and a dense array of information pathways interconnecting them (the connections or pathways). Each node typically has a scalar value that represents the likelihood that the proposition it represents is true, and the pathways encode relationships of consistency among the propositions. Nodes representing mutually consistent propositions (where the truth of one would increase one's confidence level for the other) are connected by pathways that cause a high confidence value for the first node to increment the confidence level of the second node; nodes representing inconsistent pathways (where the truth of one leads one to doubt the other) are connected by pathways that have the opposite effect. Computation in such networks consists of setting initial values for some of the nodes, letting constraints propagate through the network in parallel, and allowing it to settle into a stable set of new values, which represents a new state of knowledge. The values for the pathways (which can be set by various combinations of innate tuning, experience with the correlations among the truth values, or deduction) are designed so that the system as a whole tends to move in the direction of global criteria such as consistency and simplicity.

As I explain in *HTMW* (pp. 103–109), constraint satisfaction networks have a number of properties that help explain common-sense reasoning in the same manner as they help explain perception. One is content-addressability. We know that human memory is not searched exhaustively, nor by fixed physical addresses or file names (as in conventional computers), nor by a huge index compiled off-line (as in search engines). Rather, a concept in one set of beliefs can activate its counterpart in another set of beliefs in a single computational step. This feature falls out of the parallel, densely interconnected architecture of constraint networks. A second and related advantage is pattern completion: when some subset of a collection of mutually relevant beliefs is activated, the remaining ones are filled in automatically. Constraint satisfaction networks, at least in principle, allow far-flung information to be applied to a current problem based on overlapping content. For example, the liquid state of mercury can call to mind the liquid state of water; the associated knowledge that liquidity is not a constant property of water but one that is dependent on its temperature can then be applied back to mercury, allowing the person to abduce that the liquidity is not a necessary property of metals but a temperature-dependent one.

Constraint networks, then, are designed to do what Fodor, with his focus on Turing Machines, claims cannot be done: maintain a system of beliefs that satisfies some global property (such as consistency or simplicity) through strictly local computations. Though constraint networks are difficult to implement in standard programming languages and computer architectures (to say nothing of Turing machines), they are reminiscent of the parallel, densely interconnected, and graded signal-processing architecture of the human brain, and there is every reason to think that this is no coincidence.

The best-known constraint satisfaction networks are those developed in the connectionist school, in which the nodes tend to represent some simple feature, the propagated constraints are scalar activation levels, and the adjustments consist of summation or some other simple aggregation (e.g. Rumelhart et al., 1986). Fodor detests connectionism, which he calls 'simply hopeless', because the connectionist models most popular among cognitive psychologists are ill-equipped to represent the logical structure of propositions (Fodor and Pylyshyn, 1988). I think Fodor is right about that class of models (Pinker, 1999; Pinker and Prince, 1988), but long before the ascendance of connectionism there were *symbolic* constraint satisfaction networks (e.g., Waltz, 1975), and there are now hybrids that explicitly combine the structure-sensitivity of symbol-processing architectures with the content-addressability and pattern-completion abilities of connectionist architectures (Hummel and Biederman, 1992; Hummel and Holyoak, 1997; Marcus, 2001; Shastri, 1999). Unless such hybrids are impossible in principle, which Fodor has not shown, his arguments about the limitations of Turing Machines and other serial architectures are irrelevant.

It would be a mug's game to try to defend current models of cognition against criticisms about their numerous shortcomings. Perhaps all these ideas will turn out to fail in the long run. But it makes little sense to argue about whether to be an optimist or a pessimist when gazing into a crystal ball. The point is that Fodor claims to have identified a *principled* reason why computational approaches will not succeed at modeling cognition, and that argument is undermined by his failure to consider architectures (such as constraint-satisfaction networks) in which the computations are not necessarily serial, discrete, or sensitive only to local properties of a representation.[5]

Constraint satisfaction networks deal with representations of graded confidence levels and computations involving probabilistic inference. As such they fall under the broad rubric of heuristic reasoning, which tends toward likely solutions rather than guaranteeing correct ones. Fodor's only mention of cognitive scientists' attempt to deal with abduction is an evaluation of heuristic approaches. 'Perhaps', Fodor writes, 'real cognition in real heads achieves an appearance of abductive success by local approximations to global processes; and perhaps the problem of calculating these approximations is solved heuristically, case by case' (p. 42). But he quickly dismisses this objection by asserting, not very convincingly, that 'there is every reason to think that' the 'inferences that are required to figure out *which* local heuristic to employ are [often] themselves abductive' (p. 42).

> If it's hard to model the impact of global considerations in *solving* a problem, it's generally equally hard to model the impact of global considerations in *deciding how* to solve a problem.... Suppose I'm unclear whether, on balance, in the current state of the market, it would be reasonable for me to invest in potato futures. Then I am likely to be equally unclear *how to decide* whether, on balance, in the current state of the market, it would be reasonable for me to invest in potato futures... I'm told that Jones advises buying potatoes; so, for practical purposes, my question whether it is wise for me to buy potatoes is reduced to the question whether it is wise for me to do as Jones advises. But what weight I ought to assign to Jones's advice itself depends a lot on what the context is. If, for example, it's *Dow* Jones, it may matter a lot that the context is financial. Deciding whether to take Jones's advice depends, in all sorts of ways, on what my prior beliefs about Jones are, just as deciding whether to buy potatoes depends, in all sorts of ways, on what my prior beliefs about the market are. There is nothing to indicate that the determinants of reliable cognitive processing become decreasingly global... as one goes up this hierarchy of decision making. (pp. 42–43)

The key word here is *reliable.* Fodor's argument here assumes that people invariably make reliable decisions under uncertainty, such as whether to invest in potato futures. But real people's decisions are not so reliable, and they would appear to be not-so-reliable in just the way one would expect if they applied heuristics based on a few readily available cues. As the recent dot-com bubble has shown, real people tend to base investment decisions on, among other things, what they hear that everyone else is doing, what their brother-in-law advises, what a cold-calling stranger with a confident tone of voice tells them, and what the slick brochures from large investing firms recommend. People, in other words, use heuristics. It is in the very nature of common-sense inference (and, for that matter, Fodor's favored examples of visual perception and sentence processing) that available cues give statistically useful but frequently fallible information. Fodor provides no evidence that human beings have a power of reliable abductive inference that is better than heuristic, and by extension, that is beyond the reach of theories of cognition in the computational framework.

The Concept of 'Modularity' in *The Mind Doesn't Work That Way*

Constraint satisfaction architecture is one part of the solution to abduction in *HTMW*, but one still needs principles on how such networks are organized into mutually relevant collections of knowledge. This is one of the motivations for the second major theme in the book, specialization or domain-specificity. Rather than comprising a single set of rules that applies across the board to all propositions in memory, the human mind organizes its understanding of reality into several domains, such as physical objects, living things, other minds, and artifacts. Each is organized around core intuitions that guide reasoning in those domains. Physical objects occupy space, persist over time, and are subject to physical forces. Living things are self-propelled and self-organized owing to a hidden essence. Minds consist of nonmaterial beliefs and goals. Artifacts are objects fashioned by a mind to bring about a goal.

A reasoning system organized in this way can, in effect, prune the combinatorial tree of inferences that make up the frame problem. To understand how a rock falls and bounces, look at its size and shape. To understand what a plant does, test its juices and fibers. To figure out what other people are likely to do, ask about their opinions and wants. To decipher a gadget, try to figure out what its inventor had in mind. These principles inhibit the system from reasoning about rocks by asking them their opinions, reasoning about chairs by putting bits of a chair under a microscope, and other possible false leads that make abduction such a hard problem.

For the most part, Fodor assimilates the concept of specialization in *HTMW* to his own notion of *modularity*. In his 1983 classic *The Modularity of Mind* Fodor defended a conception of a mental module as an informationally encapsulated processor. Here is how he explains it in *TMDWTW*: 'A certain piece of information ... or rule of inference is, in principle, relevant to [a] creature's success both in tasks drawn from domain *A* and in tasks drawn from domain *B*. But though the creature reliably uses the information to perform one kind of task, it seems unable to do so when it is required to perform tasks of the other kind' (p. 62). One paradigm case is the fact that consciously knowing that a visual illusion *is* an illusion does not make the illusion go away; this suggests that some aspect of visual perception is modular. Another example is that a perfectly sensible reading of a sentence may be unavailable to a person if his parsing mechanism has trouble assigning a correct syntactic parse to the sentence. For example, *Ashley said that Sue will leave yesterday* seems contradictory, even though it has a grammatical and plausible interpretation in which Ashley said it yesterday. This suggests that sentence parsing is modular.[6]

Fodor acknowledges that a mind with some kind of modular design could, in principle, meet the abduction challenge. But he immediately attempts to demolish the suggestion that the human inference system in fact has such a design. Syntax and vision, he argues, might be modules, but domains of reasoning cannot be.

As with the concept of computation, the concept of modularity has a number of meanings, and it's important to understand what work the concept does in *HTMW*. *HTMW* took pains to distinguish modules in Fodor's strong sense of encapsulated processors with modules in a much weaker sense of domain-specific functional organization (e.g., pp. 30–31, pp. 314–315). The subsystems in *HTMW* are not categorically sealed off from information that could be relevant to them, and they were posited not just to serve as a mail router for incoming information but rather to dictate what *kinds* of inferences and goals should be triggered by that information. A module for sexual attraction, for example, doesn't just make people pay attention to siblinghood; it says specifically, 'don't find your sibling sexually attractive.'

To be fair, in *TMDWTW* Fodor does distinguish among his own encapsulated processors and my functionally specialized mechanisms (chap. 4). But after making this distinction, he blurs it all over again. He identifies the central thesis of *HTMW* as 'massive modularity', which 'means that there is a more or less encapsulated processor for each kind of problem it can solve' (p. 64). But as mentioned, in *HTMW* (pp. 30–31, 314–315) the specializations need *not* be strictly encapsulated (though they are biased to consider some kinds of information before others), and their number is by no means 'massive'. Given the complexity of human behavior, a theory that posits some two dozen emotions and reasoning faculties (distinguishing, for example, fear from sexual jealousy from the number sense) is far from profligate (especially compared to Fodor's tolerance of the possibility that people are born with 50,000 concepts).

Fodor's imputation of his own version of modularity to *HTMW* is intended, I believe, to be charitable. A massive number of encapsulated modules *could* meet the abduction challenge if it were true, he concedes, since it would confine an inference engine to the information relevant to solving a problem. But in fact, he goes on to argue, it is *not* true, so that option is not available. His objection to multiple reasoning systems is based on the same diagnosis of regress that he invoked when arguing against heuristics. Fodor claims that the problem of routing information to the appropriate reasoning system—for example, detecting that an event is an example of a social exchange in order to activate a cheater-detecting mechanism—requires nothing less than a full solution to the abduction problem, leaving us where we started: 'Nobody has *any idea* what kind of cerebration is required for figuring out which distal stimulations are social exchanges' (p. 76).

In fact, psychologists have had an idea for more than half a century, at least since Fritz Heider (Heider and Simmel, 1944) showed that people automatically interpret certain patterns of moving dots as agents that seek to help and hurt each other—just the conceptual elements that are relevant to social exchange. Fodor never mentions this phenomenon, though he does make a rather odd argument against the general idea that domain-specific reasoning systems might be triggered by psychophysical cues. Any attempt to ground cognition in sensation would be tantamount to British empiricism, Fodor writes, and evolutionary psychologists (and other advocates of domain-specificity) claim not to be empiricists. The argument is odd because it is a form of genre criticism: shoehorning people into an orthodoxy and criticizing them for not adhering to it.

Of course, spatiotemporal trajectories are not the only or even the primary way that people recognize cognitive domains such as social exchange. Let's grant that not all perceptual information is earmarked by some psychophysical cue that can be used to shunt it to the most relevant reasoning system. Let's say that the input to one system may come from the output of another system. Perhaps the social exchange system is fed by an intuitive psychology that infers people's goals from their behavior. Perhaps sexual emotions are fed, in part, by a system for inferring who is related to the self. Perhaps some of these input systems are domain-general with respect to reasoning systems, feeding a number of them with information about objects or bodies or actions. This may speak against the mind as a collection of encapsulated modules, each wired directly to the eyeballs. But it does not speak against the mind as a network of subsystems that feed each other in criss-crossing but intelligible ways—the organ system metaphor on which *HTMW* is based.[7]

The Dismissal of Evolution in *TMDWTW*

Fodor advances four arguments that evolution has nothing to add to our understanding of how the mind works.

1. Fitness and truth. Treating the mind as an organ whose ultimate function is to promote Darwinian fitness, Fodor claims, has no advantage over the biologically untutored view that the mind is an organ whose function is to arrive at the truth. 'There is nothing in the "evolutionary," or the "biological," or the "scientific" worldview that shows, *or even suggests,* that the proper function of cognition is other than the fixation of true beliefs' (p. 68). To suggest otherwise, he claims, is 'neo-Darwinist anti-intellectualism'.

Putting aside the scope error in the anti-intellectualism charge, Fodor's claim that 'truth is cognition's proprietary virtue' runs into an obvious empirical problem: many kinds of human beliefs are systematically false. Members of our species commonly believe, among other things, that objects are naturally at rest unless pushed, that a severed tetherball will fly off in a spiral trajectory, that a bright young activist is more likely to be a feminist bankteller than a bankteller, that they themselves are above average in every desirable trait, that they saw the Kennedy assassination on live television, that fortune and misfortune are caused by the intentions of bribable gods and spirits, and that powdered rhinoceros horn is an effective treatment for erectile dysfunction. The idea that our minds are designed for truth does not sit well with such facts.

And contrary to Fodor's claim that nothing in the evolutionary worldview 'even *suggests*' that the function of cognition is something other than believing true things, here are five things that suggest exactly that.

First, computing the truth has costs in time and energy, so a system designed for useful approximations (one that 'satisfices' or exhibits bounded rationality) might outcompete a system designed for exact truth at any cost. There is little point, for example, in spending twenty minutes figuring out a shortcut that saves you ten minutes in travel time.

Second, outside the realm of mathematics and logic, there is no such thing as a universal true-belief-fixer. Inductive inference systems must make fallible assumptions about the world, such as that surfaces are mostly cohesive, human languages conform to a universal grammar, and people who grow up with you are your biological siblings. If the world for which the system was designed has changed, those beliefs may be systematically false. Visual illusions are a prime example. In other words, there is an important difference between a system designed to fixate likely beliefs in an ancestral world and a system designed to fixate true beliefs in this world.

Third, beliefs have a social as well as an inferential function: they reflect commitments of loyalty and solidarity to one's coalition. People are embraced or condemned according to their beliefs, so one function of the mind may be to hold beliefs that bring the belief-holder the greatest number of allies, protectors, or disciples, rather than beliefs that are most likely to be true. Religious and ideological beliefs are obvious examples.

Fourth, publicly expressed beliefs advertise the intellectual virtuosity of the belief-holder, creating an incentive to craft clever and extravagant beliefs rather than just true ones. This explains much of what goes on in academia.

Fifth, the best liar is the one who believes his own lies. This favors a measure of self-deception about beliefs that concern the self.

The idea that the mind is designed for truth is not completely wrong. We do have some reliable notions about the distribution of middle-sized objects around us and the quotidian beliefs and desires of our friends and relatives. But the statement that the mind is designed to 'find out truths' would seem to be a rather misleading summary of the past fifty years of research on human reasoning.

2. Consilience. Fodor is puzzled by the idea that psychology might benefit by being connected to evolutionary biology, an idea that he calls 'a little odd. The New Synthesis is, after all, prepared to allow that psychology and botany, for example, actually don't have much to say to one another; let those chips fall where they may' (pp. 80–81). Similarly, he argues, astrophysical theory has few implications for botany, quantum mechanics is irrelevant to demography, and lunar geography does not constrain cellular mitosis. Why should it be any different for 'your favorite theory about how the mind works and your favorite theory of how evolution works?' (p. 82).

Here is why it should be different. The subject matter of psychology is the functioning of the brain. The subject matter of botany is plants. The brain is not a plant. Now, the subject matter of evolutionary biology is living things. The brain *is* a living thing. Therefore, the relationship between psychology and evolution is not the same as the relationship between psychology and botany (or the relationship between lunar geography and cellular mitosis, and so on). If anything is 'a little odd', it is Fodor's failure to distinguish pairs of disciplines whose subject matters are in a superset-subset relation from pairs of disciplines whose subject matters are disjoint. Fodor repeats his non-sequitur when he writes, 'It simply isn't true that all the sciences are mutually relevant'. The issue, of course, is not whether *all* the sciences are mutually relevant but whether evolutionary biology and psychology (and other pairs of sciences with overlapping subject matters) are mutually relevant.

Indeed, Fodor extends his argument from 'not all' to 'most not': 'Quite the contrary', he writes, 'most sciences are quite strikingly mutually irrelevant... It's generally hard work to get theories in different sciences to bear on one another' (p. 83). This strikes me as a remarkable misreading of the current state of science. A glance at a university catalogue or funding agency provides literally dozens of examples in which pairs of sciences are mutually relevant: astrophysics, astrobiology, atmospheric chemistry, biochemistry, biogeography, biophysics, chemical biology, geophysics, geochemistry, molecular biology, molecular genetics, physical chemistry, and on and on. A growing plaint among scientific and academic policymakers is that disciplinary divisions are fossils of nineteenth-century ways of organizing knowledge and an impediment to scientific progress.

3. Teleology. Fodor argues that invoking *function* in a psychological explanation is logically independent of invoking *natural selection*. The strong connection between function and selective history in evolutionary psychology, Fodor writes, is

> ...an uncomfortable feature of the Darwinian account of teleology, one that makes it hard to believe that it could be the one that biological/psychological explanation requires. Imagine, just as a thought experiment, that Darwin was comprehensively wrong about the origin of species... Would it then follow that the function of the heart is not to pump the blood? Indeed, that the heart, like the appendix, has no function? (p. 85)

But far from being an 'uncomfortable' feature, the logical independence of biological functionality and natural selection is what gives Darwinism its empirical content. A common (and lazy) criticism of the theory of natural selection is that it is circular. According to the criticism, Darwinism means 'survival of the fittest' but 'the fittest' is defined as 'what survives'. Or, natural selection says only that whatever gets selected gets selected. By noting that biological functionality can be identified independently of any invocation of natural selection, Fodor, to his credit, shows why such arguments are fallacious. Natural selection is a falsifiable scientific explanation of how biological functionality arises, not a part of the concept of functionality itself.

On the other hand, from a scientist's perspective functionality without natural selection is unacceptably incomplete. Adaptive organs such as the eye or heart are staggeringly improbable arrangements of matter, and we need an explanation as to how they come to exist. Faced with this puzzle, the only alternatives to natural selection are deliberate engineering by a deity or extraterrestrial; some kind of mysterious teleological force that allows future benefit to affect present design; and simply not caring. The last appears to be Fodor's preference, but there is no reason that other scientists should be so incurious.

Natural selection, moreover, does more than solve the puzzle of how biological functionality arises. It can also feed back to revise and constrain our characterization of a function itself. For example, if the explanation of biological functionality in terms of natural selection is correct, we can rule out adaptations that work toward the greater good of the species, the harmony of the ecosystem, beauty for its own sake, benefits to entities other than the replicators that create the adaptations (such as horses which evolve saddles), functional complexity without reproductive benefit (e.g. an adaptation to compute the digits of pi), and anachronistic adaptations that benefit the organism in a kind of environment other than the one in which it evolved (e.g., an innate ability to read, or an innate concept of 'carburetor' or 'trombone').

Natural selection also has a positive function in scientific discovery, impelling psychologists to test new hypotheses about the possible functionality of aspects of psychology that previously seemed functionless. Numerous success stories are recounted in *HTMW*, such as the hypothesis that social emotions (sympathy, trust, guilt, anger, gratitude) are adaptations for policing reciprocity in non-zero sum games, and that an eye for beauty is an adaptation for detecting health and fertility in potential mates. Conversely, other psychological traits, such as music and religion, are recalcitrant to any rigorous analysis of adaptiveness in the evolutionary biologist's sense; they are better explained as by-products of adaptations. None of this research would be possible if psychologists had satisfied themselves with a naive notion of function instead of the one licensed by modern biology.

4. Complexity. Fodor's final dismissal of evolution consists of a rejection of the argument that adaptive complexity requires an appeal to natural selection:

> ... the complexity of our minds, or of our behavior, is simply irrelevant to the question of whether our cognitive architecture evolved under selection pressure (p. 87). ... It's entirely possible that quite small neurological reorganizations could have effected wild psychological discontinuities between our minds and the ancestral ape's. (p. 87–88)

The problem with this argument is that it confuses complexity with *adaptive* complexity, that is, improbable functionality. Fodor may be correct that as-yet-unknown changes in the developmental program for a primate brain could increase its complexity, for example, by giving it more neurons, a more intricate tangle of connections, or a more tortuous 3–D shape. But this is entirely different from increasing its *functionality* by making it better equipped to solve problems such as mate selection, coalition building, or toxin avoidance. The reason is that the proximate physical mechanisms that constitute our neurodevelopmental program—axon guidance signals, neural growth factors, cell adhesion molecules, and so on—cannot 'see' their effects on the functioning of the whole organism in its social and physical milieu. Natural selection *can* see those effects, and thereby can shape, over generations, just those developmental variations that enhance them.

Fodor, ironically, concedes a related point:

> …what is surely not conceivable is that relatively small, fortuitous changes in brain structure should produce massive increments in a creature's stockpile of true, contingent beliefs.…barring the rarest of accidents, it's simply not conceivable that a large database of logically independent, contingent beliefs that was formed fortuitously (e.g., in consequence of random alterations of brain structure) could turn out to be generally true. To get the feel of the thing, imagine cutting up the Manhattan telephone directory and then pairing all the numbers with all the names at random. How often do you suppose the number thus assigned to someone would be the number that he actually has? (pp. 93–94)

But Fodor's argument concerning beliefs that are contingently true in an environment applies in equal force to biological mechanisms that are contingently *fit* in an environment—that is, to mechanisms that attain some improbable state that enhances the organism's chances at reproduction. As Richard Dawkins (1986) has put it, 'However many ways there may be of being alive, it is certain that there are vastly more ways of being dead, or rather not alive. You may throw cells together at random, over and over again for a billion years, and not once will you get a conglomeration that flies or swims or burrows or runs, or does *anything*, even badly, that could remotely be construed as working to keep itself alive' (p. 9).

Summary and Conclusion

In *HTMW,* I defended a theory of how the mind works that was built on the notions of computation, specialization, and evolution. Specifically, it holds that the mind is a naturally selected system of organs of computation. Fodor claims that 'the mind doesn't work that way' because (1) Turing Machines cannot do abduction, (2) a massively modular system *could* do abduction but cannot be true, and (3) evolution adds nothing to our understanding of the mind. In this paper, I have presented four reasons that Fodor's argument doesn't work.

First, the claim that the mind is a computational system is distinct from the claim that the mind has the architecture of a Turing Machine or some other serial, discrete, local processor. Therefore the practical limitations of Turing Machines are irrelevant.

Second, abduction—conceived as the cumulative accomplishments of the scientific community over millennia—is distinct from human common-sense reasoning. Therefore Fodor's gap between human cognition and computational models may be illusory.

Third, biological specialization, as seen in organ systems, is distinct from Fodorian encapsulated modules. Therefore the limitations of Fodorian modules are irrelevant.

Fourth, Fodor's arguments dismissing the relevance of evolution to psychology are unsound. Human cognition is not exclusively designed to arrive at true beliefs. Evolutionary biology is more relevant to psychology than botany is to astronomy. Biological function without natural selection is woefully incomplete. And adaptive complexity requires a non-fortuitous explanation, just as true beliefs do.

Some final thoughts. It should go without saying that we *don't* fully understand how the mind works. In particular, we don't have a complete theory of how the mind accomplishes feats of common sense and scientific inference. Scientific psychology is not over. On the other hand, Fodor has failed to show that there is some known, *in-principle* chasm between the facts of human cognition and the abilities of biologically plausible computational systems. Chicken Little is wrong, and more, not less, research needs to be done.

Notes

1. Supported by NIH grant HD 18381. I thank Clark Barrett, Arthur Charlesworth, Helena Cronin, Dan Dennett, Rebecca Goldstein, and John Tooby for invaluable comments.
   Fodor discusses *HTMW* together with a second book, Henry Plotkin's *Evolution in Mind* (Plotkin, 1997), which is similar in approach. But Fodor focuses on *HTMW*, as will I.
2. These are not the only quotations in *TMDWTW* in which Fodor equates computation with Turing Machines. For example, he suggests in another place that 'we will *all* have to give up on the Turing story as a general account of how the mind works, and hence, a fortiori, that we will have to give up on the generality of the [synthesis of computation and evolution in *HTMW*]' (pp. 46–47).
3. Despite Fodor's frequent invocation of Turing and Quine in *TMDWTW*, he does not actually cite anything by them. I will assume that the arguments Fodor has in mind come from Turing's 'Computing Machinery and Intelligence' (Turing, 1950) and Quine's 'Two Dogmas of Empiricism' (Quine, 1960).
4. Actually it is unclear whether Fodor is making the strong mathematical claim that he has identified a function that cannot be computed by a Turing machine at all, or that he has merely identified a function that Turing Machines cannot do with humanlike speed and

efficiency. The latter may be the upshot of his discussion of the 'minimal' computational theory of mind.

5. See (Barrett, 2005), for discussion of another computational architecture for cognition that escapes the limitations of Turing machines and related designs.

6. As it happens, few psycholinguists believe that sentence parsing is as modular as Fodor argued, though I believe he was probably not completely wrong about it either; see Pinker, 1994, chapter 7.

7. See (Barrett, 2005) for similar arguments, using 'enzymes' rather than organ systems as the central metaphor.

References

Attneave, F. 1982: Pragnanz and soap bubble systems: A theoretical exploration. In J. Beck (ed.), *Organization and Representation in Perception*. Mahwah, NJ: Erlbaum.

Barrett, H. C.2005: Enzymatic computation and cognitive modularity. *Mind & Language, 20*, 259–287.

Dawkins, R. 1986: *The Blind Watchmaker: Why the Evidence of Evolution Reveals a Universe Without Design*. New York: Norton.

Feldman, J. and Ballard, D. 1982: Connectionist models and their properties. *Cognitive Science, 6*, 205–254.

Fodor, J. A. 1968: *Psychological Explanation: An Introduction to the Philosophy of Psychology*. New York: Random House.

Fodor, J. A. 1975: *The Language of Thought*. New York: Crowell.

Fodor, J. A. 1981: *RePresentations: Philosophical Essays on the Foundations of Cognitive Science*. Cambridge, MA: MIT Press.

Fodor, J. A. 1983: *The Modularity of Mind*. Cambridge, Mass.: MIT Press.

Fodor, J. A. 1994: *The Elm and the Expert: Mentalese and its Semantics*. Cambridge, Mass.: MIT Press.

Fodor, J. A. 2000: *The Mind Doesn't Work That Way: The Scope and Limits of Computational Psychology*. Cambridge, MA: MIT Press.

Fodor, J. A. and Pylyshyn, Z. 1988: Connectionism and cognitive architecture: A critical analysis. *Cognition, 28*, 3–71.

Heider, F. and Simmel, M. 1944: An experimental study of apparent behavior. *American Journal of Psychology, 57*, 243–259.

Hummel, J. E. and Biederman, I. 1992: Dynamic binding in a neural network for shape recognition. *Psychological Review, 99*, 480–517.

Hummel, J. E. and Holyoak, K. J. 1997: Distributed representations of structure: A theory of analogical access and mapping. *Psychological Review, 104*, 427–466.

Marcus, G. F. 2001: *The Algebraic Mind: Reflections on Connectionism and Cognitive Science*. Cambridge, MA: MIT Press.

Marr, D. and Poggio, T. 1976: Cooperative computation of stereo disparity. *Science, 194*, 283–287.

Pinker, S. 1979: Formal models of language learning. *Cognition, 7*, 217–283.

Pinker, S. 1994: *The Language Instinct*. New York: HarperCollins.

Pinker, S. 1997: *How the Mind Works*. New York: Norton.

Pinker, S. 1999: *Words and Rules: The Ingredients of Language*. New York: HarperCollins.

Pinker, S. and Prince, A. 1988: On language and connectionism: Analysis of a Parallel Distributed Processing model of language acquisition. *Cognition, 28*, 73–193.

Plotkin, H. 1997: *Evolution in Mind*. London: Allen Lane.

Quine, W. V. O. 1960: Two dogmas of empiricism. In *From a Logical Point of View*. New York: HarperCollins.

Rumelhart, D. E., Smolensky, P., McClelland, J. L., and Hinton, G. E. 1986: Schemata and sequential thought processes in PDP models. In J. L. McClelland and D. E. Rumelhart (eds.), *Parallel Distributed Processing: Explorations in the Microstructure of Cognition: Psychological and Biological models*. (Vol. 2). Cambridge, MA: MIT Press.

Shastri, L. 1999: Advances in SHRUTI: A neurally motivated model of relational knowledge representation and rapid inference using temporal synchrony. *Applied Intelligence*, 11, 79–108.

Tooby, J. and Cosmides, L. 1992: Psychological foundations of culture. In J. Barkow, L. Cosmides and J. Tooby (eds.), *The Adapted Mind: Evolutionary Psychology and the Generation of Culture*. New York: Oxford University Press.

Turing, A. M. 1950: Computing machinery and intelligence. *Mind*, 59, 433–460.

Waltz, D. 1975: Understanding line drawings of scenes with shadows. In P. H. Winston (ed.), *The Psychology of Computer Vision*. New York: McGraw-Hill.

Wilson, E. O. 1998: *Consilience: The Unity of Knowledge*. New York: Knopf.

11

Deep Commonalities between Life and Mind

I hate festschrifts: volumes of original essays commissioned to honor an aging scholar. I hate them for the same reason that economists hate Christmas gifts: they destroy value, because the benefit of the gift to the recipient is invariably a fraction of the cost of the gift to the donor. As the German etymology suggests, festschrifts hark back to an earlier era in academia, in which few enough books were published in a given field that any new one would be noticed. Nowadays a festschrift is a tiny cork bobbing in the mighty torrent of books, journals, and Web forums that gush out of the academic spillway every hour. Though I am sure that the honoree is pleased by the tribute, the psychic benefit to him or her is disproportionate to the number of person-hours that are put into it. Like brides- maids' dresses and Christmas gifts, festschrifts persist because no one dares to be the only friend or colleague or student of the honoree who is so ungrateful or disloyal or niggardly as to sit out the celebration. Bah, humbug!

Though most of my festschrift contributions are (sorry, pals) repurposed essays I had written for some other outlet, this one, for a volume honoring Richard Dawkins, is differ- ent. I used the invitation as an opportunity to develop some ideas about deep common- alities between life and mind that were inspired by Dawkins's writings, particularly the apparent indispensability of teleological concepts like "goal" and "purpose." In fact I take some of Dawkins's ideas farther, I think, than he would be willing to take them himself. Dawkins insisted that the title of his 1976 bestseller was strictly metaphorical. But when a version of this essay was published in The Times, *the editors titled it "Yes, Genes Can be Selfish."*

I am a cognitive scientist, someone who studies the nature of intelligence and the workings of the mind. Yet one of my most profound scientific influences has been Richard Dawkins, an evolutionary biologist. The influence runs deeper than the fact that the mind is a product of the brain and the brain a product of evolution; such an influence could apply to someone who studies any organ of any organism. The significance of Dawkins's ideas, for me and many others, runs to his characterization of the very nature of life and to a theme that runs throughout his writings: the possibility of deep commonalities between life and mind.

Scientists, unlike literary scholars, are ordinarily not a fitting subject of exegesis and thematic analysis. A scientist's writings should be transparent, revealing facts and explanations directly. Yet I find that Dawkins's ideas repay close examination, not because he is a guru issuing enigmatic pronouncements for others to ponder, but because he continually engages the deepest problems in biology, problems that continue to challenge our understanding.

When I first read Dawkins I was immediately gripped by concerns in his writings on life that were richer versions of ones that guided my thinking on the mind. The parallels concerned both the content and the practice of the relevant sciences.

The first critical theme is an attention to adaptive complexity as the paramount phenomenon in need of an explanation, most forcibly expressed in *The Blind Watchmaker* and *Climbing Mount Improbable*. In the case of life, we have the remarkable adaptations of living things: echolocation, camouflage, the vertebrate eye, and countless other 'organs of extreme perfection and complication,' in Darwin's words, which represent solutions to formidable engineering problems. In the case of mind, we have the remarkable powers of human cognition: the ability to recognize objects and materials, plan and execute movement, reason and remember, speak and understand.

I shared, moreover, Dawkins's impatience with fellow scientists who provide passable accounts of relatively peripheral aspects of their subject matter, but who, when it came to mechanistic explanations for adaptive complexity, were too easily satisfied with verbal formulae and vague hand-waving. Dawkins did not disguise his exasperation with Stephen Jay Gould's claims that he had revolutionized the theory of evolution with addenda such as punctuated equilibrium, species selection, and exaptation. These addenda, Dawkins pointed out, did not address the main problem of adaptive complexity in life and so left the core of the theory of natural selection (which does solve the problem) untouched. Many cognitive scientists, I often grumble, also content themselves with verbal substitutes for explanatory mechanisms, such as 'strategies', 'general intelligence', 'plasticity', or 'extracting regularities'.

The discomfort with inadequate explanations of key phenomena underlies another resonance—the conviction that in some areas of science there is an indispensable role for the exploration of ideas, their logical adequacy, and their explanatory power, rather than equating science with the obsessive gathering of data. Biology today, especially molecular biology, is massively weighted toward laboratory work, and any hint of theory is considered scholastic or archaic. In the case of molecular biology this attitude is particularly amnesic, because at the dawn of the field in the 1940s there was an obsession with the theoretical preconditions constraining any putative candidate for the machinery of life (as expressed, for example, in the influential treatise 'What is Life?' by Erwin Schrödinger, a theoretical physicist).

Dawkins has been unapologetic in insisting that a complete biology must lay out the implications of its theories, perhaps most forcibly in his essay 'Universal Darwinism', which audaciously argued that natural selection is not only the best theory of the evolution of life on earth, but almost certainly the best theory of the evolution of life anywhere in the universe. I believe that in cognitive science, too, the demands on adequate theories are so stringent as to carve out an essential place for theoretical analysis. In Dawkins's case, this encourages a blurring of his writing for his fellow scientists and for informed nonspecialists: his more popular books certainly cannot be considered 'popularization', nor is his most technical book, *The Extended Phenotype,* restricted to specialists. This is an example I try to emulate.

A second major theme in Dawkins's writings on life with parallels in the understanding of the mind is a focus on *information.* In *The Blind Watchmaker* Dawkins wrote, 'If you want to understand life, don't think about vibrant, throbbing gels and oozes, think about information technology'. Dawkins has tirelessly emphasized the centrality of information in biology—the storage of genetic information in DNA, the computations embodied in transcription and translation, and the cybernetic feedback loop that constitutes the central mechanism of natural selection itself, in which seemingly goal-oriented design results from the directed adjustment of some process by its recent consequences. The centrality of information was captured in the metaphor in Dawkins's book title *River Out of Eden,* the river being a flow of information in the generation-to-generation copying of genetic material since the origin of complex life. It figured into his *Blind Watchmaker* simulations of the evolutionary process, an early example of the burgeoning field of artificial life. It also lies behind his influential theory of memes, which illustrates that the logic of natural selection applies to any replicator which carries information with a certain minimum degree of fidelity. Dawkins's emphasis on the ethereal commodity called 'information' in an age of biology dominated by the concrete molecular mechanisms is another courageous stance. There is no contradiction, of course, between a system being understood in terms of its information content and it being understood in terms of its material substrate. But when it comes down to the deepest understanding of what life is, how it works, and what forms it is likely to take elsewhere in the universe, Dawkins implies that it is abstract conceptions of information, computation, and feedback, and not nucleic acids, sugars, lipids, and proteins, that will lie at the root of the explanation.

All this has clear parallels in the understanding of the mind. The cognitive revolution of the 1950s, which connected psychology with the nascent fields of information theory, computer science, generative linguistics, and artificial intelligence, had as its central premise the idea that knowledge is a form of information, thinking a form of computation, and organized behavior a product of feedback and other control processes. This gave birth to a new science of cognition that continues to dominate psychology today, embracing computer simulations of cognition as a fundamental theoretical tool, and the framing of hypotheses about computational architecture (serial versus parallel processing, analogue versus digital computation, graphical versus list-like representations) as a fundamental source of experimental predictions. As with biology, an emphasis on information allows one to discuss cognition in a broader framework than the one which happens to embrace the particular species found on earth; the framework can encompass the nature of processes we would wish to consider intelligent anywhere in the universe. And, as in biology, an emphasis on information unfortunately must withstand a strong current toward experimental studies of physical mechanisms (in this case the physiology of the brain) accompanied by a mistrust of theory and analysis. Again there is no contradiction between studying information processing systems and studying their physical implementation, but there has been a recent tendency to downplay the former, at a cost of explanatory adequacy.

The parallel use of information-theoretic concepts in biology and cognitive science (particularly linguistics) is no secret, of course, and it is evident in the way that genetics has borrowed so much of its vocabulary from linguistics. DNA sequences are said to contain letters and punctuation, may be palindromic, meaningless, or synonymous, are transcribed and translated, and are even stored in libraries. Biologists occasionally describe development and physiology as following rules, most notably in the immunologist Niels Jerne's concept of the 'generative grammar of the immune system'.

A final shared theme in life and mind made prominent in Dawkins's writings is the use of mentalistic concepts in biology, most boldly in his title *The Selfish Gene*. The expression evoked a certain amount of abuse, most notoriously in the philosopher Mary Midgley's pronouncement that 'Genes cannot be selfish or unselfish, any more than atoms can be jealous, elephants abstract or biscuits teleological' (a throwback to the era in which philosophers thought that their contribution to science was to educate scientists on elementary errors of logic encouraged by their sloppy use of language). Dawkins's main point was that one can understand the logic of natural selection by imagining that the genes are agents executing strategies to make more copies of themselves. This is very different from imaging natural selection as a process that works toward the survival of the group or species or the harmony of the ecosystem or planet. Indeed, as Dawkins argued in *The Extended Phenotype*, the selfish-gene stance in many ways offers a more perspicuous and less distorting lens with which to view natural selection than the logically equivalent alternative in which natural selection is seen as maximizing the inclusive fitness of individuals. Dawkins's use of intentional, mentalistic expression was extended in later writings in which he alluded to animals' knowing or remembering the past environments of their lineage, as when a camouflaged animal could be said to display a knowledge of its ancestors' environments on its skin.

The proper domain of mentalistic language, one might think, is the human mind, but its application there has not been without controversy either. During the reign of behaviorism in psychology in the middle decades of the twentieth century, it was considered as erroneous to attribute beliefs, desires, and emotions to humans as it would be to attribute them to genes, atoms, elephants, or biscuits. Mentalistic concepts, being unobservable and subjective, were considered as unscientific as ghosts and fairies and were to be eschewed in favor of explaining behavior directly in terms of an organism's current stimulus situation and its past history of associations among stimuli and rewards. Since the cognitive revolution, this taboo has been lifted, and psychology profitably explains intelligent behavior in terms of beliefs and desires. This allows it to tap into the world of folk psychology (which still has more predictive power when it comes to day-to-day behavior than any body of scientific psychology) while still grounding it in the mechanistic explanation of computational theory.

In defending his use of mentalistic language in biological explanation, Dawkins has been meticulous in explaining that he does not impute conscious intent to genes, nor does he attribute to them the kind of foresight and flexible cleverness we are accustomed to in humans. His definitions of 'selfishness', 'altruism', 'spite', and other traits ordinarily used for humans is entirely behavioristic, he notes, and no harm will come if one remembers that these terms are mnemonics for technical concepts and heuristics for generating predictions rather than direct attributions of the human traits.

I sometimes wonder, though, whether caveats about the use of mentalistic vocabulary in biology are stronger than they need to be—whether there is an abstract sense in which we can *literally* say that genes are selfish, that they try to replicate, that they know about their past environments, and so on. Now of course we have no reason to believe that genes have conscious experience, but a dirty secret of modern science is that we have no way of explaining the fact that *humans* have conscious experience either (conscious experience in the sense of raw first-person subjective awareness—the distinction between conscious and unconscious processes, and the nature of self-consciousness, are tractable, everyday scientific topics). No one has really explained why it *feels like something* to be a hunk of neural tissue processing information in certain complex patterns. So even in the case of humans, our use of mentalistic terms does not depend on a commitment on how to explain the subjective aspects of the relevant states, but only on their functional role within a chain of computations.

Let's take the computational theory of mind to its logical conclusion. It seems to me that if information-processing gives us a good explanation for the states of knowing and wanting that are embodied in the hunk of matter called a human brain, there is no principled reason to avoid attributing states of knowing and wanting to other hunks of matter. To be specific, nothing prevents us from seeking a generic characterization of 'knowing' (in terms of the storage of usable information) that would embrace both the way in which people know things (in their case, in the patterns of synaptic connectivity in brain tissue) and the ways in which the genes know things (presumably in the sequence of bases in their DNA). Similarly, we could frame an abstract characterization of 'trying' in terms of negative feedback loops, that is, a causal nexus consisting of repeated or continuous operations, a mechanism that is sensitive to the effects of those operations on some state of the environment, and an adjustment process that alters the operation on the next iteration in a specific direction, thereby increasing the chance that that aspect of the environment will be caused to be in a given state. In the case of the human mind, the actions are muscle movements, the effects are detected by the senses, and the adjustments are made by neural circuitry programming the next iteration of the movement. In the case of the evolution of genes, the actions are extended phenotypes, the effects are sensed as differential mortality and fecundity, and the adjustment consists of the number of descendants making up the next generation.

A characterization of beliefs and desires in terms of their informational rather than their physical incarnation may overarch not just life and mind and but other intelligent systems such as machines and societies. By the same token it can embrace the various forms of intelligence that are implicit in the bodies of animals and plants, which we would not want to attribute either to fully humanlike cogitation nor to the monomaniacal agenda of replication characterizing the genes. When the coloration of a viceroy butterfly fools the butterfly's predators by mimicking that of a more noxious monarch butterfly, there is a kind of intelligence being manifest. But its immediate goal is to fool the predator rather than replicate the genes, and its proximate mechanism is the overall developmental plan of the organism rather than the transcription of a single gene.

In other words the attribution of mentalistic states such as knowing and trying can be hierarchical. The genes, in order to effect their goal of making copies of themselves, can help build an organ whose goal is to fool a predator. The human mind is another intelligent mechanism built as part of the intelligent agenda of the genes, and it is the seat of a third (and the most familiar) level of intelligence: the internal simulation of possible behaviors and their anticipated consequences which makes our intelligence more flexible and powerful than the limited forms implicit in the genes or in the bodies of plants and animals.

Inside the mind, too, we find a hierarchy of sub-goals (to make a cup of coffee, put coffee grounds in the coffeemaker; to get coffee grounds, grind the beans; to get the beans, find the package; if there is no package, go to the store; and so on). Computer scientists often visualize hierarchies of goals as a stack, in which a program designed to achieve some goal often has to accomplish a subgoal as a means to its end, whereupon it 'pushes down' to an appropriate subroutine, and then 'pops' back up when the subroutine has accomplished the subgoal. The subroutine, in turn, can call a subroutine of its own to accomplish an even smaller and more specialized sub-goal. (The "stack" image comes from a memory structure that keeps track of which subroutine called which other subroutine; it works like a spring-loaded stack of cafeteria trays.) In the image I am trying to draw for you here, the best laid plans of mice and men are the bottom layers of the stack. Above them is the intelligence implicit in their bodies and genes. The topmost goal is the replication of genes which is the essence of natural selection.

It would take a good philosopher to forge bulletproof characterizations of 'intelligence', 'goal', 'want', 'try', 'know', 'selfish', 'think', and so on, that would embrace minds, robots, living bodies, genes, and other intelligent systems. (It would take an even better one to figure out how to reintroduce subjective experience into this picture when it comes to human and animal minds.) But the promise that such a characterization is possible—that we can sensibly apply mentalistic terms to biology without shudder quotes—is one of Dawkins's legacies. If so, we would have a substantive and deep explanation of our own minds, in which parochial activities like our own thinking and wanting would be seen as manifestations of more general and abstract phenomena.

The idea that life and mind are in some ways manifestations of a common set of principles can enrich the understanding of both. But it also calls for strict vigilance in not confusing the two manifestations—not forgetting what it is (a gene? an entire organism? the mind of a person?) that knows something, or that tries something, or that wants something, or that acts selfishly. I suspect that the biggest impediment to accepting the insights of evolutionary biology in understanding the human mind is people's tendency to confuse the various entities to which a given mentalistic explanation may be applied.

One example is the common tendency to assume that Dawkins's portrayal of 'selfish genes' implies that organisms in general, and people in particular, are ruthlessly egoistic and self-serving. In fact nothing in the selfish-gene view predicts that this should be so. Selfish genes are perfectly compatible with selfless organisms, since the genes' goal of selfishly replicating themselves can be implemented via the sub-goal of building organisms that are wired to do unselfish things such as being nice to relatives, extending favors in certain circumstances, flaunting their generosity under other circumstances, and so on. (Indeed much of *The Selfish Gene* consists of explanations of how the altruism of organisms is a consequence of the selfishness of their genes.) Another example of this confusion is the common claim that sociobiology is refuted by the many things people do that don't help to spread their genes, such as adopting children or using contraception. In this case the confusion is between the motive of genes to replicate themselves (which does exist) and the motive of people to spread their genes (which doesn't). Genes effect their goal of replication via the subgoal of wiring people with certain goals of their own, but replication per se need not be among those sub-subgoals: it's sufficient for people to seek sex and to nurture their children. In the environment in which our ancestors were selected, people pursuing those goals automatically helped the relevant genes pursue theirs (since sex tended to lead to babies), but when the environment changes (such as when we invented contraception) the causal chain that used to make subgoals bring about superordinate goals is no longer in operation.

I suspect that these common fallacies arise from applying a Freudian mindset to evolutionary psychology. People conceive of the genes as the deepest, truest essence of a person, the part that harbors his deepest wishes, and think of conscious experience and overt behavior as a superficial veneer hiding these ulterior motives. This is a fallacy because the motives of the genes are entirely different from the motives of the person—they are a play within a play, not the interior monologue of a single cast of players.

More generally, I think it was the ease of confusing one level of intelligence with another that led to the proscription of mentalistic terms in behaviorism and to the phobia of anthropomorphizing organisms (and later genes) in biology. But as long as we are meticulous about keeping genes, organisms, and brains straight, there is no reason to avoid applying common explanatory mechanisms (such as goals and knowledge) if they promise insight and explanation.

The promise of applying common tools to life and mind, and the danger in failing to distinguish which is the target of any particular explanation, can also, I think, be seen in discussions of the relevance of memes to human mind and culture. Dawkins has suggested that his discussion of memes was largely meant to illustrate the information-theoretic nature of the mechanism of natural selection—that it was not particular to DNA or carbon-based organisms or life on earth but applied to replicators of any sort. Others have treated his suggestions about memes as an actual theory of cultural change, some cleaving to a tight analogy between the selection of genes and the selection of memes, others exploring a larger family of models of cultural evolution, epidemiology, demographics, and gene-culture coevolution. I think the mind-life parallel inherent in memetics holds out the promise of new ways of understanding cultural and historical change, but that it also poses a danger.

Many theorists, partly on the basis of Dawkins's arguments about the indispensability of natural selection in explaining complex design in living things, write as if natural selection, applied to memes rather than genes, is the only adequate explanation of complex design in human cultural achievements. To bring culture into biology, they reason, one must show how it evolved by its own version of natural selection. But that doesn't follow, because the products of evolution don't have to *look like* the process of evolution. In the case of cultural evolution they certainly don't look alike—human cultural products are not the result of an accumulation of copying errors, but are crafted through bouts of concerted brainwork by intelligent designers. And there is nothing in Dawkins's Universal Darwinism argument that makes this observation suspect. While it remains true that the origin of complex design on earth requires invoking selection (given the absence of any alternative mechanisms adequate to the task), in the case of complex design in culture we do have an alternative, namely the creative powers of the human brain. Ultimately we have to explain the complexity of the brain itself in terms of genetic selection, but then the ladder can be kicked away and the actual process of cultural creation and transmission studied without prejudice.

A final connection. Religion has become a major theme of Dawkins's recent writings, and here too life and mind figure into the argument in related ways. The appearance of complex design in the living world was, of course, a major argument for belief in God throughout history, and a defensible one before it was undermined by the ability of natural selection to generate the appearance of design without a designer. As Dawkins wrote in *The Blind Watchmaker,* 'Although atheism might have been logically tenable before Charles Darwin, Darwin made it possible to be an intellectually fulfilled atheist'. I believe that a parallel development has taken place with regard to beliefs about the mind. The complexity of human intelligence strikes many people as compelling evidence for the existence of a soul in the same way that the complexity of life was seen as evidence for the existence of a designer. Now that intelligence may be explicable in material terms, as a kind of information processing in neural circuitry (with the circuitry itself explicable by natural selection), this second source of intuitive support for spiritual beings is being undermined. Just as evolutionary biology made it possible to be intellectually fulfilled without creationism, computational cognitive science makes it possible to be intellectually fulfilled without dualism.

12

Rationales for Indirect Speech

The Theory of the Strategic Speaker

with J A M E S   L E E

Though I am often identified as an evolutionary psychologist, this is my only empirical paper which explicitly applies evolution to a concrete research problem. The problem, which lies at the intersection of psycholinguistics and social psychology, is why so much of human conversation is filled with innuendo, euphemism, politeness, and other forms of shilly-shallying. Why don't people just say what they mean?

The puzzle weighed on me ever since the "development office" (nice euphemism) of my university employer started asking me to serve as the bait in their fund-raising dinners, in which a high-rolling alumnus or philanthropist is wined and dined until the moment is right to pop the question of a major cash donation, usually couched in euphemisms like "vision" and "leadership." The engineered conviviality, with a lascivious proposition hanging in the air the whole time, reminded me of nothing so much as a hot date, and the psychologist in me wondered why the two scenarios seemed so similar. I sketched out a theory in The Stuff of Thought, and when James Lee, now a rising star in behavioral genetics and evolutionary psychology, first arrived at Harvard as a graduate student, I asked if he wanted to work with me on ways to make it more precise and to subject it to empirical tests. This is the result. In addition to the intellectual and empirical work he put into the project, James deserves credit for the literary allusions that begin and end the paper.

In the film *Schindler's List* (Spielberg, 1993), after some of Schindler's Jewish workers have been deported to Auschwitz, he negotiates with an SS commandant for their release. The commandant says, "It is not my task to interfere with the processes that take place down here. What makes you think that I can help you?" Schindler replies, "Allow me to express the reason," and empties a satchel of diamonds onto the table. The commandant says, "I could have you arrested." Schindler's response: "I'm protected by powerful friends. You should know that." This leaves the commandant at a loss. Finally he says, "I'm not saying that I am accepting them. All I say is that

I am not comfortable with them on the table." The commandant then scoops up the diamonds and jams them into his pocket.

No one who watches this conversation can avoid filling in the subtext of bribes, threats, solicitations, and denials that pass between these characters. Yet the terms of those transactions are never stated explicitly. Schindler does not say, "If you release my workers, I will give you the diamonds" or "If you have me arrested, I will have you punished." Nor does the commandant say, "If you reward me, I will release the workers" or "I accept your offer but will deny it to third parties."

Linguists refer to such innuendoes as *off-record indirect speech acts* (P. Brown & Levinson, 1987). They may be distinguished from "on-record" indirect speech acts such as *Can you pass the salt?*, which have become so conventionalized that hearers rarely perceive the literal meaning (Gibbs, 1983; Holtgraves, 1994). Here are some other recognizable examples of off-record indirect speech:

- "I hear you're the foreman of the jury in the Soprano trial. It's an important civic responsibility. You have a wife and kids. We know you'll do the right thing." [a threat]
- "Gee, officer. I was thinking that maybe the best thing would be to take care of the ticket here, without going through a lot of paperwork." [a bribe]
- "Would you like to come up and see my etchings?" [a sexual advance]
- "We're counting on you to show leadership in our Campaign for the Future." [a solicitation for a donation]

Off-record indirect speech is a phenomenon with both scientific and practical importance. The puzzle for social psychology and psycholinguistics is why people so often communicate in ways that seem inefficient and error-prone rather than stating their intentions succinctly, clearly, and unambiguously. The practical importance lies in the many legal cases that hinge on the interpretation of indirect speech. Examples include the 1991 Senate confirmation hearing for Supreme Court nominee Clarence Thomas, which debated whether his sexual banter with supervisee Anita Hill was a sexual come-on; the 2008 arrest of Massachusetts State Senator Dianne Wilkerson, whose acceptance of $2,000 "in appreciation of her efforts" to obtain a liquor license for a client was treated as a case of bribery; and the 2009 offer by Robert Halderman to sell a screenplay to David Letterman depicting his sexual relationships with staffers, which led to Halderman's arrest for attempted blackmail. The ambiguities of indirect speech are also a major source of misunderstanding and conflict within personal relationships (Tannen, 1991).

Indirect speech has long been studied by linguists and philosophers (Cole & Morgan, 1975; Grice, 1975; Horn, 2003; Lakoff, 1973), who have documented the relationship between the form of an utterance and the intended meaning of the speaker, and the processes by which speakers encode these meanings and hearers recover them. A widespread assumption is that people tacitly respect Grice's (1975) *cooperative principle*: that a speaker and hearer cooperate to move a conversation forward, the hearer filling in whatever propositions are necessary to preserve the assumption that the speaker is trying to be informative, truthful, clear, and relevant.

This literature says little about the social psychological question of why speakers veil their utterances in the first place, given that indirect speech, by definition, flouts the cooperative principle's maxims to be clear, concise, truthful, and relevant. The social motives behind indirect speech have been explored in important synthetic works by P. Brown and Levinson (1987) and Clark (1996). In their theory of politeness, P. Brown and Levinson extended the cooperative principle to the speaker and hearer's cooperation in maintaining *face* (from the idiom *to save face*)—the degree of approval and autonomy that a person can claim in social interactions (Goffman, 1967). Because a speaker's request for attention or favors is a threat to the hearer's face, speakers soften their requests with several kinds of politeness. These include assurances of sympathy (*positive politeness*, as in compliments and terms of endearment and familiarity) and acknowledgments of deference (*negative politeness*, as in apologies, hedges, and interrogatives). In this theory, politeness strategies are arranged on a continuum of face-restoring power: positive politeness, negative politeness, on-record indirect speech, and off-record indirect speech.

Clark's *joint action theory* also places cooperation at the center of language use. He introduces the theory as follows:

> Language use is really a form of *joint action*. A joint action is one that is carried out by an ensemble of people acting in coordination with each other. As simple examples, think of two people waltzing, paddling a canoe, playing a piano duet, or making love. (Clark, 1996, p. 3)

A key rationale for indirect speech in this theory is the joint striving for *equity*. If costs and benefits are not balanced for a speaker or hearer, it threatens their face, leads to distress, and sets up a shared goal of redressing the imbalance through compensating action or speech or a reinterpretation of the goods at stake (Walster, Walster, & Berscheid, 1978). In one of Clark's examples,

> Alan offers Barbara some Manzanilla sherry, and she accepts. When Alan proposes the offer, he puts his face at risk. What if she takes the sherry without adequate recompense? And when Barbara takes up his proposal, she puts her own face at risk. What if she cannot repay him for the favor? (Clark, 1996, p. 294)

Clark noted that Barbara might save face by saying *Yes please* (deferring to his autonomy) or *That'd be lovely* (augmenting his self-worth). In politeness theory, these would be classified as examples of negative politeness and on-record indirect speech, respectively.

Despite the many theoretical and empirical achievements of these pure-cooperation theories, they are less successful in explaining certain aspects of off-record indirect speech. Prima facie, pure-cooperation theories appear inconsistent with the fact that off-record indirect speech is often accompanied by significant interpersonal *conflict,* as in the Thomas, Wilkerson, and Letterman legal cases. Nor does the complete harmony of joint actions such as waltzing, canoeing, or sex seem like an apt analogy to the substantial tension and misunderstanding that surrounds indirect speech. Just consider the kind of conversation that often *precedes* sex, namely, the nervous, tentative, and wary exchanges that go into seducing and propositioning. Emotionally fraught and potentially conflictual propositions, such as bribes, threats, and sexual come-ons, are rarely discussed in the literature on cooperation theories, despite their being among the prime scenarios in which off-record indirect speech is called for. Such come-ons may be highly indirect, but they are unlikely to be clad in the kinds of constructions that protect the hearer's face in other requests, such as *Please, Do you think you might,* or *I'm sorry to have to ask but.*

Empirical research designed to test politeness theory also casts doubt on its conjecture that off-record indirect speech lies at the maximally polite end of a continuum of strategies (Dillard, Wilson, Tusing, & Kinney, 1997; Holtgraves & Yang, 1990). Raters often deem off-record indirect speech to be *less* polite than negative (deferential) politeness, and sometimes as downright rude (e.g., as in *Didn't I already ask you to empty the dishwasher?*).

A second empirical complication for pure-cooperation theories is that positive and negative politeness and the face threats that call for them have been found to differ not just in degree but also in kind. Positive politeness (sympathy) tends to accompany threats to solidarity, such as criticizing a friend, whereas negative politeness (deference) tends to accompany threats to power, such as an onerous request. The neglect of qualitative differences among kinds of relationships also raises questions about the appeal to equity in Clark's (1996) theory. If, following Alan's offer of sherry to Barbara at a dinner party, she were to attempt to restore equity by offering to pay him for the drink, or if he were to ask her to return the favor in the form of a sexual kiss, the exchange would result not in a reduction of emotional tension but an elevation, experienced as puzzlement, awkwardness, or shock.

We suggest that the limitations of traditional cooperation theories in explaining off-record indirect speech acts may be remedied by two insights from evolutionary biology. The first is that social relationships among conspecifics never involve a perfect overlap of interests (and hence full cooperation) but always entail at least a partial conflict of interest (Trivers, 1985). This in turn affects their mode of communication in ways that may be expected to flout the cooperative principle.[1] Dawkins and Krebs (1978) proposed that animal signals are often attempts to manipulate the behavior of receivers to the signaler's advantage. This would make signaling the product of an evolutionary arms race between strategic signalers and skeptical receivers, who in turn attempt to deduce the state of signalers to their own advantage. At an equilibrium under natural selection, however, it is likely that both signaler and receiver benefit from the exchange; otherwise the signaling system should cease to exist (Maynard Smith & Harper, 2003). Therefore we should expect a long-standing system of communication among living things to reflect a complex mixture of cooperation *and* conflict.

The second insight is that relationships among conspecifics are expected to fall into discrete kinds, in which the dyads follow qualitatively different sets of strategies depending on their genetic relationship, history, sex, and relative strength. These biologically significant relationship types include dominance, mutualism, parenting, reciprocal altruism, short-term mating, and long-term pair bonding. The hypothesis that humans differentiate their relationships into different kinds has been called *relational models theory* (Fiske, 1991, 1992) and *relationship-specific social psychology* (Wilson & Daly, 1997). It has profound implications for communication, suggesting that the tensions introduced into a relationship by a speech act may not fit along a single continuum (e.g., of face threat or equity imbalance) but may involve uncertainty over which of several possible models of relationship should be in force, each prescribing a different degree and kind of cooperation.

Motivated by these considerations, we have sketched a theory that explains off-record indirect speech in terms of the strategies of speakers in negotiating relationship types under conditions of uncertainty (Pinker, Nowak, & Lee, 2008), which game theorists call *identification problems* (Schelling, 1960). Rather than presupposing full cooperation between speaker and hearer, the theory posits that indirect speech is deployed to negotiate whether and what kind of cooperation should be in effect between them. The logic of this *strategic speaker theory*—that indirect speech supplies plausible deniability in identification problems—is most easily explained with scenarios in which the speaker's expected costs and benefits can be quantified. Such a scenario occurs, for example, when a motorist detained by a police officer contemplates a bribe to evade a traffic ticket. A simple game-theoretic model, which formalizes the intuition of "plausible deniability," specifies the conditions under which indirect speech is the optimal solution for a speaker in such a situation.

Crucially, the same game-theoretic logic applies to purely social situations, such as making a sexual overture or bribing a maitre d', where there may be no legal risks or quantifiable incentives. We suggest that the negotiation of which relational model should be in force defines a payoff matrix that is isomorphic to the one governing the bribe scenario, but where the costs are emotional rather than financial or legal. Indirect speech allows plausible deniability of a breach of a relationship type and thus avoids the aversive social and emotional consequences that would be triggered by such a breach.

Finally, the strategic speaker theory, when extended to higher orders of deniability, can explain why indirect speech is used even when there is little uncertainty in the speaker's intent or the hearer's values regarding the relationship switch. By connecting the qualitative distinctions among relationship types with the digital nature of language, the theory explains why a thinly disguised request that fools no one is still more socially acceptable than the same request expressed baldly. In this article, we develop the theory in full, work out its psychological implications, and report several studies that test its predictions.

Part 1: Indirectness as a Distinct Strategy From Politeness

We motivate the need for the theory of the strategic speaker by showing that pure-cooperation theories, though successful in explaining politeness and on-record indirect speech, are less successful in explaining off-record indirect speech. This extends the conclusions of earlier studies finding that off-record indirect speech does not seem to be an extreme form of politeness but serves largely different purposes (Dillard et al., 1997; Holtgraves & Yang, 1990).

In politeness theory the magnitude of any potential face threat is a monotonically increasing function of three factors: (a) the *social distance* between speaker and hearer, (b) the *power* of the hearer relative to the speaker, and (c) the *degree of imposition* inherent in the speaker's request. Increases in any of these factors lead speakers to use politeness strategies to nullify the resulting face threat. As mentioned, politeness theory posits four strategies that fall along a continuum: positive politeness (sympathy, concern, or camaraderie); negative politeness (respect or deference); and indirectness (the use of a wording that does not literally amount to a request), further subdivided into on-record (pro forma or clichéd) and off-record (novel and oblique) requests. A minor face threat might warrant only positive politeness, whereas a serious threat might need to be cloaked in indirect speech. According to this logic, indirect speech acts are more polite when they are off record because only then can the speaker plausibly deny that he has made a request.

We now present a study which shows that people sometimes favor direct (but polite) requests, even when social distance, power gap, and degree of imposition are manipulated to levels comparable to those in scenarios favoring indirectness. These results indicate that politeness and indirectness do not reside on the same scale but are rather distinct mechanisms elicited by different types of social encounters.

Experiment 1

Politeness theory posits that once a summed face threat crosses a certain threshold, speakers making requests should shift their preference from being direct (but polite) to being indirect. We test this prediction by manipulating the three face-threat factors and showing that they indeed affect politeness but do not push speakers into indirectness. Conversely, social scenarios that pose identification problems (in particular, about whether a hearer is willing to switch the qualitative nature of the relationship) elicit indirectness rather than politeness.

METHOD

Participants. Participants filled out a questionnaire hosted by Amazon Mechanical Turk (www.mturk.com) at home without any supervision by an experimenter.[2] Participants had to be at least 18 years old and fluent English speakers. One hundred twenty-eight participants began the questionnaire; 114 completed it. Participants were given $5 as compensation.

Materials. The questionnaire consisted of four fictional scenarios: (a) a man asking a woman for sex at the end of a date (seduction), (b) a driver attempting to bribe a police officer in order to avoid a ticket (bribe), (c) a professor threatening a talented student with the loss of a scholarship if she does not work in his lab (threat), and (d) a new employee at a finance firm asking a coworker or supervisor for help with a difficult statistical analysis (favor). All four scenarios are given in Appendix A.

The favor scenario was designed to allow for straightforward manipulations of the face-threat variables. Each participant saw eight distinct versions of this scenario in a within-participants design. The eight cells resulted from crossing three factors with two levels each: (a) whether the hearer is another new employee or the speaker's supervisor (a manipulation of power), (b) whether the hearer was the speaker's roommate in college for 3 years or someone whom the speaker hardly knows (a manipulation of social distance), and (c) whether the speaker needs 10–15 min of the hearer's time or more than 3 hr (a manipulation of imposition).

Each scenario was followed by several questions. The first three questions asked participants to rate, on a scale from 1 to 5, the following aspects of the scenario: (a) the extent to which one character was in a position of authority over the other, (b) how socially distant the characters were, and (c) how much of an imposition it would be to grant the speaker's request. The latter question gave participants a *don't know* option in addition to the ratings from 1 to 5.

Participants were then given five different speech acts and asked to rate, on a scale from 1 to 7, how likely it would be for the speaker to use each one to convey the request. The five speech acts were designed to be (a) blunt, (b) positively polite, (c) negatively polite, (d) somewhat indirect, and (e) very indirect. Within each scenario participants always rated the speech acts in this order. The positively and negatively polite speech acts were worded in accordance with the diagnostic features documented by P. Brown and Levinson (1987). The blunt speech act employed a bare minimum of politeness. The blunt and polite speech acts were all unambiguous regarding the nature of the speaker's request. In contrast, the two off-record indirect speech acts did not literally amount to requests. Here we give the speech acts used in the favor scenario:

- "Please help me out with this analysis." [blunt]
- "So, [hearer], one workaholic to another. I, uh, was thinking that it would be really good for the whole company if I got this report done on time. Could you please help me with it?" [positively polite]
- "I'm really sorry to bother you, and I wouldn't ask this if it wasn't hugely important. But do you think it might be possible to step through this analysis with me? It would be a real life-saver." [negatively polite]
- "I really admire you, [hearer]. You have the perfect background for this. I wish someone could have told me in school that this stuff would be really invaluable in my work." [somewhat indirect]
- "Oh, I can't believe this. I'm probably going to miss the deadline because of this problem." [very indirect]

After rating each of the speech acts, participants had to select the one that they thought was closest to what the speaker would actually say, with the option of rephrasing the closest selection in their own words if desired. This was to ensure that the selection would not be overly affected by the specific wordings that we chose.

Procedure. The 11 scenarios (seduction, bribe, threat, and eight cells of favor) were arranged in 32 distinct orders. The different versions of the favor scenario were always adjacent. The favor scenarios as a group were rotated along with the bribe, seduction, and threat scenarios in a Latin square. For each of these four possible orderings, the favor scenarios were rotated among themselves in a Latin square. There were eight such orderings of the favor scenarios, leading to 32 orders in total. A maximum of four participants were allowed to complete each order.

RESULTS

We first tested the validity of participants' ratings of face threat by seeing whether each rating scale in the favor scenario was most strongly influenced by the corresponding manipulation in the design of the materials. Ratings of the power gap were influenced most strongly by our manipulation of the power gap (*effect size* = 1.6 Likert points, 4 times that of the next strongest manipulation), though they were somewhat influenced by the other manipulations as well ($p < .01$). The ratings of social closeness were significantly affected only by the manipulation of social closeness itself ($p < .001$). The ratings of imposition were most strongly influenced by the manipulation of imposition (*effect size* = 1.1 Likert points, 3 times that of the next largest manipulation), though they were also affected by the other manipulations

Table 12.1 **Results of Experiment 1: Within-Participants Manipulation**

Speech act	Intercept[a]	Power gap	Social distance	Imposition
Blunt	4.52	−0.37***	−1.17***	−0.03
Positively polite	3.11	−0.25**	−0.09	0.03
Negatively polite	4.58	0.20*	0.54***	0.12
Somewhat indirect	3.51	0.28**	−0.02	0.26**
Very indirect	3.67	−0.46***	−0.77***	0.26**

[a] The average Likert rating of how likely it would be for the speaker to use the speech act when power gap, social distance, and degree of imposition were all set at the lowest level.

*p <.05.   ** p <.01.   *** p <.001.

(p <.001). Thus the ratings of the face-threat variables are sensitive to the underlying constructs.

We next examined whether manipulations of the face-threat factors in the favor scenarios had the effects on language predicted by politeness theory. We estimated the effect of each face-threat manipulation on participants' endorsement of each speech act by restricted maximum likelihood (REML), treating participant variability as a random effect (see Table 12.1). Each entry in the last three columns reflects the effect of increasing the magnitude of the face-threat factor on the attractiveness of the speech act in that row.

The blunt speech act was surprisingly popular. In fact, when all face-threat factors theoretically favored minimal politeness, the blunt and negatively polite speech acts received nearly equal mean ratings. As the face-threat factors were manipulated to favor more politeness, the ratings of these two speech acts diverged in precisely the manner predicted by politeness theory, with the negatively polite speech act becoming more popular and the blunt speech act less so. The effects of manipulating degree of imposition were not significant for either the blunt or negatively polite speech act, but the signs of these effects were correctly predicted.

The positively polite speech act was surprisingly unpopular and relatively insensitive to manipulations. It may be that the presumption of friendliness and shared goals inherent in positive politeness strikes participants as manipulative or presumptuous in this kind of situation. This confirms earlier suggestions that the positive and negative politeness strategies may not always be ordered along a single dimension (Holtgraves, 2002; Lim & Bowers, 1991; K. Tracy, 1990).[3]

As predicted by politeness theory, the somewhat indirect speech act received higher ratings as power gap and degree of imposition were increased. However, the ratings of this speech act never approached those given to the negatively polite speech act; participants consistently indicated that the negatively polite speech act was most appropriate in this scenario. The very indirect speech act became disfavored as the face-threat factors were manipulated to favor politeness. The participants' forced-choice responses were consistent with their ratings: The negatively polite speech act was the most popular choice in all eight cells, its share ranging from 34 percent in the cell calling for the least politeness to 60 percent in the cell calling for the most. This dispreference for indirect speech suggests that politeness theory, while accounting for the use of negative politeness in conversation, fails to account for the use of off-record indirect speech.

The second critical test comes from the seduction, bribe, and threat scenarios, which embody identification problems. Here we found a very different pattern from the preference for negative politeness holding in the favor scenario: Participants favored the two indirect speech acts over the three direct ones. To quantify this effect, we scored each forced-choice response as 1 if it endorsed one of the indirect speech acts and 0 otherwise. When these responses in each of the seduction, bribe, and threat scenarios were compared to the responses in the cell of the favor scenario where all face-threat factors favored maximal politeness, McNemar's test for paired dichotomous data showed that participants were more likely to endorse an indirect speech act in all three nonfavor scenarios—seduction: $\chi^2(1, N = 114) = 57.1, p <.001$; bribe: $\chi^2(1, N = 113) = 15.3, p <.001$; and threat: $\chi^2(1, N = 114) = 52.7, p <.001$. In the seduction scenario, 91 percent of participants opted for indirectness; in the bribe scenario, 58 percent; in the threat scenario, 86 percent. In the different cells of the favor scenario, in contrast, indirectness garnered between 21 percent and 34 percent of the responses. Responses to the Likert rating scales showed the same pattern.

Of course, it is crucial to show that the preference for indirect speech in the seduction, bribe, and threat scenarios was not just a consequence of their posing greater degrees of face threat than the favor scenario. It was not. Ratings of the three face-threat factors for these scenarios were comparable to or lower than those for the cell of the favor scenario favoring maximal politeness (see Table 12.2). As a rule of thumb, any pairwise difference within a column of Table 12.2 exceeding 0.3 is statistically significant at $\alpha = .05$. The only scenario that equaled or exceeded the favor scenario in ratings of the face-threat factors is the bribe scenario. However, in all three of the nonfavor scenarios, participants overwhelmingly favored indirect over direct requests, and out of the nonfavor scenarios it was in fact the bribe scenario that was most likely to elicit endorsement of a direct request.

One other finding highlights the mismatch between politeness theory and scenarios involving social identification problems. Intuitively, the question about the degree to which a sexual proposition from a man to a woman requests an "imposition" is ill-formed. If the woman doesn't want to have sex with the man, the prospect is so aversive that "imposition" seems an inadequate term; if she does want to, then it is not an "imposition" at all. To a lesser extent this applies to other scenarios

Table 12.2 **Results of Experiment 1: Degree of Face Threat across Scenarios**

Scenario	Power gap	Social distance	Imposition[a]
Favor[b]	4.29	4.22	4.14
Seduction	1.73	2.64	4.49
Bribe	4.68	4.49	4.08
Threat	3.89	2.92	3.60

[a] Participants who selected *don't know* were ignored in calculating these means. [b] The cell in which power gap, social distance, and degree of imposition were all set at the highest level.

involving identification problems: A police officer may be corrupt (and accept a bribe) or honest (and rebuff it); the target of a threat may find it expedient to accede to the threat, or he may defy the threatener (either to put the onus on him to enforce it or to deter similar threats in the future). For this reason, when asking the participants to rate the degree of imposition, we gave them the option *don't know*. In the different cells of the favor scenario, the proportion of participants choosing the *don't know* option ranged from 2 percent to 8 percent. In contrast, in the seduction scenario, 48 percent of the participants chose the *don't know* option; in the bribe scenario, 12 percent chose it; and in the threat scenario, 19 percent chose it. The difference between the number of *don't know* responses in the maximal cell of the favor scenario and the numbers in the seduction and threat scenarios were significant by McNemar's test, $\chi^2(1, N = 114) = 38.9, p < .001$, and $\chi^2(1, N = 114) = 5.76, p < .05$, respectively.

DISCUSSION

We confirmed the predictions of politeness theory on the relative preference between blunt and negatively polite (deferential) speech in asking favors. Increasing the three face-threat factors (power gap, social distance, degree of imposition) led participants to shift their predictions of the wording of a speaker's request for a favor from bluntness to negative politeness. However, no matter how high the ratings of the face-threat factors became, participants did not make the further shift from the negatively polite speech act to either of the indirect speech acts. This was despite the fact that ratings of the face-threat factors for some of the cells matched or exceeded the corresponding ratings in the seduction, bribe, and threat scenarios, in which participants strongly favored the indirect speech acts.

We conclude that these scenarios differ along dimensions other than the three face-threat factors. We suggest that the appeal of the *don't know* option when rating degree of imposition reveals the critical difference. When a less competent person asks a more competent person for a favor, he or she is always making some imposition, however small. But in seductions (and other interactions where the values of the hearer are not known to the speaker), the request does not have this character. For example, at the end of a pleasant evening, the woman might be perfectly willing to have sex with the man, if only she can be certain of what exactly he is requesting.

In the favor scenario, then, the values of the hearer are "identified" in that the speaker knows the request poses some imposition. In the other scenarios, however, different hearers might hold qualitatively different attitudes toward the speaker's request. The results of this study indicate that the use of indirect speech in conditions of uncertainty about the degree and nature of cooperation desired by the speaker requires an explanation beyond that provided by politeness theory and other pure-cooperation theories.

Part 2: Plausible Deniability as a Solution to the Identification Problem

To illustrate the appeal of indirect speech in identification problems, we begin with a subtype of conversation in which the costs and benefits may be quantified. Consider a motorist who has been pulled over for speeding and is considering two options: accepting the ticket or offering a bribe to the police officer. Which offers the better expected payoff? The answer is that it depends on the *values* of the officer he is facing. Bribery is a criminal offense which is punished much more harshly than a traffic violation, so if the officer is a scrupulous enforcer of the law, a bribe would lead to a more severe penalty for the driver than the ticket. The speaker thus faces an identification problem: There are two types of hearers, cooperators and antagonists. An attempted initiation of a joint endeavor with an antagonist will backfire to result in the worst possible outcome, and the speaker cannot tell the two types apart.

Suppose that the driver in the bribe scenario were constrained to obey Grice's (1975) cooperative maxims to be informative, succinct, truthful, relevant, and clear. Such a driver would therefore offer the bribe in direct speech, as an overt quid pro quo. The form of the identification problem faced by such a driver is depicted in the first two rows of the payoff matrix in Table 12.3. The driver can either accept the ticket or offer a direct bribe such as *If you let me go without a ticket, I'll give you fifty dollars*. Given the large potential cost inherent in offering a bribe to an honest officer, however, the driver might instead refrain from bribing and swallow the smaller cost of the ticket.

But now suppose that the driver is allowed to deviate from the maxims by veiling the bribe in an obscure, ambiguous, or irrelevant comment, such as *So maybe the best thing would be to take care of that here* (represented as the third row of Table 12.3).[4] Suppose that a dishonest officer can detect the bribe in the innuendo using mechanisms of implicature documented by linguists (P. Brown & Levinson, 1987; Clark, 1996; Grice, 1975; Holtgraves, 2002; Horn, 2003; Searle, 1975). And suppose that

Table 12.3 **Payoff Matrix for Speeding Motorist**

	Type of officer	
Driver's strategy	*Dishonest officer*	*Honest officer*
Don't bribe	Traffic ticket	Traffic ticket
Direct bribe	Go free	Arrest for bribery
Indirect bribe	Go free	Traffic ticket

an honest officer, hearing the same innuendo, could not make a bribery charge stick in court by the high standard of proof beyond a reasonable doubt. Then the indirect speech may allow the driver to combine the large benefit of bribing a dishonest officer with the relatively small cost of submitting to an honest one.

Though the appeal of indirect speech in attaining plausible deniability may seem like common sense, more rigorous examination shows that indirectness is not advantageous across the board but only with a particular configuration of expected payoffs. The circumstances under which indirect speech is optimal can be derived from a simple game-theoretic model (Pinker et al., 2008). Let y denote the expectation of the cost borne by the driver. This cost depends on: (a) q, the proportion of officers who are honest; (b) c_0, the cost of the bribe; (c) c_1, the cost of the ticket (which must be greater than the cost of the bribe, or else it would never pay to bribe); (d) c_2, the cost of an arrest for bribery (which must be greater than the cost of the ticket, or else it would always pay to bribe); and (e) p, the probability that an officer will interpret the driver's statement as an attempted bribe and act accordingly—accepting the bribe or arresting the driver, depending on whether the officer is cooperative (corrupt) or antagonistic (honest). p increases monotonically with the directness of the statement, d, which is the crucial linguistic variable. It reflects the number of inferential steps that must be carried out in the implicature to get from the literal content of the sentence to the meaning intended by the speaker. Critically, the linguistic variable of directness must correspond to the decision-theoretic variable of the probability that a signal reflects one state of affairs or another.

It can be shown that if corrupt and honest officers use the same decision function when acting on a driver's statement, indirect speech is never optimal. There exists a critical proportion of officers who are honest, $q_c = (c_1 - c_0)/(c_2 - c_0)$, such that if $q > q_c$, the optimal strategy for the driver is not to attempt a bribe at all ($p = 0$), and if $q < q_c$, the optimal strategy for the driver is to offer a direct bribe in clear and unmistakable terms ($p = 1$). Under these assumptions, therefore, the model predicts that indirect speech should never be attractive to a speaker. If the proportion of antagonistic listeners is high, he should remain silent; if it is low, he should offer the bribe overtly.

There is, however, a set of conditions in which indirect speech *is* optimal: when the two types of hearers *differ* in their probabilities of responding to the speaker's first move. Suppose that a corrupt officer must meet a threshold of certainty (say 80 percent) that a driver's utterance is an attempted bribe before he will remove the cash from a proffered wallet and send the driver on his way. Now, if an honest officer must meet an even higher threshold (say 99 percent) before he will arrest the driver for bribery, a rational driver should pitch his utterance at a directness level intended to induce a level of certainty in the hearer somewhere between 80 percent and 99 percent. (Of course, the driver need not be aware of the rationale behind his choice of words.)[5]

The critical assumption is that over some range of directness, a hearer antagonistic to the speaker sets a higher threshold for action than one who is completely cooperative. This is plausible in the case of an attempted bribe, because even if an honest officer believes just as strongly as his corrupt counterpart that a given utterance is a bribe, he might be less willing to act on his belief because of the doubtful prospects of a successful prosecution, the risk of a lawsuit for wrongful arrest, the additional paperwork, and other costs. These contingencies could easily be modeled in the payoff matrix for the hearer.

Note how this model differs from the traditional assumption that indirect speech is governed by pure cooperation: The strategic speaker is using indirectness not to work with the hearer in pursuing a joint goal (in this case, to enforce the law) but rather to subvert that goal.

The theory's central concept of deniability is related, but not identical, to the concept of *defeasibility* in the linguistic literature on implicature (Grice, 1975; Horn, 2003). An implicature is said to be defeasible if it is not logically entailed by the utterance and can be canceled or suspended without contradiction. For example, *Some men are chauvinists* naturally leads listeners to infer that the speaker also means that some men are not chauvinists. But that implicature is not logically entailed and can be canceled, as in the sequence *Some men are chauvinists; indeed, all are.* (Similarly: *They got married and had a baby, but not in that order.*) Though deniability requires defeasibility, the reverse is not true; defeasibility does not require that the speaker have a self-interested reason to cancel the implicature with antagonistic hearers but not with cooperative hearers. In the standard examples in linguistics, defeasibility is exploited purely for rhetorical purposes, and the utterance is meant to be understood in the same way by all hearers.

Plausible deniability is also distinct from the maxim "provide options" in theories of politeness (P. Brown & Levinson, 1987; Lakoff, 1973), which underlies a range of constructions of deferential politeness such as *If you please* and *Do you think you might*. This maxim is intended to ease the face threat of a request directed to a cooperative hearer, with no strategic consequences; it is not a strategy designed to protect the interests of the speaker when addressing a potentially antagonistic hearer. Indeed, Experiment 1 gave participants the choice between a provide-options construction (*Do you think it might be possible*) and an indirect request and found that the two are preferred in complementary circumstances.

The model of a strategic speaker has testable implications. First, the indirectness of speech should be perceived not just as a social gesture that redresses the hearer's face (such as the use of constructions like *Please, Can you,* and other politeness reflexes) but as one that monotonically affects the hearer's interpretation and decision. That is, people should sense that the abstract linguistic variable of directness, which underlies an unlimited range of wordings, corresponds to the hearer's probability of action, and they should deploy that correspondence strategically, so as to minimize their quantifiable costs according to the payoff matrix implicit in the situation. The use of directness should thus be sensitive to variables that that go into that payoff matrix, such as the proportion of cooperative and antagonistic speakers in the population and the costs of consummating or failing to consummate a cooperative relationship, but that are omitted from theories of indirect speech that assume the relationship between speaker and hearer to be universally cooperative. Thus directness should vary even when the face-threat variables emphasized in politeness theory (power, distance, and imposition) are held constant. If, in contrast, speakers calibrate their linguistic directness only to face threat, not to payoffs and probabilities, it would undermine the hypothesis that indirectness is deployed strategically in cases where cooperation is uncertain.

The second critical prediction is that when speakers do favor indirect speech, they should also perceive that cooperative hearers (in this case, dishonest cops) have lower thresholds of action along the directness continuum than uncooperative hearers (in this case, honest cops). If there is no such difference, then strategic speaker theory would clearly be falsified, because it is only under those circumstances that indirect speech is optimal.

Experiment 2

To test the strategic speaker theory in a scenario in which costs, benefits, and decisions can be specified precisely, we had participants imagine that they were tempted to bribe a police officer. The theory does not, of course, claim that speakers develop the use of indirect speech specifically so that they can bribe officials with cash, but rather that they easily generalize the strategies of indirectness they use in everyday conversation to these more specialized (and, for our purposes, quantifiable) situations.

METHOD

Participants. Fifty-one fluent English speakers were recruited from the Harvard undergraduate student body to fill out an online questionnaire without compensation; 26 completed it.

Materials. The questionnaire was hosted on www.survey-monkey.com and was taken at home without supervision. Participants were asked to imagine themselves on a road trip through a fictitious former republic of the Soviet Union. The first part of the questionnaire was intended to familiarize participants with the scenario and payoff structures.

An excerpt from a guidebook informs participants that because corruption and bribery are rampant in this part of the world, a traveler must understand how to act in an encounter with a police officer. The guidebook then gives four versions of a scenario in which the participant imagines being pulled over by an officer who claims, falsely, that the participant was speeding. Each version differed in the values of the variables predicted to be relevant to the optimal choice of speech act: (a) the proportion of police officers in the area who are honest, (b) the cost of the expected bribe, (c) the cost of the ticket, and (d) the cost of being arrested for bribery (see Table 12.4). In each case the scenario concludes by asking participants to consider how they would phrase an offer of a bribe to extricate themselves from the situation.[6]

Participants selected one speech act from a menu of five options in response to each familiarization scenario and received one of three possible kinds of feedback on the outcome. The choice of feedback depended on the predicted outcome of the participant's response given the parameter values of the scenario:

Table 12.4 **Levels of Experimental Factors in Experiment 2**

Trial[a]	% honest (q)	Bribe (c_0)	Ticket (c_1)	Fine (c_2)
Familiarization 1	.75	$40	$280	$400
Familiarization 2	.25	$40	$280	$400
Familiarization 3	.25	$10	$280	$290
Familiarization 4	.50	$50	$350	$500
Experimental A	1	$50	$450	$500
Experimental B	1	$20	$40	$200
Experimental C	0	$40	$80	$400
Experimental D	0	$70	$630	$700
Experimental E	.90	$50	$100	$500
Experimental F	.10	$30	$60	$300
Experimental G	.90	$30	$60	$300
Experimental H	.10	$40	$360	$400

[a] The experimental trials were not administered in the listed order but according to a Latin square.

- You encountered a willing officer, but he still wrote you a ticket.
- You encountered a willing officer. He takes your bribe and drives off.
- You encountered an unwilling officer. He punishes you for attempting to bribe an officer, and you have to pay [the amount of the fine].

Participants were told to imagine themselves with $2,000 at the start of these encounters and to keep track of their total after each successive loss (ticket, successful bribe, punishment for attempted bribery). Fields in the questionnaire were provided for participants to type in their totals.

At this point the experimental trials began. Participants were told that they would visit eight different counties on a road trip, each leading to an encounter with a policeman whose status as a corrupt officer (cooperator) or honest officer (antagonist) was unknown.

Eight combinations of values were used in the experimental trials, summarized in Table 12.4. In half of the conditions, the ratios of bribe:ticket:fine were 1:9:10; in the other half, they were 1:2:10. All else being equal, the ticket inflicts a greater loss on the driver in the former conditions, so these should tilt participants toward more direct speech acts. The scalar differences do not affect these predictions. In addition, a higher proportion of officers who are honest should tilt participants toward less direct speech acts. Participants were encouraged to pay attention to the numbers, which were highlighted in bold.

After each experimental trial, participants were shown the following four speech acts in randomized order:

- "I'm very sorry, officer. If I give you a fifty, will you just let me go?" [overt]
- "I'm very sorry, officer. But I'm actually in the middle of something right now, sort of an emergency. So maybe the best thing would be to take care of this here...without going to court or doing any paperwork." [nearly overt]
- "I'm very sorry, officer. I know that I'll have to pay for my mistake." [indirect]
- "I'm very sorry, officer. I've really learned my lesson." [very vague]

Participants were asked to allot 100 "probability points" among these four speech acts, each allotment corresponding to the strength of the participant's liking for the speech act. The wording of each of these speech acts was distinct from all of those used in the familiarization trials; this was to ensure that participants were not merely learning to associate rewards and punishments with particular linguistic formulas or constructions. Participants were instructed not to carry out the allotment task unless they were certain that they understood it. No feedback was provided after participants indicated their judgments.

The speech acts used in the experimental trials were chosen in the following way. In a pilot study, 30 Harvard University students were asked to rate the directness of eight wordings of a bribe on a scale from 0 to 100. From these eight wordings, we selected four that showed separation from each other in a parallel boxplot (p <.01 by the Wilcoxon signed rank test) and designated them as *very vague, indirect, nearly overt*, and *overt* accordingly. (The two wordings of intermediate directness were the same as those used in the Experiment 1 bribe scenario.)

As an additional check that participants interpreted a speaker's directness as a cue for probability of intent, we asked them to estimate, for each of the four wordings, the probability that a corrupt officer would interpret it as an attempted bribe and carry out the exchange. And to test the critical prediction about differing thresholds for cooperative and antagonistic hearers, the questionnaire asked for the probability that an honest officer would respond to that sentence by arresting the driver for attempted bribery.

Procedure. All participants completed the familiarization trials in the same order. Before the start of the experimental trials, participants were asked to select the top choice in a drop-down menu displaying the numbers 1 through 8 in a random order. The participant was then directed by a link to a sequence of experimental trials corresponding to that number. These sequences were generated by a Latin square.

RESULTS

We summarized each participant's responses to the experimental trials by treating the allotment of points as a probability distribution over the four sentences. We then assigned the sentences the values 1, 2, 3, and 4 in order of increasing directness and calculated the expectation. This quantity can be interpreted as the expected directness of the participant's bribe. We treated this as the outcome variable in mixed linear models estimated by REML, incorporating participant variability as a random effect and the relative cost of the ticket and the proportion of officers who are honest as fixed effects. The relative cost of the ticket was dichotomized as $1/0$.

Three participants gave the same stereotyped response (equal weight to all options or all weight on one) to four or more consecutive experimental trials and were removed from the dataset, leaving 23 for analysis. At least two participants completed each of the cells.

Figure 12.1 displays the cell means. The fixed effect of ticket cost was statistically significant, $t(18) = 2.19$, p <.05. The fixed effects of the proportion of officers who are honest, relative to a baseline of no honest officers, were also significant, $t(18) = 4.77, p$ <.001; $t(18) = 14.25, p$ <.001; $t(18) = 15.88, p$ <.001. These findings are consistent with the predictions of the strategic speaker model.

Figure 12.2 shows the perceived probabilities that the two types of officers will respond to speech acts varying in directness, a test of the hypothesis that indirect speech is used strategically. Setting aside a couple of outliers, we see that the direct offer was believed to lead deterministically either to an arrest or to a consummated

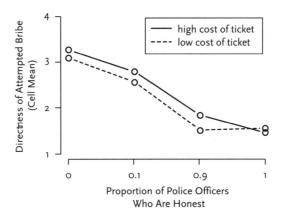

Figure 12.1. Mean preferred directness of an attempted bribe in Experiment 2. Increments along the *x*-axis are merely ordinal.

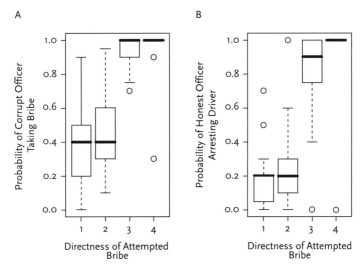

Figure 12.2. Parallel boxplots of Experiment 2 participants' estimations of probabilities that (a) corrupt officers will interpret the speech acts as bribes and take the money and (b) honest officers will interpret the speech acts as attempted bribes and arrest the driver.

transaction. For the three speech acts of varying indirectness, participants tended to believe that honest officers are less likely to arrest the driver for attempted bribery than corrupt officers are to accept the implicit offer. These tendencies were statistically significant by the signed rank test ($p < .01$). The results confirm that the linguistic variable that differentiates "vague" from "overt" sentences (as judged by the participants in the pilot study) is related to the perceived probability that a hypothetical speaker will interpret and act on the sentence as an actual request, with predicted asymmetries between cooperative and antagonistic speakers.

DISCUSSION

This study confirms two predictions of the strategic speaker model. The first is that the choice of directness in speech is affected not just by the traditional variables of power, status, and imposition but by the payoff structure inherent in the different possible interpretations and actions of the hearer. Note that participants were never told to attend to the directness of the response options; nor did the familiarization trials expose them to those wordings. They had to infer that the directness dimension was relevant to the payoffs and extend it to their choice of new wordings. The finding that participants applied linguistic directness to maximizing payoffs under uncertainty is consistent with the hypothesis that the directness of a speech act is an adaptive response to a game-theoretic identification problem.

The second confirmed prediction of the strategic speaker model is that people assume that the threshold for appropriate action set by an antagonistic hearer to be higher than the one set by a cooperative hearer. This condition allows an off-record indirect speech act to be the optimal solution to an identification problem.

Of course, scenarios in which the costs and benefits of a hearer's interpretation can be quantified are not the most common context in which indirect speech is used. In everyday life, we would expect that intangible social and emotional costs, not just money, define the payoff matrices that call for indirect speech. One finding in this experiment underscores that expectation. Figure 12.1 shows that when conditions favored a bald proposition (0 percent policemen honest), participants often did not conform to the seemingly rational response of placing their entire probability mass on the most direct speech act, but rather opted to be relatively vague. This bias is not attributable to experimental noise or a tendency of the participants to avoid extreme responses. When the payoffs militated toward the opposite extreme and ruled out an attempted bribe entirely (100 percent policemen honest), responses were bunched more tightly at the vague end of the scale. Nothing in the model (at least when implemented with dollar values) predicts this asymmetry. Participants must have felt that there is some emotional cost incurred in a botched encounter with a police officer over and above any state-enforced penalties. We now turn to the intangible social and emotional costs that are the more typical payoffs for the strategic speaker.

Part 3: Relationship Negotiation

Though everyday social life may lack the formal regulations that allow plausible deniability to be quantified, it often presents similar contingencies in the currency of emotional discomfort. Consider a case that is close to bribing a police officer: bribing a restaurant maitre d' in order to be seated immediately despite having no reservation. No one has ever been fined or imprisoned for attempting to bribe a maitre d', yet in a telling real-life example, a writer given this assignment by a magazine editor reported that he always tendered the bribe indirectly (*Is there any way to shorten my wait?*) rather than directly (*I will give you $20 if you seat me immediately*; Feiler, 2000). Similarly, the common expectation is that a man propositioning a woman after dinner would use an indirect come-on (*Would you like to come up for a cup of coffee?*) rather than a direct one (*Would you like to come up and have sex?*). Once again, no one would lead the man away in handcuffs if the woman were to rebuff his advance, yet he acts *as if* someone might do so, just as in the scenario with the driver and the police officer.

To apply the model of the strategic speaker to cases where tangible costs are absent, we must identify the intangible costs that define the requisite payoff matrix. One possibility is the implicit currency of social equity invoked by Clark (1996), who noted that actions leading to an equity imbalance between speaker and hearer prompt them to redress it with compensating actions or verbal gestures. The problem for this account is that a bribe or a sexual favor offers the opportunity for perfect equity if it is mutually agreed upon, yet merely broaching such a possibility can lead to enormous emotional tension. This suggests that emotional tension is not just a matter of equity imbalances. Not all relationships are governed by equity, and those that are may differ in which resources may be legitimately entered into the balance sheet. We suggest that it is the very process by which two people choose to enter an equity relationship (or not) that gives rise to the relevant emotional costs.

Qualitative differences among relationship types, and the emotional costs of uncertainty regarding which one applies, have been explored in cross-cultural detail by Fiske and his collaborators (Fiske, 1991, 1992; Fiske & Tetlock, 1997; Haslam, 1994a, 1994b). They proposed that humans use just four discrete *relational models* to govern their interactions. Each is defined by a distinct calculus for the apportionment of resources, and each has a distinct evolutionary basis. Humans assign every relationship and resource to one of the four models, but the assignments can vary with the culture and sometimes can be renegotiated dynamically by individual dyads.

The first model is *communal sharing*. Arising from the evolutionary forces of *kin selection* (Hamilton, 1964; Maynard Smith, 1964) and *mutualism* (Tooby & Cosmides, 1996), it applies to relationships among family members, between spouses, and among close friends with a strong overlap of interests. Partners in a relationship of communal sharing bond through signals of physical union such as bodily contact and common meals or rituals, and the hallmark of such relationships is the free sharing of resources with minimal regard for equity balances.

The second is *authority ranking*, which governs individuals at different levels of a dominance hierarchy. Signaled by signs of size, strength, and priority, it empowers a dominant individual to seize resources at will (Maynard Smith, 1982), again with little concern for equity.

The third model is *equality matching*, which implements the evolutionary logic of *reciprocal altruism* (Trivers, 1971) and other ways of apportioning resources on an equitable basis. It governs relationships among acquaintances, neighbors, and trad-ing partners, is defined by more-or-less explicit mechanisms of ensuring equity, and may be negotiated by verbal contracts.

Fiske's taxonomy includes a fourth model called *market pricing*, which applies to transactions among buyers, sellers, lenders, and middlemen in a modern monetary economy. Unlike the other three relationship types, market pricing is not a universal feature of human societies (D. E. Brown, 1991) and does not come naturally even to participants in a complex modern economy (Caplan, 2002). People instead tend to regress toward equality matching, with its face-to-face exchanges of tangible quanti-ties. For this reason we do not distinguish equality matching and market pricing.

When two people perceive that one of these relational models applies to their interaction in a given context, each tacitly accepts the designated kinds of transac-tions as socially legitimate. Transactions appropriate to other models, in contrast, elicit feelings of awkwardness or, if they are deliberate and sustained, moralistic anger (Fiske & Tetlock, 1997; Tetlock, 2003). For example, a husband can help himself to an hors d'oeuvre from his wife's plate or vice-versa (communal sharing), but an employee cannot snatch an hors d'oeuvre from the plate of his supervisor (violation of authority ranking). Similarly, the sale of a car or house can feel perfectly comfort-able between strangers or acquaintances (equality matching or market pricing), but it becomes awkward if conducted between close friends (a violation of communal sharing). As these examples suggest, within a given culture relational models are not assigned to dyads across the board but may be differentiated according to the resource. A professor and graduate student may implement communal sharing in most social resources (e.g., priority in line in a cafeteria) but authority ranking in professional resources (e.g., use of lab equipment); platonic opposite-sex friends may obey communal sharing for most resources other than sexuality.

When one party breaches the relational model currently in force, the result is one of the "self-conscious emotions" such as awkwardness, embarrassment, or shame (Haidt, 2003; J. L. Tracy, Robins, & Tangney, 2007). These are aversive emotions that pain speakers in the present and motivate them to avoid similar affronts in the future. Blushes, restless eye movements, stammering, confusion, and other invol-untary signs of shame may thus serve as *honest signals* of the speaker's remorse and concomitant resolve to refrain in the future from similar offenses (Hauser, 1996; Maynard Smith & Harper, 2003). This interpretation is consistent with the fact that displays of shame and awkwardness appear only in the presence of others and tend to be particularly intense in the presence of the wronged individual.

When the violation of a relational model is not accidental or transient but delib-erate and protracted, the actions are not just embarrassing but are stigmatized by taboo and may be formally criminalized. This may happen when a person proposes to allot resources that are normally governed by communal sharing or author-ity ranking according to the rules of equality matching or market pricing instead. Examples include prostitution; extortion; the solicitation of a quid pro quo sexual favor; the sale of votes, organs, or adoption rights; and buying one's way out of jury duty or military service (Fiske & Tetlock, 1997; Tetlock, Kristel, Elson, Green, & Lerner, 2000). People care intensely about the prescriptions of relational models because these models are the means by which humans agree on how to distribute the resources (material, emotional, and sexual) needed by all members of their communities for survival and reproduction.

We can now characterize the intangible costs that can drive a strategic speaker to indirect speech. Many propositions assume a relational model governing the resource in question: An onerous command assumes authority ranking; an offer to exchange assumes equality matching; a proposition for consensual sex assumes communal sharing; and so on. A speaker resorts to indirect speech when the relational model assumed by the speech act clashes with the model that currently holds between the speaker and hearer, avoiding the risk of awkwardness or shame in the same way that a briber avoids the risk of an arrest.

Consider the writer assigned to bribe a maitre d'. He reported that the assignment filled him with dread as he kept "imagining the possible retorts of some incensed maitre d': 'What kind of establishment do you think this is?' 'How dare you insult me?'" (Feiler, 2000). The reason for the anxiety, we suggest, is that whereas the relationship conventionally assumed by a maitre d' toward diners is one of authority ranking, according to which he seats diners when and where he pleases, the writer was proposing a reciprocity transaction appropriate to equality matching, according to which the maitre d' would be obligated to seat him in exchange for accepting the bribe.

This situation is now isomorphic to the identification problem in the officer–driver scenario, but now the incentives are not monetary or legal but emotional, reckoned in the awkwardness triggered by a mismatch of relational models. Table 12.5 presents the new payoff matrix. If an honest maitre d' sets a higher evidentiary standard for acting on an attempted bribe, then the optimal strategy for the diner is to employ indirect speech, such as "Is there any way to shorten my wait?"— which is in fact what the magazine writer spontaneously did (Feiler, 2000).

The reason an honest maitre d' might set a higher evidentiary standard for overtly rebuffing a bribe (compared to the one a corrupt one would set for accepting it) is also parallel to the case of the honest officer: His own payoff matrix differs from that of his corrupt counterpart. In particular, he has to anticipate the lost business from the customer and onlookers that would ensue if a diner stoutly and plausibly defended his innocence. In Part 4, we explore a more general explanation for the higher standard required by antagonistic hearers.

Note that Fiske's theory of relational models helps to explain the overall tendency to avoid directness (superimposed on the strategic use in response to the monetary payoffs) found in Experiment 2. A police officer wields a very strong dominance relationship over a detainee (far greater than that between a maitre d' and a diner). The emotional costs of impugning this relationship may have been

Table 12.5 **Payoff Matrix for Diner without a Reservation, Including the Relational Models Assumed by Speaker and Hearer**

	Type of maitre d'	
Diner's strategy	Dishonest maitre d'	Honest maitre d'
Don't bribe	Long wait (Authority/Authority)	Long wait (Authority/Authority)
Direct bribe	Instant seating (Equality/Equality)	Awkwardness (Equality/Authority)
Indirect bribe	Instant seating (Equality/Equality)	Long wait (Authority/Authority)

enough to discourage some participants from endorsing the blatant offer of a bribe even in the conditions where all officers were said to be corrupt and the financial costs should have militated toward directness.

Part 4: Higher-Order Deniability

Before turning to a further experiment testing the strategic speaker theory, we address an additional puzzling phenomenon surrounding off-record indirect speech. Regardless of whether a rebuffed proposition leads to a tangible cost (Part 2) or an emotional cost triggered by a relational model mismatch (Part 3), the strategic speaker model requires *uncertainty* on the part of the speaker regarding the hearer's values and on the part of the hearer regarding the speaker's intent. But Experiment 2 showed that speakers tended toward indirect speech even when there was no uncertainty about the hearer's values (i.e., when all officers were known to take bribes). And in everyday conversation, many indirect speech acts are so pro forma or transparent as to leave little doubt about the speaker's intent. If there is no uncertainty about either what the speaker means or whether the hearer is on the speaker's side, then how can an indirect speech act minimize the speaker's expected cost? The remaining puzzle, then, is the use of indirect speech acts even when deniability seems to be neither plausible nor required.

We propose that a special property of relational models combines with a special property of language to allow indirect speech to generate higher order kinds of deniability. Fiske and his collaborators argued that relational models are discrete systems and that for any given resource and context, a pair of people conform to only one of them (Haslam, 1994a, 1994b). And it has long been noted that language is perceived as a digital medium: one that conveys information in a discrete, context-independent, all-or-none manner, rather than a blended or graded manner (Pinker, 1994, 1999, 2007). The discreteness of language is apparent in the distinctness of words and phonemes and their arbitrary relationship to meaning: One cannot express an action partway between batting and patting with a sound partway between *bat* and *pat,* nor can the action of talking while walking be predictably expressed by the sound *twalking.*

More generally, we suggest that people implicitly perceive direct speech as being capable of expressing intentions unambiguously, losslessly, and recursively—each a feature of digital transmission. These features in turn allow indirect speech to provide forms of *higher-order plausible deniability* about the choice among relational models in a range of situations where simple plausible deniability is absent. Note that the hypothesis is not that language is in fact context-independent or certain in transmission (the very existence of indirectness and vagueness shows that it is not), only that direct speech is *perceived* as such, and that this affects people's tuning of the directness of their speech.

The first corollary of the digital-language hypothesis is that direct speech is perceived as *certain*. If, as Fiske proposed, relational models are discrete systems, then in the mutual signaling of which model applies, people must implement a mapping from a continuous domain of contexts to a discrete range of relational models. In other words, whereas the degree of certainty regarding the speaker's intention varies continuously, the prevailing relational model between two individuals can be only in one state or the other. How do two people come to a tacit agreement as to which model applies to their interactions?

This is an example of what game theorists call *coordination games,* scenarios in which several options are available to a pair of agents and they are both best off if they agree upon one of them, regardless of which it is (Clark, 1996; Schelling, 1960). In coordination games, agents often use *landmarks* or *focal points* as solutions. An example is the way that people negotiating over a price will often split the difference between their original positions or settle on a round number. In the case of people tacitly negotiating a relational model, the certainty of direct speech may similarly serve as a symbolic landmark, using the rest of the scale of indirectness as grounds for giving each other "the benefit of the doubt." For example, along the range of signals that probabilistically convey sexual intentions (physical proximity, suggestive remarks, relative seclusion, etc.), a woman may continue to treat the relationship as platonic all the way up to the point of an indubitable sexual proposition. Only at this point must she either rebuff the proposition, preserving the existing relationship type, or accept it. Under this corollary, indirect speech is useful as long as it allows for deniability to be *possible,* even when the deniability is not plausible.

A second corollary is that language is sensed to convey information *losslessly.* Just as a digital file containing text, music, or images can be transmitted and copied without degradation, the message conveyed by direct speech may be perceived as faithfully transmissible in chains of gossip—unlike indirect speech, where the underlying intention is uncertain and the context, history, and private details may be necessary to recover it (Clark & Schaefer, 1992). Gossip is widely recognized as an important component in the evolution of human cooperation (Nowak & Sigmund, 2005; Ohtsuki & Iwasa, 2006), and its prevalence in present-day social life supplies a motive for speakers to protect their reputations. Hearers in these encounters may also have similar motives, because communal disapproval of relationship-crossing transactions often extends to both parties. Thus, even a hearer known to the speaker with near certainty to be a willing cooperator may prefer that the request be tendered indirectly in order to maintain plausible deniability to outsiders or authorities. (Recall that in the dialogue from *Schindler's List* (Spielberg, 1993), the commandant hearer who granted Schindler's request tried to maintain plausible or possible deniability to third parties even in the speaker's presence.) Under this corollary, indirect speech is a means of protecting reputation from a virtual audience. Although the hearer may be nearly certain of the ulterior meaning and even act on it, the increasingly corrupted nature of the hearsay evidence available to third parties may attenuate any decrement in the reputations of the transacting parties. That is, with indirect speech, deniability is plausible *to a virtual audience,* even if it is plausible to neither the speaker nor the hearer.

A third form of higher-order plausible deniability arises from the fact that the syntactic rules of language define a recursive system: A sentence may contain a sentence of the same kind (e.g., *She thinks that he knows that she likes him*; Chomsky, 1957; Pinker, 1994). This allows speakers to convey recursive propositions, in which one idea (*She likes him*) is embedded in another (*He knows that she likes him*). When two or more parties have recursive representations of one another's state of knowledge about some proposition, their understanding is called *mutual knowledge, common knowledge,* or *common ground* (Chwe, 2001; Clark & Marshall, 1981; Lewis, 1969; Smith, 1982).[7] That is, two agents A and B have common knowledge of the proposition x when A knows x, B knows x, A knows that B knows x, B knows that A knows x, and so on. The reason that focal points, in particular, solve coordination problems is that they easily become common knowledge.

Logicians have shown that there are many logical differences between common knowledge and mere shared individual knowledge, but the simplest illustration comes from the story of the emperor's new clothes. When the little boy cried out that the emperor was naked, he did not tell the onlookers anything that they could not see with their own eyes. But he changed their state of knowledge nonetheless, because now everyone knew that everyone *else* knew that the emperor was naked, and this prompted them to challenge his authority through laughter. More precisely, if we denote the proposition THE EMPEROR IS NAKED by x, then we can see that the boy's exclamation augmented the presence of x in each hearer's knowledge base with the proposition y, by which we denote EVERYONE KNOWS x AND y, where y is recursively embedded in itself (Clark, 1996). For our purposes, the two morals of the parable are that direct language is an effective shared basis for common knowledge and that common knowledge is an effective way of proposing a change to a relational model. Common knowledge may even *inevitably* ratify such a proposal, overriding any intentions to the contrary. No matter how much fear the emperor's subjects may feel toward him—and hence no matter how strong the motive to pretend that they have not noticed the obvious—a state of common knowledge does not permit them this pretense without surrendering their tacit claims to rationality and honesty.

According to this corollary, then, direct speech (but not indirect speech) generates common knowledge, and relationships are maintained or nullified by common knowledge of intentions specific to the relational model. In this light, consider the man's invitation to view his etchings and his date's demurral. She may believe with near certainty that the invitation was a sexual solicitation, and he may believe just as strongly that she has turned it down. In other words, first-order or individual knowledge is present. But how certain is she that he understands the knowingness of her refusal? She may suspect that he is overly optimistic and cannot take a hint. On the other side, how certain is he that she has registered his understanding of her knowing refusal? "Maybe she thinks I'm dense," he might say to himself. As both speaker and hearer reel out successively deeper levels of the recursion, each level inherits the uncertainty from the previous levels and introduces some of its own. This process can quickly lead to great uncertainty at a given level of common knowledge, even if confidence at the first level is high.

The creation of higher-order uncertainty may be an important objective of indirect speech. Although our moral psychology demands that we condemn clear violations of relational models, there are also costs associated with acknowledging such a violation, especially if speaker and hearer are enmeshed in circumstances that commit them to a continuing relationship. Moreover, it may be in the interest of both parties to avoid acknowledging the violation in order to keep alive the possibility of renegotiating the relationship in the future. These dynamics may help explain a phenomenon noted by Darwin (1872/1998): that blushing and other symptoms of awkwardness often cause the beholder to feel awkward as well. A gauche direct request can embarrass a hearer by placing her in the unwanted position of being an enforcer and constraining her future options. For these reasons people may be reluctant to acknowledge relational breaches lightly, and indirect speech can cater to this reluctance by attenuating the common knowledge that would render ignoring the breach an impossible charade.

Because the lack of common knowledge provides this "out," unwilling hearers might raise their standard for how close an offer must be to a direct request before they are bound to give an appropriately antagonistic response. This may provide a sufficiently general reason for the higher standard of certainty required by antagonistic hearers before they must denounce the violation of the prevailing relational model, even in the absence of a tangible payoff structure that penalizes too-hasty whistle-blowing.

These hypotheses about focal points and mutual knowledge build on Clark's (1996) account of indirect speech, while differing from it in one crucial respect.

Clark showed how an enormous body of common knowledge, including common-sense understanding of the physical and social world and command of the vocabulary and grammar of the language, is necessary for communication to proceed (he called this body of knowledge *common ground*). Each successful communicative act in the conversation adds to the common ground. In the handling of requests, a pre-condition for the commitment of both speaker and hearer is common knowledge of each party's ability and willingness to carry out the joint project. An on-record pre-request, designed to add the hearer's ability or willingness to their common ground, can serve as an indirect proxy for the focal request itself. (For example, because a person can accede to a request to pass salt only if he or she is physically capable of passing salt, the pre-request *Can you pass the salt?*, which adds an acknowledgment of that capability to common ground, can serve as a proxy for the imperative *Pass the salt.*) Acceptance of the pre-request then locks both parties into an extended procedure to complete the joint project. But while this explanation applies naturally to on-record indirect speech, we propose that the crucial feature of an off-record indirect request is that it serves to keep the mental states of speaker and hearer *out of* common knowledge (common ground), granting both parties the freedom to treat the proposal and response in a personally convenient manner that may happen to contradict what the relational models proscribe.[8]

In sum, as a result of the qualitative nature of relational model choice and the perceived digital nature of language, indirect speech allows for higher-order deniability of the challenge to a relational model. This higher-order deniability includes deniability that is possible (even if not plausible), deniability that is plausible to a virtual audience (even if not to the speaker and hearer), and deniability of common knowledge (even if not of individual knowledge). In this way both speaker and hearer maintain their face—which, in this context, encompasses the self's projection of rationality, honesty, and proper regard for the relational models and other moral strictures.

Experiment 3

This experiment tests the strategic speaker theory as applied to relational model negotiation and higher-order deniability by assessing people's judgments of what the characters in a fictitious scenario are thinking and feeling as they produce and interpret dialogue that varies in directness. The critical predictions are as follows.

First, the linguistic variable of directness (as assessed by raters in a pilot study) should correlate with participants' assessments of the probability that a hearer interprets an indirect speech act as a relationship-changing request. (This is similar to the test in Experiment 2, but from the hearer's point of view rather than the speaker's.)

Second, the perceived probability that an antagonistic hearer would rebuff the request and act to the disadvantage of the speaker should also rise monotonically with directness, but at some levels the probability that an antagonistic hearer rebuffs the request must be lower than the probability that a cooperative hearer grants the request. (Recall that this inequality is necessary in the strategic speaker model for indirect speech to be optimal; it should also hold when the costs are not easily quantified in terms of dollar amounts and the like.)

Third, if speakers anticipate that hearers use certainty as a focal point in changing a relational model, and thus use indirect speech for possible (but not necessarily plausible) deniability, then participants should make a categorical distinction between direct speech and even highly suggestive indirect speech: The former should be judged as 100 percent certain in intent, the latter as less than 100 percent.

Fourth, if speakers anticipate that a relationship-changing proposition is less likely to be conveyed successfully by gossip if it is expressed by indirect than by direct speech (and thus use indirectness for plausible deniability to third parties), direct speech should be interpreted as confidently by a third party as by the hearer (indeed, with 100 percent certainty), whereas indirect speech should be interpreted with decreasing confidence with additional links in a gossip chain.

Fifth, if speakers anticipate that direct speech brings a relationship-changing proposition into common knowledge, and thus use indirect speech to achieve plausible deniability of that common knowledge, then participants should judge that direct speech is interpreted with the same certain or near-certain level of confidence regardless of the degree of embedding of the proposition in the mental states of the speaker and hearer.

METHOD

Participants. Thirty-one Harvard undergraduates filled out a paper questionnaire for course credit or pay ($10).

Materials. The questionnaire presented the bribe, seduction, and threat scenarios used in Experiment 1, each one concluding with the speaker putting his request to the hearer.

The questionnaire contained four versions of all three scenarios, and each participant saw all four versions in a within-participants design. Each scenario text concluded with one of four phrasings of the request. In each case the four phrasings were chosen from an original list of eight on the basis of ratings solicited in the pilot study described in Experiment 2. The criteria for choosing the four phrasings in this study were the same: separation in a parallel boxplot and significant differences between adjacent sentences by the signed rank test. (Thus, the phrasings used in the bribe scenario were identical in Experiments 2 and 3.) The scenario text was followed by a series of questions eliciting participants' interpretations of the thoughts and feelings of the characters in the scenario.

The questions conformed to the schematic outline set forth below. (Additional questions pertaining to hypotheses not discussed in this article are omitted here but may be obtained by request.) The speaker (S) makes a request to the hearer (H) through an indirect speech act. H declines. Later, H tells a third party (T) what S said.

1. Does H understand what S really means? [certainty as a focal point]
2. In this question and *all of the questions that follow,* assume that what S really meant by his last statement was indeed an illicit request, and that H ignores the request. Does S think that H understands what S really means? [common knowledge, 1st-order hearer]
3. How clear is S's real meaning in what he says? [reliability check]
7. Does H think that S thinks H understands what S really means? [common knowledge, 2nd-order hearer]
8. Suppose that S *does* realize that H knowingly turned down his request. Does S think that H thinks that S thinks that H understands what S really means? [common knowledge, 2nd-order speaker]
9. Suppose that H *is* certain that S knows H meant to turn down the request. Does H think that S thinks that H thinks that S thinks that H understands what S really means? [common knowledge, 3rd-order hearer]
10. Does T understand what S really meant? [virtual audience, 3rd-party]
11. Would S think that T understands what S really meant? [virtual audience, speaker's anticipation]
12. Miscellaneous scenario-specific question.

Question 3, a check on whether the participants agreed with our pilot sample's assessments of the relative directness of the speech acts, was answered on a Likert scale ranging from 1 to 7. For the other questions, participants circled one of seven options: *0 percent, 1 percent, 2 percent–49 percent, 50 percent, 51 percent–98 percent, 99 percent, 100 percent.* We instructed participants to write down a specific percentage in a provided space if they choose either *2 percent–49 percent* or *51 percent–98 percent,* thus creating a quantitative scale of subjective certainty from 0 to 100 percent.

The actual wording of the scenarios was carefully designed to make the scenario plausible and to lead the participant one step at a time to the state of knowledge that is necessary to interpret the common knowledge questions. In particular, participants were asked to put themselves in the shoes of the speaker or hearer and answer in the first person, eliminating one level of remove from the characters' mental states. The component propositions were introduced sequentially, rather than in a single embedded sentence. Different verbs were used for each mental state of the speaker and hearer (e.g., *understand, think, know, realize*), rather than repeating the verb. And each number on the rating scale was explained with a full sentence that participants could agree or disagree with, rather than having them compose their own complex interpretation and map it onto the scale. For example, the wording of the question tapping the participants' judgment about the speaker's second-order knowledge was as follows:

Suppose that Kyle *does* realize that the officer knowingly turned down his attempted bribe. Put yourself in Kyle's position. Which of the following is the *most likely* thing that Kyle is thinking at this point?

0%: "The cop thinks that I didn't understand that he turned down my bribe. I'm absolutely certain of that (or at least as certain as anyone can ever be of another person's thoughts)."

1%: "The cop almost certainly thinks that I didn't understand that he turned down my bribe."

2%–49%: "The cop probably thinks that I didn't understand that he turned down my bribe." *50%:* "Does the cop know that I understood that he turned down my bribe? Or does he think that I didn't understand? Really, it could go either way."

51%–98%: "The cop probably knows that I understood that he turned down my bribe."

99%: "The cop almost certainly knows that I understood that he turned down my bribe."

100%: "The cop knows that I understood that he turned down my bribe. I'm absolutely certain of that (or at least as certain as anyone can ever be of another person's thoughts)."

The complete text of all questions in the bribe scenario is reproduced in Appendix B of the original paper.

Procedure. Participants were run up to three at a time in a 1-hr session under the supervision of an experimenter. The order of the scenarios was randomized for each subject, whereas the order of the versions within each scenario was fixed. The versions of the scenario were never presented in order of increasing or decreasing directness of the culminating speech act. At the end of each session, participants were asked if they understood all of the questions. All answered in the affirmative.

Parallel boxplots were used to assess the effect of increasing directness on the outcome variables. Formal statistical testing was carried out by fitting linear mixed models to the responses as a function of directness level (treated as a quantitative variable with equal increments between levels), with participant variability as a random effect, by REML.

RESULTS AND DISCUSSION

The responses were qualitatively similar across the three scenarios. In most cases the results for one scenario reveal all features of interest. Results of the formal statistical tests are reported in Table 12.6; all p values are less than .001. The table entries are

Table 12.6 **Estimated Effects of Directness on Interpretations of Propositions in Experiment 3**

Question[a]	Hypothesis	Scenario		
		Seduction	Bribe	Threat
3		−1.40	−1.14	−1.74
12	Consequence of plausible deniability	−1.07[b]	16.9[c]	12.5[d]
1	Certainty as a focal point	26.9	18.1	30.6
2	Common knowledge, 1st-order hearer	23.5	22.3	27.7
10	Virtual audience, 3rd party	21.8	14.9	27.5
11	Virtual audience, speaker anticipation	19.8	15.5	27.1
7	Common knowledge, 2nd-order hearer	21.3	17.0	25.6
8	Common knowledge, 2nd-order speaker	16.7	14.0	21.0
9	Common knowledge, 3rd-order hearer	18.6	12.7	20.8

[a] The order of questions in the table mirrors the order in which the corresponding hypotheses were introduced in the text. [b] This question asked participants to rate on a 1–7 Likert scale the ease with which the man and his date are able to resume their previous nonromantic relationship. [c] This question asked participants to estimate the probability that the driver will be convicted at trial of attempted bribery. [d] This question asked participants to estimate the probability that the professor will be sanctioned by the university disciplinary board.

regression coefficients that capture the effect size; they may be interpreted as the expected change in the participants' responses resulting from a one-step increase in the directness of the offer.

Plausible deniability of an offer that breaches a relational model. The strategic speaker theory predicts that the linguistic variable of directness correlates with the probability that a hearer will interpret the speech act in its ulterior sense. The responses to the first question, which asked participants to put themselves in the hearer's position and estimate the probability that the hearer would interpret the statement as a bribe, come-on, or threat, bear this out (see Figure 12.5).

The theory also predicts that these interpretations should be linked in the minds of the speaker and hearer with differing consequences.

Question 12 in the bribe scenario asked subjects to give their estimated probability that a jury would find the driver guilty in a trial for attempted bribery. Question 12 in the threat scenario asked subjects to give their estimated probability that a university disciplinary board would sanction the professor for threatening the student. The responses are displayed in Figure 12.3. Participants clearly perceived, from their third-person vantage point, the advantage of phrasing a proscribed speech act in an indirect manner.

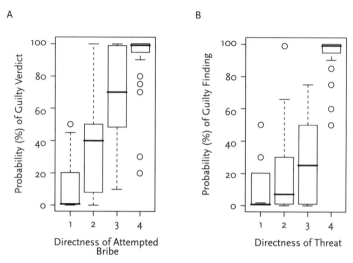

Figure 12.3. Parallel boxplots of Experiment 3 participants' estimations of probabilities that (a) the driver will be convicted at trial of offering a bribe to the officer and (b) the professor will be sanctioned by a university disciplinary board for threatening the student.

These are formal costs, like those in Experiment 2, and thus do not prove that the requisite cooperator–antagonist asymmetry in decision thresholds applies in purely informal social interactions governed by Fiske's relational models. A modified version of the seduction scenario offers the possibility of a critical test. We presented the scenario to a new sample of 83 Mechanical Turk respondents and asked them to consider, separately, how Lisa would react to the various speech acts under two circumstances:

(a) if she were attracted to Michael and would accept a proposition to sleep with him, or (b) if she wanted to maintain a professional or platonic relationship, was offended by his proposition, and would rebuff this advance, shun him in the future, and gossip about him (see Appendix A). In two blocks of items, one for each possibility of Lisa's values (order counterbalanced), participants rated the probability that she would react in the specified way for each of the four speech acts. As predicted, for each indirect speech act, participants thought that a willing Lisa's acceptance of the proposition would be more probable than an unwilling Lisa's open antagonism (see Figure 12.4; $p < .001$).

Certainty as a focal point and possible (vs. plausible) deniability. The effect of directness on the reported certainty of the hearer regarding the speaker's intent was clearly positive in all three scenarios (see Table 12.6). The slopes of these best fitting straight lines, however, do not tell the whole story.

Figure 12.5 shows that all of the participants but one judged the direct overture in the bribe scenario to be interpreted by the hearer with 100 percent certainty. The

A   B

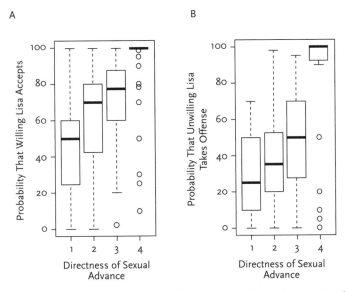

Figure 12.4. Parallel boxplots of participants' estimations of probabilities that (a) a willing Lisa would accept Michael's sexual proposition and (b) an unwilling Lisa would take offense.

Figure 12.5. Boxplot of participant responses to Question 1 of the bribe scenario in Experiment 3: "How certain is the officer that the speech act is really an attempted bribe?" The speech acts are labeled explicitly rather than numbered in order of increasing directness.

unanimity of the participants, and their choice of a single extreme value on the rating scale, is unusual in behavioral experiments and testifies to a strong perception of the digital nature of language—specifically, that a directly worded request is ubiquitously understood to indicate a speaker's intention with certainty. Also unusual is the categorical differentiation between direct and indirect speech: Whereas the direct bribe was judged by all the participants but one as 100 percent certain, the thinly veiled bribe was judged by most of them as exactly one percentage point less certain: The mode, median, and 75th percentile of responses were at exactly 99 percent. This striking pattern suggests that there is a qualitative psychological difference between a direct proposition and even the most obvious indirect one, and it supports the hypothesis that one rationale for indirect speech is a kind of higher-order plausible deniability, in particular, the deniability of certainty. That is, the speaker uses indirect speech to skirt the focal point of certainty, thereby conveying a relationship-threatening request without forcing the parties to alter their assumed relationship.

As mentioned, the seduction scenario, with its absence of legal or financial penalties, offers several pure tests of the hypothesis that indirect speech is a cost-minimizing strategy in relational model negotiation. The experiment included an additional question for this scenario designed to test the effect of directness on the social relationship between speaker and hearer, in which participants were asked how easy it would be, in the wake of the request, for the man and woman to resume their normal friendship and day-to-day interaction. Figure 12.6 confirms that more indirect propositions were perceived as making it easier for them to do so. Although the medians of the two intermediate levels appear to contradict the overall trend, the mean difference between these two levels is not statistically significant.

The virtual audience and plausible deniability to third parties. Figure 12.7 shows the mean responses to the seduction scenario with respect to the extent to which the woman believes that the man intended to make a sexual advance and

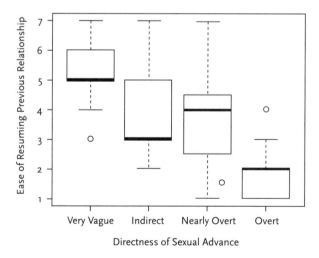

Figure 12.6. Boxplot of participant responses to Question 12 of the seduction scenario in Experiment 3: "How easily will the man and woman be able to resume their normal friendship and day-to-day interaction?"

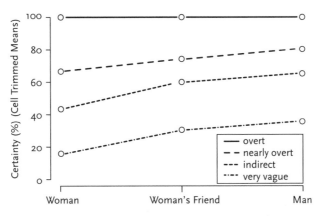

Figure 12.7. Line plots of participant responses in Experiment 3 (seduction scenario) to questions regarding the degree of certainty possessed by the hearer regarding the speaker's intent, by a third party regarding the speaker's intent, and by the speaker regarding the third party's interpretation. Going from left to right, the tick marks on the *x*-axis correspond to Questions 1, 10, and 11. The top and bottom three responses within a cell were trimmed before calculating the cell's mean. Increments along the *x*-axis are merely categorical.

the extent to which the woman's friend believes the same after hearing about the encounter. Because the relevant consideration is not so much how a third party would interpret the speaker's intent but how the speaker *anticipates* this interpretation, we also solicited judgments of the man's anticipation of the friend's interpretation. With direct speech, the level of certainty is pinned to 100 percent for the hearer's interpretation, the third party's interpretation, and the speaker's anticipation of that interpretation. With the indirect speech acts, the certainty is less in all three cases. Note that with indirect speech, increasing distance from the actual time and place of the utterance results in *increasing* certainty: The woman's friend was thought by participants to be more certain than the woman herself that the man intended something racy by his remark, despite the fact that she was not present, and the man thinks that the friend is more certain than she actually is. Similar trends are apparent in the other two scenarios. Several explanations of this anomaly are possible (perhaps the speaker is misled by immediate experience in a way that a neutral observer is not), but they are not essential to the test of the hypothesis that indirect speech affords plausible deniability to third parties. The relevant point is that with direct speech, no uncertainty exists in any direction: Present and absent parties are both completely certain of the intent, and the speaker knows it.

Deniability of mutual knowledge. To distinguish common knowledge from individual knowledge, it is necessary to separate the degree to which the speaker believes that the hearer believes something from the degree to which the hearer actually believes it (and so on for successive degrees of embedding of beliefs within beliefs). We thus phrased Questions 7–9 in such a way as to elicit the participants' judgments of the character's certainty at one level of the embedding, given certainty by the characters at all previous levels. For example, if A is the officer's probability (in the Bayesian sense, i.e., degree of subjective belief) that the driver's speech act was in fact an offer of a bribe, and if B is the officer's probability that the driver understands that the officer knowingly refused his offer, then the question regarding the latter proposition in effect asks for $P(B|A)$—the officer's probability conditioning on absolute certainty that the driver's speech act was indeed an attempted bribe. Using the basic fact of probability that $P(B \cap A) = P(B|A)P(A)$, we can calculate a joint probability representing the participant's judgment of a character's degree of certainty at a given level of common knowledge after propagating the participant's assessments of uncertainty at all previous levels of the recursion.

For example, the officer's degree of certainty (as assessed by the participant) that the driver knows that he understood the speech act as an offer of a bribe depends both on the officer's belief in the driver's knowledge given that a bribe has indeed been offered and on the officer's belief that the driver was actually offering a bribe. Multiplying the participant's assessments of these two beliefs thus yields the participant's estimate of the degree to which the officer accepts the higher-order belief. Note that this procedure does not constrain the possible outcomes: Participants were free to indicate that a conditional belief is certain while the condition itself is doubtful, or vice versa, in any combination, and in different ways for direct and indirect propositions.

The effects of mental-state embedding on the interpretation of propositions varying in directness can be seen in Figure 12.8. The first point in each line plot

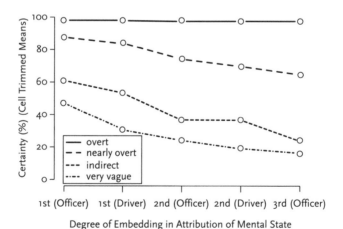

Figure 12.8. Judgments of the degree of first-order and common knowledge possessed by the driver and officer in Experiment 3. Going from left to right, the tick marks on the x-axis correspond to Questions 1, 2, 7, 8, and 9. For Questions 7, 8, and 9 the implied joint probabilities are shown. The top and bottom three responses within a cell were trimmed before calculating the cell's mean. Increments along the x-axis are merely categorical.

represents the officer's degree of certainty that the statement was an offer of a bribe, the second point the driver's degree of certainty that the officer knows that the statement was an offer of a bribe, and so on. Note that for the most direct speech act the estimates of perceived certainty remain essentially pinned to 100 percent, no matter the degree of embedding in the attribution of mental state. With all the indirect propositions, in contrast, the estimates of certainty decline with each level of recursive embedding, increasingly so as the statement becomes vaguer. The corresponding plots for the seduction and threat scenarios are similar. The perception that direct speech is certain at all levels of recursive embedding is all the more striking given the cognitive load imposed by embedded propositions. Though the difficulty of interpreting embedded degrees of belief may have reduced participants' degree of certainty that the speaker and hearer held those beliefs in the case of indirect speech, it clearly did not impede them when the same beliefs were conveyed by direct speech. This confirms the observation by Clark (1996) that people can apprehend a state of mutual knowledge directly, through the use of perceptual and linguistic cues, rather than explicitly spelling out the multiply nested propositions in their minds. Direct speech (but not indirect speech) appears to be one of those cues.

General Discussion

We have proposed a theory to explain why people so often insinuate a request indirectly rather than stating it baldly. The theory of the strategic speaker is based on the premise that off-record indirect speech is not just a social ritual but has a strategic rationale, and on the premise that language does not always involve pure cooperation between speaker and hearer but an uncertain mixture of cooperation and conflict. Off-record indirect speech is used to negotiate that uncertainty.

The core of the strategic speaker theory is a simple game-theoretic model showing that indirect propositions can allow for plausible deniability: A hearer favorably disposed to the request can accept it, whereas an uncooperative hearer cannot react antagonistically to it. The hypothesis that the use of indirect speech is a strategic response to the payoff structure defined by a mixture of cooperative and antagonistic hearers was supported in Experiment 2, which showed that speakers prefer to frame a bribe in more indirect forms as the hearer is more likely to be adversarial and a failure to strike a deal with a cooperative hearer becomes more costly. Similar support came from findings of Experiments 2 and 3, showing that the directness of a proposition is not just a linguistic variable governing the number of inferential steps that take one from the overt meaning to the implicated one, but predicts the estimated probability that a hearer will interpret the proposition as expressing the implicated meaning. Crucially, both experiments found that antagonistic hearers required more directness than cooperative hearers before acting on their interpretations; this condition was a critical prediction of the hypothesis that indirect speech is an optimal strategy in identification games.

The theory was shown to apply not just to conversations with costs that are quantifiable in money or other tangible resources but to conversations that bear on the kind of relationship that holds between the speaker and the hearer (communal sharing, authority ranking, equality matching). The emotional costs of a breach in the current relational model can create a need for plausible deniability and thereby push a speaker toward indirectness even when there are no overt costs. The informal observation that off-record indirect requests are ubiquitous in everyday life, despite the absence of quantifiable costs and rewards, was supported by judgments from Experiment 3 showing that in an imagined sexual proposition, indirect speech is perceived as more likely to allow the speaker and hearer to resume that relationship should a proposition be rebuffed, and that the critical asymmetry between antagonistic and cooperative hearers' threshold for action pertains to social as well as legally regulated actions.

Finally, the theory may be extended to higher forms of plausible deniability, owing to the discrete nature of relational models and the perceived digital nature of language. This combination allows a direct speech act to serve as a focal point in coordination games, to generate common knowledge, and to propagate a message with high fidelity along a chain of gossip. Indirect speech thus differs qualitatively from direct speech even when a speaker is highly confident of a hearer's values or a hearer is highly confident of a speaker's intent. The ability of indirect speech to avert the relationship-changing focal point of certainty was supported by a scatter of judgments among experimental participants regarding the probability that an indirect statement actually conveyed a request (always less than 100 percent certainty), in contrast with their near-unanimity that a direct one conveyed it with 100 percent certainty. Moreover, the ability of indirect speech to subvert relationship-changing common knowledge was supported by our finding a steadily deteriorating degree of certainty about the intent of an indirect request (but not of a direct request) as it was embedded in successively deeper layers of a speaker wondering whether a hearer knew what the speaker thought about what the hearer thought, and so on.

The theory of the strategic speaker builds on the insights of pure-cooperation theories such as P. Brown and Levinson's politeness theory and Clark's joint action theory, while differing from them in the treatment of off-record indirect speech. Both theories, we noted, do not deal explicitly with emotionally fraught and potentially conflictual verbal transactions such as bribes, threats, and sexual come-ons. And both conceptualize social transactions in dimensional terms, as negotiating a scalar quantity of face threat or equity imbalance. The theory of the strategic speaker, in contrast, proposes that indirect speech is a solution to potential conflicts of interest among speakers and that it negotiates a choice among qualitatively distinct and incommensurable relationship types. The theories were empirically contrasted in two ways.

According to politeness theory, indirectness is at the extreme end of a continuum of methods (including sympathetic politeness, deferential politeness, and conventionalized indirectness) by which a speaker redresses the threat to a hearer's face posed by a request. Experiment 1 showed that when the attitude of the hearer toward the request was identified within certain boundary conditions set by their relational model, increasing the face threat posed by a request was perceived to call for deferentially polite, but still direct, speech. Participants expected off-record indirectness only when a speaker addressed a hearer whose attitude toward the speech act was not identified and could range between the two extremes defined by different relational models.

According to joint action theory, speakers work to maximize their common acknowledgment of focal points and other forms of common knowledge (common ground). Experiment 3 showed that in the circumstances that call for off-record indirect speech, speakers work to *avoid* focal points and to keep certain knowledge *out of* common ground. Indeed, keeping knowledge out of common ground is a transparent interpretation of the expression *off the record* itself: The metaphorical "record" is common knowledge or common ground.

The current results provide evidence of a new kind—from psycholinguistics—for the theory of Fiske (1991, 1992, 2000) that humans expect their relationships to fall into a discrete number of models and that a given relational model fosters resource transfers that promote the evolutionary rationale of the relationship and forbids those that contradict it, with self-conscious emotions as the enforcement mechanism. The finding that common knowledge and a virtual audience are important rationales for signaling these relationships underscores Fiske's observation that relational models are not agreed upon through negotiations between the parties but depend on a larger implicit understanding. That is, the rules of inclusion and exclusion implied by networks of communal sharing, the assignment of social rank, and the viability of reciprocal exchanges depend critically on the consensus of the community. Once the mechanisms enabling this consensus are implemented, a request in violation of a prevailing relational model may be greeted with indignant anger, in turn fostering preemptive embarrassment, awkwardness, or shame. However, because of the fluidity of human social dynamics, persons looking to reap the greatest possible gain from joint projects must test the bounds of their nominal relationship types and determine whether different ones might be consummated. In order to secure these provisional adjustments from willing cooperators while minimizing the possibility of being shamed by antagonists and gossipers, speakers resort to off-record indirect speech acts.

The harmony between the qualitative distinctions among relational models and the digital nature of language helps explain why a speaker can avoid exposure by an antagonist even in cases where the euphemism in which the request is couched seems flimsy and ineffectual. The difference in initial clarity between a barefaced request and a thinly veiled innuendo might be small, but the gap between them might lead the hearer to decide that a direct request is the only logical place to draw a threshold for declaring a violation of the prevailing relational model. The high fidelity of language also ensures that a bald proposition, but not an innuendo, retains its clarity as the speech acts reverberate through chains of third parties and recursive understanding. This becomes important if potential antagonists are unwilling to openly rebuff the party who first breaches their existing relational model because neither wants to follow through on the social and emotional consequences of acknowledging the breach. In the deliberately created absence of common knowledge, both speaker and hearer can test for a willingness to change the relationship or carry out minor expedient actions that contradict its rules, all without being forced to confront the face-effacing corollary that they are opportunistic, hypocritical, irrational, or easily exploited.

We suspect that the strategic use of indirect speech to keep certain problematic facts out of common knowledge can be extended to explain a variety of emotionally fraught social phenomena, including hypocrisy, taboo, tact, euphemism, piety, mock outrage, ostensible invitations, political correctness, and other examples of emperor's new clothes and elephants in the living room. To take one example, Bandura (1999) suggested that the use of euphemisms may enable people to perpetrate atrocities while protecting their commonly acknowledged identity as moral agents (see also Orwell, 1946). When hearing the dialogue from *Schindler's List* (Spielberg, 1993), one is struck by the euphemisms used to describe the slaughter taking place inside the concentration camps: "special treatment," "the processes that take place down here," and so on. In one of the film's final scenes, after the announcement of the German surrender, Schindler challenges the SS guards to carry out their orders to kill the thousand Jews assembled before them. "Or," he says, "you could leave. And return to your families as men instead of murderers." A long silence follows Schindler's denuding of the emperor. Finally one of the guards breaks ranks and leaves. And then another. And then another.

References

Bandura, A. (1999). Moral disengagement in the perpetration of inhumanities. *Personality and Social Psychology Review, 3,* 193–209.

Brown, D. E. (1991). *Human universals.* New York, NY: McGraw-Hill.

Brown, P., & Levinson, S. C. (1987). *Politeness: Some universals in language usage.* New York, NY: Cambridge University Press.

Caplan, B. (2002). Systematically biased beliefs about economics: Robust evidence of judgmental anomalies from the Survey of Americans and Economists on the Economy. *Economic Journal, 112,* 433–458.

Chomsky, N. (1957). *Syntactic structures.* The Hague, the Netherlands: Mouton.

Chwe, M. S. Y. (2001). *Rational ritual: Culture, coordination, and common knowledge.* Princeton, NJ: Princeton University Press.

Clark, H. H. (1996). *Using language.* Cambridge, England: Cambridge University Press.

Clark, H. H., & Marshall, C. R. (1981). Definite reference and mutual knowledge. In A. K. Joshi, B. L. Webber, & I. A. Sag (Eds.), *Elements of discourse understanding* (pp. 10–63). New York, NY: Cambridge University Press.

Clark, H. H., & Schaefer, E. F. (1992). Dealing with overhearers. In H. H. Clark (Ed.), *Arenas of language use* (pp. 248–297). Chicago, IL: University of Chicago Press.

Coen, E. (Producer), & Coen, J. (Director). (1996). *Fargo* [Motion picture]. Universal City, CA: Polygram Filmed Entertainment & Working Title Productions.

Cole, P., & Morgan, J. L. (1975). *Syntax and semantics Vol. 3: Speech acts.* New York, NY: Academic Press.

Darwin, C. (1998). *The expression of the emotions in man and animals* (3rd ed.). New York, NY: Oxford University Press. (Original work published 1872)

Dawkins, R., & Krebs, J. R. (1978). Animals signals: Information or manipulation? In J. R. Krebs & N. Davies (Eds.), *Behavioural ecology: An evolutionary approach* (pp. 282–309). Oxford, England: Blackwell.

Dillard, J. P., Wilson, S. R., Tusing, K. J., & Kinney, T. A. (1997). Politeness judgments in personal relationships. *Journal of Language and Social Psychology, 16,* 297–325.

Feiler, B. (2000, October). Pocketful of dough. *Gourmet, 99–101.*

Fiske, A. P. (1991). *Structures of social life: The four elementary forms of human relations.* New York, NY: Free Press.

Fiske, A. P. (1992). The four elementary forms of sociality: Framework for a unified theory of social relations. *Psychological Review, 99,* 689–723.

Fiske, A. P. (2000). Complementarity theory: Why human social capacities evolved to require cultural complements. *Personality and Social Psychology Review, 4,* 76–94.

Fiske, A. P., & Tetlock, P. E. (1997). Taboo trade-offs: Reactions to transactions that transgress the spheres of justice. *Political Psychology, 18,* 255–297.

Gibbs, R. W. (1983). Do people always process the literal meanings of indirect requests? *Journal of Experimental Psychology: Learning, Memory, and Cognition, 9,* 524–533.

Goffman, E. (1967). *Interaction ritual: Essays on face-to-face behavior.* New York, NY: Anchor Books.

Grice, H. P. (1975). Logic and conversation. In P. Cole & J. L. Morgan (Eds.), *Syntax and semantics Vol. 3: Speech acts* (pp. 41–58). New York, NY: Academic Press.

Haidt, J. (2003). The moral emotions. In C. L. M. Keyes, K. R. Scherer, & H. H. Goldsmith (Eds.), *Handbook of affective sciences* (pp. 852–870). Oxford, England: Oxford University Press.

Hamilton, W. D. (1964). The genetical evolution of social behaviour I and II. *Journal of Theoretical Biology, 7,* 1–52.

Haslam, N. (1994a). Categories of social relationship. *Cognition, 53,* 59–90.

Haslam, N. (1994b). Mental representation of social relationships: Dimensions, laws, or categories? *Journal of Personality and Social Psychology, 67,* 575–584.

Hauser, M. D. (1996). *The evolution of communication.* Cambridge, MA: MIT Press.

Holtgraves, T. M. (1994). Communication in context: Effects of speaker status on the comprehension of indirect requests. *Journal of Experimental Psychology: Learning, Memory, and Cognition, 20,* 1205–1218.

Holtgraves, T. M. (2002). *Language as social action: Social psychology and language use.* Mahwah, NJ: Erlbaum.

Holtgraves, T. M., & Yang, J. N. (1990). Politeness as universal: Cross-cultural perceptions of request strategies and inferences based on their use. *Journal of Personality and Social Psychology, 59,* 719–729.

Horn, L. R. (2003). Implicature. In L. R. Horn & G. Ward (Eds.), *Handbook of pragmatics* (pp. 3–28). Malden, MA: Blackwell.

Isaacs, E. A., & Clark, H. H. (1990). Ostensible invitations. *Language in Society, 19,* 493–509.

Kasher, A. (1977). Foundations of philosophical pragmatics. In R. E. Butts & J. Hintikka (Eds.), *Basic problems in methodology and linguistics* (pp. 225–242). Dordrecht, the Netherlands: Reidel.

Lakoff, R. (1973). The logic of politeness; or minding your P's and Q's. In C. Colum, T. C. Smith-Stark, & A. Weiser (Eds.), *Papers from the Ninth Regional Meeting of the Chicago Linguistics Society* (pp. 292–305). Chicago, IL: Chicago Linguistics Society.

Lewis, D. K. (1969). *Convention: A philosophical study.* Cambridge, MA: Harvard University Press.

Lim, T. S., & Bowers, J. W. (1991). Facework: Solidarity, approbation, and tact. *Human Communication Research, 17,* 415–450.

Maynard Smith, J. (1964, March 14). Group selection and kin selection. *Nature, 201,* 1145–1147.

Maynard Smith, J. (1982). *Evolution and the theory of games.* Cambridge, England: Cambridge University Press.

Maynard Smith, J., & Harper, D. (2003). *Animal signals.* Oxford, England: Oxford University Press.

Nowak, M. A., & Sigmund, K. (2005, October 27). Evolution of indirect reciprocity. *Nature, 437,* 1291–1298.

Ohtsuki, H., & Iwasa, Y. (2006). The leading eight: Social norms that can maintain cooperation by indirect reciprocity. *Journal of Theoretical Biology, 239,* 435–444.

Orwell, G. (1946). Politics and the English language. *Horizon, 13,* 252–265.

Pinker, S. (1994). *The language instinct: How the mind creates language.* New York, NY: Morrow.

Pinker, S. (1999). *Words and rules: The ingredients of language.* New York, NY: Basic Books.

Pinker, S. (2007). *The stuff of thought: Language as a window into human nature.* New York, NY: Penguin Books.

Pinker, S., Nowak, M. A., & Lee, J. J. (2008). The logic of indirect speech. *Proceedings of the National Academy of Sciences, USA, 105,* 833–838.

Raggedclown. (2006, September 8). Dave Allen on the vagaries of the English language [Video file]. Retrieved from http://www.youtube.com/watch?v=4IfoUM6a4bA

Sampson, G. (1982). The economics of conversation. In N. Smith (Ed.), *Mutual knowledge* (pp. 200–210). Orlando, FL: Academic Press.

Schelling, T. C. (1960). *The strategy of conflict.* Cambridge, MA: Harvard University Press.

Searle, J. R. (1975). Indirect speech acts. In P. Cole & J. L. Morgan (Eds.), *Syntax and semantics Vol. 3: Speech acts* (pp. 59–82). New York, NY: Academic Press.

Smith, N. (1982). *Mutual knowledge.* Orlando, FL: Academic Press.

Sperber, D., & Wilson, D. (1986). *Relevance: Communication and cognition.* Oxford, England: Blackwell.

Spielberg, S. (Producer & Director). (1993). *Schindler's list* [Motion picture]. Universal City, CA: Amblin Entertainment.

Tannen, D. (1991). *You just don't understand: Men and women in conversation.* New York, NY: Ballantine Books.

Tetlock, P. E. (2003). Thinking the unthinkable: Sacred values and taboo cognitions. *Trends in Cognitive Sciences, 7,* 320–324.

Tetlock, P. E., Kristel, O. V., Elson, S. B., Green, M. C., & Lerner, J. S. (2000). The psychology of the unthinkable: Taboo trade-offs, forbidden base rates, and heretical counterfactuals. *Journal of Personality and Social Psychology, 78,* 853–870.

Tooby, J., & Cosmides, L. (1996). Friendship and the banker's paradox: Other pathways to the evolution of adaptations for altruism. *Proceedings of the British Academy, 88,* 119–143.

Tracy, J. L., Robins, R. W., & Tangney, J. P. (2007). *The self-conscious emotions: Theory and research.* New York, NY: Guilford Press.

Tracy, K. (1990). The many faces of face-work. In H. Giles & P. Robinson (Eds.), *Handbook of language and social psychology* (pp. 209–226). London, England: Wiley.

Trivers, R. L. (1971). The evolution of reciprocal altruism. *Quarterly Review of Biology, 46,* 35–57.

Trivers, R. L. (1985). *Social evolution.* Reading, MA: Cummings.

Walster, E. H., Walster, G. W., & Berscheid, E. (1978). *Equity: Theory and research.* Rockleight, NJ: Allyn & Bacon.

Wilson, M., & Daly, M. (1997). Relationship-specific social psychological adaptations. In G. Bock & G. Cardew (Eds.), *CIBA Foundation Symposium on characterizing psychological adaptations* (pp. 253–268). Chichester, England: Wiley.

Seduction, Bribe, Threat, and Favor Scenarios

SEDUCTION

Michael and Lisa are coworkers and fairly good friends. Michael finds Lisa very attractive, but he has no idea whether she has any romantic feelings toward him. One day Michael asks Lisa if she wants to have dinner with him. Lisa agrees. Michael picks up Lisa at eight and drives her to a local restaurant. The food and wine are excellent, and the two of them have a great conversation. Michael picks up the check.

At ten-thirty Michael starts driving Lisa back to her apartment. He slows down while driving past his own apartment building and remarks that he lives only ten minutes away from her.

"Wow. I feel like we've been talking about so much, but it's only ten-thirty." [very vague]
"My friend just emailed me those pictures from our trip to Europe that I was telling you about. Do you want to come over and have a look?" [indirect]
"You know, I have a really terrific view from my balcony. You can see the whole city, the lights, the ocean... would you like to come over and have a look?" [almost overt]
"I find you really attractive, and I enjoyed being with you tonight a lot. Would you like to come over and have sex?" [overt]

BRIBE

Kyle is in a hurry to drive from San Francisco to Los Angeles. Since it is late at night and there are hardly any cars on Interstate 5, Kyle floors it and starts making great time. Before too long, however, Kyle is pulled over by a Highway Patrol officer. The officer comes up beside Kyle's window and shines a bright flashlight on Kyle's face. The officer says, "Hey, buddy. Did you know that the speed limit here is seventy miles per hour? You were doing over ninety." Kyle says, "I didn't realize I was going so fast." The officer says, "Well, you were. Please show me your driver's license."

Kyle has a history of moving violations, so he is worried that another ticket will boost his insurance costs and result in the suspension of his license. He slowly gets out his wallet and holds it out to the officer. The corner of a 50-dollar bill is protruding from his wallet ever so slightly.

> "I'm very sorry, officer. I've really learned my lesson. From now on, you can be sure that I'll be more careful." [very vague]
> "I'm very sorry, officer. I know that I was speeding, and that I'll have to pay for my mistake. [indirect]
> "I'm very sorry, officer. But I'm actually in the middle of something right now, sort of an emergency. So maybe the best thing would be to take care of this here... without going to court or doing any paperwork." [almost overt]
> "I'm very sorry, officer. If I give you a fifty, will you just let me go?" [overt]

THREAT

Jennifer, a prospective graduate student, has submitted an application for an American Science Foundation Fellowship—an extremely prestigious honor with a financial award of over $30,000 a year. Jennifer earned straight A's in college, scored a perfect 1600 on the GRE, and has already been a coauthor on path-breaking articles published in the high-profile journals *Nature Genetics* and *PLoS Biology*. In short, Jennifer is a rising superstar and unquestionably worthy of a Fellowship.

One day Professor Jim Owens crosses paths with Jennifer in a hallway of the biology building. Jennifer was the best student in many of Professor Owens's courses, and they worked together on her senior thesis as true collaborators. This summer Jennifer has an offer to work in the lab of Josh Singer, which would provide her with the opportunity to broaden her experience and learn a new set of research skills.

Professor Owens asks Jennifer if she has a moment so that he can talk to her in his office. Jennifer says sure. Professor Owens happens to consult for the committee responsible for awarding Fellowships—something that Jennifer is well aware of.

> "Jennifer, I was reading the materials in your ASF Fellowship application and found your evolutionary arguments quite intriguing. I was wondering whether you would be interested in working in my lab this summer? We'll be doing some microarray experiments that might be able to test your ideas. If

we get good results, I'm sure we'll be able to write some great papers together."
[very vague]

"Jennifer, I just reviewed your AFS Fellowship application. I'm willing to
endorse it myself, but I suspect that the committee will still take a close look
at all of the outstanding candidates out there. I think what you need to do is
supplement your application with even more experience -- maybe even be
a coauthor on another big paper. In fact, there's a spot for you in my lab this
summer, if you're willing to take it." [indirect]

"Jennifer, I just reviewed your AFS Fellowship application. To be honest,
your qualifications are just not strong enough to warrant a Fellowship. But
there's a way out: why not work in my lab this summer? We're understaffed
and could use the help. And with this additional credential, I'm virtually
certain that the committee would look favorably on your application."
[almost overt]

"Listen, Jennifer. My lab is understaffed right now, and I'll need you to work
under me this summer on my latest project. Otherwise, you're not getting a
Fellowship. I'll make sure that the committee passes you over." [overt]

FAVOR

[Note: In the version given here, the experimental factors of power gap, social distance, and degree of imposition are all set at their highest levels.]

Will has just started his high-pressure job as a financial analyst. One of his first
tasks is to analyze data from the last few quarters and write up his findings in a
report.

Will comes to work very early on the day that his report is due. At about 7 a.m.
it dawns on him that a proper analysis of this time-series data requires expertise
with stochastic processes. Will was enrolled in his college's course on stochastic
processes for a single day; after staring blankly at the professor's mathematical scribbling for the entire class period, he promptly dropped the course.

Will steps outside his office to see who else might be at work this early. He finds
that Brian is occupied with some task in his own office.

Will is a newcomer, so he barely knows Brian. Although Brian is not that much
older than Will, Brian has a Ph.D. in statistics and is currently the head of the company's research division. He was one of the company's three founders.

If Will does not finish his report in the next few hours, he will be in a world of
trouble. The only way that he can finish the report is to ask Brian to go over the
analysis together with him. Will knows that this would take around three hours.
Brian would have to clear his morning to help Will, even though the report would
not benefit Brian's own division.

Will catches Brian on his way to the bathroom, gives him a friendly greeting, and
quickly explains the situation.

Notes

This research was supported by National Institutes of Health Grant HD-18381. We thank Alex Levin and Jennifer Kan for helping to design materials and run participants in Experiment 2.

1. See Kasher (1977), Sampson (1982), and Sperber and Wilson (1986) for other analyses of indirect speech that do not depend on the cooperative principle.
2. Materials for all experiments are available from the authors upon request.
3. In a well-known routine (see Raggedclown, 2006), the Irish comedian Dave Allen notes that terms of solidarity like *chum, amigo,* and *buddy* are often used aggressively, as in *Listen to me, pal!* and *All right, mate, you want it, you can come and get it!* Presumably this is because a presumption of intimacy when none exists is seen as a perquisite of a dominant individual.
4. The example is taken from a scene in the movie *Fargo* (Coen & Coen, 1996).
5. Pinker et al. (2008) noted that the same result holds if the hearers obey a continuous function for the probability of their decision, rather than a step function with a discrete threshold. The model can also be extended to a discourse of escalating propositions along the directness continuum which probe the hearer's decision function in smaller increments (e.g., "What a beautiful morning. I'm very sorry for speeding. I know I'll have to pay for my mistake. I admire officers doing their duty. Can I make a contribution to the policeman's benevolent association? Is there some way we could avoid the paperwork and settle it here?").
6. Pilot testing revealed a tendency for participants to favor the most indirect speech act possible across the board. To reduce this floor effect, we added context asking participants to imagine that on the previous night they encountered the officer off-duty in a bar.
7. Some writers use *mutual knowledge* interchangeably with *common knowledge*; others reserve it for shared individual knowledge and distinguish it from common knowledge. We use the unambiguous *common knowledge.*
8. A related speech act is the *ostensible invitation* (Isaacs & Clark, 1990), in which a speaker offers an insincere invitation, which the hearer recognizes as such and refuses, both tacitly understanding that the speaker has indicated he values the relationship. Isaacs and Clark (1990) noted that the invitation and refusal are "on record," whereas the speaker's motive is "off record." These are what we would call common and individual (first-order) knowledge, respectively. We note that as with other off-record indirect speech acts, an ostensible invitation must be worded so as to leave uncertainty about the interpretation, with some probability that the listener will misinterpret it.

13

The Cognitive Niche

Coevolution of Intelligence, Sociality, and Language

The year 2009 marked the 200th birthday of Charles Darwin and the 150th anniversary of the publication of The Origin of Species. *Among the many scientific celebrations held that year were a series of conferences sponsored by the National Academy of Sciences called "In the Light of Evolution," including one on the evolution of* Homo sapiens. *This paper, which I delivered at the conference, is the most succinct statement of my Theory of Everything. It also acknowledges another major influence on my thinking, the anthropologist John Tooby and the psychologist Leda Cosmides and their analyses of how we should think about the evolution of the human mind.*

The bicentennial of Darwin's birth and sesquicentennial of the publication of the *Origin of Species* have focused the world's attention on the breathtaking scope of the theory of natural selection, not least its application to the human mind. "Psychology will be based on a new foundation," Darwin famously wrote at the end of the *Origin*, "that of the necessary acquirement of each mental power and capacity by gradation. Light will be thrown on the origin of man and his history."

Far less attention has been given to the codiscoverer of natural selection, Alfred Russel Wallace, despite his prodigious scientific genius, and it is unlikely that the bicentennial of his birth in 1823 will generate the same hoopla. One reason was that Wallace turned out to be less prescient about the power of natural selection as an explanation of adaptive complexity in the living world. In particular, Wallace notoriously claimed that the theory of evolution by natural selection was inadequate to explain human intelligence:

> Our law, our government, and our science continually require us to reason through a variety of complicated phenomena to the expected result. Even our games, such as chess, compel us to exercise all these faculties in a remarkable degree.... A brain slightly larger than that of the gorilla

would...fully have sufficed for the limited mental development of the savage; and we must therefore admit that the large brain he actually possesses could never have been solely developed by any of those laws of evolution, whose essence is, that they lead to a degree of organization exactly proportionate to the wants of each species, never beyond those wants....

Natural selection could only have endowed savage man with a brain a few degrees superior to that of an ape, whereas he actually possesses one very little inferior to that of a philosopher. (1, pp. 340, 343)

The upshot, claimed Wallace, was that "a superior intelligence has guided the development of man in a definite direction, and for a special purpose" (1, p. 359).

Few scientists today accept Wallace's creationism, teleology, or spiritualism. Nonetheless it is appropriate to engage the profound puzzle he raised; namely, why do humans have the ability to pursue abstract intellectual feats such as science, mathematics, philosophy, and law, given that opportunities to exercise these talents did not exist in the foraging lifestyle in which humans evolved and would not have parlayed themselves into advantages in survival and reproduction even if they did?

I suggest that the puzzle can be resolved with two hypotheses. The first is that humans evolved to fill the "cognitive niche," a mode of survival characterized by manipulating the environment through causal reasoning and social cooperation. The second is that the psychological faculties that evolved to prosper in the cognitive niche can be coopted to abstract domains by processes of metaphorical abstraction and productive combination, both vividly manifested in human language.

The Cognitive Niche

The term cognitive niche was proposed by Tooby and DeVore (2) to explain the constellation of zoologically unusual features of modern *Homo sapiens* without resorting to exotic evolutionary mechanisms.

Their account begins with the biological commonplace that organisms evolve at one another's expense. With the exception of fruit, virtually every food source of one animal is a body part of some other organism, which would just as soon keep that body part for itself. As a result, organisms evolve defenses against being eaten. Animals evolve speed, stealth, armor, and defensive maneuvers. Plants cannot defend themselves with their behavior, so they resort to chemical warfare, and have evolved a pharmacopeia of poisons, irritants, and bitter-tasting substances to deter herbivores with designs on their flesh. In response, eaters evolve measures to penetrate these defenses, such as offensive weapons, even greater speed or stealth, and organs such as the liver that detoxify plant poisons. This in turn selects for better defenses, selecting for better offenses, and so on, in a coevolutionary arms race, escalating over many generations of natural selection.

Tooby and DeVore (2) suggest that humans exploit a cognitive niche in the world's ecosystems. In biology, a "niche" is sometimes defined as "the role an organism occupies in an ecosystem." The cognitive niche is a loose extension of this concept, based on the idea that in any ecosystem, the possibility exists for an organism to overtake other organisms' fixed defenses by cause-and-effect reasoning and cooperative action—to deploy information and inference, rather than particular features of physics and chemistry, to extract resources from other organisms in opposition to their adaptations to protect those resources. These inferences are played out internally in mental models of the world, governed by intuitive conceptions of physics, biology, and psychology, including the psychology of animals. It allows humans to invent tools, traps, and weapons, to extract poisons and drugs from other animals and plants, and to engage in coordinated action, for example, fanning out over a landscape to drive and concentrate game, in effect functioning like a huge superorganism. These cognitive stratagems are devised on the fly in endless combination suitable to the local ecology. They arise by mental design and are deployed, tested, and fine-tuned by feedback in the lifetimes of individuals, rather than arising by random mutation and being tuned over generations by the slow feedback of differential survival and reproduction. Because humans develop offenses in real time that other organisms can defend themselves against only in evolutionary time, humans have a tremendous advantage in evolutionary arms races. Even before the current anthropogenic mass extinction, prehistoric humans are believed to have caused significant extinctions of large fauna whenever they first entered an ecosystem.

The theory of the cognitive niche helps explain many zoologically unusual features of *H. sapiens:* traits that are universal across human cultures (3) but are either unique or hyperdeveloped (especially in combination) with respect to the rest of the animal kingdom. Three in particular make our species stand out.

Technological Know-How. Humans use and depend upon many kinds of tools, which involve multiple parts and complicated methods of fabrication. The tools are deployed in extended sequences of behavior and are acquired both by individual discovery and by learning from others. They are deployed to capture and kill animals, to process foods (including cooking, fermenting, soaking, peeling, and crushing them to remove toxins and increase the availability of nutrients), and to generate and administer medicinal drugs (4, 5). This reasoning is supported by "intuitive theories"—folk understandings of physics (in particular, objects, substances, and the forces that impinge on them), geometry (places, paths, and directions), biology (essences that give organisms their form and propel their growth, motion, and physiological processes), and psychology (internal, immaterial beliefs and desires) (6–10).

Cooperation among Nonkin. Humans cooperate with other humans: they trade goods, favors, know-how, and loyalty, and act collectively in child-rearing, gathering, hunting, and defense. This cooperation extends to other humans who are not related to them, in shifting partnerships, coalitions, and trading relationships, and thus must be explained not by kin selection but by mutualism or reciprocity (11).

The evolution of cooperation by reciprocal altruism requires a number of cognitive adaptations, which in fact appear to be well-developed in humans (11). They include the recognition of individuals (12); episodic memory for their actions (13); an ability to classify those actions in terms of whether they violate a reciprocity contract (14, 15); a suite of moral emotions such as sympathy, gratitude, anger, guilt, and trust, which impel an individual to initiate cooperation, reward reciprocators, and punish cheaters (11, 16); and the drives to ascertain the competence, integrity, and generosity of others (through gossip and other forms of due diligence) and to burnish one's own reputation for these traits (17, 18).

Because humans cooperate by at least three different kinds of relationship, governed by incompatible rules for the distribution of resources—reciprocal altruism, mutualistic sharing, deferring to dominant individuals—dyads can dynamically switch among kinds of relationship according to their history, kinship, social support, the resource at stake, and the context (19). The demands of this negotiation account for many of the complex aspects of human social life such as politeness, hypocrisy, ritual, and taboo (20, 21).

Grammatical Language. Although many animals communicate, humans appear to be unique in using an open-ended combinatorial system, grammatical language. In grammatical language, signals (words) are arbitrarily paired with concepts, and can be rearranged in novel hierarchical configurations (phrases embedded within phrases) in such a way that the meaning of the sequence can be computed from the meanings of the individual symbols and the way that they are arranged (22–24). The semantic meanings of the symbols (nouns, verbs, prepositions, tense markers, and so on) are related to the basic cognitive categories that define intuitive theories: objects, substances, motion, causation, agency, space, time (9, 25). The syntactic arrangements serve to express relationships among these concepts such as who did what to whom, what is where, and what is true of what (9). Although every language must be learned, humans have an ability to coin, pool, and learn new words and rules and thus are not dependent on some other species as teachers (as is the case with apes), or even on a longstanding linguistic community, to develop and use language (26).

Grammatical language has clear advantages in the transmission of information. Because it allows messages to be composed out of elements, rather than drawn from a finite repertoire, it confers the ability to express an unlimited number of novel messages (27, 28). Journalists say that when a dog bites a man, that is not news, but when a man bites a dog, that *is* news: the power of grammar is that it allows us to convey news, by arranging familiar words in novel combinations. Like other digital combinatorial systems in biology (RNA, DNA, proteins), language can generate vast numbers of structured combinations. The number of possible sentences (each corresponding to a distinct message) is proportional to the number of words that may appear in a position in a sentence raised to the power of the length of the sentence. With an approximate geometric mean of 10 choices available at every position in a sentence, one can estimate that a typical English speaker can easily produce or comprehend at least 10^{20} distinct sentences (29). This in turn makes it possible for language users to share an unlimited number of messages concerning specific events (who did what to whom, when, where, and why), generalized expertise (to accomplish this, do that), and flexible social contracts (if you do this for me, I'll do that for you).

Anyone who is skeptical that sophisticated reasoning, collaboration, and communication can bring survival advantages in a prehistoric lifestyle need only read ethnographic accounts of hunting or gathering in contemporary foraging peoples. One of many examples of hunter-gatherer ingenuity can be found in this description from the anthropologist Napoleon Chagnon of how the Yanomamö hunt armadillo:

> Armadillos live several feet underground in burrows that can run for many yards and have several entries. When the Yanomamö find an active burrow, as determined by the presence around the entry of a cloud of insects found nowhere else, they set about smoking out the armadillo. The best fuel for this purpose is a crusty material from old termite nests, which burns slowly and produces an intense heat and much heavy smoke. A pile of this material is ignited at the entry of the burrow, and the smoke is fanned inside. The other entries are soon detected by the smoke rising from them, and they are sealed with dirt. The men then spread out on hands and knees, holding their ears to the ground to listen for armadillo movements in the burrow. When they hear something, they dig there until they hit the burrow and, with luck, the animal. They might have to try several times, and it is hard work—they have to dig down two feet or more. On one occasion, after the hunters had dug several holes, all unsuccessful... one of them ripped down a large vine, tied a knot in the end of it, and put the knotted end into the entrance. Twirling the vine between his hands, he slowly pushed it into the hole as far as it would go. As his companions put their ears to the ground, he twirled the vine, causing the knot to make a noise, and the spot was marked. He broke off the vine at the burrow entrance, pulled out the piece in the hole, and laid it on the ground along the axis of the burrow. The others dug down at the place where they had heard the knot and found the armadillo on their first attempt, asphyxiated from the smoke. (30, pp 78–79.)

This jackpot was a reward for extraordinary feats of folk reasoning in taxonomy, physiology, physics, and geometry, some passed down from earlier generations, some improvised on the spot. And it depended on cooperative behavior among many individuals, coordinated by language.

Other Extreme Human Traits. Other zoologically unusual features of *H. sapiens* may be explained by the theory of the cognitive niche. The vast range of habitats and foods exploited by our species may in part have been facilitated by natural selection of the genes in local populations to ambient conditions such as solar radiation, diet, and disease (31–34). But these local genetic adaptations pale in comparison with those made possible by human technology. The Inuit's colonization of high latitudes may have been facilitated by adaptive changes in body shape and skin pigmentation, but it depended much more on parkas, kayaks, mukluks, igloos, and harpoons. This underscores that the cognitive niche differs from many examples of niches discussed in biology in being defined not as a particular envelope of environmental variables (temperature, altitude, habitat type, and so on), nor as a particular combination of other organisms, but rather the opportunity that any environment provides for exploitation via internal modeling of its causal contingencies.

Our extended childhoods may serve as an apprenticeship in a species that lives by its wits, and our long lives may reflect a tilt in the tradeoff between reproduction and somatic maintenance toward the latter so as to maximize the returns on the investment during childhood. The dependence of children's readiness for adulthood on their mastery of local culture and know-how may also shift the balance in male parental investment decisions between caring for existing offspring and seeking new mating opportunities. This in turn may have led to biparental care, long-term pair bonding, complex sexuality (such as female sexuality being unlinked from fertility, and sexual relationships subject to variation and negotiation), and multigeneration parental investment (35). Support for these hypotheses comes from the data of Kaplan (36), who has shown that among hunter-gatherers, prolonged childhood cannot pay off without long life spans. The men do not produce as many calories as they consume until age 18; their output then peaks at 32, plateaus through 45, then gently declines until 65. This shows that hunting is a knowledge-dependent skill, invested in during a long childhood and paid out over a long life.

Finally, the division of humankind into cultures differing in language, customs, mores, diets, and so on, is a consequence of humans' dependence on learned information (words, recipes, tool styles, survival techniques, cooperative agreements, and customs) and their peripatetic natures. As splinter groups lose touch with their progenitors over time, the know-how and customs that the two groups accumulate will diverge from one another (37).

Hominid Evolution and the Cognitive Niche. Given that the opportunity to exploit environments by technology and cooperation are independent of particular ecosystems, why was it Pliocene hominids that entered (or, more accurately, constructed) the cognitive niche and evolved sophisticated cognition, language, and sociality, rather than a population from some other taxon or epoch? This kind of historical question is difficult, perhaps impossible, to answer precisely because the unusualness of *H. sapiens* precludes statistical tests of correlations between the relevant traits and environments across species. But if we consider the cognitive niche as a suite of mutually reinforcing selection pressures, each of which exists individually in weaker form for other species, we can test whether variation in intelligence within a smaller range, together with a consideration of the traits that were likely possessed by extinct human ancestors, supports particular conjectures.

Obviously any orthogenetic theory (such as Wallace's) stipulating that the emergence of our species was the goal of the evolutionary process is inconsistent with the known mechanisms of evolution. It is also apparent that intelligence, which depends on a large brain, is not a free good in evolution (38). Its costs include the metabolic demands of expensive neural tissue, compromises in the anatomy of the female pelvis necessary for bearing a large-headed offspring, and the risks of harm from birth, falls, and the mutation and parasite load carried by such a complex organ. The proper framing of the question must ask which circumstances made the benefits of intelligence outweigh the costs. The hypothesis is that the hominid ancestors, more so than any other species, had a collection of traits that had tilted the payoffs toward further investment in intelligence.

One enabling factor may have been the possession of prehensile hands (an adaptation to arboreality) in combination with bipedality (presumably an adaptation to locomotion). We know from the fossil record that both prehensile hands and bipedality preceded the expansion of the brain and the development of tool use (39). Perhaps the availability of precision manipulators meant that any enhanced ability to imagine how one might alter the environment could be parlayed into the manufacture and carrying of tools.

A second contributor to the evolution of intelligence among hominid ancestors may have been an opportunistic diet that included meat and other hard-to-obtain sources of protein (5). Meat is not only a concentrated source of nutrients for a hungry brain but may have selected in turn for greater intelligence, because it requires more cleverness to outwit an animal than to outwit fruit or leaves.

A third may have been group living, again with the possibility of positive feedback: groups allow acquired skills to be shared, but also select for the social intelligence needed to prosper from cooperation without being exploited.

Indirect support for the hypothesis that sociality and carnivory contributed to the evolution of human intelligence comes from comparative studies showing that greater intelligence across animal species is correlated with brain size, carnivory, group size, and extended childhoods and lifespans (40, 41). I am unaware of any review that has looked for a correlation between possession of prehensile appendages and intelligence, but it is tantalizing to learn that octopuses are highly intelligent (42).

Coevolution of Cognition, Language, and Sociality. Many biologists argue that a niche is something that is *constructed*, rather than simply entered, by an organism (43, 44). An organism's behavior alters its physical surroundings, which affects the selection pressures, in turn selecting for additional adaptations to exploit that altered environment, and so on. A classic example is the way beavers generated an aquatic niche and evolved additional adaptations to thrive in it. The particulars of a *cognitive* niche are similarly constructed, in the sense that initial increments in cooperation, communication, or know-how altered the social environment, and hence the selection pressures, for ancestral hominids. It is surely no coincidence that the psychological abilities underlying technological know-how, open-ended communication, and cooperation among nonkin are all hyperdeveloped in the same species; each enhances the value of the other two. (A similar feedback loop may connect intelligence with the life-history and behavioral-ecology variables mentioned in the preceding section.)

An obvious interdependency connects language and know-how. The end product of learning survival skills is information stored in one's brain. Language is a means of transmitting that information to another brain. The ability to share information via language leverages the value of acquiring new knowledge and skills. One does not have to recapitulate the trial-and-error, lucky accidents, or strokes of genius of other individuals but can build on their discoveries, avoiding the proverbial waste of reinventing the wheel.

Language not only lowers the cost of acquiring a complex skill but multiplies the benefit. The knowledge not only can be exploited to manipulate the environment, but it can be shared with kin and other cooperators. Indeed, among commodities, information is unusually conducive to being shared because it is what economists call a "nonrival good": it can be duplicated without loss. If I give you a fish (a rival good), I no longer have the fish; as the saying might have gone, you cannot eat your fish and have it. But if I teach you to fish, it does not mean that I am now amnesic for the skill of fishing; that valuable commodity now exists in twice as many copies. Language can multiply this proliferation: for the minor cost of a few seconds of breath, a speaker can confer on a listener the invaluable benefit of a new bit of know-how. Crucially, a commodity that confers a high benefit on others at a low cost to the self is a key ingredient in the evolution of cooperation by reciprocal altruism, because both parties can profit from their exchange over the long run (11). The ability to share know-how through language thus may have been a major accelerant in the evolution of cooperation because it gave humans both the incentive and the means to cooperate. People traded not only goods but know-how and favors, and the negotiations were not limited to what could be exchanged there and then but to goods and favors transferred at widely separated times.

Language may foster cooperation, but it also depends on it, because there is no advantage in sharing information with adversaries (as we see in the expression "to be on speaking terms"). The inherent synergies among language, intelligence, sociality, enhanced paternal and grandmaternal investment, extended lives and childhoods, and diverse habitats and food sources suggest that these features cohere as a characterization of the cognitive niche, with enhancements in each serving as an additional selection pressure for the others. As far as timing is concerned, we would expect that the corresponding adaptations coevolved gradually, beginning with the first hominid species that possessed some minimal combination of preconditions (e.g., bipedality, group living, omnivory), increasing in complexity through the lineage of species that showed signs of tool use, cooperation, and anatomical adaptations to language, and exploding in behaviorally modern *H. sapiens*.

Evaluating the Theory of the Cognitive Niche

The theory of the cognitive niche, I believe, has several advantages as an explanation of the evolution of the human mind. It incorporates facts about the cognitive, affective, and linguistic mechanisms discovered by modern scientific psychology rather than appealing to vague, prescientific black boxes like "symbolic behavior" or "culture." To be specific: the cognitive adaptations invoked by the theory of the cognitive niche comprise the "intuitive theories" of physics, biology, and psychology; the adaptations for cooperation comprise the moral emotions and mechanisms for remembering individuals and their actions; the linguistic adaptations comprise the combinatorial apparatus for grammar and the syntactic and phonological units that it manipulates.

The selection pressures that the theory invokes are straight-forward and do not depend on some highly specific behavior (e.g., using projectile weapons, keeping track of wandering children) or environment (e.g., a particular change in climate), none of which were likely to be in place over the millions of years in which modern humans evolved their large brains and complex tools. Instead it invokes the intrinsic advantages of know-how, cooperation, and communication that we recognize uncontroversially in the contemporary world. Science and technology, organizations (such as corporations, universities, armies, and governments), and communication media (such as the press, mail, telephones, television, radio, and the internet) are, respectively, just the exercise of cognition, sociality, and language writ large, and they singly and jointly enable the achievement of outcomes that would be impossible without them. The theory of the cognitive niche simply extrapolates these advantages backward in time and scale.

Moreover, the theory requires no radical revision to evolutionary theory: neither the teleology and creationism of Wallace, nor mechanisms that are exotic, extreme, or invoked ad hoc for our species. Although grammatical language is unique to humans, and our intelligence and sociality are hyperdeveloped, it is not uncommon for natural selection to favor unique or extreme traits, such as the elephant's trunk, the narwhal's tusk, the whale's baleen, the platypus's duckbill, and the armadillo's armor. Given the undeniable practical advantages of reasoning, cooperation, and communication, it seems superfluous, when explaining the evolution of human mental mechanisms, to assign a primary role to macromutations, exaptation, runaway sexual selection, group selection, memetics, complexity theory, cultural evolution (other than what we call "history"), or gene–culture coevolution (other than the commonplace that the products of an organism's behavior are part of its selective environment).

The theory can be tested more rigorously, moreover, using the family of relatively new techniques that detect "footprints of selection" in the human genome (by, for example, comparing rates of nonsynonymous and synonymous base pair substitutions or the amounts of variation in a gene within and across species) (32, 45, 46). The theory predicts that there are many genes that were selected in the lineage leading to modern humans whose effects are concentrated in intelligence, language, or sociality. Working backward, it predicts that any genes discovered in modern humans to have disproportionate effects in intelligence, language, or sociality (that is, that do not merely affect overall growth or health) will be found to have been a target of selection. This would differentiate the theory from those that invoke a single macromutation, or genetic changes that affected only global properties of the brain like overall size, or those that attribute all of the complexity and differentiation of human social, cognitive, or linguistic behavior to cultural evolution. It is not necessary that any of these genes affect just a single trait, that they be the *only* gene affecting the trait ("the altruism gene," "the grammar gene," and so on) or that they appear de novo in human evolution (as opposed to being functional changes in a gene found in other mammals). The only requirement is that they contribute to the modern human version of these traits. In practice, the genes may be identified as the normal versions of genes that cause disorders of cognition (e.g., retardation, thought disorders, major learning disabilities), disorders of sociality (e.g., autism, social phobia, antisocial personality disorder), or disorders of language (e.g., language delay, language impairment, stuttering, and dyslexia insofar as it is a consequence of phonological impairment). Alternatively, they may be identified as a family of alleles whose variants cause quantitative variation in intelligence, personality, emotion, or language.

Several recent discoveries have supported these predictions. The gene for the transcription factor FOXP2 is monomorphic in normally developing humans, and when it is mutated it causes impairments in speech, grammar, and orofacial motor control (47, 48). The human version shows two differences from the version found in great apes, at least one of them functional, and the ape homolog shows only a single, nonfunctional difference from the one found in mice. The pattern of conservation and variation has been interpreted as evidence for a history of selection in the human lineage (49). In addition, several genes expressed in development of auditory system differ in humans and chimpanzees and show signs of selection in the human lineage. Because the general auditory demands on humans and chimps are similar, it is likely that they were selected for their utility in the comprehension of speech (50). And the human ASPM gene, which when mutated causes microcephaly and lowered intelligence, also shows signs of selection in the generations since our common ancestor with chimpanzees (51). It is likely that many more genes with cognitive, social, and linguistic effects will be identified in the coming years, and the theory of the cognitive niche predicts that most or all will turn out to be adaptively evolved.

Emergence of Science and Other Abstract Endeavors

Even if the evolution of powerful language and intelligence were explicable by the theory of the cognitive niche, one could ask, with Wallace, how cognitive mechanisms that were originally selected for physical and social reasoning could have enabled *H. sapiens* to engage in the highly abstract reasoning required in modern science, philosophy, government, commerce, and law.

A key part of the answer is that, in fact, humans *do not* readily engage in these forms of reasoning (9, 10, 52). In most times, places, and stages of development, people's abilities in arithmetic consist of the exact quantities "one," "two," and "many," and an ability to estimate larger amounts approximately (53). Their intuitive physics corresponds to the medieval theory of impetus rather than to Newtonian mechanics (to say nothing of relativity or quantum theory) (54). Their intuitive biology consists of creationism, not evolution, of essentialism, not population genetics, and of vitalism, not mechanistic physiology (55). Their intuitive psychology is mind-body dualism, not neurobiological reductionism (56). Their political philosophy is based on kin, clan, tribe, and vendetta, not on the theory of the social contract (57). Their economics is based on tit-for-tat back-scratching and barter, not on money, interest, rent, and profit (58). And their morality is a mixture of intuitions of purity, authority, loyalty, conformity, and reciprocity, not the generalized notions of fairness and justice that we identify with moral reasoning (16).

Nonetheless, *some* humans were able to invent the different components of modern knowledge, and all are capable of learning them. So we still need an explanation of how our cognitive mechanisms are capable of embracing this abstract reasoning.

The key may lie in a psycholinguistic phenomenon that may be called *metaphorical abstraction* (9, 59–61). Linguists such as Ray Jackendoff, George Lakoff, and Len Talmy have long noticed that constructions associated with concrete scenarios are often analogically extended to more abstract concepts. Consider these sentences:

1. a.   The messenger went from Paris to Istanbul.
   b.   The inheritance went to Fred.
   c.   The light went from green to red.
   d.   The meeting went from 3:00 to 4:00.

The first sentence (a) uses the verb *go* and the prepositions *from* and *to* in their usual spatial senses, indicating the motion of an object from a source to a goal. But in 1(b), the words are used to indicate a *metaphorical* motion, as if wealth moved in space from owner to owner. In 1(c) the words are being used to express a change of state: a kind of motion in state-space. And in 1(d) they convey a shift in time, as if scheduling an event was placing or moving it along a time line.

A similar kind of extension may be seen in constructions expressing the use of force:

2. a.   Rose forced the door to open.
   b.   Rose forced Sadie to go.
   c.   Rose forced herself to go.

2(a) conveys an instance of physical force, but 2(b) conveys a kind of metaphorical *interpersonal* force (a threat or wielding of authority), and 2(c) an *intrapersonal* force, as if the self were divided into agents and once part could restrain or impel another.

Tacit metaphors involving space and force are ubiquitous in human languages. Moreover, they participate in the combinatorial apparatus of grammar and thus can be assembled into more complex units. Many locutions concerning communication, for example, employ the complex metaphor of a sender (the communicator) putting an object (the idea) in a container (the message) and causing it to move to a recipient (the hearer or reader): We *gather* our ideas to *put* them *into* words, and if our words are not *empty* or *hollow*, we might *get* these ideas *across to* a listener, who can *unpack* our words to *extract* their *content* (62).

These metaphors could be, of course, nothing but opaque constructions coined in rare acts of creation by past speakers and memorized uncomprehendingly by current ones. But several phenomena suggest that they reflect an ability of the human mind to readily connect abstract ideas with concrete scenarios. First, children occasionally make errors in their spontaneous speech, which suggest they grasp parallels between space and other domains and extend them in metaphors they could not have memorized from their parents. Examples include *I putted part of the sleeve blue* (change of location → change of state), *Can I have any reading behind the dinner?* (space → time), and *My dolly is scrunched from someone... but not from me* (source of motion → source of causation) (63, 64). Second, several experiments have shown that when people are engaged in simple spatial reasoning it interferes with their thoughts about time and possession (9). Third, adults often experience episodes of spontaneous reminding in which an idea was activated only because it shared an abstract conceptual structure with the reminder, rather than a concrete sensory feature. For example, an episode of a barber not cutting a man's hair short enough may remind him of a wife not cooking his steak well enough done. A futile attempt at evenly darkening successive regions of a photo in Photoshop may remind a person of a futile attempt to level a wobbly table by successively cutting slices off each of its legs (9, 65, 66). This process of analogical reminding may be the real-time mental mechanism that allows cognitive structures for space, force, and other physical entities to be applied to more abstract subject matter.

The value of metaphorical abstraction consists not in noticing a poetic similarity but in the fact that certain logical relationships that apply to space and force can be effectively carried over to abstract domains. The position of an object in space is logically similar to the value of a variable, and thus spatial thinking can be co-opted for propositional inferences. In the realm of space, if one knows that A moves from X to Y, one can deduce that A is now at Y, but was not at Y in the past. An isomorphic inference may be made in the realm of possession: If A is *given* by Michael to Lisa, it is now *owned* by Lisa, but was not owned by her in the past.

A similar isomorphism allows reasoning about force to be co-opted for reasoning about abstract causation, because both support counterfactual inferences. If A forces B to move from X to Y, then if A had not forced it, B would still be at X. Similarly, If Michael forced Lisa to be polite to Sam, then if Michael had not forced her, she would not have been polite to Sam.

The concepts of the value of a variable (which is parallel to position in space) and of the causation of change (which is parallel to the application of force) are the basic elements of scientific thinking. This suggests that a mind that evolved cognitive mechanisms for reasoning about space and force, an analogical memory that encourages concrete concepts to be applied to abstract ones with a similar logical structure, and mechanisms of productive combination that assemble them into complex hierarchical data structures, could engage in the mental activities required for modern science (9, 10, 67). In this conception, the brain's ability to carry out metaphorical abstraction did not evolve to coin metaphors in language, but to multiply the opportunities for cognitive inference in domains other than those for which a cognitive model was originally adapted.

Evidence from science education and the history of science suggest that structured analogies and other mental reassignments in which a concrete domain of cognition is attached to a new subject matter are crucial to the discovery and transmission of scientific and mathematical ideas (8, 68–70). Children learn to extend their primitive number sense beyond "one, two, many" by sensing the analogies among an increase in approximate magnitude, position along a line, and the order of number words in the counting sequence. To learn chemistry, people must stretch their intuitive physics and treat a natural substance not as having an essence but as consisting of microscopic objects and connectors. To understand biology, they put aside the intuitive notions of essences and vital forces and think of living things the way they think of tools, with a function and structure. To learn psychology and neuroscience, they must treat the mind not as an immaterial soul but as the organ of a living creature, as an artifact designed by natural selection, and as a collection of physical objects (neurons).

Wallace, recall, also wondered about the human ability to participate in modern institutions such as governments, universities, and corporations. But like humans' puzzling ability to do science, their puzzling ability to take part in modern organizations is partly a pseudoproblem, because in fact the rules of modern institutions do not come naturally to us.

Sociality in natural environments is based on concepts and motives adapted to kinship, dominance, alliances, and reciprocity. Humans, when left to their own devices, tend to apply these mindsets within modern organizations. The result is nepotism, cronyism, deference to authority, and polite consensus—all of which are appropriate to traditional small-scale societies but corrosive of modern ones.

Just as successful science requires people to reassign their cognitive faculties in unprecedented ways, successful organizations require people to reassign their *social* faculties in evolutionarily unprecedented ways. In universities, for example, the mindset of communal sharing (which is naturally applied to food distribution within the family or village) must be applied to the commodity of ideas, which are treated as resources to be shared rather than, say, traits that reflect well on a person, or inherent wants that comrades must respect if they are to maintain their relationship. The evaluation of ideas also must be wrenched away from the mindset of authority: department chairs can demand larger offices or higher salaries but not that their colleagues and students acquiesce to their theories. These radically new, biologically unnatural rules for relationships are the basis for open debate and peer review in scholarship, and for the checks and balances and accounting systems found in other modern institutions (9).

Conclusion

The evolution of the human mind is such a profound mystery that it became the principal bone of contention between the two codiscoverers of the theory of natural selection. It has been an impetus to creationism and spiritualism in their day and in ours, and continues to be a source of proposed complications and elaborations of evolutionary theory. But in a year celebrating Darwin's life and work, it would be fitting to see if the most parsimonious application of his theory to the human mind is sufficient, namely that the mind, like other complex organs, owes its origin and design to natural selection.

I have sketched a testable theory, rooted in cognitive science and evolutionary psychology, that suggests that it is. According to this theory, hominids evolved to specialize in the cognitive niche, which is defined by the triad of reasoning about the causal structure of the world, cooperating with other individuals, and sharing that knowledge and negotiating those agreements via language. This triad of adaptations coevolved with one another and with life-history and sexual traits such as enhanced parental investment by both sexes and by multiple generations, longer childhoods and lifespans, complex sexuality, and the accumulation of local knowledge and social conventions in distinct cultures.

Although adaptations to the cognitive niche confer obvious advantages in any natural environment, they are insufficient for reasoning in modern institutions such as science and government. Over the course of history and in their own educations, people accommodate themselves to these new skills and bodies of knowledge via the process of metaphorical abstraction, in which cognitive schemas and social emotions that evolved for one domain can be pressed into service for another and assembled into increasingly complex mental structures.

References

1. Wallace AR (1870) The limits of natural selection as applied to man. *Contributions to the Theory of Natural Selection: A Series of Essays*, ed Wallace AR (MacMillan, New York).
2. Tooby J, DeVore I (1987) The reconstruction of hominid evolution through strategic modeling. *The Evolution of Human Behavior: Primate Models*, ed Kinzey WG (SUNY Press, Albany, NY).
3. Brown DE (1991) *Human Universals* (McGraw-Hill, New York).
4. Kingdon J (1993) *Self-Made Man: Human Evolution from Eden to Extinction?* (Wiley, New York).
5. Wrangham RW (2009) *Catching Fire: How Cooking Made Us Human* (Basic Books, New York) pp v.
6. Leslie AM (1994) ToMM, ToBY, and agency: Core architecture and domain specificity. *Mapping the Mind: Domain Specificity in Cognition and Culture*, eds Hirschfeld LA, Gelman SA (Cambridge Univ Press, New York).
7. Spelke ES, Breinlinger K, Macomber J, Jacobson K (1992) Origins of knowledge. *Psychol Rev* 99:605–632.
8. Carey S (2007) *Origins of Concepts* (MIT Press, Cambridge, MA).
9. Pinker S (2007) *The Stuff of Thought: Language as a Window into Human Nature* (Viking, New York).
10. Pinker S (1997) *How the Mind Works* (Norton, New York).
11. Trivers R (1971) The evolution of reciprocal altruism. *Q Rev Biol* 46:35–57.
12. Kanwisher N, Moscovitch M (2000) The cognitive neuroscience of face processing: An introduction. *Cogn Neuropsychol* 17:1–13.
13. Klein SB, Cosmides L, Tooby J, Chance S (2002) Decisions and the evolution of memory: Multiple systems, multiple functions. *Psychol Rev* 109:306–329.
14. Cosmides L, Tooby J (1992) Cognitive adaptations for social exchange. *The Adapted Mind: Evolutionary Psychology and the Generation of Culture*, eds Barkow JH, Cosmides L, Tooby J (Oxford Univ Press, New York).
15. Cosmides L, Tooby J (2010) Whence intelligence? *Proc Natl Acad Sci USA*.
16. Haidt J (2002) The moral emotions. *Handbook of Affective Sciences*, eds Davidson RJ, Scherer KR, Goldsmith HH (Oxford Univ Press, New York).
17. Nowak MA, Sigmund K (1998) Evolution of indirect reciprocity by image scoring. *Nature* 393:573–577.
18. Ridley M (1997) *The Origins of Virtue: Human Instincts and the Evolution of Cooperation* (Viking, New York) 1st American Ed, pp viii, 295.
19. Fiske AP (1991) *Structures of Social Life: The Four Elementary Forms of Human Relations* (Free Press, New York).
20. Pinker S, Nowak MA, Lee JJ (2008) The logic of indirect speech. *Proc Natl Acad Sci USA* 105:833–838.

21. Lee JJ, Pinker S (2010) Rationales for Indirect Speech: The Theory of the Strategic Speaker *Psychological Review* 117:785–807..

22. Pinker S (1991) Rules of language. *Science* 253:530–535.

23. Jackendoff R (2002) *Foundations of Language: Brain, Meaning, Grammar, Evolution* (Oxford Univ Press, New York).

24. Chomsky N (1972) *Language and Mind* (Harcourt Brace, New York) Extended ed.

25. Jackendoff R (1990) *Semantic Structures* (MIT Press, Cambridge, MA).

26. Senghas A, Kita S, Özyürek A (2004) Children creating core properties of language: Evidence from an emerging sign language in Nicaragua. *Science* 305:1779–1782.

27. Nowak MA, Plotkin JB, Jansen VA (2000) The evolution of syntactic communication. *Nature* 404:495–498.

28. Pinker S (1999) *Words and Rules: The Ingredients of Language* (HarperCollins, New York).

29. Miller GA, Selfridge J (1950) Verbal context and the recall of meaningful material. *Am J Psychol* 63:176–185.

30. Chagnon NA (1992) *Yanomamö: The Last Days of Eden* (Harcourt Brace, New York).

31. DiRienzo A (2010) Human population diversity. *Proc Natl Acad Sci USA.*

32. Bustamante C (2010) Genomic footprints of natural selection. *Proc Natl Acad Sci USA.*

33. Jablonski N (2010) The skin that makes us human. *Proc Natl Acad Sci USA.*

34. Tishkoff S (2010) Paleo-demography from extant genetics. *Proc Natl Acad Sci USA.*

35. Hawkes K (2010) The evolution of human life history. *Proc Natl Acad Sci USA.*

36. Kaplan H, Robson AJ (2002) The emergence of humans: The coevolution of intelligence and longevity with intergenerational transfers. *Proc Natl Acad Sci USA* 99:10221–10226.

37. Richerson P (2010) How cultures evolve. *Proc Natl Acad Sci USA.*

38. Wallace D (2010) Peopling the planet: Out of Africa? *Proc Natl Acad Sci USA.*

39. Wood B (2010) Evolution of the hominids. *Proc Natl Acad Sci USA.*

40. Lee JJ (2007) A g beyond Homo sapiens? Some hints and suggestions. *Intelligence* 35: 253–265.

41. Boyd R, Silk JB (2006) *How Humans Evolved* (Norton, New York), 4th Ed.

42. Mather JA (1995) Cognition in cephalopods. *Adv Stud Behav* 24:317–353.

43. Odling-Smee FJ, Laland KN, Feldman MW (2003) *Niche Construction: The Neglected Process in Evolution* (Princeton Univ Press, Princeton, NJ).

44. Lewontin RC (1984) Adaptation. *Conceptual Issues in Evolutionary Biology*, ed Sober E (MIT Press, Cambridge, MA).

45. Kreitman M (2000) Methods to detect selection in populations with applications to the human. *Annu Rev Genomics Hum Genet* 1:539–559.

46. Przeworski M, Hudson RR, Di Rienzo A (2000) Adjusting the focus on human variation. *Trends Genet* 16:296–302.

47. Vargha-Khadem F, et al. (1998) Neural basis of an inherited speech and language disorder. *Proc Natl Acad Sci USA* 95:12695–12700.

48. Lai CSL, Fisher SE, Hurst JA, Vargha-Khadem F, Monaco AP (2001) A novel forkhead-domain gene is mutated in a severe speech and language disorder. *Nature* 413: 519–523.

49. Enard W, et al. (2002) Molecular evolution of FOXP2, a gene involved in speech and language. *Nature* 418:869–872.

50. Clark AG, et al. (2003) Inferring Nonneutral Evolution from Human-Chimp-Mouse Orthologous Gene Trios. *Science* 302:1960–1963.

51. Evans PD, et al. (2004) Adaptive evolution of ASPM, a major determinant of cortical size in humans. *Hum Mol Genet* 13:489–494.

52. Pinker S (2002) *The Blank Slate: The Modern Denial of Human Nature* (Viking, New York).

53. Carey S (2009) *Origins of Concepts* (MIT Press, Cambridge, MA).

54. McCloskey M (1983) Intuitive physics. *Scientific American* 248:122–130.

55. Atran S (1998) Folk biology and the anthropology of science: Cognitive universals and cultural particulars. *Behav Brain Sci* 21:547–609.

56. Bloom P (2003) *Descartes' Baby: How the Science of Child Development Explains What Makes Us Human* (Basic Books, New York).

57. Daly M, Wilson M (1988) *Homicide* (Aldine de Gruyter, Hawthorne, NY).

58. Fiske AP (2004) Four modes of constituting relationships: Consubstantial assimilation; space, magnitude, time, and force; concrete procedures; abstract symbolism. *Relational Models Theory: A Contemporary Overview*, ed Haslam N (Erlbaum Associates, Mahwah, NJ).

59. Lakoff G, Johnson M (1980) *Metaphors We Live By* (Univ of Chicago Press, Chicago).

60. Jackendoff R (1978) Grammar as evidence for conceptual structure. *Linguistic Theory and Psychological Reality*, eds Halle M, Bresnan J, Miller GA (MIT Press, Cambridge, MA).

61. Talmy L (2000) *Force Dynamics in Language and Cognition. Toward a Cognitive Semantics 1: Concept Structuring Systems* (MIT Press, Cambridge, MA).

62. Reddy M (1993) The conduit metaphor: A case of frame conflict in our language about language. *Metaphor and Thought*, ed Ortony A (Cambridge Univ Press, New York), 2nd Ed.

63. Bowerman M (1983) Hidden meanings: The role of covert conceptual structures in children's development of language. *The Acquisition of Symbolic Skills*, eds Rogers DR, Sloboda JA (Plenum, New York).

64. Pinker S (1989) *Learnability and Cognition: The Acquisition of Argument Structure* (MIT Press, Cambridge, MA).

65. Hofstadter DR (1995) *Fluid Concepts and Creative Analogies: Computer Models of the Fundamental Mechanisms of Thought* (Basic Books, New York), pp ix, 518 pp.

66. Schank RC (1982) *Dynamic Memory: A Theory of Reminding and Learning in Computers and People* (Cambridge Univ Press, New York).

67. Gentner D (2003) Why we're so smart. *Language in Mind: Advances in the Study of Language and Thought*, eds Gentner D, Goldin-Meadow S (MIT Press, Cambridge, MA), pp 195–235.

68. Gentner D, Jeziorski M (1989) Historical shifts in the use of analogy in science. *The psychology of Science: Contributions to Metascience*, eds Gholson B, Shadish WR, Beimeyer RA, Houts A (Cambridge Univ Press, New York).

69. Spelke E (2003) What makes us smart? Core knowledge and natural language. *Language in Mind: Advances in the Study of Language and Thought*, eds Gentner D, Goldin-Meadow S (MIT Press, Cambridge, MA).

70. Boyd R (1993) *Metaphor and Theory Change: What is "Metaphor" a Metaphor for? Metaphor and Thought*, ed Ortony A (Cambridge Univ Press, New York), 2nd Ed.

Author Biography

Steven Pinker, a native of Montreal, received his B.A. from McGill University in 1976 and his Ph.D. in psychology from Harvard in 1979. After serving on the faculties of Harvard and Stanford for a year each, he moved to MIT in 1982, where he spent twenty-one years before returning to Harvard in 2003 as the Johnstone Family Professor of Psychology.

Pinker is a cognitive scientist who has carried out research on language and its connections to cognition, social relationships, child development, neural information processing, human evolution, and theories of human nature. This work has won many prizes, including the Troland Award from the National Academy of Sciences, the Henry Dale Prize from the Royal Institution of Great Britain, the George Miller Prize from the Cognitive Neuroscience Society, and the Early Career Award and McCandless Prize from the American Psychological Association.

Pinker has also written accessible books which synthesize cognitive science, evolutionary biology, and behavioral genetics into a comprehensive picture of how the mind works, how it evolved, and how we ought to bring these ideas to bear on theories of politics and morality. They include *The Language Instinct, How the Mind Works, Words and Rules, The Blank Slate, The Stuff of Thought,* and most recently, *The Better Angels of Our Nature*. These books have been shortlisted for the Pulitzer Prize, the Samuel Johnson Nonfiction Prize, and the Royal Society Science Book Prize, and have won prizes from the Linguistics Society of America, the American Psychological Association, The Cundill Foundation for History, and the Foundation for the Future. Pinker has also received four prizes for graduate and undergraduate teaching, including a Harvard College Professorship, and has been designated Humanist of the Year, *Time* magazine's Hundred Most Influential People in the World Today, and *Prospect* and *Foreign Policy's* "World's Top 100 Public Intellectuals." He is Chair of the Usage Panel of the *American Heritage Dictionary,* and also writes frequently in the popular press, including *The New York Times, Prospect, Slate,* and *The New Republic.*

Credits

1. Pinker, S. (1979). Formal models of language learning. *Cognition, 7*, 217–283.
2. Pinker, S. (1988). A computational theory of the mental imagery medium. In M. Denis, J. Engelkamp, & J. T. E. Richardson (Eds.), *Cognitive and neuropsychological approaches to mental imagery, 17–32*. Amsterdam, Netherlands: Martinus Nijhoff.
3. Prince, A., & Pinker, S. (1988). Rules and connections in human language. *Trends in Neurosciences, 11*, 195–202.
4. Tarr, M. J., & Pinker, S. (1990). When does human object recognition use a viewer-centered reference frame? *Psychological Science, 1*, 253–256.
5. Pinker, S., & Bloom, P. (1990). Natural language and natural selection. *Behavioral and Brain Sciences, 13*, 707–784.
6. Pinker, S. (1993). The acquisition of argument structure. In H. Nakajima & Y. Otsu (Eds.), *Argument structure: Its syntax and acquisition, 127–151*. Special Publications of the English Linguistic Society of Japan, Volume 1. Tokyo: Kaitakusha.
7. Pinker, S., & Prince, A. (1996). The nature of human concepts: Evidence from an unusual source. *Communication and Cognition, 29*, 307–361.
8. Pinker, S. (2004). Why nature and nurture won't go away. *Daedalus, 133*, Fall, 5–17.
9. Pinker, S., & Jackendoff, R. (2005). The faculty of language: What's special about it? *Cognition, 95*, 201–236.
10. Pinker, S. (2005). So how *does* the mind work? *Mind and Language, 20*, 1–24.
11. Pinker, S. (2006). Deep commonalities between life and mind. In A. Grafen & M. Ridley (Eds.), *Richard Dawkins: How a scientist changed the way we think*, 130-141. New York: Oxford University Press.
12. Lee, J. J., & Pinker, S. (2010). Rationales for indirect speech: The theory of the strategic speaker. *Psychological Review, 117*, 785–807.
13. Pinker, S. (2010). The cognitive niche: Coevolution of intelligence, sociality, and language. *Proceedings of the National Academy of Science USA, 107*, 8893–8999.

Name Index

Subject Index

2½-D sketch 75

adaptation 80, 114–116, 118–120, 126, 130,
  131–134, 137, 154, 206–208, 210, 208, 229,
  230–2323, 236, 239,246, 247, 251, 254, 260,
  270, 288–289, 349, 354–355
argument structure 160 ff.
artificial intelligence 4, 66, 84, 135, 138, 181, 296
artificial language learning 28
associationism 84, 92, 99
attention 79, 100

Baldwin effect 145
Bayesian Models 2, 15–17
behavioral genetics 215, 223, 302, 367
behaviorism 84, 135, 214, 297, 300
The Better Angels of Our Nature 228, 367
binding problem 90, 99
The Blank Slate 2, 214, 228, 367
Blocking Principle 188

children 1–4, 11–13, 17–19, 21, 23, 25–27, 31, 32,
  36, 51–55, 57–59, 74, 86, 91, 97–100, 111, 115,
  129, 136–138, 145, 147, 151, 160–163, 166,
  168–178, 180, 182, 183, 191, 193, 196–198,
  218–220, 223–225, 229, 234, 237, 239–242,
  245, 252, 254, 272, 273, 300, 354, 357, 360, 361
chimpanzees 146, 150–151
Chomsky hierarchy 7, 9, 19
classical categories 181, 183, 184, 188, 192–195,
  198, 199, 204–206, 209, 210
cognitive architecture xi, 85, 274, 279, 288
cognitive psychology *see* cognitive science
cognitive revolution 84, 269, 296, 297
cognitive science xi, 1, 3, 60, 65, 66, 80, 84, 85,
  110, 154, 195, 215, 228, 258, 270, 273, 278, 279,
  295, 296, 301, 362, 367
computational theory of mind 66, 153, 269–271,
  276, 291, 298

connectionism 85, 85, 95, 100, 195, 198, 275,
  276, 281
consciousness 297
context-free grammars 37, 44
cooperation 149, 252, 261, 304–307, 313, 315,
  316, 327, 339, 340, 344, 350–352, 354–357
culture 129, 138, 215, 216, 224, 259, 261, 300,
  301, 322, 357–8

dative alternation 167, 170
deep structure 44
distributional analysis 22–24
domain specificity *see also* modularity 58, 283, 285

emotion 214, 225, 234, 305, 306, 321, 322, 324,
  325, 340, 342
empiricism 52, 57, 84, 285
epigenetics 216
evolution xi, 110–113, 115–121, 126–130, 133,
  136–140, 143–146, 149, 152, 153, 200, 202,
  206, 208, 215, 218, 221, 229–232, 236, 237,
  239, 247, 251, 255, 256, 258, 262, 269, 270, 273,
  285, 287–290, 294, 295, 298, 300–302, 327,
  349, 350, 352, 354–359, 362, 367
evolutionary psychology 215, 226, 270, 273, 287,
  300, 302, 362
explanatory adequacy 49, 273

family resemblance 95, 96, 181–186, 188, 189,
  192–196, 198–200, 202, 205–210

gender 60, 124, 140, 142, 218, 226, 243
genetics 111, 115, 116, 119, 130, 131, 137,
  140–144, 147, 150, 151, 165, 207, 218–219,
  220–224, 226, 245–247, 260, 272, 295, 301,
  306, 354, 358
Google 2, 84
googol 2
gradualism 114